Series on Technology
and Social Priorities

NATIONAL ACADEMY
OF ENGINEERING

CITIES
AND THEIR VITAL SYSTEMS

INFRASTRUCTURE
PAST, PRESENT, AND FUTURE

Jesse H. Ausubel and Robert Herman
Editors

NATIONAL ACADEMY PRESS
Washington, D.C. 1988

National Academy Press • 2101 Constitution Avenue, NW • Washington, DC 20418

NOTICE: The National Academy of Engineering was established in 1964, under the charter of the National Academy of Sciences, as a parallel organization of outstanding engineers. It is autonomous in its administration and in the selection of its members, sharing with the National Academy of Sciences the responsibility for advising the federal government. The National Academy of Engineering also sponsors engineering programs aimed at meeting national needs, encourages education and research, and recognizes the superior achievement of engineers. Dr. Robert M. White is president of the National Academy of Engineering.

Funds for the National Academy of Engineering's Symposium Series on Technology and Social Priorities were provided by the Andrew W. Mellon Foundation, Carnegie Corporation of New York, and the Academy's Technology Agenda Program. This publication has been reviewed by a group other than the authors according to procedures approved by a Report Review Committee. The views expressed in this volume are those of the authors and are not presented as the views of the Mellon Foundation, Carnegie Corporation, or the National Academy of Engineering.

Library of Congress Cataloging-in-Publication Data

Cities and their vital systems.

(Series on technology and social priorities)
Bibliography: p.
Includes index.
1. Cities and towns—United States—Growth—
Congresses.   2. Infrastructure (Economics)—United
States—Congresses.   3. United States—Public works—
Congresses.   I. Ausubel, Jesse.   II. Herman, Robert.
III. National Academy of Engineering.   IV. Series.
HT371.C585   1988   363'.0973   88-12517
ISBN 0-309-03786-7

Printed in the United States of America

ADVISORY COMMITTEE ON TECHNOLOGY AND SOCIETY

Chairman

ROBERT M. WHITE, President, National Academy of Engineering

Members

RUTHERFORD ARIS, Regents' Professor, Department of Chemical Engineering and Materials Science, University of Minnesota

DAVID P. BILLINGTON, Professor of Civil Engineering, School of Engineering and Applied Science, Princeton University

HARVEY BROOKS, Benjamin Peirce Professor of Technology and Public Policy, Emeritus, Harvard University

HARLAN CLEVELAND, Professor of Public Affairs and Planning, University of Minnesota

DONALD N. FREY, Chairman and CEO, Bell & Howell Company

JOHN H. GIBBONS, Director, Office of Technology Assessment, U.S. Congress

MARY L. GOOD, President, Engineered Materials Research, Allied-Signal Inc.

HENRY R. LINDEN, Executive Advisor, Gas Research Institute

JAMES BRIAN QUINN, William and Josephine Buchanan Professor of Management, Amos Tuck School of Business, Dartmouth College

FREDERICK C. ROBBINS, Department of Epidemiology and Biostatistics, School of Medicine, Case Western Reserve University

WALTER G. VINCENTI, Professor Emeritus of Aeronautics and Astronautics, Stanford University

ALVIN M. WEINBERG, Distinguished Fellow, Institute for Energy Analysis, Oak Ridge Associated Universities

Preface

Infrastructure is the term applied to large-scale engineering systems and includes a variety of public works, such as roads, bridges, and sewer systems, as well as privately managed utilities such as electric power and telephone service. Much publicity has been given infrastructure in recent years as news of collapsing bridges and crowded airports makes evident our dependence on infrastructure.

Recent studies have considered the urgent problems of financing and maintaining current public works. However, what of major long-range perspectives on infrastructure needs and development? To address these issues, the National Academy of Engineering conducted a workshop entitled "The Evolution of Future Infrastructures" in Woods Hole, Massachusetts, in August 1986. Focusing primarily on problems inherent in urban areas, the workshop aimed to strengthen and focus research on infrastructure; to raise critical infrastructure issues for society, industry, and government; and to describe better for people the new sociotechnical systems that may grow around and for them. It also attempted to identify technological possibilities for the next 30–50 years in systems such as transportation, communication, water, and energy.

The discussions at the workshop having persuaded us that a volume on infrastructures would be useful, we continued with the project, focusing on this book. We deliberately adopted an expansive definition of infrastructure. While the emphasis in the book is on the great networks and nodes that immediately come to mind in such areas as power supply and transportation, we also seek to understand other aspects of our built environment that are lasting and, more generally, what it is that physically makes up or characterizes a city. We emphasize the technology, history, and theory of infrastructure. The very important issues of politics and finance are alluded to, but to be covered adequately, would require a separate volume of equal size. Art and design considerations similarly merit in-depth consideration beyond what is possible in this single volume.

I would like to thank Carnegie Corporation of New York and the Andrew W. Mellon Foundation for their funding of this activity. The Evolution of Future Infrastructures Workshop was the sixth in a series of events conducted under grants given the NAE to pursue studies of importance to technology and society. Certainly no subject is more fundamental to society or more affected by technology than our major infrastructural systems.

I believe that this volume has far-reaching implications and want to express my sincere thanks to the participants in the workshop for their creative contributions and to the authors who persevered through a lengthy process of revision and review. I would also like to note insightful contributions by Alfred Blumstein, Leonard Duhl, John Eberhard, Denos Gazis, and Richard Rothery, whose comments I hope are captured in the introductory essay. David Billington and Thomas Larson provided valuable responses to the draft essays. Special thanks are due Robert Herman, chairman of the workshop, for his imagination and enthusiasm, and Jesse H. Ausubel, director of the NAE Program Office, for the planning and execution of this activity, including a remarkable adventure across Vineyard Sound that revealed a resilient local transport infrastructure, and to both of them for their excellent editing of the volume. I also want to express my gratitude to the Advisory Committee on Technology and Society (p. *iii*) for its oversight, to Penelope J. Gibbs for administration of the activity, and to NAE editor H. Dale Langford and Caroline G. Anderson, administrative secretary with the NAE Program Office, for their work in preparing the manuscript for publication.

ROBERT M. WHITE
President
National Academy of Engineering

Contents

vii

CITIES
AND THEIR VITAL SYSTEMS

1

Cities and Infrastructure: Synthesis and Perspectives

ROBERT HERMAN AND JESSE H. AUSUBEL

The subject of this book is infrastructure, the built environment in which we live, the way we use it, and how it may evolve in the future. Cities are the summation and densest expression of infrastructure, or more accurately, a set of infrastructures, working sometimes in harmony, sometimes with frustrating discord, to provide us with shelter, contact, energy, water, and means to meet other human needs. The infrastructure is a reflection of our social and historical evolution. It is a symbol of what we are collectively, and its forms and functions sharpen our understanding of the similarities and differences among regions, groups, and cultures. The physical infrastructure consists of various structures, buildings, pipes, roads, rails, bridges, tunnels, and wires. Equally important and subject to change is the "software" for the physical infrastructure, all the formal and informal rules for operation of the systems.

Reflecting on the history of human endeavor, we are impressed by the creative achievements expressed through the arts, and engineering and science. The infrastructure is a dramatic statement that embodies all of these aspects. Many of the most esteemed, valued, and visible achievements of mankind have been in the domain of infrastructure: the watercourses and gardens of Babylon, the lighthouse at Alexandria, the roads and aqueducts of the Romans, the Suez and Panama canals. The control of water resources constituted the principal problem of early Chinese history, as agriculture was afflicted by frequent floods and droughts. The maintenance and repair of the canals and dikes of the large river valleys were the central administration's main duties and

1

became symbolic of a well-organized and efficient government (Witt-fogel, 1958).

Walls encircling towns were once perhaps the most important infra-structure for many settlements. Walls were built to provide security and at the same time served to control access to a city, allowing inspection of incoming travelers and collection of tolls. Gate taxes were a major source of income for medieval towns, and building and maintaining walls required tremendous financial outlay and technical efforts. The greatest engineers, such as Leonardo da Vinci, were extensively employed in the design and construction of walls and fortifications. Remarkably, as re-ported in the chapter by Lynn Hollen Lees and Paul M. Hohenberg in this book, the population of the cities that built some of the greatest structures was that of a small town by modern standards (see Table 3-1, p. 78). For example, the populations of the great cathedral cities of the Middle Ages—Cologne, Milan, and others—were typically only about 50,000 souls. The populations of the cities of the Italian renaissance—an era unsurpassed in building achievements—were less than 150,000.

Many of the symbols and landmarks of U.S. history, the turnpikes that carried the wagons west, the Erie Canal, the transcontinental railroad, the Brooklyn and Golden Gate bridges, the great dams of the Southwest and Northwest, the interstate highway system, the skyscrapers and subways are infrastructure. Many of the heroes of American history, including Morse (telegraph), Bell (telephone), and Edison (electric power) are fath-ers of infrastructure systems. Matching the heroic and visible legacy are the little-noticed and often unattributed accomplishments of infrastructure systems, especially improved public health connected to supplies of fresh, clean water and prompt removal of wastes.

Both public and economic welfare have been motives for infrastructure development. Spurred by a severe yellow fever epidemic, Philadelphia was the first large U.S. city to construct a municipal water supply system (1779–1801). The first modern urban sewerage system was constructed in Brooklyn in 1857. According to Joel Tarr (1984), water supply rep-resented a situation in wh ch a number of interests, such as businesses and industries, homeowne s, fire insurance companies, and those con-cerned with public health joined to demand the construction of large public works in order to secure more adequate water supplies at reasonable cost. City boosters considered waterworks crucial in the competition between municipalities for population, trade, and industry.

How vital is infrastructure? One need only think of what life is like when each person is individually responsible for disposal of all wastes, carrying messages, collecting and purifying water, and gathering fuel.

The range, safety, depth, and variety of contacts we commonly now experience are in large part functions of the quality of our infrastructure.

What are "public works" and what are private works? In the United States we sometimes identify infrastructure only with public works. In this book we examine both the conventional public works, such as roads and bridges, and the privately owned or managed infrastructure. The historical and international perspectives developed in this book effectively downplay the differences between the two. In some countries, telecommunications systems are a government-owned utility; in some countries, private. There are private and public water companies. There are private and public power companies. Often, a new, young infrastructure system is introduced by private enterprise and then becomes publicly regulated or owned as it matures into an indispensable "utility."

Infrastructure systems are systems for the delivery of services. As such, the underlying questions are how broadly and explicitly should cost be distributed? Who has ownership and control? Institutional arrangements are a means to an end, and the ends for infrastructure systems are such features as quality, flexibility, adaptability, reliability, and cost-effectiveness. In different countries and regions at different times, one or another form of ownership and governance for infrastructure may be preferable. Some networks and facilities tend more naturally toward monopoly, and so in the United States these have typically come under government management or regulation.

As a society, we should strive for a high level of access for individuals, groups, and organizations for the services available through infrastructure. To generalize the stated goal of the early days of the American Telephone and Telegraph Company, we should strive for universal, affordable service with regard to water supply and wastewater removal, energy, and transport, as well as communications. In part, infrastructure is designed to overcome uneven distribution of natural resources. As Cesare Marchetti points out in Chapter 7, infrastructure enables us to extend our range and control over our lives. Infrastructure is often in the foreground when we speak of the quality of life, and images of infrastructure, whether positive ones of aesthetic structures or negative ones of time spent waiting in queues, are central to our image of healthy cities and societies.

There are choices to be made with respect to infrastructure. Anyone flying over North America and Europe immediately notes the drastically different configurations of settlement. Like the diverse solutions for the design of local area computer networks discussed by Dean Gillette in Chapter 10, each infrastructure system at the outset may be realized in many different forms. But infrastructures also quickly grow rigid and costly to modify. We could benefit considerably from better understanding of the implications of alternative designs from technological and social perspectives.

What in fact is the state of the infrastructure? Is it deteriorating more rapidly than we are restoring or replacing it? Are systems being expanded rapidly enough to accommodate likely demands, for example, for growth in passenger and cargo air transport? The essays in this book suggest that in truth we do not know well the condition of our infrastructure. Simple, partial physical inventories are available for some components of the infrastructure. For many key systems, and for many cities, we are unable to specify much at all. Our diagnosis of the vital systems of cities and the nation remains primitive, and therefore the basis of most forecasts is questionable.

Some claim that the infrastructure of the United States is in a critical stage of decay. Is this so? In our view, the quantitative data and evidence are strong in a few areas and less clear in many others. A need and a question are raised by this judgment. The need is the deceptively simple one for more documentation of the historical and current performance of infrastructure. The question is the relationship between chronological age and quality of service provided. The relationship between age and decay is by no means clear-cut or linear for all infrastructure systems. It depends on several highly variable factors, including quality of original design, defects in construction, climate, and how facilities are used.

Some old infrastructures, whether physically sound or not, simply have no use with respect to their original function. If technological generations come quickly, as in telecommunications at present, designing and building systems and devices for a short life span may be appropriate. The fact that tens of millions of telephones built decades ago could still work today has little value because they lack the features that are now desired by consumers. With some old roads, the problem may not be age but other characteristics, such as width. With power plants, the problem may not be a decline in the quality of service they provide but that we have not determined how to relicense plants for another generation of operation. Moreover, some infrastructure elements, such as churches and many public buildings, given proper maintenance, appear to improve and increase in value with age. Infrastructure may not routinely mellow with age like a fine violin, but we should be cautious of drawing dramatic conclusions from listings simply giving the age of structures.

On the other hand, the mentality of producing goods that are expected to be used for only a short time is almost certainly self-defeating in many infrastructure areas. Why throw away roads or houses? As John S. Adams points out in Chapter 6, new housing for the poor in the United States is usually cheap and thus has built-in susceptibility to early decay and demise. Good engineering and design can change this prospect. To illustrate, some housing that was thought to be cheap when constructed, such as much nineteenth century English working-class housing or the row houses of Baltimore, has proved to be long-lived or at least readily adapted to new uses.

Although we must not assume too much about the link between aging and decay, there is a clear need for more widespread adoption of a life cycle approach to infrastructure systems. In the final chapter of the book, Gregg Marland and Alvin M. Weinberg make a telling case for this approach by asking three fundamental questions about a variety of infrastructure systems: What actually is the characteristic longevity of a given infrastructure? How long *could* it last? How long *should* it last? For all our sociotechnical systems there is birth, growth, development, and then, to varying degrees, senescence and death. As argued by W. Brian Arthur in Chapter 4, we do not appreciate sufficiently the importance of the early life history of systems, the time during which they take on a relatively fixed character. Neither do we appreciate the extent to which the growth of systems, and patterns of substitution among technologies for such infrastructure needs as energy and transport, are predictable. In their chapters, Cesare Marchetti and Nebojsa Nakicenovic provide striking examples of how well-documented life histories of infrastructure systems may enable us to forecast future infrastructure needs and how these needs are most likely to be met.

There is another simple yet compelling reason for taking an approach that emphasizes the full potential of a system through time and not merely the short-term investment decision. As Marland and Weinberg observe, sites for infrastructure are virtually eternal. The process of siting, designing, and building infrastructure facilities, whether airports, sewage treatment plants, incinerators, power plants, roads, or prisons, is characteristically long, often measured in decades. In turn, the function fulfilled at the site endures for generations and, not infrequently, centuries. The needs for infrastructure to supply energy and communications, for example, never end; specific components, systems, and technologies used are of course replaced eventually. It is time to achieve a better balance in our thinking about how to build systems, with an emphasis on both how the systems decay and how to maintain them.

Cities and the systems that serve them suffer both acute and chronic disease. Throughout human history many cities have been abruptly destroyed by wars and natural hazards, such as earthquakes and volcanic activity. We need to understand better the built-in attributes of infrastructure systems that lead to potential vulnerabilities from these forces and such events as power failures and major accidents with hazardous materials. It is possible to build resilience to disasters into infrastructure, although it sometimes requires costly outlays and also foresight about where evolving vulnerabilities lie. Some formerly devastating problems are now largely under control; fire, for example, was once the scourge of cities, but firefighting and improved engineering and design of structures now effectively keeps fire damage at an acceptable level.

The chronic diseases that afflict our roads, pipes, and other facilities should be a simpler matter to treat effectively. Much of the decay is apparent and predictable, and long-term strategies are feasible. We have usually reserved long-term efforts for the building of systems, such as the 30-year plan for the development of the interstate highway system. Such plans should be pursued more frequently for the maintenance and retirement of systems as well.

It appears that there are opportunities to be more systematic in the study and management of waning infrastructures. Marland and Weinberg (see p. 191) propose a framework for succinctly characterizing the causes of decline of bridges, dams, roads, and power plants. Could this framework also be applied to harbors, canals, railroads, post offices, and lending libraries? What are the relative roles of misuse, overuse, abuse, crime, neglect, and obsolescence in the decline of systems?

We should not underestimate the possibility of finding pleasing new uses for old infrastructure. Most harbors no longer serve the purposes for which they were designed in the nineteenth or early part of this century; movement of cargo is being widely replaced by housing and parks as the main waterfront uses. Canals in the United States are now largely used for recreational boating. Railroad tracks have been superseded by bike paths, and railway stations by restaurants. The Gare d'Orsay in Paris, a monumental infrastructure achievement of the railway era, has become France's museum of the nineteenth century. What will become of post offices, public libraries, and, eventually perhaps, airports?

An interesting trend in transport and energy technologies evident in several chapters in this volume is that infrastructures appear to be decaying or losing their share of the market for which they compete at progressively lower rates. Is this because each new system is larger in its fullest realization than the previous dominant mode, and thus more lives must be changed each time we abandon, decommission, or reduce a system? Alternatively, are we as a society tending toward preserving all systems in parallel as a form of sociotechnical insurance?

This book queries whether we are asking the right questions about the waxing infrastructures as well as about those that are waning. Nakicenovic and Thomas Craig present compelling evidence that we are not yet adequately coming to grips with the likely dimensions of the air transport system, not only today, but as envisioned 10 or 30 years in the future. Harvey Brooks and Dean Gillette outline a comparable series of issues about the communications infrastructure, which continues to grow vigorously but perhaps without sufficient careful checking against social goals.

Demographers emphasize the need to take into account demographic and behavioral considerations in infrastructure planning. The changing age profile of the U.S. population is predictable with considerable accuracy extending decades into the future. We know, for example, that the greatest percentage growth in U.S. population will be in those who are very old, that is, over 85. Our planning should reflect this and other demographic trends. We also need to understand better the mutual influence of behavior on infrastructure and of infrastructure on behavior. What should be done about "crimes" against the infrastructure: misuse, abuse, vandalism, and destruction? To what extent can we educate people to use the infrastructure more respectfully? In turn, what is the influence of infrastructure on antisocial and criminal behavior? Is it true that beauty defuses anger? How much stress might be relieved by more efficient and reliable provision of services such as transport?

The topic of behavior also raises the most fundamental question: what are the objectives of infrastructure? What is being maximized, minimized, or made adequate? Leonard Duhl (1986) has argued that we should examine the city from the point of view of human requirements. He urges us to build the "healthy city," defined in large part as one that learns from its experiences and uses the experiences to create a better quality of life. Many of our cities fail this test.

It is clearly a continuing challenge to represent the interests of users with regard to quality, safety, and satisfaction in the design and operation of infrastructure systems. The builders and operators of systems tend to provide the dominant vision, often with goals of maximizing system efficiency or size in ways that may not match users' preferences. A difficulty in this regard is the lack of detailed information on performance. However, there are vexing questions about how even to measure the economic productivity or social contribution of, for example, a bridge or a road system. In addition, how do we measure the quality of infrastructure services, such as air transport? It is universally agreed that we would like the time spent engaged with the infrastructure to be of a high quality, but how is this quality defined, measured, and denominated? The quality of a system is the result of an intimate interdependence among the various parts of the system itself, the provider, and the user. We have examples of infrastructure services, such as water supply, for which quality is generally uniformly high to all customers, even in the poorest urban areas. In the same jurisdiction, however, waste removal services may be highly variable in quality.

We tend to characterize infrastructure too little in terms of the individual. How do those in different segments of the population view infrastructure? Infrastructure for transportation appears quite different to the young, the old, and the handicapped. Access to water and sanitation remains a problem for the homeless. At what cost can high-quality infrastructure be made more friendly and accessible to larger fractions of the population and remain so? What are the social implications of alternative designs of infrastructure systems? Infrastructure, whether a village well or domed stadium, can be an organizing element in social life, and we would benefit from seeking to understand the transformations that will accompany shifts in infrastructure.

It would be helpful in allocating resources to infrastructure to have better and more readily available quantitative information on the interaction between infrastructure and individuals. For example, what is the time budget of individuals with regard to various forms of infrastructure? What fraction of the population at different times of day on average is in the air, in automobiles, on the telephone, or directly using water? How do these patterns of use vary from city to city and culture to culture? It would be informative to know the distribution of the labor force over the various infrastructure systems, how it differs between societies and how it changes over time. How is the labor force in infrastructure in different societies divided between construction of systems on the one hand and operations and maintenance on the other? Have there been changes over time in the proportion of the labor force working in communications, sanitation, water supply, energy, or transport?

It would be interesting to have more comparative data on effort and expenditure with regard to various infrastructure areas. How many worker-hours does it take to supply a gallon of fresh water in different cities and countries? How has the time and human effort required to secure and distribute water changed over the years? How many cubic feet of trash are removed by a given amount of individual effort in different countries? How many square feet of building area exist per person in different countries? How many communications of all kinds are transmitted per unit time by each person in different cities and societies? How do per capita water and energy use and travel vary? Data responding to several of these questions exist, but it is our impression that these data have not been effectively applied in many infrastructure studies or designs. A comparative, quantitative social science of infrastructure could be useful in indicating paths to improved performance.

Improved performance will certainly also come from technology. Probably the most widely appreciated cluster of technological innovations for infrastructure came in the second half of the nineteenth century. Such breakthroughs as steel building skeletons, elevators, electric lighting, indoor plumbing, central heating, telephones, and underground transportation had a profound influence on the built environment. Will there be a comparable burst of innovation in coming years? "Hard" technological advances might be foreseen in transport (larger and faster aircraft, magnetically levitated trains). Hazardous waste is an area in which there is a desperate need for technical solutions that could be widely accepted with a high level of confidence. The "utilidor" for infrastructure elements has been proposed as an interesting extension of a packaging concept that is widely and effectively used on a smaller scale in modern building design. But perhaps the current era will be remembered more for advances in enabling technologies, such as synthetic materials for a full spectrum of specifications, and applications of operations research to a range of systems from auto and air traffic control to elevators.

Just as integration of technological and behavioral aspects of infrastructure is critical, so too is examination of interactions of various infrastructure subsystems. In designing, building, repairing, or researching portions of the system, we too often forget the important interactions among system elements. Sometimes financial, political, or technical constraints lead to compartmentalized thinking and management of portions of the system. How tightly interlocked are different infrastructures? Railroads, coal use, and the telegraph grew together. So did autos and highways, oil use, and telephones. Could air transport have developed without radio and other high-speed telecommunications? In fact, it appears that transportation and communications systems may advance in tandem.

There is a complex and changing mix of competition and dependency among infrastructure systems. The airplane and the automobile compete for intercity passengers but are also jointly necessary to make most trips between given pairs of destinations. We have numerous instances of specific solutions—for example, siting of airports without appreciation of landside needs—that are put in place in a way that inevitably creates problems that surface later to haunt us. We are confident that research on specific infrastructure problems will be improved considerably when performed in the broader context, and a series of such efforts will eventually provide deeper insights and vision into the complex overall problem.

Institutional, legal, and political issues are never remote from systems so central to social organization and power. Technically feasible "fixes" such as interbasin transfers of water and development of nuclear power in the United States are either simply not socially acceptable or are blocked by political and economic concerns. Several authors, especially Brooks and Royce Hanson, stress issues of authority and legitimacy. Indeed, the concept of a "public utility" is at the intersection of all social interests.

What conclusions can we draw about the infrastructure from the chapters in this volume and the efforts associated with their production?

• In the near term, the preference for incremental improvement will almost always be dominant, and, in fact, the question of how to attain higher levels of efficiency within the existing system should always be asked. However, the challenge of infrastructure is more one of "portfolio management," and the corresponding need is to make investments that will generate yield on all time scales, from months to generations and centuries.

• Some major systems are clearly inadequate to meet current or projected demand. The most obvious are air and road transport and waste disposal. Adequate steps are not being taken to accommodate even conservative projections of increases in air travel. Other transport problems, such as parking, are almost totally overlooked. We have 120 million cars in the United States today and may have twice that many in several decades. Where will they all be housed? Are there ways to prevent the levels of congestion and delays in suburbs and outlying areas from approaching those of center cities? Vision is also lacking in waste disposal. Will there be a national infrastructure for hazardous waste? Will water supply and waste disposal be safely and effectively integrated?

• The organization of research and development in infrastructure is deficient. The emphasis is too heavily on solving narrow problems; inadequate efforts are going into research that embeds specific problems in an intelligently defined context or that looks at connections between various elements and problems. Much could be gained by linking the research and development systems for different modes within areas such as transportation and energy, as well as between areas, for example, transportation and communications. Experimentation by practitioners is also not used as it might be. In wastewater management, for example, there may be as great a need to encourage knowledgeable practitioners to experiment as there is for academic research. A major question is how to do meaningful, fundamental research on large, real systems. The importance of the development and understanding of historical data about infrastructure must also be emphasized.

• Several areas of research in engineering and science offer promise for many infrastructure systems. Operations research can be especially significant in the areas in which there are questions of traffic and transportation. Materials research and associated fields, such as sensors and nondestructive evaluation, may contribute to better and less costly system construction, performance, and maintenance. Telematics is both an infrastructure and—through the use of such concepts as the global positioning system and intelligent highways—a means for improving the use and operation of other infrastructures.

• Finally, we wish to stress not only the social and engineering challenges but also the tremendous intellectual excitement available in studies of cities and infrastructure. The chapters of this book demonstrate that this is a rich field for creative thinking. Paradigms, perspectives, and methods from many fields, including several areas of engineering, physics, operations research and systems analysis, economics, geography, sociology, demography, law, and history are represented in the book, and every author ends with fascinating, unanswered questions.

Let us now turn to a review of, and commentary on, the contributions that follow.

Suppose a Martian geographer or sociologist came to Earth and wanted to develop a taxonomy of human settlements and to describe the general characteristics of their temporal evolution. The chapter by Robert Herman et al. is such an effort to develop an objective, dynamic characterization of cities. It is an empirical attempt to use basic principles to find sets of small numbers of objective variables to describe actual cities in space and time. These variables in turn are used to generate a taxonomy of cities whose features follow similar tracks in time and that may thus be useful in prediction.

Herman and coworkers develop a history of the infrastructure of the city of Austin, Texas, and perform a comparison among contemporary features of eight U.S. cities. Some remarkable and intriguing facts emerge: water consumption per capita in Austin has remained constant since 1950; energy consumption per capita continues to grow exponentially; and the number of residents for each restaurant has held steady at roughly 600 since the turn of the century, notwithstanding the much-discussed emergence of a service society. A second area of discovery is that there are underused data resources for infrastructure studies. Quantitative examination of such sources as city directories and yellow page telephone books are one pleasing example. It would be fascinating and valuable to extend the analyses undertaken by Herman and coworkers to other cities in the United States and to cities in other countries to understand what is truly invariant, what is culturally dependent, and what is inherent in different stages of city development.

Lees and Hohenberg provide historical and sociological perspectives on how cities have grown in the Western world. They stress that cities are open systems, whether their main role is as the dominant central place of a system of settlements or as one among equally significant cities in a network. In fact, the single best descriptor of a city is dependence; a city cannot be a closed self-sustaining entity. Connectedness is thus the essence of systems of cities, and the systems may take various forms. They can be maritime empires or urban leagues united in trade. Leicester, for example, was one link in a chain of cities stretching from the north of England to central Italy that was organized in the Middle Ages around the production, processing, and marketing of wool.

Lees and Hohenberg illustrate that city growth is neither uniform nor automatic, but consistent patterns are linked to structure and function. Urban systems do not require compactness or symmetry, since transportation and communication technologies allow many feasible configurations. There may be some boundary conditions, however. In his chapter, Marchetti proposes that the ability to travel between any two points in roughly one hour defines the limits of a city. This does not accord with the traditional city planner's definition of a city based on administrative or geographical boundaries. Lees and Hohenberg, in turn, note that the distance—measured in time of travel—between cities of a given size or rank tends to be more or less uniform.

Lees and Hohenberg also discuss the dynamics of growth and change of cities and their infrastructure. Growth is not uniform in time; there are periods of explosive growth. An interesting example is the development of capitals, for example, in Spain and Italy. Capitals can continue to be oversized because of their political dominance, well after economic justification has declined. Indeed, the desire for glory or the need to maintain public order in crisis often leads to physical improvements. The economically paradoxical size of political capitals may be explained by viewing them as capitals of information.

Arthur asks how history affects the pattern of cities. Do chance events, including seemingly small occurrences, play a significant role, or does necessity determine what unfolds? For example, is it accidental that Silicon Valley developed as it has, or was it inevitable based on certain natural resources and other endowments? Arthur argues that cities become according to what they are; a mixture of economic determinism and historical chances, not either alone, forms the evolving patterns we see.

Arthur also proposes that cities exist in large part because of agglomeration economies. Most firms need to be near other firms in their own and other industries for supplies or as consumers of their products and services. Thus, there is a self-reinforcing attraction to existing and growing agglomerations.

Cities we have inherited depend partly on needs for services that arise at particular geographical locations, but also result from where skilled people happen to go. Determinism alone cannot explain city patterns without reference to chance events, coincidences, and past events. Without knowledge of these circumstances or those yet to come, Arthur argues that we cannot predict with accuracy the shape of urban systems in the future.

Thus, our infrastructure both records our past and shapes the present and future, except that early events or fluctuations act to push us into particular states or structures that the system eventually "locks into." With regard to infrastructure, we become locked into both particular spatial configurations and also technological choices. Sometimes we may settle to our later regret on local optima found with respect to restricted boundary conditions. For example, early historical competition among railroads in England resulted in adoption of narrow gauges that were better in handling turns but inferior in speed and comfort. The main reason for the eventual dominance of narrow gauge was not technological superiority; rather, George Stephenson simply built more narrow gauge in the early competition with the wide gauge of Isambard Brunel, and conversion from broad to narrow gauge was easier than the reverse. In the mid-1950s a series of minor circumstances appears to have acted in favor of light-water nuclear reactors over potentially superior competing alternatives. Arthur's argument about the importance of early decisions in the life history of systems has profound implications for infrastructure.

Martin J. Beckmann presents an economic model of urban growth. Consistent with Arthur, Beckmann argues that cities are characterized by increasing rather than constant or diminishing economic returns as the scale of an organization or operation grows. His conclusion is that under reasonable assumptions, the prediction of economic theory is that the urban sector must always grow relative to the agricultural sector and that this process will continue in the future. Substitution of services for industrial production as the main function of a city does not change this. The implication is that there is no end in sight to the increase in city size. The growth of "giant cities" such as Mexico City may confirm Beckmann's theoretical viewpoint.

Adams discusses the evolution of urban infrastructure at national and local scales. He identifies a series of epochs characterized by different transportation technologies: wagon and sailing vessel; steamboat and early railroad; long-haul trains; automobiles, trucks, and airplanes. Adams stresses the complementarity and synergy among modes of transport, in contrast to Nakicenovic and Marchetti, who stress the struggle for survival among them. At any given time, a city or individual is dependent on several modes, and in combination they provide services that could not be offered by a technological monoculture.

An interesting question is whether communication will become the next "epochal" infrastructure. In fact, communication has traditionally been associated with transportation, though it now may receive greater attention in its own right. Letters and packages have been carried by wagons, sailing vessels, pony express, trucks, and airplanes. Is there a qualitative difference between traditional and modern means of carrying information, that is, between the mails, telegraph, radio, and new lightwave communication? Is the epochal designation earned by the growth of infrastructures that are dedicated exclusively to transport of information and not goods?

Adams points out the difficulty faced by planners in the transition periods between epochs. "A group of urban planners in 1880 might have been fairly successful at outlining growth patterns for the ensuing 20 or 30 years, but how would such a group have fared in 1920, when their experience with the characteristics of a rail-dominated transportation network was about to become obsolete?" (p. 111)

Like Hanson and Brooks, Adams faces the question of who should pay for infrastructure. One issue is the extent to which one mode of transport or one sector should subsidize another. More generally, there are questions of distributive justice and fairness. In this context, he raises the key question of how we can take the economic temperature of a city: Do we look at bond ratings? Should we measure the change in number of jobs within its boundaries?

Adams also reviews the availability, condition, and cost of housing units in the largest cities and urban/suburban dynamics. Housing, unlike some other infrastructural elements, is never obsolete in a broad sense, though it may be dated in style, deteriorated in quality, or lacking some modern technological features.

Marchetti approaches the question of infrastructure at both its most global and most fundamental levels. From biological thought, he borrows the notion that the goals of infrastructure are range and control. The final objective must be to have the whole earth comfortably and efficiently as one's territory, and this requires a hierarchy of complementary infrastructures for transportation and communication. Marchetti argues that there is limited range for substitution between transportation and communication. Rather, each feeds the growth of demand for the other.

In the area of transportation, time and money are allocated by individuals to different means of travel to maximize range. People in all societies in fact travel on average about 75 minutes per day, hence Marchetti's notion of a city as a spatial configuration that can be traversed in about one hour. Ancient cities satisfied this definition, and the majority of modern cities do as well. Naturally, means adequate to distances are required. Ancient Athens was a pedestrian city, whereas Peking had public wagon transportation from a remarkably early date. Indeed, any agglomeration that cannot be traversed in about an hour must fragment into several entities, according to Marchetti's view. The introduction of air shuttles in many corridors like Boston-Washington and San Diego-San Francisco is co-agulating these into a functional unity. To make genuine cities of the megalopolises that are developing in various urban corridors in Japan, the United States, and Europe, Marchetti suggests that very rapid magnetically levitated trains will come into commercial operation around the year 2000, providing a sort of super-subway. To achieve the true global village, aircraft that can travel between major cities in one hour are a necessity, and indeed research efforts are under way on hypersonic airplanes that could in three or four decades provide an ''Orient Express'' shuttle service between, for example, Tokyo and New York.

Marchetti emphasizes the extraordinary regularity and universality, and hence predictability, of infrastructure development. The growth of the network of telegraph wires in the United States (Figure 2 in Chapter 7) is one of many examples of a perfectly consistent process; the smooth curve shows none of the social, political, and industrial conflict that must have accompanied this growth. The spread of railroads and subway systems throughout the world can also be successfully analyzed as a single, global process, with each city or country falling into line with military precision. Marchetti also discerns pulses of growth arising from technological innovation, ''long waves'' that have periods of about 50 years and characterize the transformation of infrastructure.

Nakicenovic provides a complementary characterization of the evolution of infrastructure systems for transportation and energy in the United States. A logistic substitution model organizes the data on these systems according to market share and overall growth into a set of patterns that have probably not been appreciated in the past for their remarkably steady behavior. The successive roles of horses and automobiles mesh with astonishing precision, as do the life cycles of canals, railroads, roads, and air routes (Figures 14 and 15 in Chapter 8). His analyses also bring out the parallel and interdependent evolution of the systems for transport and energy.

Extrapolating Nakicenovic's analyses leads to significant predictions. On the one hand, no breakthroughs in transport are required for the rest of the century, rather improvements must be made in those systems and technologies currently in place. On the other hand, to handle predicted increased demand for air transport, around the year 2000 stretched jumbo jets carrying 1,000 people will be needed. Alternatively, supersonic or hypersonic aircraft carrying about 300 passengers could contribute significantly toward meeting the projected demand for intercity transportation. Nakicenovic also concludes that in the United States only about half of the eventual number of road vehicles that will saturate the country are currently in use. In 50 more years some 300 million road vehicles are projected for the United States. Like Marchetti, with whom Nakicenovic developed the theoretical underpinnings of the approach presented in Chapters 7 and 8, Nakicenovic argues that natural gas will be the fuel of choice for a new pulse of growth in the world economy; considerable expansion and extension of the gas pipeline network thus lies ahead.

Craig discusses air traffic congestion in a detailed case study. All transportation analysts are predicting growth in the volume of air traffic accompanied by continued and often worsening congestion. Indeed, the major problem with travel infrastructure for the rest of the century will be in aviation. As Craig points out, innovative engineering and management will be required in relation to both air and ground traffic control. The so-called landside problems of the air transport system create massive and largely unresearched issues of how to process astonishingly large numbers of people through hubs, and how to connect the air transport system to other modes of transport. The airport can be regarded as essentially the location at which autos meet aircraft, and these ''intermodal'' connections are generally ignored by research organizations and funding agencies that tend to focus on the pure problems of each mode, like highway paving and air traffic safety, rather than the links between modes.

What will be the great cities of the air? Historically, cities have always emerged with each new infrastructure. The growth of Chicago and Berlin, for example, was intimately connected to the growth of railways. What cities will emerge as the highest-level hubs in the continuing expansion of aviation? Amsterdam? Singapore? Brasilia, which, like a 1951 Buick LeSabre, has an automotive heart but a shell designed to look like an airplane? We also wonder when airports will begin to be recognized as the new city centers, as they become central places for more and more socioeconomic activity.

Gillette examines the conjunction of computers and telecommunication devices that makes up the telematics infrastructure. The integration of these systems became possible for widespread applications in the 1970s. It is a metaphor for the entire structure of society: to what extent are processes and knowledge centralized or distributed? What are the topologies and flows of data? Gillette points out that this system is still in the early, turbulent stage of growth that we recognize as the subject of Arthur's analysis. Alternatively, this is the variable, undetermined part of the growth curve in the Marchetti-Nakicenovic perspective. Telematics is a system in which many variants are competing. In time, certain structures will emerge and dominate for better or worse.

Can the pace of innovation in telematics be maintained by existing institutional arrangements? In contrast to areas such as water supply, in which it is generally held that progress toward better systems will be costly, in this instance it is believed that better systems will cost less. Components of greater capacity and lower cost are certainly in the offing. Although telematics will develop primarily on the basis of technology, Gillette also raises a number of social issues, such as privacy and intrusion, that may be created by or constrain the technology.

Brooks points out that telecommunications infrastructure is a different problem from all of the others addressed in this book. It is not a problem of decay or lack of investment. The problem is the shortening of the life cycle of the technologies and what to do in the face of the richness of opportunities. Moreover, substitution among communication technologies does not seem to be as significant as symbiosis. The question is how the technologies fit together. Indeed, customers are interested in the service and do not concern themselves with whether their voice is carried by copper or silicon. Yet, certainly there is competition within communication technologies, with copper wires, satellites, and optical fibers—or electrons and photons—battling for niches and market share.

Distributive effects are of central importance. What is the relation between high technology for a few and the service available to the many? Is there a trickle-down effect? Are developments in communications technologies a force for hierarchy or equality? Will they allow or encourage dispersion over forces for centralization and economies of scale? Will telecommunications attain a pattern of hubs and spokes similar to air travel and tend to reinforce the hierarchy of urban centers? In turn, what will be the impact of modern telecommunications on the configuration of the city itself?

Brooks reports that Japan is experimenting with regional development centered on the telecommunications infrastructure. The Japanese are building experimental cities of about 200,000 people with wideband communication, videotext, and interactive systems. An interesting question raised by Brooks is whether there are meaningful ways to assess the volume of service in telecommunications. Is saturation in the offing? Do we have insatiable appetites for transmission of information in contrast to areas such as water, energy, or transport in which saturation appears to be a valid concept, albeit at high levels?

Hanson stresses the importance of the changing context in which our infrastructures operate. In the case of water supply, we need to be as alert to problems arising from outside the systems as we are to internal ones. Hanson emphasizes that at least two external factors, the pollution of groundwater and the climatic changes caused by man-made emissions of greenhouse gases, may be critical. By expanding an energy infrastructure for burning coal, oil, and gas, the main sources of greenhouse gases, we may be undermining our planning for the water infrastructure.

At the same time Hanson notes that forecasts of water demand have not been reliable; estimates have often been overblown. We noted earlier the finding of an almost constant level of per capita demand over four decades in Austin. In addition, estimates of costs to replace water supply systems based largely on age have been unreliable. The age of water mains is not firmly correlated with failures, as Marland and Weinberg also discuss.

Water was perhaps the first infrastructure around which civilizations were built, for example, the hydraulic civilizations of Mesopotamia and China. Water is unique and of primary importance. It has often been a reason for, and an instrument of, war. Hanson proposes that there must be real progress in technology (for example, desalinization) and in institutional arrangements for its distribution or there will be conflict. In the United States there is enough water overall, but not locally and everywhere. In many other parts of the world, especially where watersheds are divided between two or more nations, the outlook for adequate and equitable distribution of water in the context of a changing and perhaps deteriorating global or regional environment is not encouraging.

In the area of wastewater, Bernard B. Berger similarly stresses the need for a systems view. Planning needs to be more and more comprehensive. There are some extraordinary successes in this area, for example, Chicago's Tunnel and Reservoir Plan (TARP)—a sewer and water overflow system that makes use of underground storage reservoirs. We speculate that such systems will be adopted by other cities over the next century so that, like subways, they are integral components of most major cities. There are enormous political and financial obstacles to constructing such systems, however, and in the meantime there is an urgent need to work on various related aspects incrementally.

Large, bold solutions for waste disposal are not only expensive but inappropriate in some situations. In addition, the technical "solutions" of one generation may not be acceptable, scientifically or otherwise, for succeeding generations. For example, Berger reports that the view that "dilution is the solution" is no longer held; neither is it acceptable to use sewage sludge as fertilizer, because of fears about toxic substances.

Cities have been the innovators in waste disposal. One concern is how the increasingly dense but less politically organized populations that are filling so many areas, for example, coastal regions, will address problems of wastewater treatment. Will higher levels of systems integration, for example, regional plans, become necessary?

C. William Ibbs and Diego Echeverry describe the need for and examples of technological progress in the construction industry. There is tentative evidence that productivity growth in construction industries is lower than in other industrial sectors in the United States. Factors such as complexity, uniqueness, and size of projects, managerial complacency, poor labor–management relations, and governmental regulations have contributed to the absence of an innovative environment.

At the same time there has been an explosive growth of competition among firms from many countries for infrastructure projects in all parts of the world, including the United States. A large number of vendors are available to do infrastructure work on a global scale. Historically, certain technologically advanced countries have designed and built (or supervised the building of) infrastructure systems. The British, for example, were responsible for building railroads all over the world, from India to South America, in the nineteenth century. Now many more nations appear to have skilled construction enterprises, and it may not be necessary to be a world economic power to compete for such contracts.

Ibbs and Echeverry identify several promising areas for research that could contribute to improved infrastructure in many modes: materials, monitoring and sensing technologies, nondestructive evaluation and testing, construction methods, robotics, management approaches, and data bases for management.

Marland and Weinberg discuss the longevity, mortality, and morbidity of infrastructure systems. Rather than dwell on the decay and death of systems, they point out that a surprising number of systems live longer than anticipated and thus give free benefits to future generations. This is true of some dams, power plants, bridges, and roads. Their chapter is a first attempt at a deeper demography of infrastructure. Many more such studies are needed. Marland and Weinberg identify three factors that determine the lifetime of infrastructure. Systems wear out. They become too expensive to maintain so that maintenance and replacement are not feasible. They are superseded by better alternatives.

Marland and Weinberg also note the permanence of routes and the eternity of sites. Even if roads and plants decay, their routes and the sites on which they are located appear to have immortality. It is easier to widen roads or add to sites than to obtain territory for new infrastructure. The man-made backbone of our society is probably well established and unlikely to change.

Marland and Weinberg hypothesize that immortalization and future uncertainty make for smaller, more decentralized units. If the perception of obsolescence is strong, then the amount that is worth spending in the first place is limited. Research and development in materials should lead to longer life without additional capital investment. In what cases should we design for immortality? Marland and Weinberg conclude with the fundamental observation that we should design in a way that structure and life expectancy are optimized for an evolving role, incremental change, and periodic replacement.

The chapters in this book show vividly that the overall problems of the physical infrastructure and the human activity associated with it present both an overwhelming and an inviting task for researchers and practicing engineers. We are confident that creative inroads can be effectively made immediately in thinking globally about the area. It is also imperative to move toward a style of infrastructure research in which more effort goes to thinking about the meaning of specific questions concerning smaller problems considered in broader contexts. The infrastructure appears as a system with fractal qualities, reproducing its essential features in a hierarchy of levels ranging from the global to the individual. Ultimately, we would like to attain a unified appreciation of the functioning of the entire infrastructure system and understand where it is headed. To use the phrase employed by Lees and Hohenberg, we would like to understand cities as systems and the systems of cities.

Such an appreciation requires a broader and deeper education for many more individuals who study, design, build, operate, and manage infrastructure systems. More of our engineers must also be historians and sociologists, and more of our city planners must understand fundamental trends and insights deriving from technology and the behavioral sciences.

It is our belief that the stronger forces in U.S. culture continue to move our society in directions that emphasize self-reliant, and sometimes atomized, structure. Our overriding goals are often to provide great autonomy and higher levels of consumption for the individual. Inevitably, much of our group character derives from the summation of the resulting individual behaviors. There are many positive features to this trend. For example, it contributes to the development of an infrastructure that provides considerably better for the aged and the handicapped. At the same time, to use Thomas Schelling's (1978) phrase, there are unwanted macroconsequences from micromotives. Indeed, we believe this is the essence of the problems of the infrastructure systems that are in crisis in the United States. For example, everyone is free to have a car and drive where they choose, and at liberty to make traffic jams. The central challenge is to improve the imagination and effectiveness with which we address longer-term, collective needs and retain a balance with individual possibilities.

The infrastructure is us. Like a seashell or a coral reef, it is an expression of the organism, a history of our lives and the technological and social evolution of our societies. It is a genetic reminder that we are what we were and will be what we are. We should not allow the infrastructure to develop only on the basis of individual utility and short-term measures of cost and benefit, or narrowly measurable attributes that are tractable with current analytic tools. We require longer-range goals of a creative and inspirational kind that blend technological and aesthetic considerations. The future quality of life is to some considerable degree in our hands when we debate decisions about infrastructure. Are beautiful structures ever obsolete?

REFERENCES

Duhl, L. J. 1986. The healthy city and your health. Health Promotion 1(1):55–60.

Schelling, T. 1978. Micromotives and Macrobehavior. New York: Norton.

Tarr, J. A. 1984. The evolution of the urban infrastructure in the nineteenth and twentieth centuries. Pp. 4–66 in Perspectives on Urban Infrastructure, Royce Hanson, ed. Washington, D.C.: National Academy Press.

Wittfogel, K. A. 1958. Oriental Despotism: A Comparative Study of Total Power. New Haven, Conn.: Yale University Press.

2

The Dynamic Characterization of Cities

ROBERT HERMAN, SIAMAK A. ARDEKANI,
SHEKHAR GOVIND, AND EDGAR DONA

The unprecedented rate of urban development over the last few generations has led to a wide variety of human problems, many of which stem from the nature and growth of a city's infrastructure. Blumenfeld (1971) has studied the consequences of urban sprawl, the process by which a metropolis (Greek for mother city—defined as the largest center of activity in a region) develops satellite cities or suburbs and evolves into a megalopolis (also Greek, meaning great city—originally a town in the Peloponnesus that the ancient Greeks unsuccessfully tried to develop into a large city). Gottman (1961) recognized this phenomenon taking place along the Boston-Washington corridor and saw in it new patterns in the use of space. He argued that this reorganization of space was inevitable because of the gregarious nature of opportunity-seeking people and leads to a high concentration of white-collar and service-oriented workers.

Geographers have also looked at the growth of the metropolitan framework. Adams (Chapter 6 in this volume) has used modes of transportation to classify urban development into four eras or epochs: sail–wagon, iron horse, steel rail, and auto–air–amenity. Each epoch sees unique metropolitan growth patterns being molded by the transportation available. Adams has also speculated about the epoch yet to come, one in which telecommunications and not transportation is the prime mover.

Dantzig and Saaty (1973) have looked at some of the problems that have been identified in today's urban environment and have proposed new ideas in space and time use. Their "compact city," which was designed using a mathematically and architecturally elegant approach, makes full use of time and the third dimension in space in reorganizing urban activities.

Studies in urban planning have not been confined to printed words and designs alone. The incorporation of Le Corbusier's ideas into the building of the metropolises of Chandigarh (India), Brasilia (Brazil), and the more recent example of Islamabad (Pakistan) suggests that ideas in urban design have a practical side, too. Such incorporation also demonstrates that if problems (especially those of scale) can be accounted for in the design process, they can be addressed effectively (Le Corbusier, 1967, 1971).

Any planning exercise that deals with the issues raised by modern urban growth must account for the unique fingerprint of each city. This requires grouping cities according to a "phylum," that is, an organic group in which all members exhibit a basic similarity of ground plan and evolve through similar stages, yet are completely dissimilar from one another.

One of the grey areas in this arena is the classification of cities on the basis of their infrastructure. It is characteristic of urban studies to establish a quantitative variable based on certain attributes of the city (such as population or area). These variables are then most often viewed in isolation from other variables, and cities are ranked or ordered on some common scale. Attempts have also been made to stratify metropolitan areas into relatively homogeneous groups on the basis of predetermined criteria (Golob et al., 1971, 1972).

There have been few attempts to examine the evolutionary path of a city and, using data across time and space, create a morphology for different urban settings. A classification scheme introduced by Herman and Montroll (1972) for characterizing countries and representing them graphically (in the form of multiaxis phase diagrams) is extended for use in this context to differentiate the form and structure of various cities.

In this chapter we shall establish a general framework for studies in the taxonomy of cities. Taxonomic studies, in the classical sense, have generally been restricted to biosystematics—the classification of living things (a process in which historical data are relevant). However, if we accept that evolution is the fundamental mode of change for both organic and inorganic systems (as expounded by Herbert Spencer [1820–1903] and Teilhard de Chardin [1881–1955] and discussed recently by Prigogine et al. [1978]), then it should be worthwhile to bring a historical perspective to the investigation of a means for differentiating among cities.

The study described in this chapter includes historical data for variables that represent several infrastructural attributes of one city, namely, Austin, Texas; it also examines the evolutionary track of the variables from the turn of the century to the present, using as its sources the City Directory of Austin (1959–1985) and the General Directory of the City of Austin (1900–1985). Similar variables are examined for eight other cities (Atlanta, Chicago, Cincinnati, Houston, Los Angeles, Miami, New York, and Seattle) for the present. Because pictorial representations of data derived from a complex situation may provide insight into the mechanisms of the system, the first set of data will be evaluated from this point of view. The second series of data will be used to determine which variables statistically discriminate or correlate best across the cities under study.

Our intention in this chapter is to explore a means of differentiating among cities according to the mutually dependent areas of a city's current character and its evolutionary path. Eventually, formal models might be constructed to describe possible changes for a set of cities with similar ground plans.

EVOLUTION OF A CITY

The figures that follow are pictorial representations of the evolutionary path taken by certain attributes of the city of Austin. Comparisons across both time and space require the use of data that are either normalized on some scale or reduced to a dimensionless quantity. It is a common practice to use population as a normalizing variable and to represent attributes on a per capita (or its reciprocal) basis. Density functions in two dimensions (involving area) have also been used previously for normalization. It would be worthwhile to investigate density functions formed in one dimension when the functions are normalized with respect to the total length of streets in a city. Figures 2-1, 2-2, and 2-3 show how three basic variables— population, area, and street miles—have changed over time. It would be interesting to observe the changes in lane miles, which reflect both road width and length, rather than street miles; unfortunately, such data are extremely difficult to obtain.

Figures 2-4, 2-5, and 2-6 show how the basic variables change with respect to one another. The density of population shows an approximate linear increase from 1900 to 1950 (Figure 2-4); from 1950 to 1980, however, the city's growth in area was faster than the corresponding growth in population. The 1985 peak represents the spurt of growth the city has had in the 1980s. Density of street miles may give a general indication of the "efficiency" of land use in Austin (Figure 2-5). The decreasing trend from 1950 onward suggests that even though the city acquired various tracts, this land was not opened up to the same extent as land acquired before 1950. Another interpretation is that the density of streets in the inner city (areas included in the city limits until 1950), may not be greater

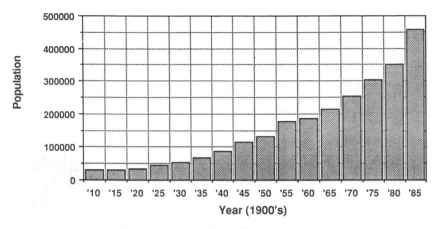

FIGURE 2-1   Population of Austin, 1910–1985.

than the density of streets in the suburban areas adjoining the city (developed after 1950), and the decline comes simply from the inclusion of
tracts of undeveloped land. The density of population per street mile has
remained fairly constant from 1955 to 1980 (Figure 2-6), which supports
(although not conclusively) the argument that the effect is due to the
inclusion of undeveloped land. One immediate conclusion to be drawn
from Figure 2-6 is that growth in the number of street miles in the city
has lagged behind growth in population over the last 70 years. This state-

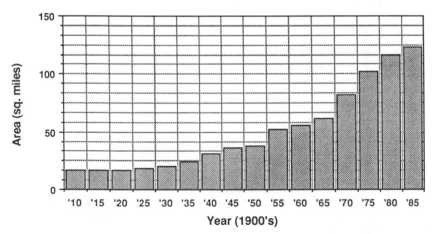

FIGURE 2-2   Area enclosed by the city limits of Austin, 1910–1985.

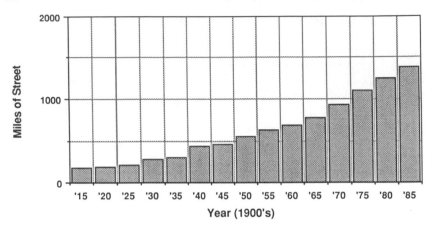

FIGURE 2-3   Miles of streets in Austin, 1915–1985.

ment reflects a simple measure of the increasing number of people sharing the use of one unit of the transportation infrastructure.

Another indicator of the load imposed on infrastructure is the number of motor vehicles in a city. Figure 2-7 shows that the total number of registered vehicles in Austin has grown at an exponential rate that is much faster than the growth in population. The number of vehicles per capita demonstrates this fact (Figure 2-8). As might be expected from the preceding discussions, both the number of vehicles per street mile and the number of vehicles per square mile have increased exponentially since

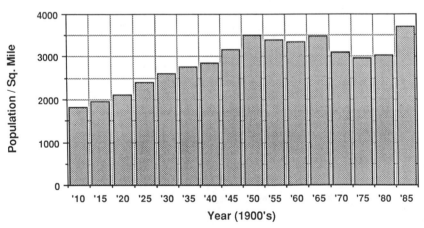

FIGURE 2-4   Population density of Austin, 1910–1985.

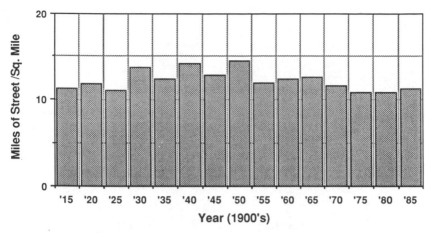

FIGURE 2-5   Density of street miles in Austin, 1915–1985.

1950 (Figures 2-9 and 2-10). It is worth noting that Figures 2-8, 2-9, and 2-10 all have a similar characteristic hump from 1920 to 1945; after 1950 they show exponential growth. This phenomenon indicates that strong correlations exist between the normalizing variables and the number of vehicles.

One of the more intriguing findings in this study arises from different functions of the number of restaurants (Figures 2-11, 2-12, and 2-13). Except for localized fluctuations, the ratio between the size of the population of Austin and the number of restaurants has been remarkably steady

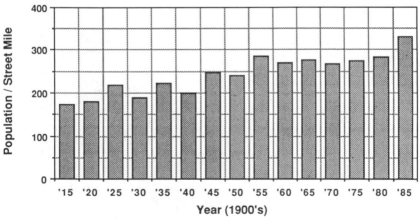

FIGURE 2-6   Population per street mile in Austin, 1915–1985.

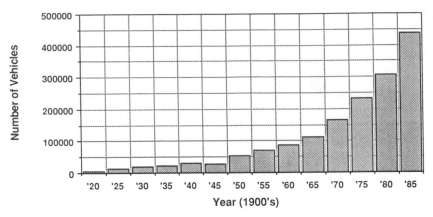

FIGURE 2-7   Total number of vehicles in Austin, 1920–1985.

from 1900 to 1985 (mean = 678, standard deviation = 159). Charts showing the number of restaurants normalized by area (mean = 4.2, standard deviation = 1.3) and street miles (mean = 0.4, standard deviation = 0.1), also exhibit a similar consistency over a long period of time (Figures 2-12 and 2-13). It would be interesting to compare these values for different cities, assuming that other cities display such characteristic numbers as well.

The ratio of population to the number of restaurants could, for example, reflect the degree to which a city is service oriented. Preliminary studies of data from San Antonio indicate that a steady-state ratio of population

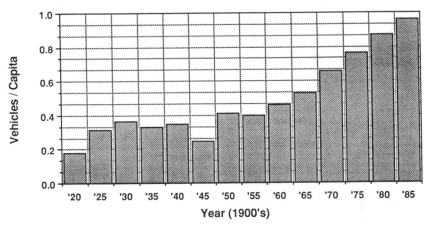

FIGURE 2-8   Number of vehicles per capita in Austin, 1920–1985.

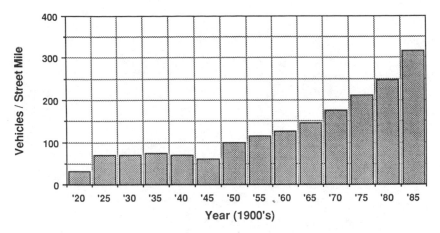

FIGURE 2-9   Number of vehicles per street mile in Austin, 1920–1985.

to the number of restaurants is not unique to Austin. In San Antonio the number of people per restaurant has a mean of 809 and a standard deviation of 359 (City Directory of San Antonio, 1900–1985).

The level of sharing of selected services (auto dealers, doctors, lawyers, and contractors) by the population (Figures 2-14 and 2-15) may represent key factors in the growth of a city. The number of doctors, including both physicians and dentists, indicates the level of health care available to the city's inhabitants. A lower population number per contractor implies higher

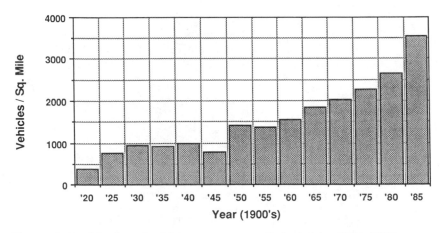

FIGURE 2-10   Number of vehicles per square mile in Austin, 1920–1985.

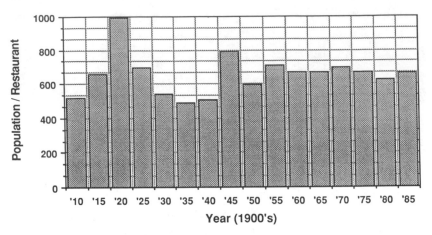

FIGURE 2-11   Population per restaurant in Austin, 1910–1985.

construction activity. The number of law firms could indicate essential aspects of the city and the type of activity on which it thrives.

Various conclusions may also be drawn by looking at the utility hookups in a city (Figures 2-16 and 2-17). One could reason that every dwelling unit would probably have its own electric meter; in the case of water, however, most apartment complexes do not have separate meters for each apartment. For the most part, charges for this utility are assessed on a fixed rate (which may be included in the rent of the apartment). Data on

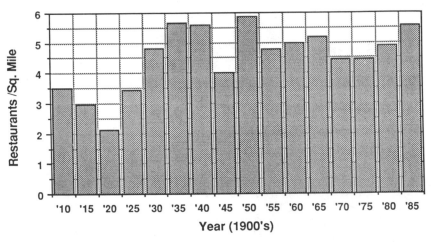

FIGURE 2-12   Number of restaurants per square mile in Austin, 1910–1985.

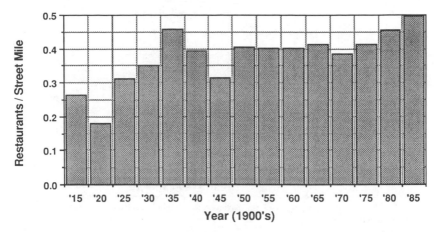

FIGURE 2-13   Number of restaurants per street mile in Austin, 1915–1985.

the number of electric meters and water meters could therefore be used to characterize the composition of the housing market (Figure 2-16). Further, the volume of telephone numbers in use may reflect not only the average family size (assuming one telephone number per family) but also the business activity of the city (Figure 2-17).

Austin's annual per capita consumption of water appears to have remained stable at 70,000 gallons since 1970 and shows no signs of increasing (Figure 2-18). This variable could be used as an indicator of geographical and climatological differences among cities. Another excel-

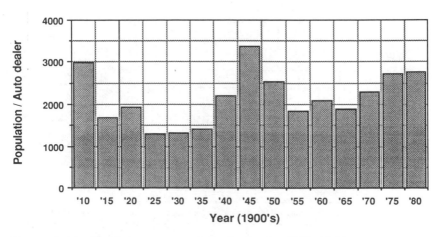

FIGURE 2-14   Population per auto dealer in Austin, 1910–1985.

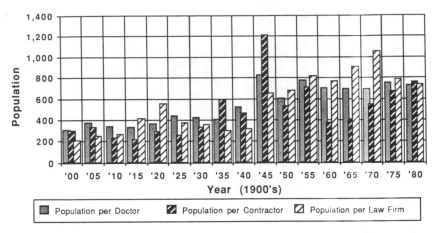

FIGURE 2-15   Population per doctor, law firm, and contractor in Austin, 1900–1980.

lent scale for the comparison of cities would be per capita annual power consumption because it measures an infrastructural attribute that is often of prime concern (Figure 2-19). Cities that use electrical energy for transportation—including escalators and elevators as well as rapid transit systems—may show higher per capita consumption of electric power than other cities. Weather and industry (among other factors) affect this variable as well. For this reason, per capita power consumption might be an excellent discriminant among cities.

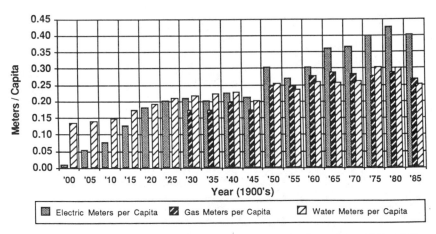

FIGURE 2-16   Electric, gas, and water meters per capita in Austin, 1900–1980.

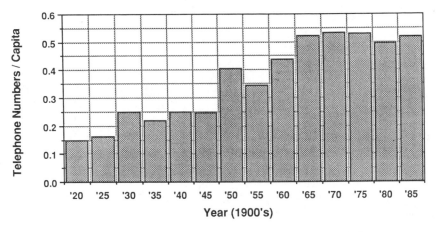

FIGURE 2-17   Telephone numbers per capita in Austin, 1920–1985.

The exponential rise in postal receipts in Austin (Figure 2-20) might not be so steep if this chart were further normalized by the corresponding year's postage rates and indexed for inflation. Current levels of postal revenues could be a strong indicator of the nature and level of the business of the city. It would also be interesting to examine the levels of overnight private letter and package delivery services.

Size rather than quantity is the most pertinent question when looking at the hospitals and banks in a city. For instance, data regarding the number of hospital beds or the number of admissions may prove to be more

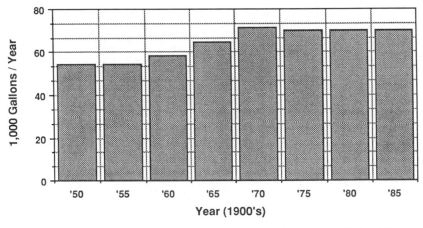

FIGURE 2-18   Annual water consumption per capita in Austin, 1950–1985.

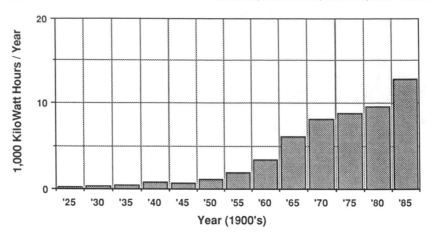

FIGURE 2-19   Annual power consumption per capita in Austin, 1925–1985.

revealing than the number of institutions. Similarly, for banks the number of customers or net assets and liabilities may be more meaningful than the number of banks.

The number of hotels and motels in relation to the size of the permanent population is one measure of the transient population of a city. As in the case of hospitals and banks, however, the question of size confounds the issue. Data on hotel revenues and the number of beds available in a city might provide more definite answers. For example, data based on the

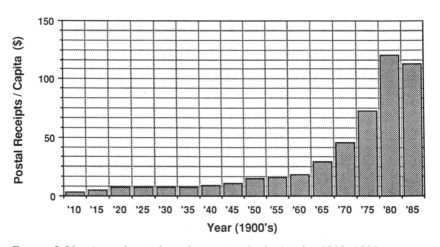

FIGURE 2-20   Annual postal receipts per capita in Austin, 1910–1985.

combined numbers of hotels and motels do not indicate the sharp increase in the number of motels after World War II and the decreasing number of hotels during the same period.

COMPARISON OF CITIES

In this study the first step in characterizing the dynamics of cities was to compare current demographic, socioeconomic, and infrastructural characteristics of several cities. Such comparisons are also fruitful in identifying key variables that may be used to characterize a single city through time.

One city was selected from each of eight major urban regions of North America. The eight regions are the Boston-New York-Washington megalopolis (Bosnywash), the Great Lakes, California, the urban South, Florida, the Gulf Shore, the Ohio Valley, and the Northwest (Figure 2-21 and Table 2-1). The selection of these regions is based on Maurice Yeates's *North American Urban Patterns* (1980) in which he subdivides North America into major urban regions using three criteria: (1) population density, (2) commuting patterns, and (3) size. For the current study, the cities of New York, Chicago, Los Angeles, Atlanta, Miami, Houston, Cincinnati, and Seattle were chosen to represent the eight regions, respectively. Recent data were used to examine 55 variables (see Table 2-2) across the eight cities.

DATA COLLECTION AND INTERPRETATION

The values of the variables listed in Table 2-2 were extracted from numerous sources and therefore are not associated with a single year. An attempt was made, however, to maintain the same year for a single variable across the eight cities. In addition, most of the data are as recent as 1980. The values of the variables for each of the eight cities, together with their years, units, and sources, are given in Appendix B. Note that no values are reported for bus ridership (variable 40) in the eight cities. Nevertheless, to emphasize the importance of considering bus ridership as a characteristic variable, bus ridership has been included in the tables of Appendix B.

Closer examination of the data in Appendix B reveals several dominant characteristics among the eight cities under study. New York City, for example, far exceeds the others in population density (23,285 persons/sq mi), followed by Chicago (13,174); notable tall buildings (118 buildings above 20 stories), followed by Chicago (45); number of theaters (671), followed by Chicago (169); hotel rooms (100 per 1,000 population), followed by Chicago (44); average residential electric bill ($90 per month),

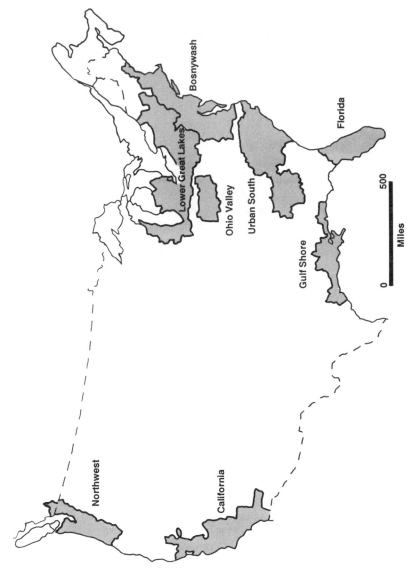

FIGURE 2-21 Location of major urban regions in North America, 1975/76. (Source: Yeates, 1980).

TABLE 2-1   Distribution of Population Among the Major Urban
Regions of North America, 1975–1976

Major Urban Region	Population (in thousands)	Size (in thousands of square miles)	Density (persons per square mile)
Bosnywash	44,384	102.58	432.7
Lower Great Lakes	37,569	128.38	292.6
California	19,668	67.75	290.3
Urban South	12,669	105.39	120.2
Florida	7,440	35.96	206.9
Gulf Shore	6,790	42.69	159.1
Ohio Valley	6,150	19.20	320.3
Northwest	5,738	45.94	124.4

SOURCE: Yeates (1980).

followed by Miami ($53); percentage of perimeter on water (76 percent),
followed by Seattle (59 percent); amount of revenue per capita ($2,370),
followed by Atlanta ($873); city expenditures per capita ($2,036), followed by Atlanta ($973); and workers using public transportation (242
per 1,000 population), followed by Chicago (189). New York City also
ranks first in miles of freeway (0.37 mi/sq mi), followed by Los Angeles
(0.33); and miles of sewer lines (20.4 mi/sq mi), followed by Chicago
(18.9).

The above characteristics identify New York as the most compact city
among the cities studied. Yet New York is a considerably less compact
city than that proposed by Dantzig and Saaty (1973) in *Compact City—
A Plan for a Liveable Urban Environment* and less compact than the more
decentralized version of this concept recently set forth by Beck (1986).
Dantzig and Saaty proposed that a circular city 8,840 feet (ft) in radius
and 16 levels high could comfortably house nearly 2 million people. This
480-ft-high domed city would have a total floor area of 141 sq mi, on a
land area of 8.81 sq mi, for a population density of 227,100 people/sq
mi, compared with New York's 23,285 people/sq mi. The city would be
capable of housing 600,000 families (300 families per 1,000 population)
in homes (each 2,400 sq ft in area) or apartments (each with a floor area
of 1,400 sq ft).

There would be three main transport modes in the compact city: horizontal mass transit (trams), vertical mass transit (elevators), and private
electric automobiles. The horizontal transit system would have 200 transit
cars with a total capacity of 737,280 passengers per day and a total track
length of about 62 mi (0.44 mi/sq mi). There would also be 256 elevator
banks with 32 cages per bank providing a vertical transportation capacity

TABLE 2-2   Variables[a] Studied in Each City

No.	Variable	No.	Variable
1	Population	28	Hospital beds
2	Area	29	Airports
3	Population density	30	Airport plane departures
4	Perimeter	31	Enplaned passengers
5	Form factor	32	Parks
6	Percentage of perimeter on water	33	Stadiums
7	Median age	34	Cemeteries
8	Average income	35	Churches
9	Revenue	36	TV stations
10	Expenditures	37	Radio stations
11	Bonded debt	38	Theaters
12	Households	39	Bus transit route length
13	Families	40	Buses
14	Workers employed in central business district	41	Rail transit track length
		42	Rail cars
15	Workers using public transit	43	Transit ridership
16	Total employment	44	Car registrations
17	School enrollment	45	Length of freeways
18	Postal revenue	46	Length of nonfreeway roads
19	Library budget	47	Bridges
20	Library books	48	Tunnels
21	Libraries	49	Water lines
22	Schools	50	Water use
23	Colleges and universities	51	Sewer lines
24	Notable tall buildings	52	Sewage treated
25	Hotels	53	Solid waste generation
26	Hotel rooms	54	Telephones
27	Hospitals and clinics	55	Residential electric bills

[a]See Appendix A for definitions of selected variables.

of 300,000 passengers per minute. The 32 radial and 26 concentric road-ways would be used by 10,000 electric automobiles (0.005 per capita) as well as bicycles on protected, parallel rights-of-way. A total of 3,130 mi of roads (22.2 mi/sq mi) would be needed. The total cost of constructing this city is estimated to be $36.5 billion in 1969 dollars. The city would contain 27 sq mi of parks (8.67 acres per 1,000 population) and 6.5 sq mi of work space. All offices and businesses would be concentrated in the central core exchange and the midplaza atrium. The city dwellers could be adequately served by 1,500 physicians and 32 clinics.

In contrast to New York, the cities of Los Angeles and Houston can be characterized as highly decentralized and thus are least like a compact city. Los Angeles is ranked highest in number of hospitals and clinics

(822), followed by Chicago (123); number of airports (4), followed by Chicago and Seattle (3); television stations (18), followed by Chicago (9); and radio stations (72), followed by Seattle (48).

Houston has the greatest perimeter (187 miles), followed by Los Angeles (144); highest average annual income ($10,958 per capita), followed by Cincinnati ($9,534), largest employment (519 per 1,000 population), followed by Seattle (506); and greatest number of public schools (1,944), followed by Miami (1,050).

A more systematic approach in comparing the eight cities under study is through a statistical technique known as factor analysis (Kendall, 1975), which has been used by Golob et al. (1972) to compare cities' needs for arterial roadways. In this technique a large number of variables are clustered into a few groups, each of which contains a set of mutually highly correlated variables. Each group is then represented by the variable that explains the greatest amount of variation in the data across, in this case, the cities studied. Therefore, a large number of variables can be reduced to only a few pertinent variables, which are used to characterize and compare the cities.

Statistical Analysis

Identifying the nine most descriptive variables to characterize the eight cities involves a twofold procedure. In the first stage the dimensionality imposed by the set of 40 variables for which data are available for all eight cities is reduced by clustering the variables into nine disjoint subsets or clusters such that any one cluster contains at least two but not more than seven variables. In the second stage the clusters are subjected to factor analysis to estimate the relative leverage exerted by each variable in the cluster. The outcome of the two-step process gives the ranking of variables within a cluster on the basis of the common variance explained.

Using this approach, we start by establishing broad categories under which the variables can be uniquely classified. Each category that contains more than seven (one less than the number of cities studied) variables is further subdivided into two subcategories: (1) wants and (2) needs. An exception is the transportation category, which is also divided into wants and needs even though it includes only six variables. This has been done to emphasize the importance of considering other transportation variables, listed in Table 2-2, in any future analyses of this type.

Although this clustering technique will not guarantee clusters with highly correlated variables, it is far more rational than a methodology based entirely on statistical considerations. In correlation methods of clustering, many variables, including those that are logically unrelated, may each fit into a cluster equally well. The correlation matrix for the variables to be clustered is shown in Table B-9 (Appendix B).

To rank the variables in clusters so that a single variable can be used to explain a large body of data, the principal-component approach in factor analysis is used. Its primary concern is to resolve a set of variables linearly in terms of a small number of underlying factors, which are themselves uncorrelated.

Mathematically, the principal-component approach is an attempt to represent a variable X_j in terms of several factors F_n's as in the following model:

$$X_j = a_{j1}F_1 + a_{j2}F_2 + \ldots + a_{jn}F_n,$$

where the coefficient a_{jn}, the factor loading, is an indication of how significant the associated factor is in representing the observed variable. The underlying characteristics of the observed variables, their inter-correlations, and the amount of variance individually explained, among other results, can be derived by analyzing the matrix of the factor loadings. Note that the total variance explained by a factor, the so-called eigenvalue, is numerically equal to the sum of the squares of the loading on that factor.

An important property of the principal-component approach is that each component makes a maximum contribution to the sum of the variances of all the observed variables. In essence the first principal component has the largest possible variance; every succeeding principal component also has to have the maximum sample variance, subject, however, to the condition that it be statistically uncorrelated with any of the preceding components. Although all the components are required to reproduce the total variance, for practical purposes, only a few components may be retained if they account for a large percentage of the total variance.

The statistical method used in this study computes eigenvalues for all principal components, but only those components with eigenvalues greater than 1.0 are considered in the analysis (SAS Institute Inc., 1982). On the basis of the retained principal components, the observed variables are then ranked according to their communality estimate, which is the amount of variance held in common with the other variables in the cluster. This amount is numerically equal to the sum of the squares of factor loadings (Kendall, 1975). The results of the analysis are shown in Table 2-3.

Data Presentation and Results

The factor analysis technique was used to select nine characteristic variables: (1) median age of the city population, (2) length of perimeter,

TABLE 2–3   Factor Analysis Results Showing the Members of Each Cluster and Their Communality Estimates

Cluster	Variables	Eigenvalues of Principal Components	Communality[a] Estimates
1. Demographic	Median age	2.415600	0.872
	Population density	1.313225	0.854
	Population	0.883587	0.800
	Families	0.340437	0.621
	Households	0.047151	0.582
2. Geographic	Perimeter	2.377001	0.969
	Area	1.161406	0.920
	Form factor	0.457670	0.837
	Percentage of perimeter on water	0.003923	0.813
3. Health	Hospital beds	2.313200	0.893
	Cemeteries	0.564199	0.836
	Hospitals	0.122600	0.584
4. Utilities	Telephones	1.321853	0.847
	Water use	1.145786	0.837
	Electric bill average	0.532361	0.783
5. Economic	Expenditures	3.200759	0.975
	Revenues	2.122249	0.970
	Postal revenue	0.818851	0.942
	Bonded debt	0.651224	0.741
	CBD[b] employment	0.175524	0.604
	Employment	0.030281	0.573
	Average income	0.001112	0.517
6. Transportation (wants)	Enplaned passengers	2.164236	0.960
	Airplane departures	0.964486	0.822
	Tunnels	0.856362	0.208
	Airports	0.014916	0.173
7. Transportation (needs)	Car registrations	1.754869	0.877
	Workers on public transit	0.245131	0.877
8. Social/cultural/ recreational (wants)	Theaters	2.566701	0.985
	Libraries	2.292634	0.963
	TV stations	1.076829	0.953
	Library books	0.683973	0.818
	Stadiums	0.343463	0.750
	Library budgets	0.032994	0.739
	Radio stations	0.003407	0.727

Continued

TABLE 2–3   Continued

Cluster	Variables	Eigenvalues of Principal Components	Communality[a] Estimates
9. Social/cultural/ recreational (needs)	Tall buildings	2.974723	0.814
	Enrollment	1.351481	0.771
	Hotel rooms	0.876889	0.748
	Universities and colleges	0.666752	0.683
	Hotels	0.122761	0.664
	Churches	0.007394	0.645

[a]Based on the retained factors with eigenvalues greater than 1.0.
[b]CBD = Central business district.

(3) number of telephone sets per capita, (4) hospital beds per 1,000 population, (5) city expenditures per capita, (6) number of enplaned passengers, (7) per capita car registrations, (8) number of theaters, and (9) number of buildings taller than 20 stories. The values of these variables were normalized for each city according to the highest value of each variable across the eight cities in the study. The normalized values in turn were used to plot "snowflake" diagrams for the eight cities. Snowflake diagrams have been used by Herman and Montroll (1972) to characterize countries by the distribution of a country's labor force across agricultural, transportation, commerce, manufacturing, service, and construction industries. The diagrams are formed by assigning one radial axis of a polygon to each characteristic variable (Figure 2-22). For each of the eight cities in the current study, the value of each variable is plotted on a scale from zero to one along the respective axes. Diagrams plotted in this way can be powerful graphical representations of the growth and development of a city. They can also be used to compare cities with each other and to examine changes in a single city over time.

Figure 2-23 shows the resulting diagrams for the eight cities studied. The variable represented by each axis of the phase diagrams is given in the figure caption and has the highest communality estimate in its respective cluster (Table 2-3). As can be seen the phase diagrams for Atlanta and Chicago are alike in shape although the area enclosed by Chicago's polygon is smaller. This shrinkage is attributable to the normalization of four of the variables on a per capita basis and to Chicago's denser population. The difference in size between these two diagrams can be an indication that, on a per capita basis, the people of Atlanta are better

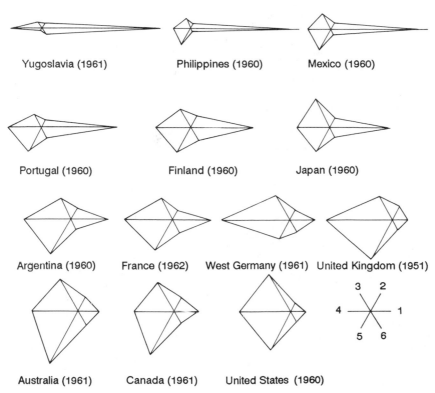

Yugoslavia (1961)   Philippines (1960)   Mexico (1960)

Portugal (1960)   Finland (1960)   Japan (1960)

Argentina (1960)   France (1962)   West Germany (1961)   United Kingdom (1951)

Australia (1961)   Canada (1961)   United States (1960)

FIGURE 2-22   Six variable snowflakes for several countries for 1960. The axes as numbered on the lower right corner are as follows: 1. Agriculture; 2. Transportation; 3. Commerce; 4. Manufacturing; 5. Service; and 6. Construction (Source: Herman and Montroll, 1972).

served than those of Chicago by the amenities represented in the diagrams. The similarity in shape and the difference in size of the snowflake diagrams are expected to remain relatively the same if other variables in clusters 2 through 9 of Table 2-3 are to be plotted on their respective axes, given that the pairwise correlations among variables are positive. Therefore, the similarity in the general shape of the diagrams for Chicago and Atlanta indicates that these two cities have similar characteristics. The relative size of the diagrams, independent of their similarity in shape, may be an indication that Chicago and Atlanta are at different positions on the same general evolutionary track.

The diagrams for Houston and Los Angeles are also somewhat similar

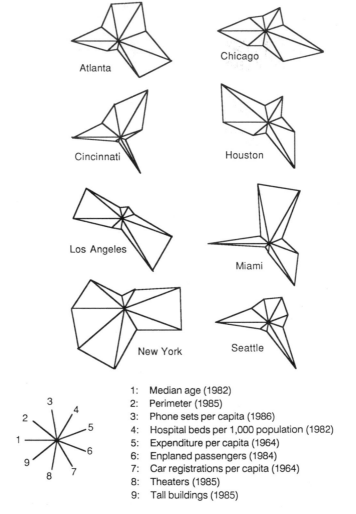

1: Median age (1982)
2: Perimeter (1985)
3: Phone sets per capita (1986)
4: Hospital beds per 1,000 population (1982)
5: Expenditure per capita (1964)
6: Enplaned passengers (1984)
7: Car registrations per capita (1964)
8: Theaters (1985)
9: Tall buildings (1985)

FIGURE 2-23 Nine variable snowflakes. The axes numbered on the left correspond to the variables numbered on the right.

in shape. They are both stretched out along axes 2 and 7, and both show small to intermediate values along axes 3, 4, 5, 8, and 9. Houston, however, is characterized by a lower number of per capita car registrations (axis 7), fewer enplaned passengers (axis 6), and a younger population (axis 1) than Los Angeles.

The diagrams for Cincinnati and Seattle are similar in shape and, unlike those of Chicago and Atlanta, are also similar in size. These similarities could suggest that Cincinnati and Seattle are at the same stage of evolution in their infrastructure. Dissimilarities can be noted along axes 3, 4, and 6; Cincinnati has a considerably higher number of telephones in use per capita, a higher number of hospital beds per 1,000 population, and a greater number of enplaned passengers, respectively. Once again it must be noted that these similarities and dissimilarities are expected to persist among most of the variables in the clusters represented by each axis. In essence, it is expected that a roughly similar diagram shape can be obtained if the variable plotted on a given axis is replaced by another variable in its cluster, provided a positive correlation exists between substituting variables.

In contrast to the other diagrams, those of Miami and New York show little resemblance to each other or to any other city in the study. Miami has high values along axes 1, 3, 4, 6, and 7; and low values along axes 2, 5, 8, and 9. New York City has high values along all axes except axes 3 (telephones) and 7 (car registrations per capita), implying that the city may not be as well served by its utilities and private transportation infrastructure as the other cities in the study.

It is remarkable that these snowflake diagrams characterize the cities under study in ways that are somewhat intuitive and certainly not surprising. For example, it is expected that Atlanta, Chicago, Los Angeles, and New York have high numbers of enplaned passengers. It is also not surprising that Atlanta, Cincinnati, and Miami all have relatively high numbers of hospital beds per 1,000 population and that New York is characterized by high per capita expenditures and numerous tall buildings. What is not so intuitive are all the variables that are correlated and clustered in the nine groups. Any attempt to explain the causality of these correlations is currently premature, considering that at present data are limited to the eight cities in this study.

Analysis of even these limited data, however, begins to indicate the value of using snowflake diagrams to characterize cities. Diagrams of a city over time can provide valuable information about its growth, decay, and evolution in relation to variables that mold its character. These diagrams could also provide insight into the age distribution of a city's key infrastructural elements such as sewer mains and bridges. Such time studies are currently being conducted for Roanoke, Virginia, using many of the variables considered in this study (Ardekani and Dona, 1987).

The proposed framework discussed in this chapter provides a means for characterizing the state of development of a city both over time and in relation to other cities. A classification scheme may then be formulated wherein all cities belonging to a given group exhibit basic similarities. It is thus feasible to examine the time evolution of these cities in relation to a particular set of variables and to make comparisons among them. Similarities can also be observed between two cities at different times. For example, the current characteristics of a city may resemble those of another city in the past. These comparisons might in turn be indicative of the future evolutionary path of the city in question.

Such inferences about a city's future state are strongest when a wide array of variables is examined and the interrelations and feedbacks among these variables are accounted for. Of great importance are the effects produced by social, political, and economic changes, which can completely alter a city's evolutionary trend. Note that it is inevitable that technological substitutions will occur, enabling a city to evolve toward greater complexity and causing a totally different infrastructural character to emerge (see Chapter 7).

Several other recommendations may also be made regarding extensions of the research described in this chapter. The significance of the underlying statistical analysis, for example, would be enhanced through the study of considerably more cities. The list of variables may also be expanded to encompass a larger number of city characteristics. On the other hand, the list of variables may be shortened to consider only a specific aspect of cities, such as their demography, transportation, commerce, or utilities. Finally, it is imperative that interpretations of the shape and size of the snowflake diagrams be extended to recognize views of a city from the perspective of various disciplines such as demography, geography, economics, and environmental health.

ACKNOWLEDGMENTS

The authors are indebted to the National Academy of Engineering for its financial support of a graduate student who pursued the data collection task. They are also grateful for the invaluable help of David Lee Han and Hans Seyffert, Jr., in collecting data and assisting with the production of the artwork. Finally, the authors would like to acknowledge Michael Allen Hoffman and Andrezei Blinkow for their assistance in collecting data on the city of Austin.

REFERENCES

Ardekani, S. A., and E. L. Dona. 1987. Characterizing the development of cities. Submitted to the ASCE Journal of Urban Planning and Development.

Atlanta Department of Community Development. 1984. City of Atlanta Comprehensive Development Plan 1984–1988. Atlanta.

Automotive Safety Foundation. 1964. Urban Freeway Development in Twenty Major Cities. Washington, D.C.

Beck, A. 1986. Utopia under glass. Journal of Civil Engineering 56(7):54–56.

Bergman, E., and T. Pohl. 1975. Geography of the New York Metropolitan Region. Dubuque, Iowa: Kendall/Hunt Co.

Blumenfeld, H. 1971. Modern Metropolis: Its Origins, Growth, Characteristics, and Planning, Selected Essays, P. D. Spreiregen, ed. Cambridge, Mass.: MIT Press.

City Directory of Austin, 1959 to 1985. Dallas, Tex.: R. L. Polk and Co.

City Directory of San Antonio, 1900 to 1985. Dallas, Tex.: R. L. Polk and Co.

City of Atlanta. 1985. Metropolitan Area Rapid Transit Authority Annual Report.

City of Chicago. 1982. Portfolio for the Future: Chicago Long Range Infrastructure Planning Needs. Chicago: Metropolitan Housing and Planning Council.

City of Chicago. 1984. Metropolitan Sanitary District of Chicago Maintenance and Operations Department Annual Report.

City of Los Angeles. 1985. Statistical Report for the Fiscal Years 1976–1985. Los Angeles Department of Water and Power.

City of Seattle. 1982. Seattle Engineering Annual Report.

Dantzig, G. B., and T. L. Saaty. 1973. Compact City—A Plan for a Liveable Urban Environment. San Francisco: W. H. Freeman.

Federal Aviation Administration. 1985. Airport Activity Statistics of Certified Route Air Carriers for 12 Months Ending Dec. 1984. Washington, D.C.: FAA Office of Management Systems.

General Directory of the City of Austin, 1900 to 1985. Galveston, Tex.: Morrison and Fourmy.

Golob, T. F., E. T. Canty, and R. L. Gustafson. 1971. Towards the Stratification and Clustering of Metropolitan Areas. General Motors Research Publication No. GMR-1093. Warren, Mich.

Golob, T. F., E. T. Canty, and R. L. Gustafson. 1972. Classification of Metropolitan Areas for the Study of New Systems of Arterial Transportation. General Motors Research Publication No. GMR-1225. Warren, Mich.

Gottmann, J. 1961. Megalopolis—The Urbanized Northeastern Seaboard of the United States. Cambridge, Mass.: MIT Press.

Grossman, D. 1979. The Future of New York City's Capital Plant. Washington, D.C.: Urban Institute.

Hendrickson, C. 1986. A note on trends in transit commuting in the United States relating to employment in the central business district. Transportation Research 20A(1):33–37.

Herman, R., and E. W. Montroll. 1972. A manner of characterizing the development of countries. Proceedings of the National Academy of Sciences 69(10):3019–3023.

Houghton Mifflin Co. 1986. Information Please Almanac, 39th ed. Boston.

Houston Chamber of Commerce. 1985. Information pamphlet.

Kendall, M. 1975. Multivariate Analysis. London: Charles Griffin & Company, Ltd.

Le Corbusier. 1967. The Radiant City. New York: Grossman-Orion Press.

Le Corbusier. 1971. The City of Tomorrow. Cambridge, Mass.: MIT Press.

Los Angeles City Planning Commission. 1981. Los Angeles City Planning 1781–1981. Los Angeles.

Martin, J., J. Avery, and S. Collins. 1983. The Book of American City Rankings. New York: Facts on File Publications.

Metcalf and Eddy, Inc. 1979. Wastewater Engineering: Collection, Treatment, Disposal and Reuse, G. Tchobanoglous, ed. New York: McGraw Hill.

Miami-Dade Water and Sewer Authority. 1985. Component Unit Fiscal Report. Sept. 30.

Newspaper Enterprise Association. 1985. World Almanac and Book of Facts. New York.
Prigogine, I., P. Allen, and R. Herman. 1978. The evolution of complexity and the laws of nature. In Goals in a Global Community, Vol. II, E. Laszlo and J. Bierman, eds. Elmsford, N.Y.: Pergamon Press.
SAS Institute Inc. 1982. SAS User's Guide: Statistics. Cary, N.C.: SAS Institute, Inc.
Seattle Water Department. 1984. 1984 Annual Report. Seattle.
Showes, V. 1979. World Facts and Figures. New York: John Wiley & Sons.
Sinnreich, M. 1980. New York, World City. Cambridge, Mass.: Oelgeshlager, Gunn and Hain.
Sunbank Marketing Department. 1985. Perspective '85. Miami.
U.S. Bureau of the Census. 1983. County and City Data Book. Washington, D.C.
Unibook, Inc. 1980. Houston, City of Density. O. M. Nergal, ed. New York: Macmillan.
Yeates, M. 1980. North American Urban Patterns. New York: Halsted Press.

APPENDIX A

Selected Study Variables: Explanatory Notes

Population   Data for this variable are based on the results of the Census of Population and Housing, conducted as of April 1, 1980. Persons enumerated were counted as inhabitants of their usual place of residence, which was not necessarily the same as a legal residence, voting residence, or domicile. Residence rules were established when a place of residence was not readily apparent (e.g., children in boarding schools below the college level were counted at their parental home, whereas college students were counted at their college residence).

Area   These data reflect annexations and boundary changes as of January 1, 1980. Included are dry land and land temporarily or partially covered by water such as marshlands, swamps, and river floodplains. Generally, streams, sloughs, estuaries, canals less than one-eighth of a statute mile in width, lakes, reservoirs, and ponds less than 40 acres in area are also included.

Form Factor   The ratio of the measured perimeter to the minimum possible perimeter for the same area.

Average Income   These data are based on the aggregate personal income in the city divided by the city resident population. Personal income is the income received from all sources, measured before the deduction of income and other personal taxes but after the deduction of personal contributions for social security, government retirement, and other social insurance programs.

Revenue   All revenues except utility, liquor stores, and insurance trust revenues. Also included are all tax revenues and intergovernmental revenues, which are amounts received from other governments as fiscal aid or as reimbursements for the performance of general government functions and other specific services for the paying government.

Expenditure   All city expenditures other than those for utilities, liquor stores, and employee retirement or other insurance trusts.

Bonded Debt   All long-term credit obligations of the government and its agencies and all interest-bearing, short-term (1-year) credit obligations unpaid at the close of the fiscal year. Although bonded debt includes judgments, mortgages, revenue bonds, general obligation bonds, notes, and interest-bearing warrants, it excludes noninterest-bearing obligations, interfund obligations, amounts held in a trust, advances and contingent loans from other governments, and individual benefits from employee retirement funds.

Households   Year-round occupied housing units. A housing unit can be a house, an apartment, a group of rooms, or a single room occupied as separate living quarters. The occupant may be a single family, one person living alone, two or more unrelated families, or related persons who share a household.

Employment   The total employed labor force divided by the total population. The labor force consists of persons at least 16 years old working as paid employees or in their own business or profession.

Enrollment   The number of persons at least 3 years old who have attended regular school or college at any time since February 1980. Regular school in this instance means nursery school, kindergarten, elementary school, and schooling that leads to a high school diploma or college degree.

Tall Buildings   Buildings at least 300 ft high or having at least 20 stories. Building height is measured from the sidewalk to the roof and includes the penthouse and tower (if present); the number of stories begins at street level.

Hotels   Both hotels and motels registered in the 1977 Census of Service Industries (Martin et al., 1983).

Hospitals   Facilities that have at least six beds and are licensed by the state as hospitals or that are operated by a federal or state agency (and therefore not subject to state and local licensing laws). Institutions and services commonly referred to as rest homes, nursing homes, old-age homes, and sanitariums are excluded.

Hospital Beds   Beds, cribs, and pediatric bassinets regularly maintained for inpatients during a 12-month period.

Library Books   Major library holdings reported in terms of volumes per 1,000 persons.

Colleges and Universities   All accredited, undergraduate degree-granting institutions that have a total institutional enrollment of 600 or more.

Airports   All airports (i.e., major, international, national, and regional) that support activities of certificated route air carriers.

Departures   All performed scheduled and nonscheduled departures.

Stadiums   All football and baseball stadiums.

Tunnels   Underwater vehicular tunnels with lengths of 3,000 ft or more and land vehicular tunnels of 2,450 ft or more.

Telephones   All public and private installed telephones that can be connected to a central exchange.

APPENDIX B

Characteristics of Eight U.S. Cities (on the following pages)

TABLE B-1 City of Atlanta

No.	Variable	Value	Unit	Year	Reference
1	Population	425,022	Persons	1980	U.S. Bureau of the Census, 1983
2	Area	136	Sq. miles	1981	Martin et al., 1983
3	Population density	3,125	Pop./sq. mile	1980	Martin et al., 1983; U.S. Bureau of the Census, 1983
4	Perimeter	69	Miles	1985	
5	Form factor	1.67		1985	
6	Perimeter on water	24	Percentage	1985	Martin et al., 1983
7	Median age	29.8	Years	1982	Martin et al., 1983
8	Average income	6,499	$/Capita	1981	U.S. Bureau of the Census, 1983
9	Revenue	873	$/Capita	1981	U.S. Bureau of the Census, 1983
10	Expenditures	973	$/Capita	1981	U.S. Bureau of the Census, 1983
11	Bonded debt	2,029	$/Capita	1981	U.S. Bureau of the Census, 1983
12	Households	382	/1,000 Pop.	1980	U.S. Bureau of the Census, 1983
13	Families	230	/1,000 Pop.	1980	U.S. Bureau of the Census, 1983
14	CBD employment	160	/1,000 Pop.	1980	Hendrickson, 1986
15	Workers on public transit	169	/1,000 Pop.	1980	Hendrickson, 1986
16	Employment	411	/1,000 Pop.	1980	U.S. Bureau of the Census, 1983
17	School enrollment	283	/1,000 Pop.	1980	U.S. Bureau of the Census, 1983
18	Postal revenue	787	$/Capita	1985	U.S. Postal Service, private communication, 1986
19	Library budget	8.72	$/Capita	1982	Martin et al., 1983
20	Library books	1,808	/1,000 Pop.	1982	Martin et al., 1983
21	Libraries	4		1979	Showes, 1979
22	Schools	676		1985	City telephone directories, 1986
23	Colleges and universities	28		1985	Newspaper Enterprise Association, 1985
24	Tall buildings	28		1985	Newspaper Enterprise Association, 1985
25	Hotels	72		1977	Martin et al., 1983
26	Hotel rooms	29	/1,000 Pop.	1977	Martin et al., 1983

27	Hospitals	56		1985	Newspaper Enterprise Association, 1985
28	Hospital beds	10.78	/1,000 Pop.	1981	Martin et al., 1983
29	Airports	1		1984	Federal Aviation Administration, 1985
30	Airplane departures	271.1	1,000/Year	1984	Federal Aviation Administration, 1985
31	Enplaned passengers	18,920.3	1,000/Year	1984	Federal Aviation Administration, 1985
32	Parks	7.48	Acres/1,000 pop.	1985	Houghton Mifflin Co., 1986
33	Stadiums	2		1985	Newspaper Enterprise Association, 1985
34	Cemeteries	8	/100,000 Pop.	1985	City telephone directories, 1986
35	Churches	3.53	/1,000 Pop.	1985	Houghton Mifflin Co., 1986
36	TV stations	8		1985	Houghton Mifflin Co., 1986
37	Radio stations	45		1985	Houghton Mifflin Co., 1986
38	Theaters	96		1985	City telephone directories, 1986
39	Bus route miles	12.35	Miles/sq. mile	1985	Martin et al., 1983; City of Atlanta, 1985
40	Buses		1,000 Riders/day		
41	Rail tracks	0.18	Mile/sq. mile	1983	Martin et al., 1983; City of Atlanta, 1985
42	Rail cars		1,000 Riders/day		
43	Transit passengers		/1,000 Pop.		
44	Car registrations	0.271	/Capita	1964	Automotive Safety Foundation, 1964
45	Freeway miles		/Sq. mile		
46	Street miles		/Sq. mile		
47	Bridges				
48	Tunnels	0		1985	Newspaper Enterprise Association, 1985
49	Water lines	16.1	/Sq. mile	1982	Atlanta Department of Community Development, 1984
50	Water use	149	Gpd^a/capita	1979	Metcalf and Eddy, Inc. 1979
51	Sewer lines	14.7	/Sq. mile	1982	Atlanta Department of Community Development, 1984
52	Sewage treatment		Gpd^a/capita		
53	Solid waste		Tons/year/capita		
54	Phone	2.3	/Capita	1986	Houghton Mifflin Co., 1986
55	Residential electric bills	40.53	$/Month	1983	U.S. Bureau of the Census, 1983

^{a}Gpd = gallons per day.

TABLE B-2 City of Chicago

No.	Variable	Value	Unit	Year	Reference
1	Population	3,005,072	Persons	1980	U.S. Bureau of the Census, 1983
2	Area	228.1	Sq. miles	1981	Martin et al., 1983
3	Population density	13,174	Pop./sq. mile	1980	Martin et al., 1983; U.S. Bureau of the Census, 1983
4	Perimeter	65	Miles	1985	
5	Form factor	1.21		1985	
6	Perimeter on water	43	Percentage	1985	
7	Median age	30.4	Years	1982	Martin et al., 1983
8	Average income	8,097	$/Capita	1981	Martin et al., 1983
9	Revenue	587	$/Capita	1981	U.S. Bureau of the Census, 1983
10	Expenditure	610	$/Capita	1981	U.S. Bureau of the Census, 1983
11	Bonded debt	359	$/Capita	1981	U.S. Bureau of the Census, 1983
12	Households	364	/1,000 Pop.	1980	U.S. Bureau of the Census, 1983
13	Families	235	/1,000 Pop.	1980	U.S. Bureau of the Census, 1983
14	CBD employment	92	/1,000 Pop.	1980	Hendrickson, 1986
15	Workers on public transit	189	/1,000 Pop.	1980	Hendrickson, 1986
16	Employment	411	/1,000 Pop.	1980	U.S. Bureau of the Census, 1983
17	School enrollment	272	/1,000 Pop.	1980	U.S. Bureau of the Census, 1983
18	Postal revenue	187	$/Capita	1985	U.S. Postal Service, private communication, 1986
19	Library budget	9.41	$/Capita	1982	Martin et al., 1983
20	Library books	1,244	/1,000 Pop.	1982	Martin et al., 1983
21	Libraries	5		1979	Showes, 1979
22	Schools	525		1985	City telephone directories, 1986
23	Colleges and universities	95		1985	Newspaper Enterprise Association, 1985
24	Tall buildings	45		1985	Newspaper Enterprise Association, 1985
25	Hotels	247		1977	Martin et al., 1983
26	Hotel rooms	44	/1,000 Pop.	1977	Martin et al., 1983

#	Item	Value	Units	Year	Source
27	Hospitals	123		1985	Newspaper Enterprise Association, 1985
28	Hospital beds	6.33	/1,000 Pop.	1981	Martin et al., 1983
29	Airports	3		1984	Federal Aviation Administration, 1985
30	Airplane departures	295.3	1,000/Year	1984	Federal Aviation Administration, 1985
31	Enplaned passengers	20,030.0	1,000/Year	1984	Federal Aviation Administration, 1985
32	Parks		Acres/1,000 pop.		
33	Stadiums	3		1985	Newspaper Enterprise Association, 1985
34	Cemeteries	2.36	/100,000 Pop.	1985	City telephone directories, 1986
35	Churches	0.4	/1,000 Pop.	1986	Houghton Mifflin Co., 1986
36	TV stations	9		1986	Houghton Mifflin Co., 1986
37	Radio stations	37		1986	Houghton Mifflin Co., 1986
38	Theaters	169		1985	City telephone directories, 1986
39	Bus route miles	9.16	Miles/sq. mile	1982	City of Chicago, 1982
40	Buses		1,000 Riders/day		
41	Rail tracks	0.94	Miles/sq. mile	1982	City of Chicago, 1982
42	Rail cars		1,000 Riders/day		
43	Transit passengers		/1,000 Pop.		
44	Car registrations	0.228	/Capita	1964	Automotive Safety Foundation, 1964
45	Freeway miles	0.311	/Sq. mile	1982	City of Chicago, 1982
46	Street miles	22.36	/Sq. mile	1982	City of Chicago, 1982
47	Bridges	1,060		1985	Newspaper Enterprise Association, 1985
48	Tunnels	0			
49	Water lines	18.3	/Sq. mile	1982	City of Chicago, 1982
50	Water use	230	Gpd/capita	1979	Metcalf and Eddy, Inc., 1979
51	Sewer lines	18.9	/Sq. mile	1982	City of Chicago, 1982
52	Sewage treatment	194	Gpd/capita	1984	City of Chicago, 1984
53	Solid waste		Tons/year/capita		
54	Phone	0.9	/Capita	1986	Houghton Mifflin Co., 1986
55	Residential electric bills	50.88	$/Month	1983	U.S. Bureau of the Census, 1983

TABLE B-3 City of Cincinnati

No.	Variable	Value	Unit	Year	Reference
1	Population	385,457	Persons	1980	U.S. Bureau of the Census, 1983
2	Area	78.1	Sq. miles	1981	Martin et al., 1983
3	Population density	4,935	Pop./sq. mile	1980	Martin et al., 1983; U.S. Bureau of the Census, 1983
4	Perimeter	71	Miles	1985	
5	Form factor	2.27		1985	
6	Perimeter on water	43	Percentage	1985	
7	Median age	30.5	Years	1982	Martin et al., 1983
8	Average income	9,534	$/Capita	1981	Martin et al., 1983
9	Revenue	861	$/Capita	1981	U.S. Bureau of the Census, 1983
10	Expenditure	792	$/Capita	1981	U.S. Bureau of the Census, 1983
11	Bonded debt	398	$/Capita	1981	U.S. Bureau of the Census, 1983
12	Households	409	/1,000 Pop.	1980	U.S. Bureau of the Census, 1983
13	Families	235	/1,000 Pop.	1983	U.S. Bureau of the Census, 1983
14	CBD employment	137	/1,000 Pop.	1980	Hendrickson, 1986
15	Workers on public transit	99	/1,000 Pop.	1980	Hendrickson, 1986
16	Employment	414	/1,000 Pop.	1980	U.S. Bureau of the Census, 1983
17	School enrollment	265	/1,000 Pop.	1980	U.S. Bureau of the Census, 1983
18	Postal revenue	352	$/Capita	1985	U.S. Postal Service, private communication, 1986
19	Library budget	12.83	$/Capita	1982	Martin et al., 1983
20	Library books	3,730	/1,000 Pop.	1982	Martin et al., 1983
21	Libraries	2		1979	Showes, 1979
22	Schools	300		1985	City telephone directories, 1986
23	Colleges and universities	17		1985	Newspaper Enterprise Association, 1985
24	Tall buildings	11		1985	Newspaper Enterprise Association, 1985
25	Hotels	30		1977	Martin et al., 1983
26	Hotel rooms	8	/1,000 Pop.	1977	Martin et al., 1983

		Value	Units	Year	Source
27	Hospitals	30		1985	Newspaper Enterprise Association, 1985
28	Hospital beds	13.02	/1,000 Pop.	1981	Martin et al., 1983
29	Airports	1		1984	Federal Aviation Administration, 1985
30	Airplane departure	38.8	1,000/Year	1984	Federal Aviation Administration, 1985
31	Enplaned passengers	1,703.8	1,000/Year	1984	Federal Aviation Administration, 1985
32	Parks	11.27	Acres/1,000 pop.	1985	Houghton Mifflin Co., 1986
33	Stadiums	1		1985	Newspaper Enterprise Association, 1985
34	Cemeteries	9.35	/100,000 Pop.	1985	City telephone directories, 1986
35	Churches	2.21	/1,000 Pop.	1985	Houghton Mifflin Co., 1986
36	TV stations	6		1985	Houghton Mifflin Co., 1986
37	Radio stations	24		1986	Houghton Mifflin Co., 1986
38	Theaters	44		1985	City telephone directories, 1986
39	Bus route miles		Miles/sq. mile		
40	Buses		1,000 Riders/day		
41	Rail tracks		Mile/sq. mile		
42	Rail cars		1,000 Riders/day		
43	Transit passengers		/1,000 Pop.		
44	Car registrations	0.257	/Capita	1964	Automotive Safety Foundation, 1964
45	Freeway miles		/Sq. mile		
46	Street miles		/Sq. mile		
47	Bridges				
48	Tunnels	0		1985	Newspaper Enterprise Association, 1985
49	Water lines		/Sq. mile		
50	Water use	137	Gpd/capita	1985	Cincinnati Water Authority, private communication, 1986
51	Sewer lines		/Sq. mile		
52	Sewage treatment		Gpd/capita		
53	Solid waste		Tons/year/capita		
54	Phone	2.0	/Capita	1986	Houghton Mifflin Co., 1986
55	Residential electric bills	39.04	$/Month	1983	U.S. Bureau of the Census, 1983

TABLE B-4 City of Houston

No.	Variable	Value	Unit	Year	Reference
1	Population	1,595,138	Persons	1980	U.S. Bureau of the Census, 1983
2	Area	556	Sq. miles	1981	Martin et al., 1983
3	Population density	2,869	Pop./sq. mile	1980	Martin et al., 1983; U.S. Bureau of the Census, 1983
4	Perimeter	187	Miles	1985	
5	Form factor	2.24		1985	
6	Perimeter on water	14	Percentage	1985	
7	Median age	28.4	Years	1982	Martin et al., 1983
8	Average income	10,958	$/Capita	1981	Martin et al., 1983
9	Revenue	472	$/Capita	1981	U.S. Bureau of the Census, 1983
10	Expenditure	481	$/Capita	1981	U.S. Bureau of the Census, 1983
11	Bonded debt	636	$/Capita	1981	U.S. Bureau of the Census, 1983
12	Households	378	/1,000 Pop.	1980	U.S. Bureau of the Census, 1983
13	Families	246	/1,000 Pop.	1983	U.S. Bureau of the Census, 1983
14	CBD employment	65	/1,000 Pop.	1980	Hendrickson, 1986
15	Workers on public transit	26	/1,000 Pop.	1980	Hendrickson, 1986
16	Employment	519	/1,000 Pop.	1980	U.S. Bureau of the Census, 1983
17	School enrollment	263	/1,000 Pop.	1980	U.S. Bureau of the Census, 1983
18	Postal revenue	178	$/Capita	1985	U.S. Postal Service, private communication, 1986
19	Library budget	8.55	$/Capita	1982	Martin et al., 1983
20	Library books	1,555	/1,000 Pop.	1982	Martin et al., 1983
21	Libraries	4		1979	Showes, 1979
22	Schools	1,944		1985	City telephone directories, 1986
23	Colleges and universities	29		1985	Newspaper Enterprise Association, 1985
24	Tall buildings	38		1985	Newspaper Enterprise Association, 1985
25	Hotels	198		1977	Martin et al., 1983
26	Hotel rooms	16	/1,000 Pop.	1977	Martin et al., 1983

27	Hospitals	59		1985	Newspaper Enterprise Association, 1985
28	Hospital beds	6.88	/1,000 Pop.	1981	Martin et al., 1983
29	Airports	2		1984	Federal Aviation Administration, 1985
30	Airplane departures	139.7	1,000/Year	1984	Federal Aviation Administration, 1985
31	Enplaned passengers	9,198.6	1,000/Year	1984	Federal Aviation Administration, 1985
32	Parks	3.60	Acres/1,000 pop.	1985	Houghton Mifflin Co., 1986
33	Stadiums	3		1985	Newspaper Enterprise Association, 1985
34	Cemeteries	1.63	/100,000 Pop.	1985	City telephone directories, 1986
35	Churches	1.10	/1,000 Pop.	1985	Houghton Mifflin Co., 1986
36	TV stations	6		1985	Houghton Mifflin Co., 1986
37	Radio stations	30		1985	Houghton Mifflin Co., 1986
38	Theaters	107		1985	City telephone directories, 1986
39	Bus route miles		Miles/sq. mile		
40	Buses		1,000 Riders/day		
41	Rail tracks	None	Miles/sq. mile	1980	Unibook, Inc., 1980
42	Rail cars	None	1,000 Riders/day	1980	Unibook, Inc., 1980
43	Transit passengers		/1,000 Pop.		
44	Car registrations	0.338	/Capita	1964	Automotive Safety Foundation, 1964
45	Freeway miles	0.12	/Sq. mile		
46	Street miles		/Sq. mile		
47	Bridges				
48	Tunnels	0		1985	Newspaper Enterprise Association, 1985
49	Water lines	250	/Sq. mile	1979	Houston Chamber of Commerce, 1985
50	Water use	9.0	Gpd/capita	1985	Houston Chamber of Commerce, 1985
51	Sewer lines	276	/Sq. mile	1985	Houston Chamber of Commerce, 1985
52	Sewage treatment	1.255	Gpd/capita	1982	Houston Chamber of Commerce, 1985
53	Solid waste	1.0	Tons/year/capita	1986	Houghton Mifflin Co., 1986
54	Phone	48.63	/Capita	1983	U.S. Bureau of the Census, 1983
55	Residential electric bill		$/Month		

TABLE B-5 City of Los Angeles

No.	Variable	Value	Unit	Year	Reference
1	Population	2,966,850	Persons	1980	U.S. Bureau of the Census, 1983
2	Area	463.9	Sq. miles	1981	Martin et al., 1983
3	Population density	6,395	Pop./sq. mile	1980	Martin et al., 1983; U.S. Bureau of the Census, 1983
4	Perimeter	144	Miles	1985	
5	Form factor	1.89		1985	
6	Perimeter on water	15	Percentage	1985	
7	Median age	31.1	Years	1982	Martin et al., 1983
8	Average income	8,469	$/Capita	1982	Martin et al., 1983
9	Revenue	571.2	$/Capita	1980	U.S. Bureau of the Census, 1983
10	Expenditures	451.2	$/Capita	1980	U.S. Bureau of the Census, 1983
11	Bonded debt	292.0	$/Capita	1980	U.S. Bureau of the Census, 1983
12	Households	383	/1,000 Pop.	1980	U.S. Bureau of the Census, 1983
13	Families	234	/1,000 Pop.	1983	U.S. Bureau of the Census, 1983
14	CBD employment	45	/1,000 Pop.	1980	Hendrickson, 1986
15	Workers on public transit	80	/1,000 Pop.	1980	Hendrickson, 1986
16	Employment	470	/1,000 Pop.	1980	U.S. Bureau of the Census, 1983
17	School enrollment	267	/1,000 Pop.	1982	U.S. Bureau of the Census, 1983
18	Postal revenue	121	$/Capita	1985	U.S. Postal Service, private communication, 1986
19	Library budget	6.55	$/Capita	1982	Martin et al., 1983
20	Library books	2,062	/1,000 Pop.	1982	Martin et al., 1983
21	Libraries	4		1979	Showes, 1979
22	Schools	750		1985	City telephone directories, 1986
23	Colleges and universities	11		1985	Newspaper Enterprise Association, 1985
24	Tall buildings	27		1985	Newspaper Enterprise Association, 1985
25	Hotels	512		1977	Martin et al., 1983
26	Hotel rooms	16	/1,000 Pop.	1977	Martin et al., 1983
27	Hospitals	822		1985	Newspaper Enterprise Association, 1985

28	Hospital beds	3.14	/1,000 Pop.	1981	Martin et al., 1983
29	Airports	4		1984	Federal Aviation Administration, 1985
30	Airplane departures	195.7	1,000/Year	1984	Federal Aviation Administration, 1985
31	Enplaned passengers	17,713.8	1,000/Year	1984	Federal Aviation Administration, 1985
32	Parks	4.88	Acres/1,000 pop.	1985	Houghton Mifflin Co., 1986
33	Stadiums	1		1985	Newspaper Enterprise Association, 1985
34	Cemeteries	1.31	/100,000 Pop.	1985	City telephone directories, 1986
35	Churches	0.66	/1,000 Pop.	1985	Houghton Mifflin Co., 1986
36	TV stations	18		1985	Houghton Mifflin Co., 1986
37	Radio stations	72		1985	Houghton Mifflin Co., 1986
38	Theaters	119		1985	City telephone directories, 1986
39	Bus route miles		Miles/sq. mile		
40	Buses		1,000 Riders/day		
41	Rail tracks		Mile/sq. mile		
42	Rail cars		1,000 Riders/day		
43	Transit passengers		/1,000 Pop.		
44	Car registrations	0.39	/Capita	1964	Automotive Safety Foundation, 1964
45	Freeway miles	0.33	/Sq. mile	1982	Los Angeles City Planning Commission, 1981
46	Street miles	13.85	/Sq. mile	1982	Los Angeles City Planning Commission, 1981
47	Bridges				
48	Tunnels	2	/Sq. mile	1985	Newspaper Enterprise Association, 1985
49	Water lines	15.1	/Sq. mile	1984	City of Los Angeles, 1985
50	Water use	180	Gpd/capita	1980	Los Angeles Department of Water and Power, private communication, 1986
51	Sewer lines	12.9	/Sq. mile	1985	City of Los Angeles, 1985
52	Sewage treatment	161.8	Gpd/capita		City of Los Angeles, 1985
53	Solid waste		Tons/year/capita		
54	Phone	0.7	/Capita	1986	Houghton Mifflin Co., 1986
55	Residential electric bills	51.97	$/Month	1983	U.S. Bureau of the Census, 1983

TABLE B-6 City of Miami

No.	Variable	Value	Unit	Year	Reference
1	Population	346,865	Persons	1980	U.S. Bureau of the Census, 1983
2	Area	34.3	Sq. miles	1981	Martin et al., 1983
3	Population density	10,112	Pop./sq mile	1980	Martin et al., 1983; U.S. Bureau of the Census, 1983
4	Perimeter	35	Miles	1985	Martin et al., 1983
5	Form factor	1.69		1985	Martin et al., 1983
6	Perimeter on water	42	Percentage	1985	
7	Median Age	38.4	Years	1982	Martin et al., 1983
8	Average income	5,898	$/Capita	1982	Martin et al., 1983
9	Revenue	472.8	$/Capita	1980	U.S. Bureau of the Census, 1983
10	Expenditure	424.7	$/Capita	1980	U.S. Bureau of the Census, 1983
11	Bonded debt	590.4	$/Capita	1980	U.S. Bureau of the Census, 1983
12	Households	386	/1,000 Pop.	1980	U.S. Bureau of the Census, 1983
13	Families	250	/1,000 Pop.	1980	U.S. Bureau of the Census, 1983
14	CBD employment	63	/1,000 Pop.	1980	Hendrickson, 1986
15	Workers on public transit	138	/1,000 Pop.	1980	Hendrickson, 1986
16	Employment	459	/1,000 Pop.	1980	U.S. Bureau of the Census, 1983
17	School enrollment	223	/1,000 Pop.	1980	U.S. Bureau of the Census, 1983
18	Postal revenue	487	$/Capita	1985	U.S. Postal Service, private communication, 1986
19	Library budget	10.96	$/Capita	1982	Martin et al., 1983
20	Library books	1,322	/1,000 Pop.	1982	Martin et al., 1983
21	Libraries	2		1979	Showes, 1979
22	Schools	1,050		1985	City telephone directories, 1986
23	Colleges and universities	6		1985	Newspaper Enterprise Association, 1985
24	Tall buildings	11		1985	Newspaper Enterprise Association, 1985
25	Hotels	118		1977	Martin et al., 1983
26	Hotel rooms	14	/1,000 Pop.	1977	Martin et al., 1983

27	Hospitals	41		1985	Newspaper Enterprise Association, 1985
28	Hospital beds	14.5	/1,000 Pop.	1981	Martin et al., 1983
29	Airports	2		1984	Federal Aviation Administration, 1985
30	Airplane departures	117.2	1,000/Year	1984	Federal Aviation Administration, 1985
31	Enplaned passengers	9,949.6	1,000/Year	1984	Federal Aviation Administration, 1985
32	Parks		Acres/1,000 pop.	1985	Houghton Mifflin Co., 1986
33	Stadiums	1		1985	Newspaper Enterprise Association, 1985
34	Cemeteries	7.2	/100,000 Pop.	1985	City telephone directories, 1986
35	Churches	2.1	/1,000 Pop.	1985	Houghton Mifflin Co., 1986
36	TV stations	7		1985	Houghton Mifflin Co., 1986
37	Radio stations	38		1985	Houghton Mifflin Co., 1986
38	Theaters	89		1985	City telephone directories, 1986
39	Bus route miles		Miles/sq. mile		
40	Buses		1,000 Riders/day		
41	Rail tracks	0.612	Miles/sq. mile	1983	Sunbank Marketing Department, 1985
42	Rail cars	5.44	1,000 Riders/day	1985	Sunbank Marketing Department, 1985
43	Transit passengers	25	/1,000 Pop.	1985	Sunbank Marketing Department, 1985
44	Car registrations	0.31	/Capita	1964	Automotive Safety Foundation, 1964
45	Freeway miles	0.16	/Sq. mile	1964	Automotive Safety Foundation, 1964
46	Street miles		/Sq. mile		
47	Bridges				
48	Tunnels	0		1985	Newspaper Enterprise Association, 1985
49	Water lines	66.4	/Sq. mile	1985	Miami-Dade Water and Sewer Authority, 1985
50	Water use	319	Gpd/capita	1979	Metcalf and Eddy, Inc., 1979
51	Sewer lines		/Sq. mile		
52	Sewage treatment		Gpd/capita		
53	Solid waste	1.683	Tons/year/capita	1985	Miami-Dade Solid Waste Department, private communication, 1986
54	Phone	3.6	/Capita	1986	Houghton Mifflin Co., 1986
55	Residential electric bills	52.96	$/Month	1983	U.S. Bureau of the Census, 1983

TABLE B-7 City of New York

No.	Variable	Value	Unit	Year	Reference
1	Population	7,071,639	Persons	1980	U.S. Bureau of the Census, 1983
2	Area	303.7	Sq. miles	1981	Martin et al., 1983
3	Population density	23,285	Pop./sq. mile	1980	Martin et al., 1983; U.S. Bureau of the Census, 1983
4	Perimeter	137	Miles	1985	Martin et al., 1983
5	Form factor	2.22		1985	Martin et al., 1983
6	Perimeter on water	76	Percentage	1985	Martin et al., 1983
7	Median age	33.3	Years	1982	Martin et al., 1983
8	Average income	8,739	$/Capita	1982	Martin et al., 1983
9	Revenue	2,370	$/Capita	1981	U.S. Bureau of the Census, 1983
10	Expenditures	2,036	$/Capita	1981	U.S. Bureau of the Census, 1983
11	Bonded debt	1,115	$/Capita	1981	U.S. Bureau of the Census, 1983
12	Households	394	/1,000 Pop.	1980	U.S. Bureau of the Census, 1983
13	Families	248	/1,000 Pop.	1980	U.S. Bureau of the Census, 1983
14	CBD employment	70	/1,000 Pop.	1980	Hendrickson, 1986
15	Workers on public transit	242	/1,000 Pop.	1980	Hendrickson, 1986
16	Employment	413	/1,000 Pop.	1980	U.S. Bureau of the Census, 1983
17	School enrollment	255	/1,000 Pop.	1980	U.S. Bureau of the Census, 1983
18	Postal revenue	175	$/Capita	1985	U.S. Postal Service, private communication, 1986
19	Library budget	10.41	$/Capita	1982	Martin et al., 1983
20	Library books	1,762	/1,000 Pop.	1982	Martin et al., 1983
21	Libraries	8		1979	Showes, 1979
22	Schools			1985	City telephone directories, 1986
23	Colleges and universities	29		1985	Newspaper Enterprise Association, 1985
24	Tall buildings	118		1985	Newspaper Enterprise Association, 1985
25	Hotels	398		1977	Martin et al., 1983
26	Hotel rooms	100	/1,000 Pop.	1977	Martin et al., 1983
27	Hospitals	100		1985	Newspaper Enterprise Association, 1985

28	Hospital beds	5.27	/1,000 Pop.	1981	Martin et al., 1983
29	Airports	2		1984	Federal Aviation Administration, 1985
30	Airplane departures	212.1	1,000/year	1984	Federal Aviation Administration, 1985
31	Enplaned passengers	20,008.3	1,000/year	1984	Federal Aviation Administration, 1985
32	Parks	3.60	Acres/1,000 pop.	1985	Houghton Mifflin Co., 1986
33	Stadiums	2		1985	Newspaper Enterprise Association, 1985
34	Cemeteries	1.87	/100,000 Pop.	1985	City telephone directories, 1986
35	Churches	0.50	/1,000 Pop.	1985	Houghton Mifflin Co., 1986
36	TV stations	6		1985	Houghton Mifflin Co., 1986
37	Radio stations	29		1985	Houghton Mifflin Co., 1986
38	Theaters	671		1985	City telephone directories, 1986
39	Bus route miles		Miles/sq. mile		
40	Buses		1,000 Riders/day		
41	Rail tracks	0.76	Miles/sq. mile	1980	
42	Rail cars		1,000 Riders/day		
43	Transit passengers		/1,000 Pop.		
44	Car registrations	0.161	/Capita	1964	Automotive Safety Foundation, 1964
45	Freeway miles	0.37	/Sq. mile	1964	Automotive Safety Foundation, 1964
46	Street miles	19.76	/Sq. mile	1980	Sinnreich, 1980
47	Bridges	1,337		1980	Grossman, 1979
48	Tunnels	8		1985	Newspaper Enterprise Association, 1985
49	Water lines	20.2	/Sq. mile	1979	Grossman, 1979
50	Water use	276	Gpd/capita	1979	Metcalf and Eddy, Inc. 1979
51	Sewer lines	20.4	/Sq. mile	1979	Grossman, 1979
52	Sewage treatment		Gpd/capita		
53	Solid waste	2.065	Tons/year/capita	1970	Bergman and Pohl, 1975
54	Phone	0.8	/Capita	1986	Houghton Mifflin Co., 1986
55	Residential electric bills	90.53	$/Month	1983	U.S. Bureau of the Census, 1983

TABLE B-8 City of Seattle

No.	Variable	Value	Unit	Year	Reference
1	Population	493,846	Persons	1980	U.S. Bureau of the Census, 1983
2	Area	91.6	Sq. miles	1981	Martin et al., 1983
3	Population density	5,391	Pop./sq. mile	1980	Martin et al., 1983; U.S. Bureau of the Census, 1983
4	Perimeter	67	Miles	1985	
5	Form factor	1.97		1985	
6	Perimeter on water	59	Percentage	1985	
7	Median age	33.0	Years	1982	Martin et al., 1983
8	Average income	8,548	$/Capita	1982	Martin et al., 1983
9	Revenue	705	$/Capita	1980	U.S. Bureau of the Census, 1983
10	Expenditure	699	$/Capita	1980	U.S. Bureau of the Census, 1983
11	Bonded debt	427	$/Capita	1980	U.S. Bureau of the Census, 1983
12	Households	444	/1,000 Pop.	1980	U.S. Bureau of the Census, 1983
13	Families	231	/1,000 Pop.	1980	U.S. Bureau of the Census, 1983
14	CBD employment	105	/1,000 Pop.	1980	Hendrickson, 1986
15	Workers on public transit	152	/1,000 Pop.	1980	Hendrickson, 1986
16	Employment	506	/1,000 Pop.	1980	U.S. Bureau of the Census, 1983
17	School enrollment	244	/1,000 Pop.	1980	U.S. Bureau of the Census, 1983
18	Postal revenue	328	$/Capita	1985	U.S. Postal Service, private communication, 1986
19	Library budget	21.33	$/Capita	1982	Martin et al., 1983
20	Library books	3,074	/1,000 Pop.	1982	Martin et al., 1983
21	Libraries	3		1979	Showes, 1979
22	Schools	480		1985	City telephone directories, 1986
23	Colleges and universities	15		1985	Newspaper Enterprise Association, 1985
24	Tall buildings	21		1985	Newspaper Enterprise Association, 1985
25	Hotels	111		1977	Martin et al., 1983
26	Hotel rooms	8	/1,000 Pop.	1977	Martin et al., 1983
27	Hospitals	27		1985	Newspaper Enterprise Association, 1985

28	Hospital beds	6.62	/1,000 Pop.	1981	Martin et al., 1983
29	Airports	3		1984	Federal Aviation Administration, 1985
30	Airplane departures	69.7	1,000/Year	1984	Federal Aviation Administration, 1985
31	Enplaned passengers	5,063	1,000/Year	1984	Federal Aviation Administration, 1985
32	Parks	9.66	Acres/1,000 pop.	1985	Houghton Mifflin Co., 1986
33	Stadiums	2		1985	Newspaper Enterprise Association, 1985
34	Cemeteries	5.67	/100,000 Pop.	1985	City telephone directories, 1986
35	Churches	1.17	/1,000 Pop.	1985	Houghton Mifflin Co., 1986
36	TV stations	4		1986	Houghton Mifflin Co., 1986
37	Radio stations	48		1985	Houghton Mifflin Co., 1986
38	Theaters	99		1985	City telephone directories, 1986
39	Bus route miles		Miles/sq. mile		
40	Buses		1,000 Riders/day		
41	Rail tracks		Miles/sq. mile		
42	Rail cars		1,000 Riders/day		
43	Transit passengers		/1,000 Pop.		
44	Car registrations	0.346	/Capita	1964	Automotive Safety Foundation, 1964
45	Freeway miles	0.29	/Sq. mile	1986	Seattle Engineering Department, private communication, 1986
46	Street miles	18.10	/Sq. mile	1986	Seattle Engineering Department, private communication, 1986
47	Bridges	170		1986	Seattle Engineering Department, private communication, 1986
48	Tunnels	2		1985	Newspaper Enterprise Association, 1985
49	Water lines	19.5	/Sq. mile	1984	Seattle Water Department, 1984
50	Water use	288	Gpd/capita	1979	Metcalf and Eddy, Inc., 1979
51	Sewer lines	11.1	/Sq. mile	1979	City of Seattle, 1982
52	Sewage treatment		Gpd/capita		
53	Solid waste	1.395	Tons/year/capita	1982	City of Seattle, 1982
54	Phone	1.4	/Capita	1986	Houghton Mifflin Co., 1986
55	Residential electric bills	26.94	$/Month	1983	U.S. Bureau of the Census, 1983

Table B-9 Matrix of Correlation Coefficients for the 40 Variables Used in the Study's Factor Analysis

Variable[a] Number	Variables																			
	2	3	4	5	6	7	8	9	10	11	12	13	14	15	16	17	18	19	20	21
2	1.0																			
3	0	1.0																		
4	.9	0	1.0																	
5	.3	−.1	.5	1.0																
6	−.5	.7	−.3	.1	1.0															
7	−.5	.4	−.5	−.1	.5	1.0														
8	.6	−.1	.7	.6	−.1	−.7	1.0													
9	0	.8	.2	.4	.7	.1	.1	1.0												
10	0	.7	.2	.3	.7	0	0	1.0	1.0											
11	−.1	0	.1	0	0	−.1	−.4	.4	.5	1.0										
12	−.4	−.2	.2	.5	.5	.2	.1	.1	.1	−.2	1.0									
13	.2	.5	.3	.3	.2	.5	.1	.3	.2	−.1	−.3	1.0								
14	−.6	−.4	−.5	−.1	.1	−.3	−.2	0	.1	.5	.2	−.6	1.0							
15	−.5	.8	−.4	.3	.8	.3	−.5	.7	.7	.4	.1	0	.2	1.0						
16	.4	−.5	.4	.3	−.3	0	.4	−.5	−.5	−.4	.3	.1	−.5	−.6	1.0					
17	.4	−.2	.3	−.1	−.4	−.9	.3	0	.1	.4	−.4	−.6	.5	0	−.4	1.0				
18	−.6	−.4	−.6	−.2	−.1	.2	−.7	−.1	0	.7	.1	−.3	.7	.2	−.3	.1	1.0			
19	−.6	−.1	−.4	.2	.6	.3	0	0	0	−.2	.9	−.2	.3	.2	.3	−.4	.1	1.0		

20	−.3	.3	−.2	.5	.2	.2	.2	−.2	0	.3	−.2	−.2	.3	0	.8	0	.2	.5
21	−.4	.8	.5	.0	.4	.4	−.1	−.2	.8	.2	.4	.2	.8	.8	.2	.8	.6	.2
23	.1	.3	−.1	.6	.1	−.1	.1	−.4	0	−.2	.1	.1	0	0	−.3	0	.3	−.5
24	.3	.8	.4	.2	.0	−.3	.4	−.3	.9	.2	.6	.2	.9	.9	.1	.9	.6	.4
25	.7	.5	.6	0	.6	−.1	−.4	.0	.2	.0	0	.3	.2	.3	−.1	.2	.1	.2
26	.2	.9	.2	.6	.2	.4	.1	−.1	.9	.1	.4	.3	.9	.9	.3	.9	.7	.5
27	.5	.0	.4	.4	.4	.0	−.1	.4	.2	−.3	0	.2	.2	−.1	.0	−.1	−.3	−.1
28	.7	.3	.7	.0	.7	−.1	−.4	.0	−.2	.3	.6	.6	.2	.2	.1	.2	.7	.5
29	.4	−.1	.2	−.1	.2	−.3	−.1	.1	−.2	−.3	.4	.5	−.2	−.2	−.3	−.2	.6	−.7
30	.3	.3	−.3	.1	.2	.3	−.3	.5	−.2	−.3	.2	.4	−.2	−.2	−.6	−.2	.4	−.7
31	.3	.3	.1	.6	.2	.1	−.1	.2	−.2	.4	.0	.4	.2	.2	−.4	−.2	.5	−.3
33	.4	.5	.2	.5	.3	.1	.3	−.1	.4	.5	.1	.1	.2	.2	−.2	.0	.4	.4
34	.8	−.1	.3	.2	.1	−.3	−.5	.7	.0	.3	−.3	.3	.3	.3	.1	.8	−.3	.0
35	.5	.4	.1	.0	.7	.5	.2	.7	−.2	−.1	.5	.2	−.9	−.9	−.6	−.9	−.3	−.7
36	.4	.5	.3	.3	.5	.4	.0	.2	−.2	.3	.2	.4	−.8	−.8	.0	.9	−.8	−.7
37	−.2	−.1	−.1	.4	.3	.2	.2	.0	−.2	−.1	.4	.2	.9	.9	.4	−.1	.7	.2
38	.3	.4	.3	.0	.1	.2	.7	.2	−.2	.1	.6	.2	−.1	−.1	.0	.3	.2	0
44	.2	.2	−.1	.2	.7	.3	.2	.4	.2	−.7	.2	.2	.3	.3	−.3	−.1	−.3	.5
48	.2	.9	−.3	.7	.0	.1	.0	.2	.2	.0	.2	.2	.9	.9	.1	.0	.8	.2
50	−.1	.7	−.1	.0	.2	−.1	.2	−.3	.7	.2	.2	.1	−.1	.1	−.3	.2	.7	−.1
54	.7	.2	−.7	.2	.0	.1	.7	.2	.6	.4	.1	.2	.3	.3	−.1	.3	.2	−.2
55	.3	.9	.4	.4	.4	.7	.3	.0	.2	.0	.7	.2	.7	.8	.7	.8	.0	.5

Continued

TABLE B-9 Continued

Variables[a]

Variable Number	23	24	25	26	27	28	29	30	31	33	34	35	36	37	38	44	48	50	54	55
23	1.0																			
24	.3	1.0																		
25	.1	.5	1.0																	
26	.3	1.0	.5	1.0																
27	−.2	0	.8	−.1	1.0															
28	−.3	−.5	−.8	−.4	−.6	1.0														
29	.1	0	.7	−.1	.7	−.7	1.0													
30	.7	.4	.4	.5	.2	−.4	.2	1.0												
31	.5	.6	.6	.7	.4	−.5	.3	.9	1.0											
33	.7	.4	0	.3	−.4	−.4	0	.5	.3	1.0										
34	−.3	−.6	−.8	−.4	−.5	.9	−.7	−.4	−.5	−.5	1.0									
35	−.4	−.5	−.7	−.5	−.4	.8	−.7	−.1	−.2	−.3	.8	1.0								
36	0	−.1	.7	−.1	.9	−.4	.6	.4	.5	−.3	−.4	−.2	1.0							
37	−.2	−.3	.5	−.3	.8	−.5	.7	.2	.3	−.3	−.3	−.1	.8	1.0						
38	.1	1.0	.5	.9	0	−.4	0	.3	.5	.2	−.5	−.5	−.1	−.2	1.0					
44	−.5	−.7	0	−.8	.5	−.1	.5	−.3	−.3	−.1	−.1	0	−.4	.7	−.7	1.0				
48	0	.9	.4	.8	−.1	−.4	0	.1	.1	.3	−.3	−.4	−.3	−.3	.9	−.6	1.0			
50	−.1	.3	.1	.2	−.3	−.1	.3	−.2	0	.1	−.3	−.4	−.4	−.1	.3	0	.4	1.0		
54	−.4	−.5	−.7	−.4	−.4	.9	−.5	−.3	.3	.2	.8	.7	.3	−.2	−.4	.1	−.3	.1	1.0	
55	.1	.9	.6	.9	.1	−.3	0	.4	.6	.5	−.5	−.4	.1	−.2	.9	−.6	.8	.3	−.3	1.0

[a]Variable numbers refer to those in Table 2, p. 38.

3

How Cities Grew in the Western World: A Systems Approach

LYNN HOLLEN LEES AND PAUL M. HOHENBERG

If there is a single defining characteristic of urban life, it is dependence. Not only are citizens interdependent, but the truly isolated city is both unviable and pointless. Unable to sustain itself, it would have no outlets for the fruits of specialization and complex organization. In the words of B. J. L. Berry, "Cities are systems within systems of cities" (1964, p. 147). During the last millennium, as settlement in Europe became predominantly urban, city systems of great complexity evolved as population grew. As conduits for goods, people, and information, they helped to distribute resources throughout vast territories. In fact, the very stuff of urban life is exchange, and the exchange process has generated extensive infrastructures to aid the distribution of commodities, ideas, and population.

The complexity of urban systems poses a challenge to planners and urban scholars. How can the interactions of market towns, capitals, ports, resorts, and manufacturing cities as well as their functions be captured by an analytical model? Because of the varied quality of urban processes, no single schema will suffice. Drawing on the disciplines of economics, geography, and history, we propose that a dual model of interurban relationships captures many important distinctions and offers a tool through which changes over time and variations among city types can be explained. It is important to note that urban growth has been neither automatic nor uniform but has exhibited consistent patterns linked to structure and function. Many of the dynamic influences on city size—demographic change, migration, transportation, technology, and communications—have affected urban fortunes through processes referred to as the *central place system* and the *network system* (Hohenberg and Lees, 1985).

A DUAL MODEL OF URBAN SYSTEMS: ECONOMIC EXCHANGE AND SPATIAL CONFIGURATIONS

The notion of a town as a central place is well established (Berry and Pred, 1961; Christaller, 1933; Lösch, 1954; Tinbergen, 1968). As a center for the exchange of goods and services, a town serves the needs of a farming area, for example, by offering an outlet for surplus production and by housing artisans as well as purveyors of cultural and political products. The central place concept can also be applied to a set of settlements. Because people need complex goods and services less frequently but are willing to travel longer distances for them, such items are offered only in larger settlements. Differing types and intensities of demand create a hierarchy of settlements in which larger towns serve territories also organized by smaller central places. Through a regular nesting and interdependence of centers, urbanization creates integrated regions that are more than the sum of their parts. Roads and railroads make visible the multiple linkages that tie a large array of settlements together. Nations and kingdoms can be visualized as groups of regions, beginning with the hinterlands of small markets and progressing through the territories directed by administrative centers to the major economic and political capitals, which in some countries coincide and in others do not.

Medieval Leicester is a good example of a regional marketplace (Brown, 1970; Hoskins, 1955; Simmons, 1974). Located approximately in the center of the English county of Leicestershire, it served as the county's commercial and cultural capital. Fairs, schools, and charities regularly brought outsiders into the town, and city dwellers themselves provided goods and services to a wide area. Besides producing staples, the city's workers made substantial amounts of woolen cloth for sale in the region. Smaller market towns, roughly equidistant from Leicester, offered simpler goods and services to the surrounding villages, but the county's highest order central place was the only locus of political authority, as well as the site of courts and tax collections. Royal administrators working from London contacted officials in Leicester, who spread information throughout the region.

Leicester also had external ties that cannot be explained through a central place model. Note the city's location at the place where a Roman road forded the river Soar. Leicester was one link in a chain of cities that stretched to London and were finally connected to central Italy. The principal activity of Leicester merchants in the later Middle Ages was the sale of raw wool to distant cloth makers, and the amounts of wool traded were far greater than what would have been necessary to buy indispensable imports or to pay the taxes and rents due the Earl of Leicester and the English king. Leicester therefore linked its region to a larger commercial network, which stretched from English east coast ports to the Low Countries and from London to manufacturing towns throughout Europe.

The example of Leicester shows how a city's trade may involve an exchange of goods with both local and distant destinations. Neither size nor position in a central place system is sufficient to predict the long-distance linkages of a settlement. Indeed, even small villages may engage in the specialized production of a traded staple, which an urban system then helps to distribute. The network of exchange thus generated is still hierarchic, but a regular geometric ordering of centers is replaced by a series of nodes, junctions, and outposts arranged according to a core–periphery logic (Figure 3-1b). Rather than a contiguous group of regions, often centrally administered, such urban systems comprise loosely linked cities that anchor trade routes. We call this type of linkage the network system (Hohenberg and Lees, 1985). Both Braudel (1979) and Wallerstein's (1974) visions of a world economy are consonant with this model. In a network system, maritime empires and urban leagues rival one another. Their wealth and influence depend not on the control of the territory but on access to long-distance transportation, luxury goods, information, and human capital. Few places in early Europe illustrate this alternative urban system better than Venice, the Queen of the Adriatic.

Venice began on an unpromising site as a small gathering of boatmen who produced fish and salt (Lane, 1973; Luzzatto, 1961). Building on its ties to Constantinople, the city became the trading gateway between a rapidly developing European periphery and a thriving eastern economy that stretched through Arab and Byzantine lands to China. In time, mercantile wealth and naval power reinforced one another to undermine the dominance of the Middle East and to create a Venetian maritime empire. Despite meager resources and a limited population, Venice was able to preserve its autonomy, if not its influence, until the early nineteenth century.

In spatial terms the central place system is territorial and geometric. Distances between cities of a given size or rank are more or less uniform, as is the relation of city size to the dimensions of the territory served (Figure 3-1a). Topographic irregularities of course modify this mosaic, but for the most part the spacing of the cities in central place systems is regular. By contrast the network system consists of linkages dictated by profit and facilitated by water transport, which blunt the effects of distance. Even in the transfer of ideas, a case in which bulk is not an issue, distance

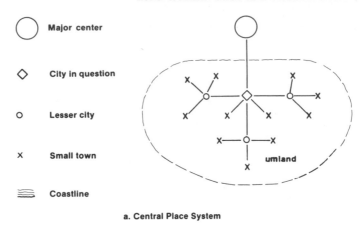

Major center

City in question

Lesser city

Small town

Coastline

umland

a. Central Place System

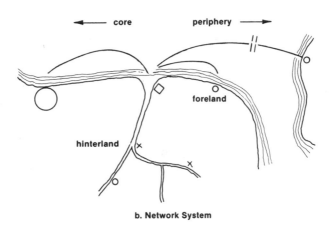

core   periphery

foreland

hinterland

b. Network System

FIGURE 3-1   Patterns of interaction for cities in two different urban systems: central place system (3-1a) and network system (3-1b). From Hohenberg and Lees (1985). Reprinted by permission.

proves a greater barrier to exchange in the central place system than in the network system. In the latter, principal centers may well be clustered, as in northern Italy and the Low Countries during the Middle Ages or along the East Coast in contemporary America; or they may surround an inland sea, each serving as a gateway to a region of the interior, as Braudel (1966) so vividly illustrated for the case of the Mediterranean. Indeed, the clustering of major centers in wealthy areas, compared to their wider spacing in many agriculturally rich but less economically active territories, is a phenomenon that the central place model cannot explain. Because this model implies that each large city commands a region in which internal exchange is more intense than external trade, it deals poorly with the active, long-distance exchanges of people and goods directed through highly urbanized areas.

An urban system does not require geographic compactness or symmetry. Instead, transportation linkages can overcome the barrier of distance, and infrastructures can be created to support asymmetrical flows of commodities and population. The huge port areas of Rotterdam and Hamburg or the railway yards in Essen were built not for the economic exchanges of a central place region but for an international trading system.

THE DYNAMICS OF GROWTH AND CHANGE

Long waves of population growth provided the human material for city building. Although statistical data for medieval and early modern times are often incomplete and unreliable, the combination of tax records, household listings, demographic registers, and censuses yields plausible estimates for the sizes of major cities and for overall patterns of growth and decline (Bairoch, 1985; de Vries, 1984; Russell, 1972). Demographers estimate that the European population rose steadily from around the year 1000 to 1350, after which it declined. Increases predominated from 1450 to 1600, and accelerated growth resumed well after 1700. Tabulations for the period 1600–1700 are disputed, but regional variations probably add up to a slight decline in overall population. Changes in the sizes of European regional capitals illustrate both the timing and the magnitude of growth (Figure 3-2). The demographic engine produced in Europe three periods when increasing numbers of people had to be accommodated by social and economic systems and by urban infrastructures. The first and third witnessed large jumps in the urban share of population; the second was marked by shifts within a more static urban sector.

Historical patterns of urbanization reflect the interaction of geography and economic development with the availability of human capital. The first, post-Roman wave of city creation rested on the secure base of rising agricultural productivity. At a time of relatively low population density and weak political centralization, the most common urban type was the market town in which the predominantly rural population could sell its surplus and buy locally manufactured goods. Central place systems of cities fed by short-distance and step-by-step migration grew up in most parts of western and southern Europe, as well as England. Long-distance trade also encouraged urban growth, primarily along waterways and seacoasts. Between the years 1000 and 1350, thousands of settlements acquired the social, economic, and legal characteristics of cities, becoming

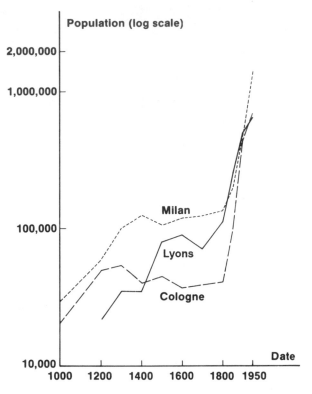

FIGURE 3-2   Growth of provincial capitals, 1000–1950. Data from Chandler and Fox (1974). From Hohenberg and Lees (1985). Reprinted by permission.

important forces in an essentially rural, sometimes feudal environment. City creation and the rapid buildup of central place urban networks were the order of the day. Castle towns and settlements with newly granted market rights multiplied all the way from Ireland through eastern Europe.

The next phase of urban development, between 1450 and 1650, was markedly different. Population growth remained relatively slow, hindered by plague, war, and famine. Economic competition undermined the prosperity of Mediterranean towns; empires in the Americas brought both costs and benefits to cities along the Atlantic coast (Hohenberg and Lees, 1985). The result was a redistribution of the urban population among regions and types of towns (de Vries, 1984). Few new cities were founded, and overall rates of urban growth slowed. Revival from the demographic losses of the fourteenth century was concentrated among the larger market towns and regional capitals. Hundreds of medieval towns, particularly in southern

France and central Europe, disappeared or became villages once more. But capital cities and ports grew explosively. Short-term declines in the urban populations of Italy, Spain, and the Low Countries were counterbalanced by the rising urbanization of England and Scandinavia. In the sixteenth century, a northern core of towns displaced the older southern cities, and rivalries among Antwerp, Amsterdam, and London replaced earlier Italian competitions for influence (Braudel, 1979).

During this period when Europe asserted its leadership over an enlarged world economy, network system linkages brought more growth than did local trade. Nevertheless, the fastest growth of city populations at this time occurred in the capitals and court cities of dynastic states, the capstones of central place systems (Table 3-1). The political centralization of kingdoms, with the associated power to levy increased taxes and rents, brought growth to the top levels of urban hierarchies at the expense of smaller towns. In several cases—for example, France, Spain, and southern Italy—centralization and exploitation led to primacy in urban size distributions as oversized capitals (Paris, Madrid, Naples) dominated an otherwise static urban ensemble. These early metropolises drew resources from the rest of the kingdom without stimulating economic growth elsewhere (Ringrose, 1983). London, which was also England's principal seaport and manufacturing town, is one of the few exceptions to the hypothesis that, at this time, great size and rapid expansion in a political capital were a sign of poor rather than good economic health in the urban system as a whole.

Two dynamics of growth, each characteristic of a different urban system, can be observed at this time. Network system centers grew on the basis of specialized activities, often that of international trade. As a result, they tended to stimulate development at sources of supply, for example, in colonies or other distant places (Wallerstein, 1974). In urban distributions, therefore, network systems encouraged the development of new cities in peripheral territories as well as the development of specialized places, such as mining towns, resorts, and ports. Growth rates were inversely related to size and tended to level off among the larger centers. But in the older central place systems of western and southern Europe, where new towns rarely arose, increasing centralization resulted in primacy with growth rates biased toward higher order urban places (Hohenberg and Lees, 1985).

Urban growth after 1750, during the long phase of population increase and industrialization that continues today, has also been channeled through both network and central place systems. Most strikingly, new cities developed in large numbers for the first time since the Middle Ages as settlers were attracted to the sites of industrial production. In particular,

TABLE 3-1 The Largest Cities in Europe, 1000–1900 (population in thousands)

1000		1400		1700		1900	
City	Pop.	City	Pop.	City	Pop.	City	Pop.
Constantinople	450	Paris	275	London	550	London	6,480
Cordova	450	Milan	125	Paris	530	Paris	3,330
Seville	90	Bruges	125	Naples	207	Berlin	2,424
Palermo	75	Venice	110	Lisbon	188	Vienna	1,662
Kiev	45	Granada	100	Amsterdam	172	St. Petersburg	1,439
Venice	45	Genoa	100	Rome	149	Manchester	1,255
Regensburg	40	Prague	95	Venice	144	Birmingham	1,248
Thessalonika	40	Rouen	70	Moscow	130	Moscow	1,120
Amalfi	35	Seville	70	Madrid	125	Glasgow	1,072
Rome	35	Ghent	70	Milan	124	Liverpool	940

SOURCE: Chandler and Fox (1974); Ringrose (1983).

when large coal deposits were opened up and heavy industry gathered near the pitheads, explosive urbanization of formerly rural areas resulted. New linkages among producers, exporters, and consumers were created to handle the increasing volume of production and trade. The Ruhr, with its rapidly expanding pattern of canals, railroads, roads, and towns, is the classic example, but England's Black Country and the Belgian Borinage should also be kept in mind (Reulecke, 1984; Steinberg, 1967). In the territory around originally small settlements, urbanization disregarded central place patterns of market centers and instead engulfed and absorbed villages and small towns alike. Many of these new "cities" lacked the urban services and functions common to central places. Financial and other services came from outside, and the internal cultural and administrative links were forged later, if at all.

Such industrial conurbations developed in ways quite foreign to the central place dynamic but readily accounted for in the network system model. Specialized activity in an isolated location implies strong ties with more distant locations because industrial settlements remained dependent for all essentials: food, finance, markets, and even people. The steel furnaces of the Ruhr were fed by iron from Lorraine and Asturias; yet they also drew on Polish workers, Russian wheat, and Hungarian cattle. Meanwhile, the region's larger banks moved to Berlin. Proximity could not preserve the influence of the older Rhenish financial centers over the Ruhr's industry (Reulecke, 1984; Steinberg, 1967).

Although network linkages fostered the early stages of industrial urbanization, a resurgence of the economic power of the larger, older central places can be seen during the late nineteenth and early twentieth centuries when technological processes made it both more feasible and more attractive to concentrate industrial activities in existing cities. Railways linked the bigger towns, and electric power transmission severed the locational pull of the pithead. Ready access to labor and markets soon outweighed the lure of cheap land and raw materials. In Europe after 1880 the result was an acceleration in the centralizing tendency of central place systems. Growth tended to be concentrated in and on the outskirts of major capitals and conurbations, and rapid migration from rural areas to major cities accentuated the imbalance. Industrial activities congregated in ports and national centers. But the expansion of service employment—ranging from retail trade and construction to intellectual, artistic, and scientific pursuits alongside finance and administration—accounted for much of the growth. The largest cities by far were those that combined a multiplicity of functions.

If a list of the 40 largest cities in Europe in 1750 is compared with similar lists for 1850 and 1950, the continued dominance of political capitals is striking. A few cities from the Mediterranean area—Venice, Palermo, and Granada—disappear from the lists, and a handful of industrial cities, such as Manchester, Birmingham, and Katowice, become urban giants. For the most part, however, the top ranks of the European urban system continued to be occupied by political capitals, which combined service and production functions with their administrative powers (see Table 3-2).

This numerical predominance of political capitals highlights the most important centripetal influence on urban systems, the increasing role of information as opposed to raw labor and materials. Over time, economies of agglomeration outweighed economies of scale and vertical integration, so crucial to heavy industrial complexes. The proximity of government offices, suppliers, competitors, and financiers has drawn entrepreneurs into the major towns.

The concentration of people and activities in large and very large cities—the growth of the threatening and imposing metropolis—could proceed only so far, however, before cost and congestion imposed a reversal in the trend. In the twentieth century, rising land prices in combination with the decentralizing potential of the internal combustion engine and the mass ownership of automobiles have permitted the dispersion of routine production tasks. In the longer run, chemical factories shifted away from Paris (Gaillard, 1977), and docks in central London were abandoned for sites downriver. Nevertheless, the long-run choices of entrepreneurs for the siting of companies are only partially explained by the direct costs of production. The extraordinary flow of new English industry into the London region, despite its higher wages, rents, and land prices, illustrates the pull of the metropolis for both managers and workers (Hall, 1966). And although the computer permits easy dispersion of personnel, the attraction of both Silicon Valley and Boston's Route 128 for new entrants in the industry shows economies of agglomeration at work in the United States.

IMPLICATIONS FOR THE DEVELOPMENT OF INFRASTRUCTURES

Urban sytems are far more than physical structures. To be sure, their roads, airports, and telephone lines have a physical existence. But remember that cities with six-digit populations long antedated railroads and turnpikes. Cities were magnets for people and ideas before modern technology developed elaborate infrastructures to link them. Feet brought new citizens from mountain villages to towns in the plain, and ships linked Greek coastal city-states to counterparts throughout the Mediterranean.

Studies of interurban systems need to include the intangible links between central places, ties that shape the formation of physical structures.

TABLE 3-2 Leading Cities of the European Hierarchy in 1750, 1850, and 1950 (population in thousands)

	1750		1850		1950	
Rank	City	Pop.	City	Pop.	City	Pop.
1	London	676	London	2,320	London	8,860
2	Paris	560	Paris	1,310	Paris	5,900
3	Naples	324	St. Petersburg	502	Moscow	5,100
4	Amsterdam	219	Berlin	446	Ruhr	4,900
5	Lisbon	213	Vienna	426	Berlin	3,707
6	Vienna	169	Liverpool	422	Leningrad	2,700
7	Moscow	161	Naples	416	Manchester	2,382
8	Venice	158	Manchester	412	Birmingham	2,196
9	Rome	157	Moscow	373	Vienna	1,755
10	St. Petersburg	138	Glasgow	346	Rome	1,655
11	Dublin	125	Birmingham	294	Hamburg	1,580
12	Palermo	124	Dublin	263	Madrid	1,527
13	Madrid	123	Madrid	263	Budapest	1,500
14	Milan	123	Lisbon	257	Barcelona	1,425
15	Lyons	115	Lyons	254	Milan	1,400
16	Berlin	113	Amsterdam	225	Glasgow	1,320
17	Hamburg	90	Brussels	208	Liverpool	1,260
18	Marseille	88	Edinburgh	194	Naples	1,210
19	Rouen	88	Hamburg	193	Leeds	1,164
20	Copenhagen	79	Marseille	193	Copenhagen	1,150
21	Florence	74	Milan	193	Athens	1,140
22	Genoa	72	Leeds	184	Bucharest	1,100
23	Granada	70	Palermo	182	Katowice	977
24	Barcelona	70	Rome	170	Brussels	964
25	Seville	68	Barcelona	167	Amsterdam	940
26	Bologna	66	Warsaw	163	Prague	938
27	Bordeaux	64	Budapest	156	Stockholm	889
28	Turin	60	Bristol	150	Lisbon	885
29	Valencia	60	Sheffield	143	Munich	870
30	Cádiz	60	Bordeaux	142	Newcastle	830
31	Stockholm	60	Venice	141	Rotterdam	803
32	Dresden	60	Turin	138	Warsaw	803
33	Prague	58	Copenhagen	135	Kiev	800
34	Brussels	55	Munich	125	Kharkov	730
35	Edinburgh	55	Prague	117	Sheffield	730
36	Lille	54	Breslau	114	Turin	725
37	Cork	53	Wolverhampton	112	Cologne	692
38	Breslau	52	Newcastle	111	Frankfurt	680
39	Koenigsberg	52	Valencia	110	Genoa	676
40	Leiden	50	Ghent	108	Lodz	675

SOURCE: Chandler and Fox (1974).

For example, one basic urban service is the provision of information. Through resident experts, schools, newspapers, and other institutions, cities provide information to their hinterlands, and critical linkages are forged by the movement of people and paper along regular channels of communication. Moreover, innovations are diffused by means of urban elites and institutions. New ideas and inventions speed across national boundaries through the channels of the network system and then are adopted by people and institutions connected in regional urban hierarchies. Power plants, telephone exchanges, and printing presses have tended to appear early in capital or very large cities and then to diffuse downward through central place systems. Although these technologies generated a tangible infrastructure, they only gave form to preexisting ties. In the twentieth century, the growth of a "wired society" permits the decentralization of many management and service activities; yet paradoxically, these activities are just the functions that cluster in metropolitan areas. Large-scale manufacturing plants, which thrive on cheap land and easy transportation, are much more likely to decentralize than management or finance, which use the amenities of the city to attract highly skilled workers and use its roads, mass transit, schools, and information services to link employees in a high-density environment. Managers have realized that creativity is fostered by the propinquities of the city.

The ability of urban populations to innovate is also shaped by the systemic, political ties of towns outside their borders. For centuries, patterns of urban governance have varied with the type of interurban connection. Whereas central places are economically somewhat insular, deriving their principal activities from local service functions, they have been politically dependent on an outside authority. Central places, after all, administer the area around them. Except for national capitals, this function is delegated from the top of the urban hierarchy. By contrast, the network system forges close economic ties among cities—often geographically distant and functionally dissimilar—with no necessary political ties. Ideally, the network city is politically autonomous because governmental centralization inhibits the fluidity of those interurban ties on which network cities thrive. The most economically successful trading cities of the past—places such as Venice, Hamburg, and Amsterdam—remained on the peripheries of European nation-states during their periods of dominance (Rokkan, 1975).

This contrast between the political dependence of central place towns and the relative independence of network centers has shaped the financing of municipal government as well as investment in major improvements. Central places, other than national capitals, have limited resources of their own. They act as conduits for revenues and expenditures controlled by the territorial administration. Such cities must compete, often unsuccess-fully, for a share of national resources. Capitals, whose buildings sym-bolize both a state and a particular regime, are best situated to profit from this competition. There, the desire for glory or the need to maintain public order in the face of crisis often results in physical improvements. This is an odd but continuing story. Compare the levels of governmental spending on streets, water supplies, and public buildings in nineteenth-century Paris or seventeenth-century Madrid with those of smaller towns in France or Spain (Evenson, 1969; Ringrose, 1983). In contrast, network cities, al-though typically oligarchic rather than democratic entities, have had greater control of their own resources as well as a lively sense of the value of the investment in both collective and individual ventures. Local funds built Amsterdam's canals, modernized Liverpool's port, and added parks to central Milan (Dalmosso, 1971; Konvitz, 1985; Vigier, 1970). Whereas formerly independent German trading cities have maintained traditions of large-scale public investment in services and municipal buildings, the level of such expenditures in France and Spain, countries where even network cities have been kept under relatively strong central control, has been low.

Urban resources and the infrastructures they generate vary with the nature of a city's exchange relations. Indeed, the adoption of new tech-nologies depends heavily on networks of communication and finance, which are generated by a city's regional and international position. The analysis of infrastructures therefore requires examination of urban systems as they have evolved through time and as they persist today.

REFERENCES

Bairoch, P. 1985. De Jéricho à Mexico. Villes et économie dans l'histoire. Paris: Gallimard.

Berry, B. J. L. 1964. Cities as systems within systems of cities. Papers and Proceedings of the Regional Science Association 13:147–163.

Berry, B. J. L., and A. Pred. 1961. Central Place Studies: A Bibliography of Theory and Application. Philadelphia: University of Pennsylvania Regional Science Research Insti-tute.

Braudel, F. 1966. La Méditerranée et le monde méditerranéen à l'époque de Philippe II. Deuxième édition. Paris: A. Colin.

Braudel, F. 1979. Civilisation Matérielle, Economie et Capitalisme. 3 vols. Paris: A. Colin.

Brown, A. E., ed. 1970. The Growth of Leicester. Leicester, England: Leicester University Press.

Chandler, T., and G. Fox. 1974. 3000 Years of Urban Growth. New York: Academic Press.

Christaller, W. 1933. Central Places in Southern Germany, trans. C. W. Baskin. Reprint. Englewood Cliffs, N.J.: Prentice-Hall, 1966.

Dalmosso, E. 1971. Milan, Capitale Economique de l'Italie. Ph.D. dissertation. Université d'Aix-Marseille.

de Vries, J. 1984. European Urbanization, 1500–1800. Cambridge, Mass.: Harvard University Press.

Evenson, N. 1969. Paris: A Century of Change, 1878–1978. New Haven, Conn.: Yale University Press.

Gaillard, J. 1977. Paris, la ville, 1852–1870. Paris: Champion.

Hall, P. 1966. The World Cities. New York: McGraw-Hill.

Hohenberg, P. M., and L. H. Lees. 1985. The Making of Urban Europe, 1000–1950. Cambridge, Mass.: Harvard University Press.

Hoskins, W. G. 1955. An Elizabethan provincial town: Leicester. Pp. 33–67 in Studies in Social History: A Tribute to G. M. Trevelyan, J. H. Plumb, ed. London: Longmans, Green.

Konvitz, J. W. 1985. The Urban Millennium: The City-Building Process from the Early Middle Ages to the Present. Carbondale: Southern Illinois University Press.

Lane, F. C. 1973. Venice: A Maritime Republic. Baltimore, Md.: Johns Hopkins University Press.

Lösch, A. 1954. The Economics of Location. New Haven, Conn.: Yale University Press.

Luzzatto, G. 1961. Storia Economica de Venezia. Venice: Centro Internazionale delle Arti e del Costume.

Reulecke, J. 1984. The Ruhr: Centralization versus decentralization in a region of cities. Pp. 403–430 in The Metropolis, 1890–1940, A. Sutcliffe, ed. Chicago: University of Chicago Press.

Ringrose, D. R. 1983. Madrid and the Spanish Economy, 1560–1850. Berkeley: University of California Press.

Rokkan, S. 1975. Dimensions of state formation and nation-building: A possible paradigm for research on variations within Europe. Pp. 601–638 in the Formation of National States in Western Europe, C. Tilly, ed. Princeton, N.J.: Princeton University Press.

Russell, J. C. 1972. Medieval Regions and Their Cities. Bloomington: Indiana University Press.

Simmons, J. 1974. Leicester Past and Present. Vol. 1, Ancient Borough to 1860. London: Methuen.

Steinberg, H. G. 1967. Sozialräumliche Entwicklung und Gliederung des Ruhrgebietes. Bad Godesberg: Bundesanstalt für Landeskunde und Raumforschung.

Tinbergen, J. 1968. The hierarchy model of size distribution of centers. Papers and Proceedings of the Regional Science Association 20:65–68.

Vigier, F. 1970. Change and Apathy: Liverpool and Manchester During the Industrial Revolution. Cambridge, Mass.: MIT Press.

Wallerstein, I. M. 1974. The Modern World System. New York: Academic Press.

4

Urban Systems and Historical Path Dependence

W. BRIAN ARTHUR

If small events in history had been different, would the pattern of cities we have inherited be different in any significant way? Could different "chance events" in history have created a different formation of urban centers than the one that exists today?

To a great degree, cities form around and depend on clusters of industry, so that without doing too much injustice to the question, we can ask whether the patterns of industry location follow paths that depend on history. The German Industry Location School debated this question in the earlier part of this century, but it was never settled conclusively. Von Thünen (1826), the early Weber (1909), Predöhl (1925), Christaller (1933), and Lösch (1944) all tended to see the spatial ordering of industry as preordained—by geographical endowments, shipment possibilities, firms' needs, and the spatial distribution of rents and prices that these induced. In their view, history did not matter: the observed spatial pattern of industry was a unique "solution" to a well-defined spatial economic problem. Early events in the configuration of an industry therefore could not affect the result. But others, the later Weber, Engländer (1926), Ritschl (1927), and Palander (1935), tended to see industry location as process-dependent, almost geographically stratified, with new industry laid down layer by layer on inherited, previous locational formations. Again, geographical differences and transport possibilities were important, but here the main driving forces were agglomeration economies—the benefits of being close to other firms or to concentrations of industry. In the simplest formulation of this viewpoint (Maruyama, 1963), an industry starts off on a uniform,

85

featureless plain. Early firms put down by "historical accident" in one or two locations; others are attracted by their presence, and others in turn by *their* presence. The industry ends up clustered in the early-chosen places. But this spatial ordering is not unique: a different set of early historical events could have steered the locational pattern into quite a different outcome, so that settlement history would be crucial.

These two viewpoints—determinism versus history-dependence, or "necessity" versus "chance"—are echoed in current discussions of how modern industrial clusters have come about. The determinism school, for example, would tend to see the electronics industry in the United States as spread over the country, with a substantial part of it in Santa Clara County in California (Silicon Valley) because that location is close to Pacific sources of supply and because it has better access there than elsewhere to airports, skilled labor, and advances in academic engineering research. Any "small events" that might affect location decisions are overridden by the "necessity" inherent in the equilibration of spatial economic forces; and Silicon Valley is part of an inevitable result. Historical dependence, on the other hand, would see Silicon Valley and similar concentrations as largely the outcome of "chance." Certain key persons— the Packards, the Varians, the Shockleys of the industry—happened to set up near Stanford University in the 1940s and 1950s, and the local labor expertise and interfirm markets they helped to create in Santa Clara County made subsequent location there extremely advantageous for the thousand or so firms that followed them. If these early entrepreneurs had had other predilections, Silicon Valley might well have been somewhere else. In this argument, "historical chance" is magnified and preserved in the locational structure that results.

Although the historical dependence-agglomeration argument is appealing, it has remained problematical. If history can indeed steer the spatial system down different paths, there are multiple "solutions" to the industry location problem. Which of these comes about is indeterminate. In the 1920s, analysts could not cope with this difficulty, and the historical chance argument did not gain enough rigor to become completely respectable.

This chapter investigates the importance of "chance" (as represented by small events in history) and "necessity" (as represented by determinate economic forces) in determining the pattern of industry location. It contrasts three highly stylized locational models in which small events and economic forces are both present and allowed to interact. In each model an industry is allowed to form, firm by firm, and build up into a locational pattern. In each model we will examine whether historical chance can indeed alter the locational pattern that emerges. Insights gained from the three models will be used to derive some general conditions under which long-run locational patterns may be affected by small historical events.

THE EVOLUTION OF LOCATIONAL PATTERNS: THREE MODELS

Model 1. Pure Necessity: Location Under Independent Preferences

Let us begin with a very simple model of the emergence of an industry location pattern. Starting from zero firms, we allow an industry to form firm by firm, with each new firm that enters deciding "at birth" which of N possible regions (or sites) it will locate in. Once located, each firm will stay put. Firms in this industry are not all alike; there are I different types. The net present value or payoff to a firm of type i for locating in region j is Π_j^i; each firm choosing selects the location with the highest return for its type. In this model, firms are independent: the presence or absence of other firms does not affect what they can earn in each region.

We now inject a small element of "chance" by assuming that the particular historical circumstances that lead to the next firm's being of a particular type are unknown. We do know, however, that a firm of type I will occur next with probability p_i. The question is: What pattern of industrial settlement will emerge in this model, and can it be affected by a different sequence of historical events in the formation of the industry?

It is not difficult to work out the probability that at any time of choice, region j will be chosen. This is simply the probability, q_j, that the newest firm is of a type that has its highest payoff in region j, which is given by $q_j = \Sigma p_k$ for $k \in K$, where K is the set of firm types that prefer j. Repeating this calculation for each of the N regions, we have a set of probabilities of choice $q = (q_1, q_2, \ldots , q_N)$ that are constant no matter what the current pattern of location is. Starting from zero firms in any region, concentrations of the industry in the various regions will fluctuate, considerably at first. But the strong law of large numbers tells us that as the industry grows, the proportions of it in the N regions must settle down to the expectation of an addition being made to each region. That is, regions' shares of the industry must converge to the constant vector q. In this simple model then, even though well-defined "chance historical events" are present, a unique, predetermined locational pattern emerges and persists.

Figure 4-1 shows a simple three-region simulation of this process, with three possible firm types that prefer (clockwise from the top) region 1, region 2, and region 3, respectively, with probabilities of occurrence .5, .25, and .25. After 16 firms have located, the regions' shares of the industry are 0.75, 0.125, and 0.125, respectively—not yet close to the

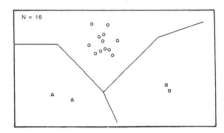 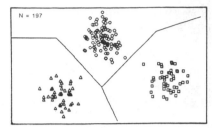

FIGURE 4-1   A three-region example of the independent preferences location model.

long-run predicted pattern. After 197 firms have located, however, the shares are 0.528, 0.221, and 0.251—much closer to the predetermined theoretical long-run shares.

In this model, chance events, represented as randomness in the sequence of firm types that enter the industry, are important early on. But they are progressively averaged away to become dominated by the economic forces represented by firms' payoffs in each region. Different sequences of firm types caused by different historical events would, with probability one, steer the system into the same locational pattern. Here, historical chance cannot affect the outcome. Necessity dominates.

Model 2. Pure Chance: Location by Spin-off

We now assume a quite different mechanism driving the regional formation of an industry—one in which chance events become all-important. Once again the industry builds up firm by firm, starting with some set of initial firms, one per region, say. This time new firms are added by ''spinning off'' from parent firms one at a time. (David Cohen [1984] has shown that such spin-offs have been the dominant ''birth mechanism'' in the U.S. electronics industry.) We assume that each new firm stays in its parent location and that any existing firm is as likely to spin off a new firm as any other. With this mechanism we have a different source of ''chance historical events'': the sequence in which firms spin off daughter firms.

It is easy to see that in this case firms are added incrementally to regions with probabilities exactly equal to the proportions of firms in each region at that time. This random process, in which unit increments are added one at a time to one of N categories with probabilities equal to current proportions in each category, is known in probability theory as a *Polya process*. We can use this fact to examine the long-term locational patterns that might emerge. From Polya theory we know that once again the industry will settle into a locational pattern (with probability one) that has unchanging proportions of the industry in each region. But although this vector of proportions settles down and becomes constant, surprisingly it settles to a constant vector that is *selected randomly* from a uniform distribution over all possible shares that sum to 1.0. This means that each time this spin-off locational process is "rerun" under different historical events (in this case a different sequence of firms spinning off), it will in all likelihood settle into a different pattern. We could generate a representative outcome by placing $N - 1$ points on the unit interval at random and cutting at these points to obtain N "shares" of the unit interval.

Figure 4-2 shows four realizations of this location-by-spin-off mechanism starting from the same three original firms in a three-region case. Each of the four "reruns" has settled into a pattern that will change but little in regional shares with the addition of further firms. But each pattern is different from the others. In this model, industry location is highly path-dependent. Although we can predict that the locational pattern of industry will indeed settle down to constant proportions, we cannot predict what proportions it will settle into. Any given outcome—any vector of proportions that sum to 1.0—is as likely as any other. "History," in the shape of the early random sequence of spin-offs, becomes the sole determining factor of the regional pattern of industry. In this model, "chance" dominates completely.

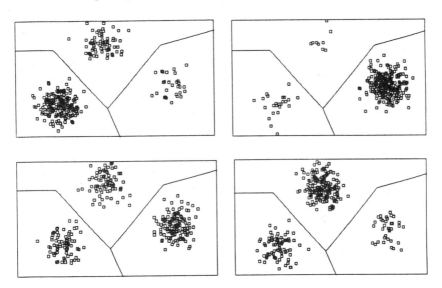

FIGURE 4-2   Four realizations of location by spin-off.

Model 3. Chance and Necessity: Location Under
Agglomeration Economies

Firms that are not tied to raw material localities and that do not compete for local customers are often attracted by the presence of other firms in a region. More densely settled regions offer better infrastructure, deeper labor markets (David, 1984), more specialized legal and financial services, better local availability of inventory and parts, and more opportunity to do business face to face. For our third model we go back to model 1 and extend it by supposing that new firms gain additional benefits from local agglomerations of firms.

Suppose now that the net present value or payoff to a firm of type i for locating in region j is $\Pi^i_j + g(y_j)$, where the "geographical benefits," Π^i_j, are enhanced by additional "agglomeration benefits," $g(y_j)$, from the presence of y_j firms already located in that region. We can recalculate the probability that region j is chosen next, given that $y_1, \ldots, y_N$ firms are currently in regions 1 through N, once again as $q_j = \Sigma p_k$ for $k \in K$, where K is now the set of firm types for which $\Pi^i_j + g(y_j) > \Pi^i_m + g(y_m)$ for all regions $m \neq j$. Notice that in this case the probability that region j is chosen is a function of the number of firms in each region at the time of choice.

Starting from zero firms in the regions, once again we can allow the industry to grow firm by firm, with the appearance of firm-types subject to known probabilities as in model 1. Again, the pattern of location of the industry will fluctuate somewhat; but in this model, if by a combination of luck and geographical attractiveness a region gets ahead in numbers of firms, its position is enhanced. We can show (see Arthur, 1986, for proof) that if agglomeration benefits increase without ceiling as firms are added to a region (that is, if the function g is monotonically increasing without upper bound), then eventually (with probability 1.0) one of the regions will gain enough firms to offer sufficient locational advantages to shut the other regions out in all subsequent locational choices.* From then on, each entering firm in the industry will choose this region, and this region's share of the industry will tend to 100 percent with the others' shares tending to 0 percent.

Figure 4-3 shows two realizations of a three-region example with agglomeration economies. The first three panels show the buildup of

---

*In the case where g is bounded, several locations can share the industry in the long run. But again, typically, there are multiple possible outcomes, so that chance events matter here too (see Arthur, 1983, 1984, 1986, 1987).

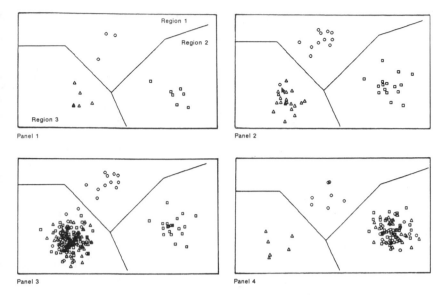

FIGURE 4-3   Two realizations of a locational process with agglomeration economies.

firms, with geographical preferences dominating in panel 1 but with region 3 in panel 2 by good fortune in the sequence of arrival of firm-types just gaining enough firms to cause another firm-type to favor it instead of its pure geographical preference. In panel 3, region 3 has come to dominate the entire industry in a Silicon Valley-like cluster. Panel 4 shows the outcome of an alternative run. Here the industry is locked in to region 2.

In this model of unbounded agglomeration economies, monopoly of the industry by a single region must occur. But which region achieves this "Silicon Valley" locational monopoly is subject to historical luck in the sequence of firm-types choosing. Chance, of course, is not the only factor here. Regions that are geographically attractive to many firm-types— regions that offer great economic benefits—will have a higher probability of being selected early on. And this will make them more likely to become the single region that dominates the industry. To use an analogy borrowed from genetics, chance events act to "select" the pattern that becomes "fixed"; but regions that are economically attractive enjoy "selectional advantage," with correspondingly higher probabilities of gaining dominance. In this third model the long-run locational pattern is due both to chance and necessity.

PATH-DEPENDENCE AND CONVEXITY

Each of our three stylized industry location models includes both determinate economic forces and some source of chance' events. Yet each behaves differently. Determinate forces, or historical chance, or a mixture of the two are in turn responsible for the long-run pattern of industry settlement that emerges.

To explain these results and to provide some precise conditions under which historical chance can be important, it is useful to introduce a general framework that encompasses all three models (as well as many others). In this general framework, suppose there are N regions and that industry locates, one firm at a time, starting from a given number of firms in each region. Different economic forces, different sources of chance events, and different mechanisms of locational choice would be possible within this framework, but we do not need to know these. What we do need to know are the probabilities that region 1, region 2, . . . , region N will be chosen next, as a function of current regional shares of the industry $x_1, x_2, \ldots, x_N$. Plotting this function (as in Figure 4-4 for the two-region case), we might expect that where the probability of a region's receiving the next firm exceeds its current proportion of the industry, it would tend to increase in proportion; and where the probability is less than its current proportion, it would tend to decrease in proportion. Moreover, as firms are added, each new addition changes proportions or shares by an ever smaller magnitude. Therefore proportions should settle down, and fluc-

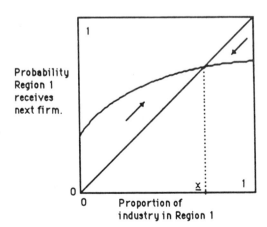

FIGURE 4-4   Proportion-to-probability mapping (arrows indicate expected motions).

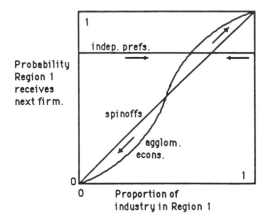

FIGURE 4-5   Probability mappings for the three models.

tuations in proportions should die away. In the long run then, we might expect that regions' proportions (the industry's location pattern) ought to converge to a point—to a vector of locational shares—where proportions equal probabilities, a point toward one that expected motions lead toward (point x in Figure 4-4). That is, this process ought to end up at a stable fixed point of the proportions-to-probabilities function. It takes powerful theoretical machinery to prove this conjecture, but it turns out to hold under unrestrictive technical conditions (see Hill, Lane, and Sudderth, 1980; and Arthur, Ermoliev, and Kaniovski 1983, 1986, 1987).* Further, and significantly for us, where there are multiple stable fixed points, each of these would be a candidate for the long-run locational pattern, with different sequences of chance events steering the process toward one of the multiple candidates.

We can now see what happened in our three locational models (Figure 4-5). The first model, "independent-preferences," has constant probabilities of choice and thus a single fixed point. Therefore, it has a unique, predetermined outcome. The second model, "spin-off," with probabilities equal to proportions, has every point a fixed point, so that "chance" could drive this locational process to any outcome. The third model, "agglomeration economies," has 0 and 1 as two candidate stable fixed

---

*The set of fixed points needs to have a finite number of components. Where the proportions-to-probabilities function itself changes with the number of firms located, as in the agglomeration case, the theorem applies to the limiting function of these changing functions, providing it exists. (See Arthur et al., 1986, 1987.)

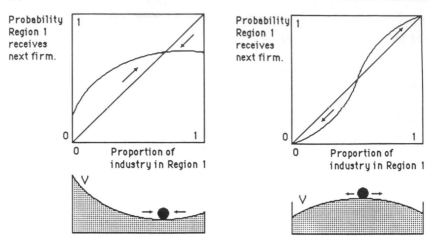

FIGURE 4-6   Convex and nonconvex potential functions.

points. Thus, the outcome is not fully predetermined, and one of the candidate solutions is "chosen" by the accumulation of chance events.

When does history matter in the determination of industry location patterns? We can now answer this question, at least for the broad class of models that fit our general framework. History—that is, the small elements outside our economic model that we must treat as random—becomes the determining factor when there are multiple solutions or multiple fixed points in the proportions-to-probabilities mapping. More intuitively, history counts when expected motions of regions' shares do not always lead the locational process toward the same share.

It is useful to associate with each probability function a potential function V whose downhill gradient equals the expected motion of regions' shares (see Figure 4-6).* Intuitively, we can think of the process as behaving like a particle attracted by gravity to the lowest points on the potential, subject to random fluctuations that die away. If this potential function is convex (looking upward at it), it has a unique minimum; therefore, the locational process that corresponds to it has a unique determinate outcome which expected motions lead toward and which historical chance cannot influence. If, on the other hand, this potential function is nonconvex, it must have two or more minima with a corresponding

---

*For dimension $N > 2$, a potential function may not exist. This would be the case if there were cycles or more exotic attractors than the single-point cycles considered here.

split in expected motions and with "historical chance" determining which of these is ultimately selected.*

To establish nonconvexity, all we need is the existence of at least one unstable point, a "watershed" share of the industry, above which the region with this share exerts enough attraction to increase its share and below which it tends to lose its share. Yet in a way, this is another definition of the presence of agglomeration economies: if above a certain density of settlement a region tends to attract further density, and if below it it tends to lose density, there must be some agglomeration mechanism present. The underlying system will then be nonconvex, and history will count.

CONCLUSIONS

Whether small events in history matter in determining the pattern of spatial or regional settlement in the economy reduces, strangely enough, to a question of topology. It reduces to whether the underlying structure of locational forces guiding the locational pattern as it forms is convex or nonconvex. And for this structure to be nonconvex, so that history will matter, some mechanism of agglomeration must be present.

Our models were highly stylized. They considered populations of firms, not people; they assumed that firms lived forever and never moved; and they dealt with the formation of only one industry over time, not several. Nevertheless, even if the mechanisms creating urban systems in the past and present are a great deal more complex, it is still likely that a mixture of economic determinism and historical chance—and not either alone—has formed the spatial patterns we observe. Certain firms, such as steel manufacturers, need to be near sources of raw materials; for them, spatial economic necessity dominates historical chance. Certain other firms, such as gasoline distributors, need to be separated from their competitors in the same industry; for them, the necessity to spread apart again dominates historical chance. But most firms need to be near other firms—if not firms in their own industry, then firms in other industries that act as their suppliers of parts, machinery, and services, or as consumers of their products and services. For this reason, firms are attracted to existing and growing agglomerations. After all, it is this need of firms to be near other firms that causes cities—agglomerative clusters—to exist at all.

Thus, it is highly likely that the system of cities we have inherited is only partly the result of industries' geographical needs, raw material lo-

---

*For some early discussion of nonconvexity's importance for the role of history, see David (1975).

cations, the presence of natural harbors, and transportation costs. It is also the result of where immigrants with certain skills landed, where early settlers met to market foods, where wagon trains stopped for the night, where banking services happened to be set up, and where politics dictated that canals and railroads be built. We therefore cannot explain the observed pattern of cities by economic determinism alone without reference to chance events, coincidences, and circumstances in the past. And without knowledge of chance events, coincidences, and circumstances yet to come, we cannot predict with accuracy the shape of urban systems in the future.

REFERENCES

Arthur, W. B. 1983. Competing technologies and lock-in by historical small events: The dynamics of choice under increasing returns. Center for Economic Policy Research Paper 43. Stanford University.

Arthur, W. B. 1984. Competing technologies and economic prediction. Options. I.I.A.S.A. Laxenburg, Austria, April: 10–13.

Arthur, W. B. 1986. Industry location patterns and the importance of history. Center for Economic Policy Research Paper 84. Stanford University.

Arthur, W. B. 1987. Self-reinforcing mechanisms in economics. In The Economy as an Evolving Complex System, P. W. Anderson and K. J. Arrow, eds. Forthcoming. New York: Addison-Wesley.

Arthur, W. B., Yu. M. Ermoliev, and Yu. M. Kaniovski. 1983. A generalized urn problem and its applications. Cybernetics 19:61–71.

Arthur, W. B., Yu. M. Ermoliev, and Yu. M. Kaniovski. 1986. Strong laws for a class of path-dependent urn processes. In Proceedings of the International Conference on Stochastic Optimization, Kiev 1984, Arkin, Shiryayev, and Wets, eds. New York: Springer, Lecture Notes in Control and Information Sciences 81.

Arthur, W. B., Yu. M. Ermoliev, and Yu. M. Kaniovski. 1987. Path-dependent processes and the emergence of macro-structure. European Journal of Operational Research 30: 294–303.

Christaller, W. 1933. Central Places in Southern Germany. Englewood Cliffs, N.J.: Prentice-Hall.

Cohen, D. L. 1984. Locational patterns in the electronics industry: A survey. Stanford University. Mimeo.

David, P. A. 1975. Technical choice, innovation and economic growth. New York: Cambridge University Press.

David, P. A. 1984. High technology centers and the economics of locational tournaments. Stanford University. Mimeo.

Engländer, O. 1926. Kritisches and Positives zu einer allgemeinen reinen Lehre vom Standort. Zeitschrift für Volkswirtschaft und Sozialpolitik. Neue Folge 5.

Hill, G., D. Lane, and W. Sudderth. 1980. Strong convergence for a class of urn schemes. Annals of Probability 8:214–226.

Lösch, A. 1944. The Economics of Location. Translated by W. G. Woglom from 2nd revised ed. New Haven, Conn.: Yale University Press, 1954.

Maruyama, M. 1963. The second cybernetics: Deviation amplifying mutual causal processes. American Scientist 51:164–179.

Palander, T. 1935. Beiträge zur Standortstheorie. Stockholm: Almqvist and Wicksell.

Predöhl, A. 1925. Das Standortsproblem in der Wirtschaftslehre. Weltwirtschaftliches Archiv 21:294–331.

Ritschl, H. 1927. Reine und historische Dynamik des Standortes der Erzeugungszweige. Schmollers Jahrbuch 51:813–870.

Thünen, J. H. von. 1826. Der Isolierte Staat in Beziehung auf Landwirtschaft und Nationalökonomie. Hamburg.

Weber, A. 1909. Theory of the Location of Industries. 1929. Chicago: University of Chicago Press.

5

An Economic Model of
Urban Growth

MARTIN J. BECKMANN

Infrastructures are basic to all economic life. The urban infrastructure is one of the most diverse and complex. To name only the most important components, it includes streets and public transportation; water supply and sewage removal; police and fire protection; judicial, educational, and health facilities; and parks and other recreational facilities. The study of infrastructure opens up an approach to a whole class of economic problems.

Characteristically, both private and public agents demand infrastructure, but most infrastructure is supplied by the public sector. Yet there are a great variety of institutional arrangements for the creation and management of infrastructure, offering a fruitful field for economic analysis and one that has been insufficiently explored. This chapter will focus on the demand side of urban infrastructure. No exact relationship will be established between the size or population of cities and the demand for infrastructure. Rather, we will consider generically the principal forces behind this demand—those forces that drive the growth or decline of individual cities and the urban system as a whole.

Explaining the rise and fall of cities is one of the fundamental problems of urban economics. Cities may exist and grow for noneconomic reasons, particularly political ones. Madrid and Washington are examples of cities that were located for purely political reasons; the rise of centralized government is the principal driving force behind their growth.

In a market economy the economic fortunes of a city clearly depend on two factors. The first is the value of goods and services that can be sold to residents with sources of income that do not derive from the city's current productive activities. This first factor includes the economic base associated with retirement income, certain welfare payments, remittances transferred from other geographic regions, and some other forms of un-earned income and the use of accumulated wealth. The second factor is the value of goods and services that can be exported to the rest of the economy. More exactly, the gross income of a city is determined by the value added in production and trade. It is this added value that generates the demand for labor and thus determines the population that can be so supported. Urban population is, in fact, an increasing function of such added value—strict proportionality would result if per capita income were constant.

Exporting goods and services to locations outside the city is of greater overall importance than exogenous sources of income in the urban economy. These exports may go to the immediate neighborhood (rural centers) or to the region of which the city is the economic capital. They may also be sold nationwide or worldwide, in which case the city's advantage derives either from localized natural resources or from spe-cialized labor resources that, often for historical reasons, choose to reside in this location.

When a city exports goods and services to a surrounding region, it is known as a central place and serves as a trade and production center of a particular region. Subregions aggregate into regions, which leads to a nesting of regions and to a hierarchy of central places (see chapter 3). The size of a central place depends on its rank in the hierarchy of central places—because this determines the size of the region to which it exports—and on the income of the region of which the city is the capital. The more prosperous the region, the greater the demand for services from its regional capital. Each central place supplies a range of goods and services, some to its immediate neighborhood, in its role as a lowest order central place. Some goods and services are produced in every city, but others are pro-duced only in central places above a certain rank. The rank of a good is the minimum rank of a central place that supplies this good. The growth of central places is a result of the growth of a region's income and of shifts in the specialization for goods and services among centers of dif-ferent ranks.

Cities that serve as supply points to distant markets produce spe-cialized products from specialized resources. When such production is concentrated in only a few cities, it is usually because of economies of scale; the joint location of several related specialized activities arises from agglomeration economies—that is, economies of joint location—wherein producers use each other's products or related or joint facilities (see chapter 4). These cities change in size when the demand for these specialized products shifts or when natural resources are discovered or exhausted.

"Resources" include capital stock as well as natural assets. Thus, when General Motors decides to set up an assembly plant in some location deemed favorable as a supply point for a regional market (identified by the company), this specialized capital (the plant) gives the location an advantage, at least temporarily, for producing a certain type of automobile.

When a city specializes in one product, its growth or decline is usually a result of the market demand for this product. The larger the potential (world) market, the stronger the potential for growth or decline. There are any number of possible products or resources to which a city may look for economic success. Spectacular growth rates for settlements have occurred based on areas as diverse as mining and defense work. In mining, growth results from the more or less accidental discovery of extractable resources, and decline occurs when the resources are depleted or sudden shifts of demand take place. In defense work, growth is mainly due to political decisions about where to locate defense contracts.

Predictions of long-term demand and demand shifts for particular products, however, have been notoriously incorrect. Prosperous cities may fall on hard times when their product is no longer in demand and when no alternative uses have been found for their specialized resources. Decline may occur either because a competitor city is producing a similar good more efficiently or because in general the market for the good has faded. Economic theory is able to predict the future of cities with specialized industries only in quite general terms. Oscillations, or cycles of boom and bust, are probably more characteristic of specialized urban economies than of diversified ones.

We can provide somewhat more illumination in the task of predicting expected changes in central places over periods that extend beyond the life span of a particular industry. These changes can be summarized as a decline of smaller central places and growth of the metropolis. Metropolitan growth is often accompanied by a decentralization or spread of the metropolitan area itself. But it appears that most new economic activities are launched in or near metropolitan centers and then are filtered down or diffused through a competition among higher order central places. Ease of transportation and other factors affect the pattern that emerges.

A deeper economic understanding of the forces behind urbanization can be gained by looking at individual cities and particular cases. Yet at the same time, we must try to understand what drives the expansion of the urban system as a whole. To keep the analysis as simple as possible, we consider as an example an economy with two goods that are produced from two resources, land and labor. Labor is assumed to be mobile, and both land and labor are assumed to be of uniform quality. The first or "agricultural" good is land intensive and characterized by constant returns to scale. The second or "industrial" good requires little land and has increasing returns to scale. (In economic parlance, "returns to scale" can be explained as follows. If all inputs are doubled and output is also doubled, returns are constant; if all inputs are doubled and output is more than doubled, returns to scale are increasing.) In addition, this economy includes transportation activity that uses only labor. (Note that capital has been omitted. Because under mild assumptions it can be shown that capital and labor are used in constant proportions in each activity, the two factors may be conveniently aggregated into a single factor called labor.)

To simulate the operation of market forces in a competitive economy, we postulate an optimum location of available labor on an unlimited amount of land. This results in maximum welfare as measured by the aggregate of consumer utilities due to the consumption of the two goods. Labor supply by each household is considered fixed, and income constraints are disregarded. This model has been analyzed at length (Beckmann and Puu, 1985).

This combination of variables produces a predictable result. If the total population is not too large, the production of the good with increasing returns is entirely concentrated in one small circular area, which we may call a city. This city is surrounded by a larger circle in which the agricultural good is produced. The density of land use declines with distance from the city and ends at a well-defined distance at which the product price in the center equals wage costs plus transportation costs to the market in the center. This is a modified version of a so-called von Thünen system (von Thünen, 1826) composed of a single metropolis and its rural hinterland.

In a central-place system, centers of each rank constitute the focal point of such von Thünen systems, and the spatial economy founded on an environment with uniform resource endowments may be understood as the combination of central places with their urban satellites and rural hinterlands. A study of economic growth in such a system would have to explain the differential growth rates of centers of various orders. The goal in this chapter is to try something simpler, namely, to examine the growth of city and rural hinterland for a simple von Thünen system. As it turns out, this is sufficiently challenging and can serve as a first step in the direction of a full analysis of economic growth in a spatial economy. Our main concern is in determining the relative growth rates of the urban and rural population.

To analyze the process of economic growth in a von Thünen economy, we explore an aggregate production function for the agricultural sector, describing agricultural output delivered to a city as a function of aggregate inputs of labor and transportation into the agricultural sector. The appendix to this chapter presents the mathematical argument for the conclusions that follow. Under reasonable assumptions, decreasing returns to scale in agriculture result from the necessity of using more and more transportation as the agricultural zone is expanded. The question of the development of the spatial economy can thus be shown to be equivalent to studying a growth process in a two-sector economy in which an urban good is produced with increasing returns to scale and an agricultural good is produced with decreasing returns to scale.

If we assume that the market achieves an efficient allocation of total available labor between urban and agricultural production, we find that urban population increases relative to rural population as total population grows. The driving force behind urban growth is the increasing returns in the production of urban goods, combined with the substitution of urban for agricultural goods, which in the aggregate are produced under diminishing returns to scale.

Figure 5-1 shows the degree of urbanization as a function of total population when $\alpha = 3/4$, $\beta_1 = 11/10$, and $\delta = 1/4$. This result should be compared with the actual proportion of urban population in the United States in the last 200 years (Figure 5-2).

Thus, the prediction of economic theory is that, under reasonable assumptions, the urban sector must always grow relative to the agricultural

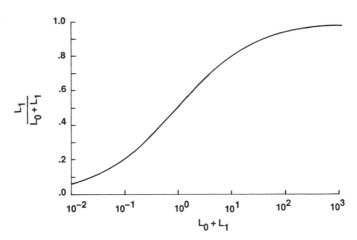

FIGURE 5-1   Urban population (L_1) as a fraction of total population ($L_0 + L_1$), calculated. L_0: rural population.

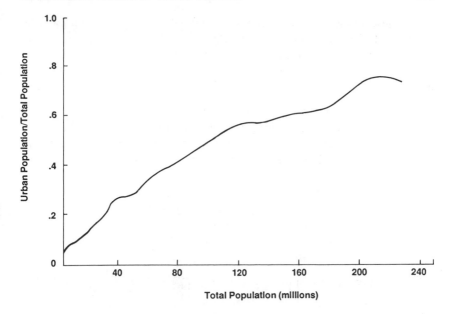

FIGURE 5-2 Urban population as a fraction of total population in the United States, 1790–1980. Data source: U.S. Bureau of the Census, Census of Population. Washington, D.C., various years.

sector and that this process will continue in the future. The substitution of services for industrial production does not change this prediction because many urban services, like industry, enjoy increasing returns to scale. From this perspective, any past reversals of the urbanization process must be viewed as resulting from economic setbacks that occurred because of wars and other catastrophes. If we accept such a viewpoint, the challenge of providing urban infrastructure can only become greater.

REFERENCES

Beckmann, M. J., and T. Puu. 1985. Spatial Economics: Flow, Density and Potential. Amsterdam: North-Holland.
Thünen, J. H. von. 1826. Der isolierte Staat in Beziehung auf Landwirtschaft und Nationalökonomie. Stuttgart: Gustav Fischer, 1966 (reprint).

APPENDIX

To analyze the process of economic growth in a von Thünen economy, we must first construct an aggregate production function for the agricultural sector, describing agricultural output Z_0 delivered to the city as a function of aggregate inputs of labor X_0 and of transportation T into the agricultural sector. Let r be the distance from the city and R the radius of the agricultural zone. The area occupied by the city will be neglected. The following notation will be used:

r distance from the center
R distance at which production intensity falls to zero
$x(r)$ labor employed in agricultural production per unit of land
$bx(r)^\alpha$ output of agricultural product per unit of land (a Cobb-Douglas function)
Z_0 aggregate agricultural output delivered to the city
X_0 aggregate labor input into agriculture
T aggregate transportation input
$Z_1 = b_1 L_1^{\beta_1}$ aggregate output of the urban good as a function of urban labor input L_1

These aggregates depend on the density of labor input $x(r)$ as follows. Output:

$$Z_0 = \int_0^R 2\pi r \, bx^\alpha(r)\mathrm{d}r. \tag{1}$$

Labor input:

$$X_0 = \int_0^R 2\pi r \, x(r)\mathrm{d}r. \tag{2}$$

Transportation input:

$$T = \int_0^R 2\pi r^2 \bullet b \, x(r)^\alpha \, \mathrm{d}r. \tag{3}$$

We maximize equation 1 subject to equations 2 and 3. The Lagrangian of this problem is

$$\int_0^R L(r)\mathrm{d}r = \int_0^R 2\pi r \, x^\alpha \, \mathrm{d}r + \lambda(L - \int_0^R 2\pi r \, x\mathrm{d}r)$$
$$+ \mu(T - \int_0^R 2\pi r^2 \, x^\alpha \mathrm{d}r).$$

Maximizing with respect to x under the integral yields

$$\alpha x^{\alpha-1} - \lambda - \mu r \alpha \, x^{\alpha-1} = 0$$

or

$$x(r) = \frac{\alpha}{\lambda} (1 - \mu r)^{\frac{1}{1-\alpha}} . \tag{4}$$

This shows that labor input per unit area $x(r)$ decreases with distance and is zero for

$$r \geq R = \frac{1}{\mu} . \tag{5}$$

Substituting for $x(r)$ from equation 4 and R from equation 5 in equations 1, 2, and 3 for Z_0, X_0, and T yields

$$Z_0 \sim \lambda^{-\frac{\alpha}{1-\alpha}} \mu^{-2}, \tag{6}$$

$$X_0 \sim \lambda^{-\frac{1}{1-\alpha}} \mu^{-2}, \tag{7}$$

$$T \sim \lambda^{-\frac{\alpha}{1-\alpha}} \mu^{-3} . \tag{8}$$

Eliminating λ and μ between equations 7 and 8 and substituting in equation 6 yields the aggregate production function for agriculture:

$$Z_0 = B \cdot X_0^{\frac{\alpha}{3-2\alpha}} T^{\frac{2-2\alpha}{3-2\alpha}} . \tag{9}$$

Note that this is a Cobb-Douglas production function with decreasing returns to scale because the exponents add to less than 1:

$$\frac{\alpha}{3-2\alpha} + \frac{2-2\alpha}{3-2\alpha} = \frac{2-\alpha}{3-2\alpha} < 1$$

for $0 < \alpha < 1$. The decreasing returns result from the necessity of using more and more transportation as the agricultural zone is expanded.

Finally, consider the allocation of a fixed amount L_0 of labor to agricultural production and transportation:

$$\underset{X_0,T}{\text{Max }} B \cdot X_0^{\frac{\alpha}{3-2\alpha}} T^{\frac{2-2\alpha}{3-2\alpha}}$$

such that

$$X_0 + T \leq L_0.$$

The efficiency conditions for this simple constrained maximum problem are

$$X_0 = \frac{\alpha}{2-\alpha} L_0 \tag{10}$$

and

$$T = \frac{2-2\alpha}{2-\alpha} L_0, \tag{11}$$

and the aggregate production function in terms of aggregate labor L_0 is then

$$Z_0 = b_0 \cdot L_0^{\frac{2-\alpha}{3-2\alpha}}. \tag{12}$$

The question thus has been shown to be equivalent to studying a growth process in a two-sector economy in which an urban good is produced with increasing returns to scale and an agricultural good is produced with decreasing returns to scale. (Transportation need no longer be considered explicitly.) In our model the urban good is either consumed in the city or transported to the city as back freight at no cost.

We assume that the market achieves an efficient allocation of total available labor L between urban and agricultural production. Economic theory shows that this is true under perfect competition. The object of the market is then to maximize welfare as measured by an aggregate utility function. Let this be specified as

$$U = aZ_0^\delta + (1-a)Z_1^\delta \tag{13}$$

in terms of aggregate outputs Z_i of the two sectors. Furthermore, we have the production functions

$$Z_i = b_i L_i^{\beta_i},$$

where

$$0 < \beta_0 < 1 < \beta_1. \tag{14}$$

A given total labor force L is then allocated to achieve

$$\max_{L_0, L_1} a b_0 L_0^{\delta\beta_0} + (1-a)b_1 L_1^{\delta\beta_1}, \tag{15}$$

such that

$$L_0 + L_1 \le L. \tag{16}$$

The Lagrangian

$$a b_0 L_0^{\delta\beta_0} + (1-a)b_1 L_1^{\delta\beta_1} + \lambda(N - L_0 - L_1)$$

is maximized when

$$\delta\beta_0 \, a \, b_0 \, L_0^{\delta\beta_0 - 1} = \lambda$$

and

$$\delta\beta_1 \, (1-a)b_1 \, L_1^{\delta\beta_1 - 1} = \lambda.$$

Thus,

$$\frac{L_1^{1-\delta\beta_1}}{L_0^{1-\delta\beta_0}} = \frac{b_1}{b_0} \frac{\beta_1}{\beta_0} \frac{1-a}{a}. \tag{17}$$

From this

$$L_1 = c \, L_0^{\frac{1-\delta\beta_0}{1-\delta\beta_1}}$$

or

$$L_1 = c \, L_0^\gamma. \tag{18}$$

Now equation 14 and $\delta\beta_1 < 1$ imply

$$\gamma > 1, \tag{19}$$

such that equation 18 shows a faster growth of urban population L_1 compared to rural population L_0.

For an illustrative calculation, let $\alpha = 3/4$ (a conventional value for labor's output elasticity), implying

$$\beta_0 = \frac{2-\alpha}{3-2\alpha} = \frac{5}{6}.$$

Let returns to scale in urban production be 10 percent (another conventional number). Then $\beta_1 = 11/10$. In the utility function, let $\delta = 1/4$, implying a sharply diminished marginal utility of consumption for either good when the other good is held constant. Then $\gamma = 95/87 = 1.097954$. Urban population as a fraction of total population may be calculated from equation 18 for different levels of total population. It depends on both γ and c. No econometric analysis has been attempted to obtain the optimal fit. Figures 5-1 and 5-2 compare actual calculated fractions.

6

Growth of U.S. Cities and Recent Trends in Urban Real Estate Values

JOHN S. ADAMS

Urban infrastructure evolves at two geographical scales. At the *national* scale the physical infrastructure connects our system of urban centers; at the *local* scale, it supports activity inside each urban area. Activity at the two scales is largely separate but entirely complementary.

At the national scale an infrastructure framework of transportation and communication channels has evolved to support production, distribution, and consumption activity, which increasingly has centered on urban areas. Indeed, the design and operation of the infrastructure has fostered the growth of the nation's system of cities while directing its evolution. The building of the infrastructure absorbed huge amounts of private capital investment; in return, it enhanced the productivity of natural and human resources devoted to producing the goods and services that people wanted to buy.

At the local scales, urban areas were organized and built up mainly as economic entities to facilitate the collection, processing, and distribution of goods, and the production and distribution of business and personal services. Locally generated public and private finances traditionally were the main sources drawn on to build and maintain much of the local infrastructure (for example, dams, bridges, roads, and utilities). In recent decades the direct costs of new local infrastructure have been paid for from public sources (borrowing, taxes, fees, investment tax credits, tax breaks, etc.) or private sources (equity investments, borrowing). The indirect costs of such infrastructure, which are often imposed on the rest of the system as a result of premature deterioration, underutilization, or abandonment of existing infrastructure, are harder to assess but are just as real.

This chapter examines the evolution of the transportation and communications aspects of the national infrastructure and then explores the dynamics of local infrastructure supply and demand as they relate to changing real estate values and new central city housing construction. In conclusion, questions are raised about what is needed in the way of urban infrastructure, what may not be needed, and who should pay for it.

DEVELOPMENT OF THE NATIONAL METROPOLITAN INFRASTRUCTURE

Urban growth nationwide can be divided into epochs that reflect the impacts of major technological innovations on the construction of urban infrastructure. The first epoch depended on the wagon and sailing vessels; the second, on steamboats and the early railroad; the third, on long-haul trains made possible by the advent of standard-gauge steel tracks; and the fourth, on autos, trucks, and airplanes powered by the internal combustion engine. The nation's current romance with computers and telecommunications prompts us to wonder about a fifth epoch, but the impact of these innovations on the geography of metropolitan areas is still unclear.

During the four epochs, changes in transportation and power generation technologies were strong propellants of population and investment redistributions because they altered relative distances between cities and defined the cost of accessibility to raw materials. In addition, they permitted workers and urban economies to specialize and to trade profitably with one another. Other kinds of innovations, such as advances in medicine and public hygiene that increased life expectancies in cities, were also important to growth. But transportation and power innovations were the changes that could bring new sources of raw materials within a city's reach or, alternatively, signal atrophy of a city's industry by increasing the accessibility of a nearby larger, more competitive center.

The sail–wagon epoch spanned the first several decades (1790–1830) of U.S. history. Nearly all the largest cities at the beginning of this epoch were ports on the Atlantic Ocean or on rivers emptying into it. But despite their water route connections and a heavy emphasis on trade, these large cities were highly independent of each other and were as much extensions of European economies as they were organizers of their own. For most of the colonial period, Boston, Philadelphia, New York City, and the other ports interacted sparingly, and the land transportation network remained primitive in the early national period. The resulting inability to penetrate the interior of the continent with satisfactory low-cost transportation and communication infrastructure delayed the struggle for hinterlands until the end of the epoch, thereby enabling most Atlantic ports to retain their places in the population size hierarchy.

The most important resource of this first epoch and the ensuing "iron horse" epoch (1830–1870) was arable land. Especially in the early 1800s the vast majority of Americans worked in primary industries, most of them as farmers. Hence, cities of rapid growth were closely associated with the nation's westward expansion; as new farmlands and timber areas opened up, cities appeared on the navigable rivers and canals to serve them, and an assortment of steam vessels were developed to carry passengers and cargo. In the 1840s the rising importance of the "iron horse" stimulated demand for iron ore and coal. As a result, boom towns grew up around areas of extraction of those resources as well, largely in the previously settled parts of the nation.

Change became more rapid during the iron horse epoch as the struggle for hinterlands began in earnest. The development of regional rail networks extended the influence of rising urban centers deeper into the surrounding agricultural regions. Some Atlantic ports grew at the expense of others, and New York City's growth far outpaced that of its rivals Boston and Philadelphia as it became the nation's first-ranked metropolis. The fastest growing cities during this epoch were the inland ports such as Detroit, Cleveland, Chicago, and St. Louis, which grew at junctures of regional rail networks and long-haul transport.

The "steel-rail" epoch (1870–1920) saw the emergence of a national rail transportation system as the standardization of track and cars and the advent of improved steel rails made long-haul trains feasible. The improvement of the rail network was a strong force in organizing new heavy industries—particularly steelmaking—and therefore also stimulated population redistribution. The large inland ports that had thrived earlier as commercial centers were now within easy rail access of bituminous coal deposits and the national market, and they soon became industrial centers. Their populations continued to grow, increasing their concentration of the population in the largest centers and thereby continuing a trend that had begun in the iron horse epoch. Although the number of large cities remained stable after growing rapidly in the previous epoch, they continued to increase their share of the national population. The steel-rail epoch also witnessed a large increase in the number of medium-sized cities as more places were brought within the national circulation patterns with the expansion and improvement of the transportation and communication infrastructure to accommodate the flows of passengers, commodities, and information.

Most of the steel-rail epoch's new major urban centers appeared around the recently opened agricultural areas of the West; a few others were associated with the deposits of copper in Montana, lead and zinc in Missouri, and iron ore on Lake Superior. Boom centers also accompanied exploitation of bituminous coal deposits. The largest group of cities to decline in relative importance during the epoch were concentrated on the Missouri-Mississippi-Ohio river systems, reflecting the rapid decline of steamboat traffic at the hands of the nationally integrated rail network.

By the end of the steel-rail epoch, the outline of today's metropolitan system was established. Nevertheless, urban evolution continued in the "auto–air–amenity" epoch (1920–1960s). Cities near the coalfields now declined while those near the oil fields grew with the demands of the automobile, home heating, and industry. An important feature of the new epoch was the relative decline in the labor force of the primary and secondary industries, signaling their diminishing impact on the prosperity of large centers. Employment swung toward the hard-to-mechanize nonbasic service activities, which mostly serve local populations, and their rising importance foretold the expanded role of inertia in metropolitan evolution. A rapidly growing national population and an increasingly sophisticated economy now ensured that large metropolitan centers could grow despite reverses in their industrial export sectors.

INFRASTRUCTURE LESSONS FROM GEOGRAPHIC HISTORY

Behind the steadily increasing proportion of Americans living in metropolitan centers lay a more complex picture of metropolitan growth. Each era featured boom and slow-growth centers as well as centers that grew at less extreme rates (these latter centers made up the majority). The growth patterns of individual urban centers were determined in large part by the state of technology and the resultant designation of important resources. With society's adoption of technological innovations, an advantageous location might become disadvantageous, and a specialized urban economy that meant boom in one epoch could spell doom in the next. Many centers prospered in two or more epochs by a combination of aggressive entrepreneurship and fortunate location within the transportation–communication network of the day. Other centers faltered because they were unable to adapt quickly enough to a new technological regime and consequently dropped in ranking in the urban size hierarchy. St. Louis and Pittsburgh, for example, grew quickly during the iron horse epoch but later fell in size relative to many American cities.

Even those centers that adjusted to changing conditions grew in different ways from one epoch to the next, as is revealed today in their physical structures. New York City is an old American metropolis that experienced a large proportion of its growth during the iron horse and steel-rail epochs, during which it became the nation's largest city and then one of the world's great industrial and financial centers. Chicago boomed in the iron horse epoch and maintained its rank thereafter. Los Angeles, on the other hand, is primarily a product of the auto–air–amenity epoch and has no real counterpart in the vast areas of New York or Chicago that were built up during the earlier eras. It would therefore be unreasonable to assume that Los Angeles will someday "grow up" to be another New York.

There are many similarities among American metropolises and the layers of infrastructure that sustain them, but the nature of metropolitan evolution ensures that no single model of growth or structure will apply equally to such diverse centers as New York, Los Angeles, Chicago, Miami, and Charleston, West Virginia. Urban policy, therefore, must be flexible enough to accommodate each city's unique characteristics and changing growth patterns. Metropolises with different physical structures, populations, and functions are likely to have different shortcomings as well. Based on our previous example, we can imagine that New York and Los Angeles have significantly different housing needs. They are also dissimilar in their needs for other infrastructure, in the kinds of pollution they suffer, in their physical resource bases, in their employment and unemployment profiles, and in their illegal alien problems. Their governmental structures and their different relationships with state and federal governments further complicate comparisons.

Moreover, it cannot be assumed that urban policies for the Los Angeles or the New York of today will be appropriate 20 years from now. The history of American urban planning fits largely into the auto–air–amenity epoch; consequently, planners have never faced the turmoil that accompanies the accelerated change in growth patterns between epochs. Urban growth in some respects has been unidirectional within epochs, but it becomes confused as society adopts an important innovation that redefines the locational significance of places within the national transportation–communication infrastructure. A group of urban planners in 1880 might have been fairly successful at outlining growth patterns for the ensuing 20 or 30 years, but how would such a group have fared in 1920, when their experience with the characteristics of a rail-dominated transportation network was on the verge of becoming obsolete?

We could derive some basic policy guidelines for individual metropolitan centers by grouping them and finding the problems common to members of each group. For example, metropolises that grew most rapidly in the same epochs and in approximately the same physical environments, that are of the same size, and that have similar employment structures usually have common needs. Because of the many ways in which metropolitan areas differ, however, comprehensive urban policies—whether initiated at the federal, state, or local level—must address unique problems as well. And, as we noted earlier, metropolitan needs change with time. An understanding of these complexities of urban policy is currently of special interest because of indications that metropolitan America is entering a new growth epoch.

PAYING FOR INFRASTRUCTURE IN THE NEW SERVICE ECONOMY

It can be argued that this new metropolitan growth epoch centers on the service industries and on an infrastructure of information handling; that the new jobs will come from the service industries; and that much of the new economic infrastructure will be built around offices, airports, computers, and telecommunications systems. But this limited view focuses merely on transactions and flows through the metropolitan economy and not on the stocks of physical and human capital that make the flows possible. Even after we measure the flows, we cannot be sure whether they mean what we think they mean. Some of what passes for productive economic activity these days looks suspiciously like the transfer of money from one set of pockets to another without the creation of anything of corresponding value.

This charge is easy to make but hard to prove. At the moment, we do not have comprehensive economic balance sheets for cities or regions as we do for companies or even families. A family or a firm can usually tell at the end of a year whether it is in better or worse shape than it was a year earlier. Such a determination is harder to make for a city, a region, or a nation. As a consequence, we focus most of our policy attention on flows and on the annual operating statements that report the flows. To a certain extent, we can take the economic "temperature" of a city by looking at its bond rating or at the annual budget of the city government or at the change in the number of jobs located within its boundaries.

But these glimpses fall well short of the full frontal view needed to assess the current infrastructure needs of our cities and society's continuing ability to pay for them. The nation's economy is fraught with instances in which potentially valuable capital investment is depreciated in value prematurely or allowed to deteriorate physically within metropolitan areas and between regions of the country in order to maintain cash flows to our expanding service industries—health care, government, legal services, finance, casualty insurance, and education, to name a few of the largest.

The expanding service industries in the boom areas of the United States appear to require new infrastructure to support their activity, but they hesitate to pay for providing it. In fact, it is often unclear how today's expanding service industries are analogous to yesterday's goods-producing and distribution industries, which received much of the infrastructure that they needed. Equally unclear is the extent to which public funds should underwrite the infrastructure needs of service industries because in many cases (Houston in the 1970s is probably a good example) it is uncertain whether their activity produces net gains for the national or regional balance sheets. What in earlier days of abundant and essentially free natural resources was a simple tug of war between saving and spending—between investment and consumption—has now escalated to a more serious and pernicious conflict. Nothing of value is free anymore. One set of forces urges long-term maintenance and improvement of physical infrastructure that will support the economical production and distribution of goods and services that people who have a measure of consumer choice really want to buy. The pull in the opposite direction often comes from rapacious elements in certain service sectors that have been able to deliver overpriced services to involuntary customers trapped by location and barriers to the entry of new service providers. The first set of forces entails earning money the old-fashioned way, and part of today's service sector follows that tradition. The second set often entails making money by systematically taking it through exploitative activity that disrupts healthy economic development, disturbs the rational evolution of our urban areas, and draws down our investments in infrastructure instead of building them up.

In metropolitan areas, large and untaxed capital gains on residential real estate accumulate in high-class suburbs, whereas corresponding uncompensated capital losses are drained from the homes and businesses of inner-city neighborhoods. Suburbs grow faster than they otherwise would. Suburban shopping centers are bigger and enjoy larger sales volumes than they otherwise would. Central city infrastructure is abandoned prematurely or lies in need of repair or replacement, for which there is no ability to pay. Meanwhile, the gain, if any, to the metropolitan economy is hard to assess.

Among the various regions of the country, capital in the form of savings and taxes is withdrawn from some areas to be spent or invested elsewhere. Populations reared and educated in one set of areas move elsewhere to live, work, or retire. Some regions appear to be winners, and others seem to be losers. Yet it is unclear whether the nation has gained by these redistributions of existing forms of wealth and capital.

INFRASTRUCTURE AT THE LOCAL SCALE

The biggest determinant of demand for urban infrastructure is population, which at the local level is measured by size and geographical

distribution. Within each locale, three broad classes of population movement affect size and distribution: (1) the long-term net movement from
rural and small-town America to large urban areas; (2) the movement from
central cities to surrounding suburbs; and (3) another long-term movement
from the Northeast and Midwest to the West and South.

Population moving out of one area and into another means added demand for infrastructure at the new location. It may also mean "wasted"
capacity at the old location—that is, capacity abandoned before reaching
the end of its useful life, still fully usable but unwanted because of the
relocation of demand and therefore lacking in economic value.

Large-scale movement from one place to another normally raises land
and housing prices at the destination and reduces them at the origin in
relation to the levels that would have obtained without the movement.
Thus, population movements affect the demand for infrastructure, and
corresponding movements in real estate prices redistribute the ability to
pay. Capital gains on real estate in new areas often escape taxes, however,
and capital losses in areas of decline and outmigration are usually uncompensated. In the following sections, these issues will be examined in the
context of (1) differential changes in the number of households from one
metropolitan region to another, (2) price changes for owner-occupied and
rental housing in three major metropolitan regions, and (3) new housing
construction in selected central cities across the country at the end of the
1970s.

HOUSEHOLDS AND HOUSING UNITS IN THE LARGEST CITIES

About one of seven U.S. residents in 1980 lived in the five leading
metropolitan areas at census time: New York, Chicago, Los Angeles,
Philadelphia, and Detroit. During the 1960s and 1970s, these top five
added households and housing units at varying rates, except for the New
York area, which suffered a slump in the 1970s (Table 6-1). Except for
Los Angeles, the central cities (areas within city limits) saw declines in
the number of households in the 1970s. For New York and Philadelphia,
the central city household declines of the 1970s were a reversal of gains
during the 1960s.

Aggregate net population and household changes over a decade or two
depend on four kinds of demographic events: births, deaths, moves in,
and moves out. For example, the Chicago standard metropolitan statistical
area (SMSA) gained 300,000 households in 1970s, but the central city
lost 45,000. Migrants who were added to the central city from the suburbs,
from outside the metropolitan area, and from abroad, plus births to res-

TABLE 6-1 Population and Housing, Selected Large SMSAs, 1960 to 1980 (in thousands)

City	1980			Households, Change			
	Population	Households	Housing Units	1960–1970	Percent	1970–1980	Percent
Chicago							
SMSA	7,104	2,487	2,653	286	15	303	14
Central city	3,005	1,093	1,174	−19	−2	−45	−4
Suburbs	4,099	1,393	1,462	305	41	347	33
Detroit							
SMSA	4,353	1,509	1,588	186	17	242	19
Central city	1,203	434	471	−16	−3	−64	−13
Suburbs	3,150	1,076	1,117	202	36	307	40
Los Angeles–Long Beach							
SMSA	7,478	2,731	2,854	216	10	299	12
Central city	2,967	1,135	1,189	150	17	50	5
Suburbs and other	4,511	1,596	1,665	66	5	260	19
New York							
SMSA	9,120	3,499	3,669	403	13	−357	−9
Central city	7,071	2,789	2,941	166	6	−32	−1
Suburbs and other	2,049	710	728	237	30	−325	−31
Philadelphia							
SMSA	4,717	1,639	1,757	213	17	159	11
Central city	1,688	620	685	26	4	−22	−3
Suburbs	3,029	1,020	1,072	187	29	182	22

NOTE: Data are based on SMSA definitions current at census dates.

SOURCES: U.S. Bureau of the Census, County and City Data Book, 1962, Tables 3 and 6, pp. 433–455, 476–575; Statistical Abstract of the United States, 1971, pp. 830–880; State and Metropolitan Area Data Book, 1982, pp. 356–445; County and City Data Book, 1972, pp. 642–653.

idents of the central city, minus those who moved out and residents who died meant a net loss of 45,000 households.

The characteristics of the households in a metropolitan area and the decisions of their members about where to live establish the social geography of the area. The social geography in turn determines much of the nature of demand for urban infrastructure and patterns of its use. In the Chicago area, as in other major urban regions, there are three main patterns of geographical variation from place to place (Berry and Kasarda, 1977; Pinkerton, 1969, 1973): variation in (1) socioeconomic status of householders, (2) stage in the life cycle of the household, and (3) race and ethnicity.

Socioeconomic Status of Households

The first pattern is the spatial variation in average socioeconomic status of householders and in the related value of the housing units they occupy. The map of social status and housing value usually shows distinct areal sectors radiating outward from the downtown. The sectors are often bounded by and aligned with major radial transport corridors linking the city center with places outside the metropolitan area. Upper-middle-class neighborhoods are found in one or more sectors of the city; other sectors are middle class in character, and the rest are distinctly working class in their measures of income, occupation, education levels, housing values, rent levels, and life-styles.

Each sector reveals a tendency to project outward the general social class character of its inner-city neighborhoods.* Working-class central city neighborhoods project their outlooks and behaviors outward into what become working-class suburbs. Upper-class inner-city areas carry their affluence, life outlooks, and styles outward into exclusive suburbs. Middle-class and upper-middle-class sectors are usually the most dynamic. They generate the most vigorous and rapidly expanding suburban extensions and leave the largest number of vacancies at their inner precincts near the downtown. These vacated areas in turn lure immigrants and native minority households who are eager to establish themselves on the low rung of the housing and neighborhood ladder as they try to repeat the upward mobility success story of those who have already achieved the comfortable suburbs. Neither the rich nor the working poor display ag-

---

*A leading early discussion of this process appears in Park et al. (1925), especially chapters 2 and 3, pp. 47–79. The most complete treatment appears in Hoyt (1939), especially chapter 2, pp. 96–104. For comprehensive recent accounts, see Abler and Adams (1976) and Adams (1987).

gressive efforts to document socioeconomic mobility through the practice of intraurban geographic mobility. Unlike the middle class, neither the rich nor the poor consider that their status has changed or that it will change soon. It is the mobile middle class that supplies most of the energy that transforms the map of social status.

Stage in the Household Life Cycle

A second geographical pattern is formed by the spatial segregation of households according to stage in the household life cycle. Small housing units built at high densities and favored by single persons, and small households at the beginning and ending stages of the household life cycle, are located mainly near the core of the central city along transit routes, near outlying commercial centers, and in suburban apartment districts, often adjacent to transport corridors and commercial land.* At the other extreme of the unit size and housing density continuum are large, single-unit houses on ample lots, catering to family households at their stage of maximum involvement with family life and child rearing. The family status of a household is basically independent of a household's socioeconomic status. Thus, the geographic patterning due to variations—usually sectoral—in the social status of an urban area is different from, and essentially unrelated to, the geographic patterning of an urban area in terms of the life-cycle stage of households and corresponding unit size and housing density. This second kind of pattern is usually concentric around the city center.

Race and Ethnicity

The third basic pattern of geographical variation in metropolitan areas is an expression of race and ethnicity. Maps of racial and ethnic patterns are significantly different from maps of family status and socioeconomic status, except in cases where social class is due in part to racial or ethnic characteristics or when family status flows in some measure from cultural practices based on ethnic roots or on practices rooted in religious belief (for example, the number of children or the persistence of extended families).

---

*On the location preferences of young unmarried persons and households without children and their willingness to pay high prices to be near goods and services they want, see Nelson (1973). For locational requirements of single and childless women in the labor force, see Roistacher and Senyoung (1980). On the general problem of family change and its impact on the city, see Frey and Korbin (1982).

To summarize, the social geography and housing patterns of each U.S. metropolitan region are composed of at least three largely independent and additive patterns of variation: a socioeconomic pattern, a family status pattern, and a racial-ethnic pattern. The locations of births, deaths, household moves in, and household moves out are regulated and shaped by the metropolitan region's social geography and related housing patterns. At the same time, natural and migration changes revise those social patterns and thereby contribute to the redesign of the housing landscape and a reordering of its patterns of use.

SOCIAL STATUS AND HOUSING VALUE OF NEIGHBORHOODS

Most residential neighborhoods of central cities decline in attractiveness or desirability in relation to their suburban counterparts. The suburbs offer newer houses, lower densities, easier movement, and the more exclusive socioeconomic environments that many households seem to prefer if they have the financial means to achieve them. The flow of causation in suburban development usually begins with land speculators and developers anticipating that new, high-priced houses can be built and sold for a profit at a specific suburban location. After the houses are built, sold, and occupied, the process is repeated but this time with less uncertainty. If the development fails or is slow to succeed, it is not repeated unless adjustments in project scale or housing styles and prices are made.

The construction, sale, and occupancy of new suburban housing draw population out of the central city and soften the housing submarkets in the inner segments of markets that were developed during earlier periods (Lansing et al., 1969). The average income levels of central city households and the average market values of central city houses fall behind these measures in the suburbs. The movement of upper-income households from city to suburb sharply raises aggregate suburban income and lowers the city average income and usually its aggregate personal income as well. Withdrawing effective demand for housing from the central city and adding it to the suburbs causes housing prices to slide in the city because the housing supply remains roughly constant while demand is reduced. At the same time, such withdrawal causes housing prices to rise in the suburbs where supply is rising only slowly but strong demand continues.

Certain portions of the central cities seem to resist these forces of decline and decay in the housing market. The evidence that they resist is the persistence of above-average housing values and above-average rents in a fast-changing metropolitan housing market. New housing, when it is built, is almost always significantly above average in value and rent levels; old housing, when it is removed from the stock and demolished, is usually well below average in value and quality. The normal life cycle of a housing unit is a succession of stages from new and expensive to old and cheap. That process is interrupted when the physical structure after construction is maintained or improved in ways that preserve or enhance its relative desirability in the midst of a regularly updated and improved housing stock.

Even though houses in the neighborhood continue to age, the obsolescence, deterioration, and eventual dilapidation process can be averted, slowed, or reversed if the attractiveness of the neighborhood is maintained or improved. The value of a housing unit depends not only on the structure itself but also on the lot on which it stands. The value of the lot depends on the neighborhood social environment, the quality of the physical environment and individuals' attitudes toward physical features, and the location of the lot with respect to the principal nodes of interaction in the local metropolitan system.* These three elements of housing value—social environment, physical environment, and location—are revealed in the central cities of the nation's three leading metropolitan areas: Chicago, Los Angeles, and New York. Inside these cities, highly valued physical amenities include quiet, cleanliness, open space, greenery, elevation, and views over water. Highly valued social environments are those with residences of upper-income groups and the retail and recreational facilities that they patronize. Where attractive physical amenities and desirable social environments coincide close to or within a vigorous downtown center, the third condition is met for maintaining housing demand and high housing prices. In neighborhoods such as these, the physical infrastructure must be maintained and regularly improved to sustain the heavy or even increasing use it receives.

Chicago

Housing Values and Rent Levels   In the city of Chicago the median value of owner-occupied housing (in tracts where owner-occupied housing predominates) and the median contract rent (in tracts where rental housing predominates) were above the respective metropolitan averages in 1980 at locations along Lake Michigan and in selected neighborhoods at the north edge of the city and in the far south side (Figure 6-1). The lake provides a natural scenic and recreational amenity of great desirability; houses with a view of the lake command high premiums when rented or

---

*For specific examples from an increasingly rich literature using this method of estimating the contribution of various elements to the value of housing, see Apps (1973), Bagby (1981), Bielby (1980), Dale-Johnson (1982), Daniels (1975), and Jackson (1979).

sold. As might be expected, the value of this amenity diminishes with increasing distance from the lake unless other factors interrupt the decline. South of downtown Chicago are four well-defined zones of above-average housing prices along the lake. The first runs from the south edge of downtown, north and south of Roosevelt Road, and along waterfront parks to McCormick Place (the Chicago Exhibition Center). The second occurs around the neighborhood of the Illinois Institute of Technology (between 31st and 35th Streets). The third surrounds the University of Chicago and the Hyde Park area (from 47th to 63rd Streets) and extends back from the lake almost a mile. The fourth zone of high value and persistently high rents runs from the 67th Street Beach to Rainbow Park Beach (79th Street). North of downtown, the high prices run in an unbroken string of tracts to the northern city boundary with Evanston and westward across the north end of the city in newer, high-quality housing.

These highly prized areas feature attractive neighborhoods, open space and other physical amenities, and excellent access to the downtown, the lake, the parks, the industrial centers, and the shopping opportunities on the city's west side. They are relatively remote from the noise, pollution, and social environment of the poor minority areas on the south side.

When developers sense that the housing market in these above-average inner-city neighborhoods is strong and likely to remain so, new housing is often added at market rates, which holds the tracts' average housing price high or raises it even higher. It is the desire of above-average-income households to maintain the value of their houses, but it is the above-average structures and environmental attributes (social, physical, locational) that attract these households from other places and in the process maintain the value of housing.

Changes in Housing Values and Rent Levels in Chicago, 1970–1980   The 1980 median contract rent in the Chicago SMSA was $214, which was 65 percent higher than the median of $130 in 1970.* The consumer price index of residential rents in the Chicago SMSA also rose more than 60 percent, from 107.6 in 1970 (1967 = 100) to 172.2 in 1980 (U.S. Bureau of the Census, 1983).

In a general metropolitan climate of rising rents, certain city tracts with a majority of rental units had rent increases above the SMSA average. Sometimes the above-average rise accompanied changes in the tracts' rental stock as a result of rehabilitation, remodeling, or clearance and replacement. Sometimes tracts were abruptly exposed to intensified de-

---

*U.S. Bureau of the Census, 1980 and 1970 Censuses of Population and Housing. Census Tracts. Chicago SMSA, Table H1.

Housing Values and Rent Levels, 1980, and Changes in Values and Rent Levels, 1970–1980

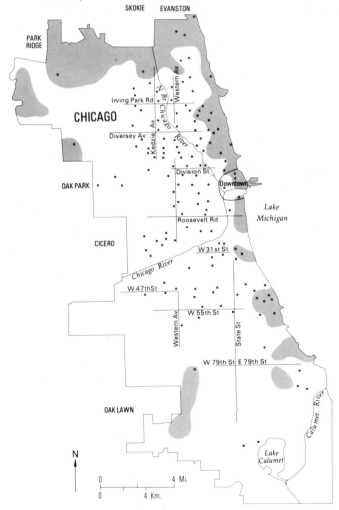

Median value of owner occupied housing (where owner occupied units predominate), or median contract rent (where rental units predominate) exceeds 1980 SMSA median.

• Median value of owner occupied housing percentage increase, 1970 to 1980 (where owner occupied units predominate), or median contract rent percentage increase, 1970 to 1980 (where rental units predominate) exceeded SMSA percentage increase.

(Maps based on sample of one-third of all tracts. Condominiums excluded from value calculations.)

FIGURE 6-1   Housing values and rent levels in Los Angeles and Chicago. Data sources: U.S. Bureau of the Census, 1970 and 1980 Censuses of Housing. Maps designed by the author.

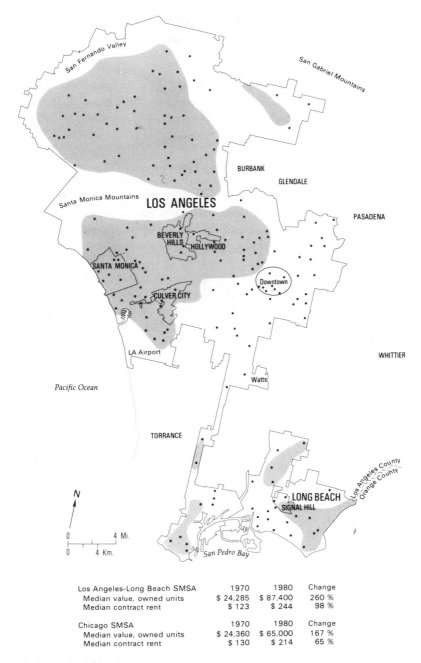

Los Angeles-Long Beach SMSA	1970	1980	Change
Median value, owned units	$ 24,285	$ 87,400	260 %
Median contract rent	$ 123	$ 244	98 %
Chicago SMSA	1970	1980	Change
Median value, owned units	$ 24,360	$ 65,000	167 %
Median contract rent	$ 130	$ 214	65 %

FIGURE 6-1   Continued.

mand without a corresponding expansion of the supply at prevailing prices, such as in newly fashionable areas or around schools and hospitals that expanded in the 1970s or at the leading edges of expanding minority neighborhoods.

The same observations can be made about owner-occupied housing in the city of Chicago and how it maintained its relative value in the metropolitan housing market in the 1970s. The median value of owner-occupied housing in the Chicago SMSA in 1980 was $65,000, up 167 percent from $24,360 in 1970. Again, as in the case of new rental units, new construction on vacant and cleared sites supplied new owner-occupied units in the largely built-up central city. But because most of the new housing in the metropolitan area was built in the suburbs in the 1970s and because most newly built housing carries prices well above the metropolitan median, it is a struggle for central city housing to retain its value relative to the entire metropolitan housing stock, which is constantly improving in quality and advancing in price.

Most of the Chicago tracts that had median rents and median values rising faster than average in the 1970s were located in the northeastern quadrant of the city (see Figure 6-1). These areas have not generally been the locations of major redevelopment activity. Thus, the higher-than-average price inflation for housing must be traceable to strong demand in those neighborhoods for a relatively fixed supply of rental and owned housing units.

Los Angeles

Housing Values and Rent Levels   The unrelenting demand pressure on the Los Angeles SMSA (i.e., Los Angeles County) housing stock, plus a continuing stream of high-priced additions to the stock, raised the median value of owner-occupied housing units from $24,285 in 1970 to $87,400 in 1980, an extraordinary rise of 260 percent. (It is especially extraordinary considering that the parallel rise in the Chicago SMSA was 167 percent, as noted in the previous section, and 126 percent in the New York SMSA, which is discussed in the next section.) The median contract rent in the Los Angeles SMSA rose 98 percent, from $123 in 1970 to $244 in 1980 (Badcock, 1984; Palm, 1981; Vance, 1976).

The median value of owner-occupied housing (in tracts where owned housing predominates) and the median contract rent (in tracts where rentals predominate) were above the corresponding metropolitan averages in northwest Los Angeles in the direction of the San Fernando Valley, west of downtown to Santa Monica, through Hollywood and Beverly Hills to the foothills of the Santa Monica Mountains. Median housing values and rents were also well above metropolitan averages on the far south side where there is a mixture of old and new on the hills near San Pedro Bay, and along much of the coast and in the newer areas of Long Beach (see Figure 6-1).

The two large districts of the city that are excluded from the regions of high values and above-average rents are the largely Hispanic east side of downtown and the region south and southwest of downtown, the region that has been the city's principal middle-class housing corridor for upwardly mobile newcomers. The first wave of newcomers were transplanted from the Midwest, coming in large numbers in the decades before and after World War I. They prospered and moved south and east (continued movement southwest was blocked by the ocean), to be followed by blacks from the western regions of the Old South and from Texas. In the 1970s and 1980s, newcomers south of downtown include large numbers of Asians (the Korean population alone is said to number 250,000). As Los Angeles increasingly becomes the nation's premier immigrant city, the historic immigrant reception neighborhoods south and east of downtown Los Angeles continue to perform their traditional function, and on a grand scale.

Changes in Los Angeles Housing Prices and Rent Levels, 1970–1980 The city of Los Angeles appears to retain a large share of the metropolitan area's exclusive neighborhoods as well as low-income minority areas. Housing in the exclusive areas appreciated faster than the SMSA average in the 1970s in the very areas that featured above-average values and rents (see Figure 6-1). In addition, values and rents rose faster than metropolitan averages in selected regions of the lower income areas south and west of downtown, which were straining to accommodate a large influx of newcomers during the 1970s when the SMSA (the county) added 436,000 persons.

New York City

Housing Values and Rent Levels The median value of owner-occupied housing in New York City (in tracts where owned housing predominates) and the median contract rent (in tracts where rentals predominate) were above the respective 1980 metropolitan averages in many parts of the city at census time (Figure 6-2). The median value of specified owner-occupied housing units in the SMSA was $64,300; the SMSA median contract rent was $220 (Stegman, 1985).

There is significant variation from borough to borough in the city's housing values and costs. Rents in Richmond and Manhattan are higher than the metropolitan averages, whereas the other boroughs fall below

Housing Values and Rent Levels, 1980, and Changes in Values and Rent Levels, 1970–1980

Median value of owner occupied housing (where owner occupied units predominate), or median contract rent (where rental units predominate) exceeds 1980 SMSA median.

Median value of owner occupied housing percentage increase, 1970 to 1980 (where owner occupied units predominate), or median contract rent percentage increase, 1970 to 1980 (where rental units predominate) exceeded SMSA percentage increase.

(Map based on sample of one-fourth of all tracts. Condominiums excluded from value calculations.)

New York SMSA	1970	1980	Change
Median value, owned units	$ 28,416	$ 64,300	126 %
Median contract rent	$ 117	$ 220	88 %

STATEN ISLAND
(RICHMOND County)

FIGURE 6-2   Housing values and rent levels in New York City. Data sources: U.S. Bureau of the Census, 1970 and 1980 Censuses of Housing. Maps designed by the author.

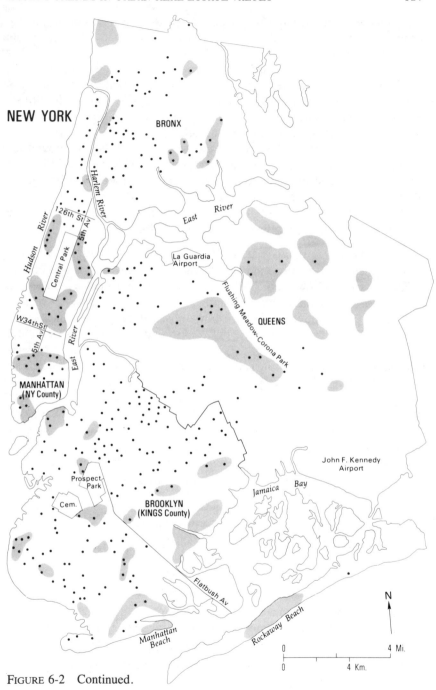

FIGURE 6-2 Continued.

them. Meanwhile, the average values of owner-occupied housing in the central city boroughs, with the exception of Manhattan, are well below the metropolitan average.

The residential districts in New York City with rents (i.e., in tracts where rental housing predominates) and housing values (i.e., in tracts where owner-occupied housing units are the majority) above the SMSA average are concentrated on Manhattan at the southern tip of the island; north of Houston Street on either side of Fifth Avenue in the vicinity of New York University; south, west, and east of Central Park; around the edges of the Bronx near the water; in Queens on either side of Flushing Meadow Park; and in scattered neighborhoods of Brooklyn near Jamaica Bay, Rockaway Beach, Manhattan Beach, park districts, and near the bridge to Manhattan (see Figure 6-2). A few newly developed tracts in central Richmond County were also above average.

Changes in Housing Values and Rent Levels in New York, 1970–1980   The median value of owner-occupied housing (excluding co-ops and condominiums) in the New York SMSA rose 126 percent between 1970 and 1980; during the same period, median contract rents rose just 88 percent.*

Many tracts throughout the five boroughs had value and rent rises in excess of the metropolitan averages. A systematic one-in-four sample of the census tracts in New York City revealed widespread inflation of rents and values in south, central, and north Manhattan and in a few locations near the older, high-density rental areas of Staten Island (see Figure 6-2). One explanation for the rises in values and rents may be the substantial amount of new housing constructed in New York City in the 1970s (213,000 structures in the five boroughs, many with two or more housing units); the high value of new structures can pull up the median for a particular tract. Demand for city rather than suburban living pushed up prices in both owner-occupied areas and in predominantly rental areas. Prices might have risen even faster if New York City had not had a strict rent control law. On the other hand, if there had been no rent control, faster inflation might have stimulated even more new construction than actually occurred.

COMPARING CENTRAL CITY AND METROPOLITAN AREA HOUSING VALUES

Suburban areas around central cities and upper-middle-class submarkets within cities and suburbs enjoyed above-average appreciation in housing

---

*U.S. Bureau of the Census, 1980 and 1970 Censuses of Population and Housing. Census Tracts. New York SMSA, Table H1.

prices in the 1970s and received a disproportionate share of the new construction that occurred during the decade. New housing is usually more expensive than existing housing, and when it is built, it not only raises the median housing values in an area but also pulls up the values of lower priced houses, which become more attractive when located near higher priced properties (Follain and Malpezzi, 1981). The dynamics of this process yield faster-than-average residential expansion in higher priced housing districts in selected suburbs and central cities. This faster-than-average growth places strains on existing infrastructure, which is normally augmented—often at public expense—to accommodate the expansion pressure. If average cost-pricing schemes are used to extend water, sewer, roads, schools, and other infrastructure, the new areas can receive high-quality services at prices below the cost of producing the services, whereas customers and residents in older settled areas pay higher costs for services that may be deteriorating. The dynamics and economics of local housing markets interact with the supply, demand, and pricing of other elements of infrastructure to yield an unstable and often inequitable marriage of the two systems. One set of zones receives free benefits while the other areas pay high prices for the services of inferior infrastructure.

Part of the instability can be traced to the fact that middle-class and upper-middle-class households accrued significant untaxed capital gains on their houses in the 1970s, and those gains lowered significantly (sometimes to zero or less) their real after-tax housing costs. Above-average disposable household income in middle-class and upper-middle-class neighborhoods combined with a high average propensity to spend, based in part on the steadily enhanced wealth position of the homeowner, contribute to a strong tax base; a healthy, vigorous, and attractive business environment that people enjoy living near and using; good practices of augmenting and tending the physical and scenic infrastructure of the area; and a self-perpetuating aura of attractiveness. Thus, in a circular, cumulative process, attractive upper-middle-class neighborhoods are created, occupied, and maintained.

Renters also like to live in these areas and will do so if they can afford to, leaving if they cannot. Above-average advances in housing prices in such neighborhoods, however, usually force many renters out even if zoning permits them. Owners are insulated from above-average value increases—they actually benefit from them—whereas renters enjoy no such protection, except in the rare case in which rents are kept well below market levels by local rent control ordinances.

Where are these prized locations? They occur usually in one or two suburban sectors that lie beyond the central city neighborhoods that enjoyed that high status at an earlier time. Occasionally, a central city will retain some neighborhoods that compete effectively with the more desirable and exclusive suburbs. If the central cities succeed in the competition—as they have in Seattle, San Francisco, St. Paul, Minneapolis, New Orleans, Miami, and some others—they can retain a significant share of the metropolitan leadership and put that leadership to work on their behalf. If they cannot, the leadership eventually abandons the central city for the suburbs, leaving a core city with a much diminished capacity to dictate the terms of its future as a place to live, work, and recreate.

Most new housing units built in recent decades have been erected on new land in suburban settings, yet construction has also continued in the city. Some new housing has been built on former railroad, port, and obsolete industrial land; some has been put into completely remodeled warehouses and factory buildings; some school buildings have been rehabilitated and converted to residential use; and some new housing has been placed in central city neighborhoods on land cleared of a former residential use. The new housing is often built at densities higher than that of the obsolete housing it replaces.

Since 1970 a significant amount of new housing has been built in or near the downtown of cities, occasionally as one element in a development program that includes several functions, such as hotels, shops, offices, and housing. Sometimes the houses, apartment buildings, condominiums, and other housing styles stand alone as separate private or publicly sponsored projects. Sometimes the new housing comes about as a result of major building rehabilitation or renovation. Occasionally, new housing is the result of a historic preservation project in the oldest part of town, which is usually the core (Laska and Spain, 1980; Mercer and Phillips, 1981; Rosenthal, 1980).

Houses built one or two at a time can succeed in the suburbs, but in the built-up central city, new residential development must go forth at a sufficiently large scale to succeed. Housing provides a bundle of services: a structure and dwelling place, the social and physical environment of the neighborhood, and accessibility to various sections of the urban area. If a residential development takes place at a sufficiently large scale—for example, 10 acres or more—it can virtually create its own physical and social environment. Then its chances of success will vary with its accessibility. If a new development on the edge of the built-up area or near the core is located in a sector of the urban area that has been traditionally favored by the elite, it is much easier to establish a social environment that will promote the success of the development.

In developments on the edge of the built-up area, large parcels of land are usually available for housing. In inner-city redevelopment, small parcels are usually the only kind available. Complex development projects and financial deals that include inner-city land acquisition for housing often favor large buildings on small parcels. For one thing, profits can be greater for a given amount of entrepreneurial and management effort on a large downtown project than on a small one. Moreover, because land acquisition for a single parcel is easier than for multiple parcels, costly delays during the land acquisition phase of development can be controlled.

In the 1970s most new housing construction occurred in the suburbs; both the central city and the downtown area received their shares of new housing construction (Figures 6-3 through 6-8). The developments in the inner city received more press attention than those in the suburbs because they were often more interesting visually and seemed to be dramatic. They were easy to notice and convenient for the press to cover. Moreover, in the context of post-World War II suburban residential trends through the 1960s, the downtown developments were somewhat unexpected and frequently triggered conflict, with the resulting media attention that generally follows.

CONCLUSIONS

The dominant technology and resources during each U.S. growth epoch defined the locations that enjoyed economic advantage over others of their day. The infrastructure that was built to support city building and trade during each epoch responded to the needs of the day and helped bring unused and underused resources into fuller production.

That principle remains true today: sound infrastructure development and maintenance will help bring resources into fuller production to provide the goods and services people want to buy. But today it is often unclear whether the fastest growing industries or locations are demonstrating a fair and healthy economic advantage over others and therefore should be accommodated with appropriate infrastructure at public expense. Sometimes industries and, as a consequence, the regions in which they are headquartered appear merely to be preying on other segments of society as a result of defective or incomplete understandings of how the urban economy works. Perhaps the costs of expanding the infrastructure should be charged more fully to the primary beneficiaries, as in the case of property owners in high-value, rapidly appreciating real estate submarkets.

In urban geography and in urban economics, what is familiar is often thought to be necessary, but it may not be. The housing industry and the fast-growth service industries should be closely scrutinized to assess their net contribution to the commonwealth and their genuine need for additional

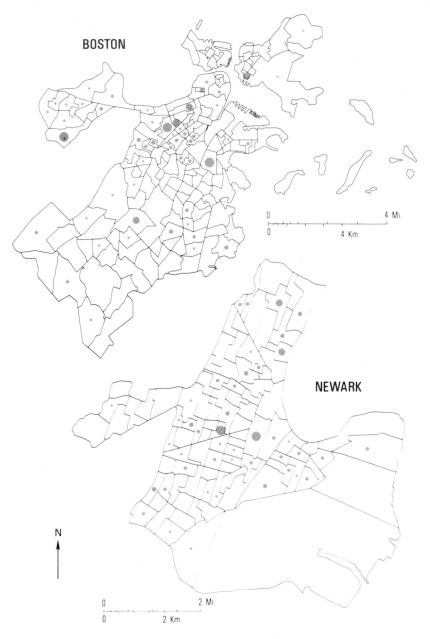

FIGURE 6-3   New central city housing in the Northeast: Buffalo, Boston, Pittsburgh, and Newark. Data source: U.S. Bureau of the Census, 1980 Census of
Housing. Maps designed by the author.

Housing Units Built 1979 through March 1980: Northeast

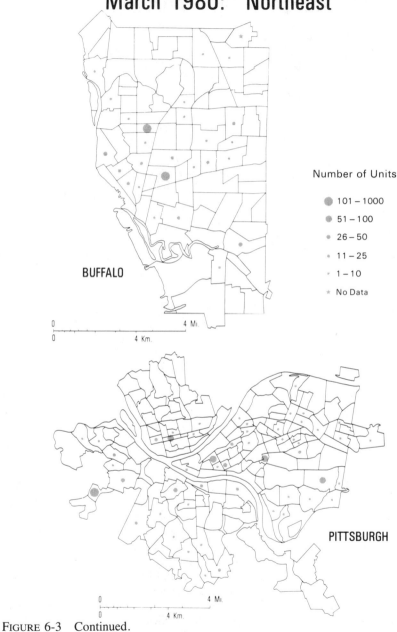

FIGURE 6-3 Continued.

Housing Units Built 1979 through March 1980: Midwest

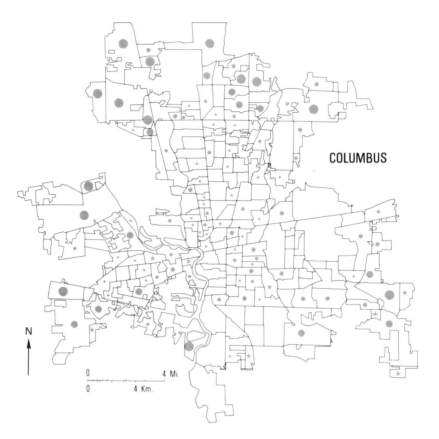

FIGURE 6-4   New central city housing in the Midwest: Milwaukee, Cleveland, and Columbus. Data source: see Figure 6-3. Significant amounts of new housing construction occurred in Milwaukee in the vigorous northwest sector, where the eight leading tracts had >1,500 new units. New units near the city center were scarce, except for the high-amenity location near the lake. The quiet and stable southside had small numbers of new units added at many locations. Except for one tract on the east edge of downtown with 180 units, and another west-side tract on the lake with 164, new housing construction in Cleveland was extremely sparse. Vigorous north-side Columbus had many hundreds of new units at various locations. The south edge of the city got the smallest share of new units.

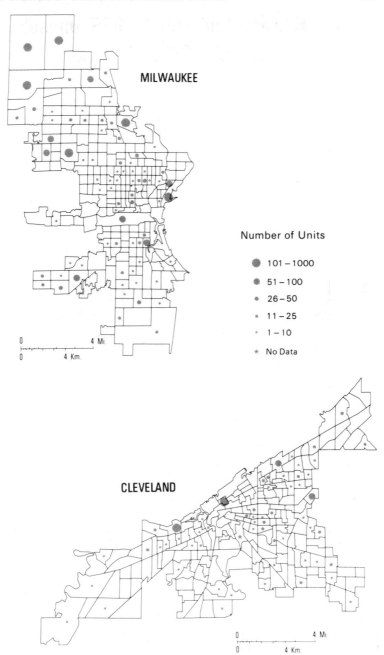

<small>FIGURE 6-4   Continued.</small>

Housing Units Built 1979 through
March 1980:   Midwest

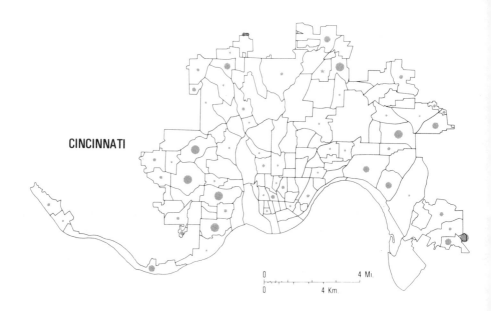

CINCINNATI

0   4 Mi.

0   4 Km.

FIGURE 6-5   New central city housing in the Midwest: Cincinnati, Kansas City, and St. Louis. Data source: see Figure 6-3. Cincinnati reported several large clusters of new housing completed on the west side, with two tracts each receiving >150 new units, and another >200. The east and north sides had significant numbers of new units in various locations, but almost no new construction occurred in the old core-city tracts. One tract near downtown Kansas City, Mo., received almost 100 new housing units, and a peripheral tract in Kansas City, Kans., had >50. Other tracts in both cities had few or none. The same was true in St. Louis. Several tracts close to downtown had a total of ~500 new housing units. Another western tract west of Forest Park by Washington University had almost 200. Elsewhere, new construction was extremely limited or nonexistent.

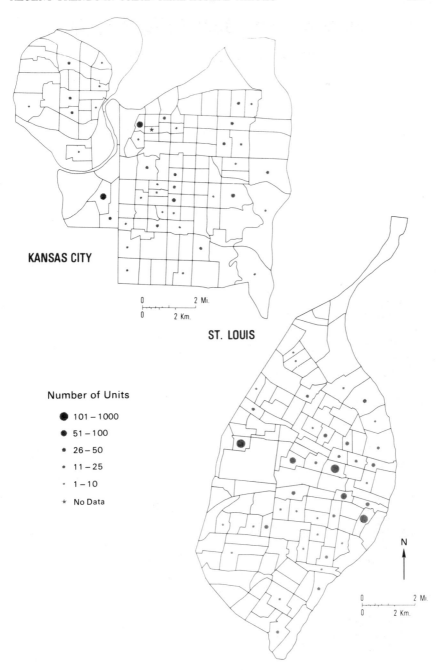

FIGURE 6-5 Continued.

Housing Units Built 1979 through March 1980: South

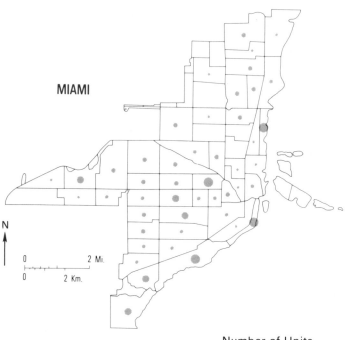

FIGURE 6-6   New central city housing in the South: Baltimore, Washington, and Miami. Data source: see Figure 6-3. Scattered development and redevelopment projects in Baltimore added >100 new housing units in each of seven tracts, but the core tracts in general had little new housing, like most tracts elsewhere in the city. New housing construction occurred throughout Washington and was especially intense around the core and in tracts to the north and east of Rock Creek Park. The largest increment was at the northeastern edge, behind the National Arboretum. In Miami, new housing construction was significant in all parts of the city, but was most intense in tracts by the ocean just north and south of downtown.

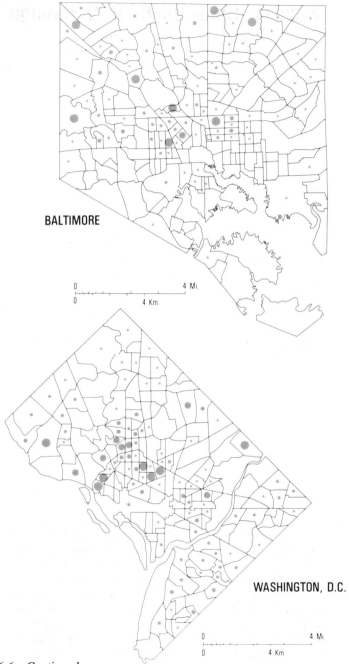

FIGURE 6-6 Continued.

Housing Units Built 1979 through March 1980: South

Number of Units

- 2501 or more (6026)
- 1001 – 2500
- 101 – 1000
- 51 – 100
- 26 – 50
- 11 – 25
- 1 – 10

FIGURE 6-7   New central city housing in the South: Dallas, Houston, and New Orleans. Data source: see Figure 6-3. The few hundred new housing units added to core tracts in Dallas do not compare with the many thousands built on the north and east sides during the same period. There was a modest rate of construction on the south and west sides as well, with a peak of >600 in one peripheral tract there. Houston was one of the nation's great boom cities of the 1970s and new housing construction throughout the city in the 1970s was part of the result. The west side got the most new units, but almost all tracts in all parts of the city got significant numbers of new units. New Orleans received significant new construction, especially in the newly developed northeastern, western, and southeastern down-river tracts. The old, historic, and often protected inner city tracts had modest rates of new construction, but the number of units in each tract is small.

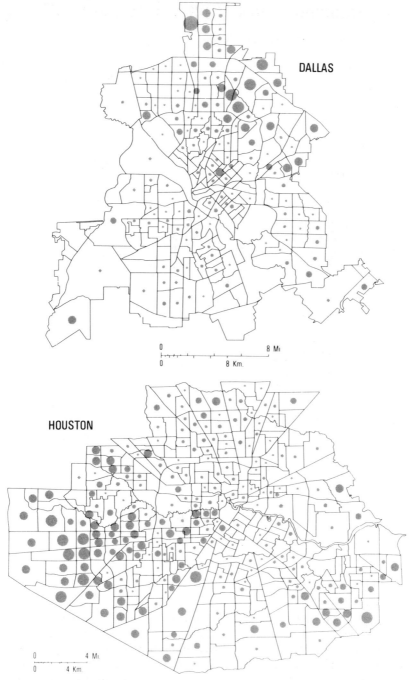

FIGURE 6-7   Continued.

Housing Units Built 1979 through March 1980: West

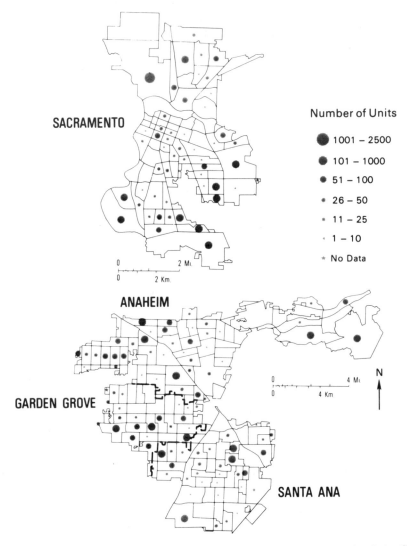

FIGURE 6-8   New central city housing in the West: Sacramento, Anaheim/Santa Ana/Garden Grove and Riverside/San Bernadino/Ontario. Data source: see Figure 6-3. Half of the core tracts of Sacramento received no new housing construction, and the other half had only modest amounts. Farther out, in the south, east, and north sides, construction was vigorous. Anaheim, Garden Grove, and Santa Ana received new housing in all parts of these cities. It is hard to see any bias toward

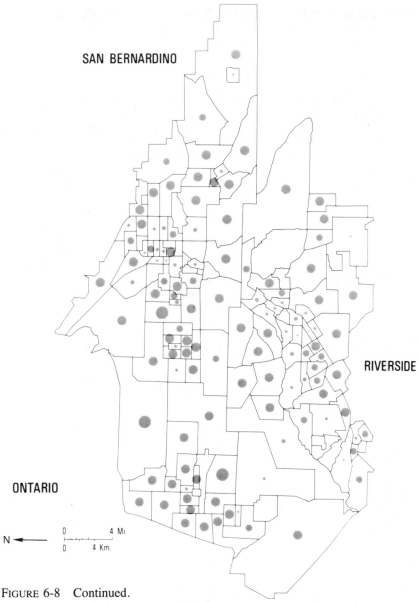

FIGURE 6-8   Continued.

the downtowns and old cores (which are not very old by East Coast standards) or away from them. The Riverside area on the south had new construction at significant levels in all parts of the city. San Bernadino was also vigorously building in all districts of the city. Only two tracts in Ontario had no construction. In all three cities, core tracts generally had new construction but at levels lower than in newer peripheral tracts.

infrastructure at public expense; otherwise, it is easy for situations to develop in which capital losers subsidize capital winners, instability increases, and infrastructure is wasted.

REFERENCES

Abler, R. F., and J. S. Adams. 1976. A Comparative Atlas of America's Great Cities: Twenty Metropolitan Regions. Minneapolis: University of Minnesota Press.

Adams, J. S. 1987. Housing America in the 1980s. New York: Russell Sage Foundation.

Apps, A. F. 1973. An approach to urban modeling and evaluation. 1. A residential model. 2. Implicit prices for housing services. Environment and Planning 5:705–717.

Badcock, B. 1984. Unfairly Structured Cities. Oxford, England: Basil Blackwell.

Bagby, D. G. 1981. The effects of traffic flow on residential property values. Journal of the American Planning Association 46:88–94.

Berry, B. J. L., and J. D. Kasarda. 1977. Contemporary Urban Ecology. New York: Macmillan.

Bielby, W. T. 1980. Evaluating Measures of Neighborhood Quality in the Annual Housing Survey. Washington, D.C.: U.S. Government Printing Office.

Dale-Johnson, D. 1982. An alternative approach to housing market segmentation using hedonic price data. Journal of Urban Economics 11:311–332.

Daniels, C. B. 1975. The influence of racial segregation on housing prices. Journal of Urban Economics 2:105–122.

Follain, J. R., and S. Malpezzi. 1981. Estimates of housing inflation for 39 SMSAs: An alternative to the consumer price index. Annals of Regional Science 14(3):41–56.

Frey, W. H., and F. E. Korbin. 1982. Changing families and changing mobility: Their impact on the central city. Demography 19(3):261–275.

Hoyt, H. 1939. The Structure and Growth of Residential Neighborhoods in American Cities. Washington, D.C.: Federal Housing Administration.

Jackson, J. R. 1979. Intraurban variation in the price of housing. Journal of Urban Economics 6(4):464–479.

Lansing, J. B., C. W. Clifton, and J. N. Morgan. 1969. New Homes and Poor People: A Study of Chains of Moves. Ann Arbor: Institute for Social Research, The University of Michigan.

Laska, S.B., and D. Spain, eds. 1980. Back to the City: Issues in Neighborhood Renovation. New York: Pergamon Press.

Mercer, J., and D. A. Phillips. 1981. Attitudes of homeowners and the decision to rehabilitate property. Urban Geography 2(3):216–236.

Nelson, R. H. 1973. Accessibility and rent: Applying Becker's time–price concept to the theory of residential location. Urban Studies 10(1):83–86.

Palm, R. I. 1981. The Geography of American Cities. New York: Oxford University Press.

Park, R. E., E. W. Burgess, and R. D. McKenzie. 1925. The City. Chicago: University of Chicago Press.

Pinkerson, J. R. 1969. City-suburban residential patterns by social class: A review of the literature. Urban Affairs Quarterly 4(4):499–519.

Pinkerton, J. R. 1973. The changing class composition of cities and suburbs. Land Economics 49(4):462–469.

Roistacher, E. A., and J. S. Senyoung. 1980. Working women and city structure: Implications of the subtle revolution. Signs 5(3):220–225.

Rosenthal, D. O., ed. 1980. Urban Revitalization. Beverly Hills, Calif.: Sage.

Stegman, M. A. 1985. Housing in New York. Piscataway, N.J.: The Center for Urban Policy Research.

U.S. Bureau of the Census. 1983. Statistical Abstract of the United States: 1984. 104th ed. Washington, D.C.: U.S. Government Printing Office.

Vance, J. E., Jr. 1976. The American city: Workshop for a national culture. Pp. 1–49 in Contemporary Metropolitan America, Vol. 1, J. S. Adams, ed. Cambridge, Mass.: Ballinger.

7
Infrastructures for Movement: Past and Future

CESARE MARCHETTI

Not snow, nor rain, nor heat,
nor night keeps them from
accomplishing their appointed
courses with all speed.

Herodotus, Histories

Man is a territorial animal; the book of history could well be considered a string of squabbles (by turns glorious or miserable but mostly bloody) over territorial dominance. The instinct of a territorial animal is to expand its territory as far as possible. Yet curiously, ancient empires never became larger than an area allowing 15-day mail service from the capital. Beyond that distance, acquisitions tended to become unstable and to split away, indicating perhaps a lunar cycle in man's submission and trust. If the greed of the king required more territory, he had to develop an appropriate infrastructure to speed the messenger service. The Persian empire is a textbook example of such development; and what Herodotus said about the King of Persia's messengers, U.S. postal workers have adopted as a credo.

When Marco Polo explored China, he witnessed many marvels, but apparently nothing struck him more than the efficient Chinese mail and messenger system and the infrastructure that supported it. Ancient civilizations did not transport much in terms of mass, even by sea, but the transportation of men and information always received the best available technology and some extraordinary engineering efforts.

This emphasis on transporting people and information is not a cultural imprint of Euroasiatic origin; the Amerindian civilizations found the same solution to the same problem. In the technological context of a neolithic culture, the Incan roads and bridges appear to be just as extraordinary an engineering and organizational feat. Their most important function was to speed messages carried by runners, who traveled up to 300 km a day

146

using a sophisticated relay system. The stimulus to set the high-speed system in motion may usually have been royal letters, but important missions were undertaken by high-ranking officials or *missi dominici,* indicating a *limited substitutability between the transportation of pure information and that of people*. Such behaviors and relationships, so deeply ingrained in the animal nature of man (the "beast"), are here forever, naturally, and can provide a solid basis for a model of the long-term development of transportation systems.

The work of Zahavi (1981) embodies mathematically the drives of the territorial animal. We could say that every man is a territorial animal and that, as such, he will try to maximize the extent of the territory he uses. Zahavi found that the constraints to this activity are time (a little more than one hour per day is dedicated to extramural movement) and energy, indexed here by money (15 percent of disposable income is dedicated to transportation expenses). Within these constraints, time and money are allocated to different means of locomotion to maximize range.

This conceptual scheme permits us to draw a general, long-term conclusion: what the system wants is low-cost speed (low cost is obviously contextual). Nowadays, most of humanity walks, giving a personal territory not far different from that of a village (about 10 square kilometers [km^2]). In Western countries, most moving people own a car, the mean speed of which is an order of magnitude greater than walking—about 50 km per hour (h). The resulting territory is then 100 times larger (1,000 km^2). Interestingly, this mean speed has remained unchanged during the last 50 years, suggesting the existence of a homeostatic mechanism.

The mean speed of air transport is about an order of magnitude larger than that of a car—about 500 km/h. Thus, the jet set has a territory that is 100 times larger than that of the car set. The final objective is obviously to have the world as one's territory, and with the world's growing population, more and more sites are becoming valuable visiting points.

To belong to a city, one must have easy access to its services. Ancient cities, be they Rome or Peking, did not become larger than a radius that could be transited by walking or riding on public transportation for one hour, and some spot checks indicate that the same is true today. This means that extremely large cities, which are now coalescing here and there, need first of all a fast transportation network. The figures in this chapter give some quantitative glimpses of the spread of transportation systems at the world level and some quantitative hints about the future.

In his delightful collection of offbeat statistics, Zipf (1972) reported on the hierarchical structure of city sizes. Cities can be considered informational machines; as such, they are served well by a hierarchical information system. But if people can move across a set of cities within the one-hour time limit using air shuttles, some high-level functions can then be split between the cities and synthesized through personal movement, just as if such people were living in different quarters of the same city. In other words, corridors such as the Bosnywash corridor in the eastern United States and the Shinkansen corridor in Japan actually operate as single cities—at least at the level of hierarchical information processing—but it is information bound to flesh, like that of the *missi dominici.*

Over the past two decades the magnetic levitation (or Maglev) train for the next Shinkansen line has made mixed progress. Indeed, the only thing that has remained constant during these years is the required one-hour transit time between its terminals, Tokyo and Osaka. The obvious implication is that the 70 million people who have gravitated to that strip of land have the aspiration and potential to become part of a single city. In the hierarchical information scheme, size is a prerequisite for power. In other words, the Shinkansen corridor, with its 70 million people, may become the hierarchical capital of the world, a position London held for more than a century.

A transportation analyst looking forward in time at the development of networks sees intense interaction among settlements on a grand scale. But how grand? As is shown later in this chapter, the context of air transportation calls for an airplane capable of operating at speeds as great as Mach 8, a development that will reduce the transit time between any two locations with suitable landing facilities to about one hour. The "grand scale" will then be the world. The world is imploding into larger and larger settlements, which makes such a global intercity air transport system logical.

Over the long term (which is probably not all that long, considering the time necessary to realize such huge and complex networks and the exponential speed at which people implode into cities), transportation must be conceived of in terms of cities. But what will such cities look like? Doxiadis and Papaioannou (1974) in their seminal book on Ecumenopolis, give some guidelines on the shape cities (i.e., the "super" city) will take; basically a chicken-wire system of large mesh with blobs and smears here and there.

In such a system, vacuum-tunnel Maglev trains would be perfect for the job of transporting people, accelerating at 8 Gs for half the trip and decelerating the other half. From my earlier analysis (1983), the Maglev system should begin operations about the year 2000. Thus, the Shinkansen experiment will give us a solid context for our thinking about the future.

METHODOLOGY

Most of the analysis undertaken here uses a version of Darwinian ideas incorporated into Lotka's (1956) equations of competition between species in ecological niches. At the first level the analogy is formal, but the fit is excellent. At the second level, biological systems and social systems are information systems. The analogy may be substantial at this level.

A second aspect of the methodology is that it is just phenomenological. Thus, only facts are examined, and they are organized using the model. Explanations are not usually given, but the reader is always free to apply his or her own to the facts described.

The methodology looks for invariants in sets of measurements. These invariants can be constants—for example, the human mortality for automobile accidents or the energy input–output ratio in energetically close agricultures—or they can be functional relationships, that is, quantitative rules or "laws." In this second area the models derived from a Darwinian concept of the working system proved to be of widest application. In these models the time dynamics is reduced to a competition between subsystems. Much has been written about these models, which have been applied extensively in genetics and ecology. A schematic treatment is reported in the appendix to this chapter.

The examples of competition between subsystems can be reduced to three cases (or models).

Case 1: The Malthusian Population

This population represents a single species growing in a niche of limited resources. This is the case of self-competition—that is, competition among individuals for resources. The classic biological example is a colony of bacteria growing in a bottle of broth. When a population cannot be enumerated, as in the case of bacteria, the growth phenomena follow the same rule—for example, the growth of a sunflower is measured by its height and the growth of a road network is measured by its length.

This case is modeled using logistic equations. Because of the many constraints that must be satisfied, it is easy to use this case improperly. For this reason many failures (in the area of human population growth, see Pearl, 1924, for example) occur when it is applied.

The Malthusian population case is mapped using three-parameter logistics. The parameters are not normally known externally; they are determined by the best fit method. Socioeconomic examples are the growth of the registered car population in Italy after World War II (Figure 7-1) and the growth of the telegraph system in the United States (Figure 7-2).

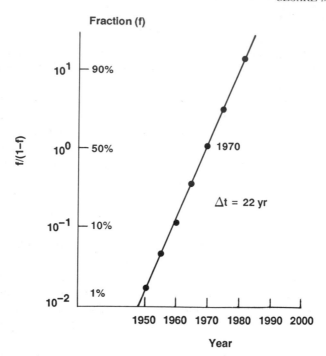

FIGURE 7-1   Car registrations following World War II in Italy. Saturation point = 20 million cars.

In Figure 7-1 the logistic equation for car registration is linearized, using the Fisher and Pry (1970) transform, $\log f/(1 - f)$. This presentation facilitates graphic handling of these data and the comparison of sets of curves in the same graph. The saturation point, not visible in the graph, is given numerically, as is the time constant (Δt), which is the time required to go from 10 to 90 percent of the saturation level.

Case 2: One-to-One Competition

In this case a new species is introduced into a niche previously occupied by another species. Haldane (1924) applied this case to biology when studying the penetration of a mutant, and Fisher and Pry (1970) applied it in a number of examples of market substitution. The treatment of case 2 is much easier than that of case 1, especially if one is interested in the ratios of population numbers or market fractions of the competitors.

Case 2 is treated with two-parameter logistics. Because one species filled the niche at time zero, the sum of the individuals gives the size of the niche. An example of this case is the substitution of cars for horses

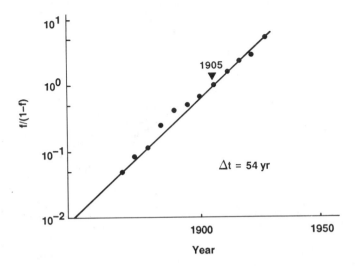

FIGURE 7-2 Miles of wire in the Western Union telegraph system in the United States. Saturation point = 2.3 million mi.

for personal transportation in the United States. The sum of horses and cars is the actual level of personal transportation. This is an example of simple substitution. Over about 20 years most of the personal transportation in the United States shifted from horse to car (see chapter 8). The substitution is not easily explained, however, because cost and speed were roughly the same.

Case 3: Multiple Competition

This case is a generalization of case 2 in which new species are introduced sequentially into the same niche; a few thus are present at any given time in a phase-in or phase-out configuration.

Case 3, which was originally developed by Marchetti and Nakicenovic (1979), is treated with a mixture of interacting logistics and transition functions. Multiple competition is in fact the rule in the real world, and the preceding cases can be considered simplifications of this general case when perturbations from other species are considered small. By determining niche shares or market shares of competitors, one can construct the life cycle of each competitor, introducing only two parameters in the equations. The parameters may change over time, but they change interactively so that no external information is needed. An example of this case is the competition among primary energies for world markets (Figure

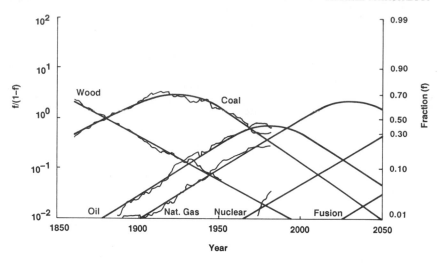

FIGURE 7-3   Primary energy substitution worldwide.

7-3). In Figure 7-3, the coordinates are those of a Fisher-Pry transform. The great stability of the dynamics of the substitution for such a long time results from the fact that price elasticity and shadow prices always have the correct values. Nakicenovic (1987) shows the same analysis for the competition of transport infrastructures in the United States.

This methodology was originally used for diagnostics—that is, to have a compact, consistent description of what happened. With the accumulation of analyzed cases, however, it became clear that actual systems are extremely stable in time although subject to variable levels of noise. That is, the subjacent equations are followed for decades and centuries, which led to the use of the diagnostics in a forecasting mode. Many precautions were taken to ensure that booby traps common to such predictions were avoided. It was then concluded that forecasting within a period corresponding to about 50 percent of the time constant of any particular subsystem is safe.

AIR TRANSPORT

This section briefly surveys the dynamics of air transport worldwide to show these models at work. The kind of object studied is immaterial, provided that the appropriate indicators of its definition are identified.

Efficient indicators for air transport can be either ton-kilometers per year (ton-km/year) or passenger kilometers per year (pass-km/year), if this subset activity is analyzed. For individual airplanes the preferred indicator is ton-kilometers per hour, the "flux" of payload.

As shown in Figure 7-4, air transport since World War II can be mapped with the utmost precision. The saturation point of 200 billion ton-km/year was calculated by best fitting. It is remarkable that the increases in the price of jet fuel in 1974 and 1979 had no effect on the performance of the system. Such homeostatic behavior is characteristic of these large systems. When an external condition changes, the system rearranges itself internally to hold its trajectory.

The air transport system is a huge "clockwork" system made up of smaller and smaller interlocking wheels. If a general Darwinian view holds for the similarity in behavior of subsystems at different hierarchical levels, the smaller wheels will also fit in the same mathematical pattern. For example, Lufthansa Airlines, which accounts for only a few percent of world air traffic, fits perfectly (Figures 7-5, 7-6, and 7-7). Figure 7-6 (ton-kilometers per year) is similar to Figure 7-5 (passenger-kilometers per year) except that it includes cargo. Passengers are by definition calculated at 80 kilograms each. In both figures, Lufthansa appears to be on a saturation course, a situation rarely perceived as such inside companies

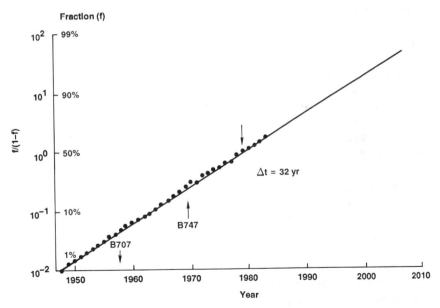

FIGURE 7-4   Air traffic (billion ton-kilometers per year) in the Western world. Saturation point = 200 billion ton-km/yr.

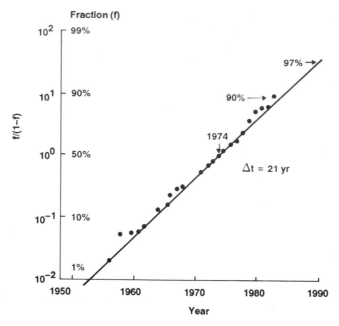

FIGURE 7-5   Lufthansa Airlines: billions of passenger-kilometers per year. Saturation point = 25 billion pass-km/yr.

themselves. Often a decline in growth rate is interpreted as overcautiousness in management and investment, and ends in excessive capitalization and debts. Figure 7-7 shows equipment, following the rules of the game, for both quantity and quality. When the management of a company does not perceive the externality of the rules, overinvestment will result—that is, the company will exceed in a nontransitory way its intrinsic saturation level of about 100 airplanes. Incidentally (transitory) mistakes appeared when the first batch of B-747s was purchased.

It is practical to measure the tools for operating an air transport system—that is, airplanes—in terms of their function. Airplanes can be classified according to their flux (how many ton-kilometers per hour they can transport). Thus, an airplane is again a very small wheel in the air transport system, quantified homogeneously. Figure 7-8 plots successful long-range passenger aircraft introduced during the last 40 years, using the dates of their first commercial appearance. This figure condenses the description of some of the deep mechanisms that connect airplane performance and air traffic. The thin dashed line represents world air traffic, expressed in passenger-kilometers per hour; the upper line represents the evolution of first-level airplane capacity, also expressed in passenger-kilometers per hour. The two lines are parallel, indicating that when first-level airplanes were introduced, their flux was a constant fraction of the traffic's flux. Because machines grow horizontally with traffic, forecasting traffic permits forecasting the performance of successful airplanes, usually a soul-wearing decision for airframe makers. In this context an essential feature for the success of the Concorde was lacking: it was too small by a factor of almost three.

About 4,000 airplanes have been in service with commercial air companies (basically, the members of the International Air Transport Association) over the last 30 years, despite an approximately 50-fold increase in traffic. Presumably, 4,000 airplanes is the minimum number needed to satisfy the time and space configuration of travel demand. (The number of oil tankers in service is about the same.)

According to the forecasting power of the equations, air traffic will

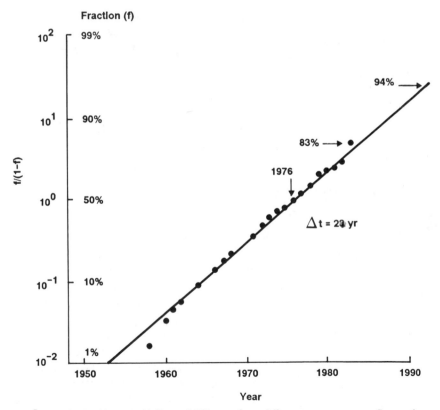

FIGURE 7-6   Lufthansa Airlines: billions of ton-kilometers per year. Saturation point = 5 billion ton-km/yr.

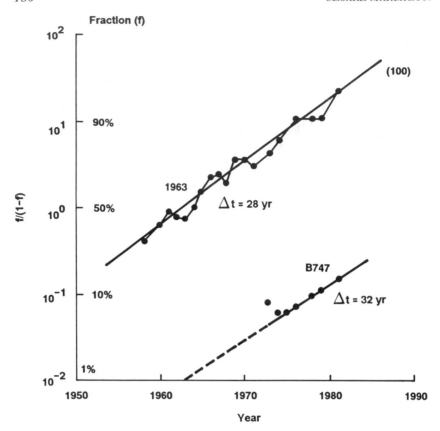

FIGURE 7-7   Lufthansa Airlines, planes in service. Saturation point = 100 planes.

increase by about 25–30 percent during the next 15 years. Thus, using the rules observed here, a stretched B-747 (Jumbo 1000) may well satisfy this demand. Airports need only plan then for an increase in throughput and pulse intensity. Engine designers should not be too preoccupied either, because lighter materials, better aerodynamics, and increased engine efficiency (requiring less fuel on board) will take care of the extra payload without the need for major engineering breakthroughs.

The situation appears more lively, however, if we zoom ahead in time. The general idea is that more income will lead to using a larger share of the traveling hour for faster (and more expensive) transport modes. An analysis of the intercity passenger-kilometers of different systems in the United States (see Figure 8-15 in Nakicenovic, this volume), reveals airways' increasing market share in intercity travel, with a possible increase of a factor of 10 during the next Kondratief (1926) long cycle of economic growth (1995–2050). The competition among different kinds of transport for intercity passengers is in the usual Darwinian form. Trains and buses appear to be noncompetitive despite the intense rumors about their revival. The "game" is now between winning airplanes and losing cars over a fairly short time ($\Delta t \approx 65$ years) with a crossover around 2005. The increase will put a strain on the size of airplanes, which may stimulate the installation of Maglev trains in the most intense corridors.

During the present Kondratief cycle, air travel at the world level has increased by a factor of more than 50. Except for the United States, however, most of the world is still in the primitive stage of air travel, and it can therefore be assumed that air travel will increase by more than an order of magnitude during the next cycle. What impact will this increase in demand have on airplane technology? Using the minimum of 4,000 planes, a ceiling the airlines seem to want, we would have to increase their flux by a factor of 10; that is, they must be 10 times faster, or have 10 times more capacity, or some combination of the two.

These airplanes will, in any event, need larger power plants. As Figure 7-9 shows, the situation is challenging. Piston engine power saturated in

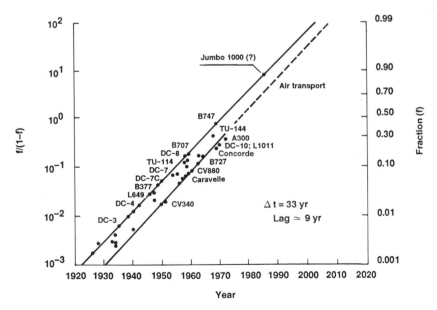

FIGURE 7-8 Passenger aircraft performance (thousands of passenger-kilometers per hour). Saturation point = 1.2 million pass-km/hr.

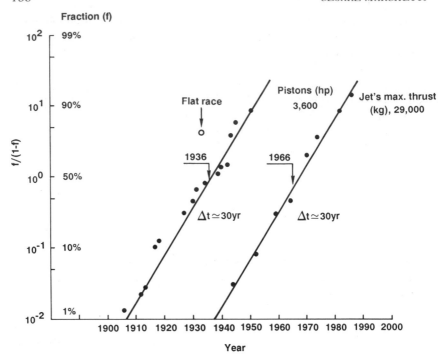

FIGURE 7-9   Aircraft engine performance.

the 1950s at a unit power of about 2.5 megawatts (MW). Jet engines are saturating now at a unit power of about 25 MW. The problem in both cases is how to bring enough air to the engine. Air is the working medium, and power is bound thermodynamically to its flux. Efficiencies are already in the 50 percent range. The cross section is limited by the fact that it grows with the square of linear dimensions, whereas engine mass and problems tend to grow with the cube. Increasingly clever designs have overcome this handicap, but, as the analysis shows, engineers seem to be out of breath. Apparently, the only way forward is to run the airplanes faster. The engines will have more power, and the payload flux will increase proportionally with speed. The jet set can then hope for another quantum leap in speed (by another factor of 10), and the world will finally shrink to the magic one-hour range.

Development of a Mach 8 Jumbo 1000 airplane will probably upset the basic structure and location of intercontinental airports. Will the traffic of Paris, Frankfurt, or Munich be absorbed by Amsterdam or London, which are so much closer to the open ocean? Or will a downward-silent hypersonic airplane be developed? Curiously, as quantified by Doxiadis and Papaioannou (1974), the world's population is already slowly migrating toward continental borders.

For continental travel a factor of 10 means that the workhorse DC-9 must shift to the 1,000-seat range. Some continental stretches are already being served by the derated short-range B-747. In this situation the Maglev train could be used as a second-level metro. In the next Kondratief cycle the airplane may be reserved for intercontinental (and possibly interplanetary?) flight, and the lower level may consist of only the Maglev metro.

1995 AND BEYOND

This section discusses what may unfold worldwide after 1995 when many elements of national infrastructures saturate—for example, roads (Figure 7-10), natural gas pipelines (Figure 7-11), and nuclear power plants (Figure 7-12). By shedding light on infrastructure at the global level, this section will provide a frame of reference for the work of Nakicenovic (see chapter 8), who describes the circumstances in the United States. In this vein a powerful process that feeds the dynamics of Western societies, the process of invention and innovation, is analyzed.

Invention, according to Mensch (1975), can be said to occur when the

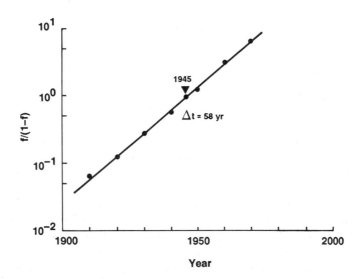

FIGURE 7-10   Miles of surfaced roads in the United States. Saturation point = 3.4 million mi.

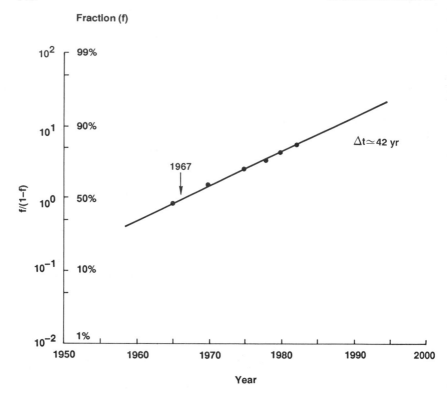

FIGURE 7-11   Natural gas trunklines (in thousands of kilometers) worldwide. Saturation point = 1 million km.

prototype works in the lab or the workshop; innovation comes when the first product (or service) is sold commercially. These definitions permit a clear and homogeneous classification of the key points in the process of moving from idea to utility. In analyzing the number of basic innovations in 10-year periods, Mensch found that this number changes about every 55 years. He describes this phenomenon as innovation waves, and he found similar behavior for invention waves.

The heuristic hypothesis that successful innovations per se are products at a different hierarchical level was used to analyze the innovation waves in the same way. To this end, the Malthusian populations of innovations (each of which is characterized only by its date of commercial introduction) were measured in relation to their "markets" (Figure 7-13). The fit also appears excellent for the inventions that preceded the successful innovations. In the figure, inventions are cumulatively mapped by the lines with

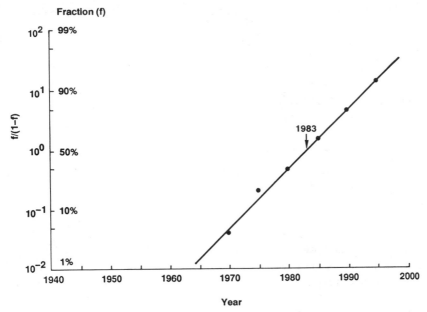

FIGURE 7-12   Installed nuclear power plants (in gigawatts) in the Western world.
Saturation point = 350 GW.

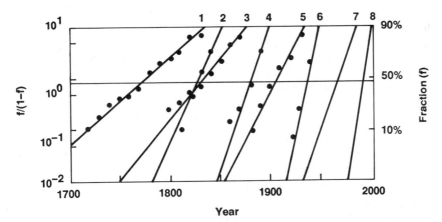

FIGURE 7-13   The "secular set" of invention and innovation waves.

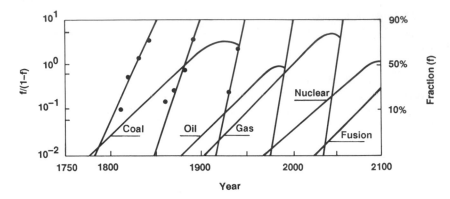

FIGURE 7-14   Innovation waves and the start of new energy sources.

odd numbers and innovations by the lines with even numbers. The distance between the center points (50 percent) of lines 2, 4, and 6 is about 55 years, a Kondratief cycle. Steepening lines indicate that the waves are more focused if the innovations are viewed as parallel processes. If they are viewed as a single process, however, one could speak of a quickening tempo. The great internal regularities of the first three pairs of waves permit calculation of the fourth. Just after the turn of the century the forecast can be verified.

Many things can be deduced from this analysis—for example, that inventors and innovators are controlled by "the system." The important point for this line of reasoning, however, is that the distance between the center points of innovation waves is a stable 55 years. In fact, the system pulsates with this rhythm in all its subsets. For example, every innovation wave of new primary energies, so important for the development of new transportation systems, is led by a new primary energy source (Figure 7-14). Today's wave has been led by nuclear energy. Hypersonic airplanes will almost certainly need liquid hydrogen for fuel, and nuclear reactors may well provide that. Once the link is established, a nuclear-hydrogen energy system may develop to revolutionize the sizing and siting of nuclear plants. It is interesting that the *actual* start for nuclear energy is correctly positioned in time with respect to the *calculated* innovation wave (wave 8 in Figure 7-13). Similar reasoning indicates that a new primary source, fusion, will be introduced in 2025.

Figure 7-15 shows the introduction of underground transportation in various cities worldwide. Every city counts for one system, and the associated date is that of the inauguration of the first underground line.

If the same exercise is carried out for railway networks worldwide, a single bunching with a time constant of about 55 years is obtained. Figure 7-16 organizes the opening dates of the first lines of future railway networks at the world level. It seems to prove the hypothesis that the development of railways worldwide must be seen as a single process. It also indicates that such subsystems as countries and regions operate interactively, the link being informational and partly commercial. Curiously, all networks now existing were started during the period indicated on the figure.

Cars were born on paved roads. In the United States, for example, paved roads were introduced before cars, and contrary to current opinion the pace of road growth was already set when the car finally appeared. Thus, the appearance of the car was not felt at all, as equations and statistics for the paved road show (see chapter 8).

Motorways, however, were created for cars. Curiously, once they had been started, motorways grew on their own, without any apparent relation to the number of cars in the country. Figure 7-17 shows the development of motorways in selected countries in Europe and for nine countries of the European Economic Community taken together. The construction of motorways in Europe follows a regular pattern, collectively and in individual countries, showing consistent time constants and saturation times. It appears that motorways are saturating in terms of total length over all of Europe. Thus, the construction of motorways does not seem to be a

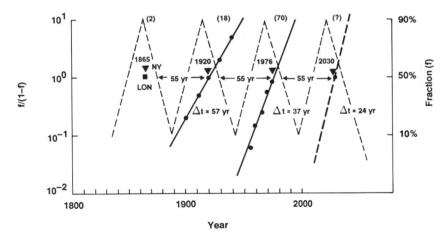

FIGURE 7-15   Underground transportation worldwide, plotted by dates when system construction began. Subway construction appears to have occurred in three pulses, beginning with systems in London and New York.

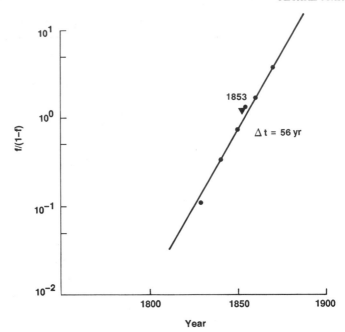

<small>$\Delta t = 56$ yr</small>

FIGURE 7-16   Railway systems for 40 countries worldwide, plotted by dates when system construction began.

good target for Keynesian tactics (i.e., more public works) to counter the effects of the current recession.

MOVING ENERGY

Energy products are the largest single item moved around on the earth's surface, and they occupy a dominant position in the world's bulk trade and internal transport. This section describes a product life cycle for each of the primary energy sources—coal, crude oil, natural gas, and nuclear power—that have a commercial (long-distance) impact. The section is intended to show where we are going in terms of energy, to indicate the potential quantities involved, and to suggest some appropriate technologies.

This analysis is based on the Darwinian competition for market shares among the primary energy sources: wood, coal, crude oil, natural gas, and "X," or a source yet to come (called fusion here). This competition has been stable over the past 150 years, with three energy crises and their related price increases, wars, and depressions having little effect on the mechanism.

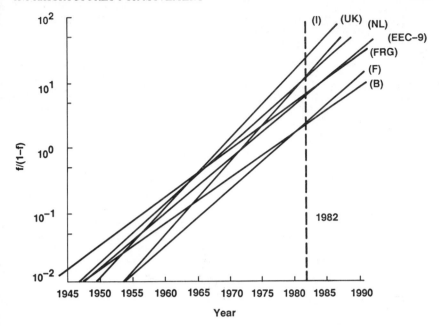

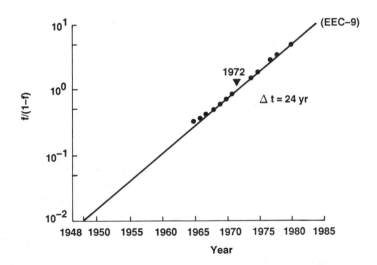

FIGURE 7-17   Construction of motorways in Europe. B: Belgium; EEC-9: European Economic Community; F: France; FRG: Federal Republic of Germany; I: Italy; NL: the Netherlands; and UK: United Kingdom.

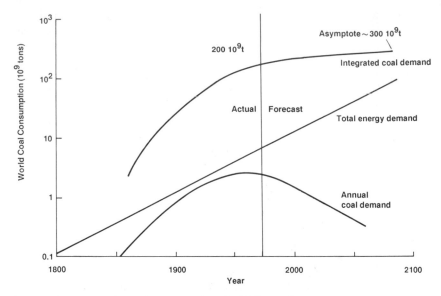

FIGURE 7-18   World coal consumption (in billions of tons).

Because absolute quantities are needed and the life cycle is measured in terms of market shares, it was necessary to assume that a mean world energy consumption growth of 2.3 percent (which has been the case during the last 200 years) is acceptable for the next 150 years. If the world population then doubles every 70 years (it now doubles every 30 years), world per capita energy consumption in 2150 will equal the present level in the United States.

Coal

Coal reached its maximum market share penetration in the 1920s, and it has been losing ground ever since. Because of the expanding total energy market, however, the absolute quantity of coal consumption continued to grow; it has now reached its maximum level (this has occurred during the last few years). Consequently, the global infrastructure for coal will shrink although its geographical distribution will inevitably change.

Despite this phase-out, the amounts that will be used cumulatively are still impressive: about 100 billion tons against the 200 billion tons already extracted (Figure 7-18). Approximately 3 billion tons of coal are processed each year. The straight line in Figure 7-18 represents total energy demand worldwide as interpolated and extrapolated from historical data, adopting the historical mean rate of growth of 2.3 percent per year. The actual coal demand curve approaches total energy demand in the 1920s when the main source of primary energy was coal, as shown by the market penetration curve (coal then covered about 80 percent of the market). This total energy demand does not contain the Kondratief oscillation; thus, it may be locally incorrect. The upper curve gives the cumulative amount of coal consumed.

Most of this coal is now used in making electricity and, at a much lower level, steel. In developed countries, nuclear energy appears to be the inevitable competitor for the base load production of electricity, and steel comes increasingly from recycling through the use of electric steel processes. Thus, the geographical distribution of coal use will presumably move toward developing countries, which are also more willing to accept the pollution burden. A special case is China, which is now almost completely dependent on coal and is ready to use 10 times as much.

Use of the same analytical methods to look at the development of the electrical system and at the share of coal-generated electricity (to see if absolute quantities match) would probably reveal that there will be too much coal. This situation opens the way to molten-iron coal burning, a process in which electricity and synthetic gas are produced at the same time.

Molten-iron coal burning is a process in which coal is dissolved in iron to remove impurities, including sulfur, before injecting oxygen in the iron bath to burn the carbon. The resulting product, 1400°C gas, is then used to produce electricity and subsequently to synthesize methanol (methanol is formed from carbon monoxide and hydrogen). Because the coal is burned at the mine, long-distance exportation of electricity and methanol would occur, thereby avoiding local pollution as well as train traffic pollution. This process, which is being studied at the Nuclear Research Center in Jülich, Federal Republic of Germany (Häfele et al., 1986), has been christened ''zero emissions.'' It is a configuration and process that may well lie within the constraints and skills of developed countries.

Oil

Oil, the so-called lifeline of Western countries, has been selling at about the same level for the past few years. According to the product life-cycle analysis (see Figure 7-3), the use of oil has just peaked in terms of market shares, and it is now peaking in terms of absolute quantities. Because the share is falling sharply, the expansion of energy markets will compensate for the fall for only another 20 years (Figure 7-19). Apparently, however, there will be no growth after the market share peaks, as there has been

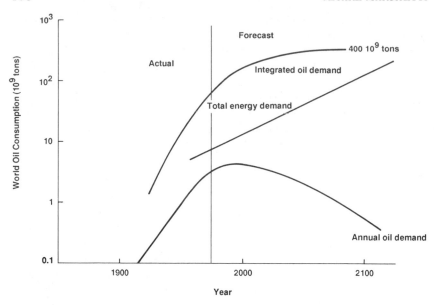

FIGURE 7-19   World oil consumption (in billions of tons).

for coal. The infrastructure for oil therefore has no reason to grow globally, although its geographic distribution may change considerably during the next 100 years, before the market share finally falls to 1 percent. Because the size of oil tankers is closely linked to the amount of oil traded overseas and because more accurate exploration reveals oil deposits closer to the final consumers, a continuous decrease in the tonnage of tankers can be expected, a trend that is already occurring. Thus, neither port facilities for megatankers nor megaterminals will be necessary.

Because the demand for coal and nuclear energy will cut into the demand for heavy oils and because progress in oil refining has made upgrading relatively easy, all of the oil on the market will probably be used to produce transportation fuels. (Natural gas may provide substantial help in refining operations by improving the hydrogen content of the feed, but this should not influence the infrastructure for gas.) Although oil appears to coast and slow down on what it achieved, the amount of oil still to be extracted is impressive, about 300 billion tons against the 100 billion already extracted. (Estimates about resources are always dated, but this 300-billion-ton estimate appears reasonable for the time span considered here.)

As it is for coal, the demand for oil can be dynamic in the spatial sense, but it is basically business as usual. Almost 4 billion tons of oil are processed per year, a mass roughly equivalent to that of coal. Its market share did not go as high as that of coal, however, because its introduction into the market was a bit "late" in historical terms.

Natural Gas

If coal and oil sound much like the railways— more of the same, but running down—the most interesting prospect seems to be natural gas, at least within our life span.

The product life cycle of gas displays nothing unusual (Figure 7-20). Because its next competitor (nuclear energy) was introduced a good 70 years later, however, natural gas has had time to gain a large market share, which will reach a maximum—like coal, 70 percent—around the year 2040. Above all, natural gas is facing a larger and larger energy market. Quantities of natural gas will then increase by an order of magnitude over present quantities.

This expansion will be realized by the development of networks in such countries as Brazil and India. The largest pipelines will also increase their capacities proportionally. This means that gas pipelines must be developed to carry 10 times as much gas as the present 58-inch (in.) pipe, the largest in use. Because the amount of gas transported grows almost in proportion to the cubic power of the diameter of a pipeline (if subsonic), a doubling of pipeline size to 120 in. can be expected. And because economic distance

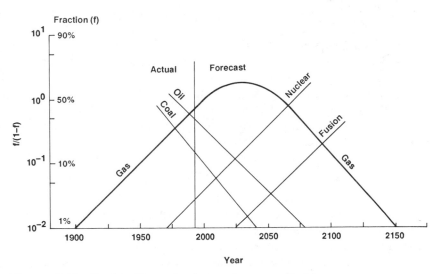

FIGURE 7-20   Product life cycle of natural gas, worldwide.

grows linearly with the diameter of a pipeline, these trunk lines can be expected to carry gas 5,000–6,000 km from the source. Obviously, the implications of such developments will be political as well as infrastructural.

No attempt is made here to unveil what will happen in the liquefied natural gas (LNG) area after 1995. It is possible that new cooling methods will make LNG more appealing and that large LNG tankers will develop in response to volume trading. This kind of analysis is probably possible using Darwinian methodology.

As for past and future extraction, natural gas production is just in its initial stage. The cumulative amount extracted to date is only a negligible share (about 2 percent) of the cumulative total: about one trillion cubic meters or, in equivalent energy, about six times that of oil.

Nuclear Energy

As shown in Figure 7-20, nuclear energy is projected to succeed natural gas as the world's primary energy source in the latter half of the twenty-first century. The real breakthrough in the use of nuclear energy will come when electricity grids are saturated sometime during the next 10 years in France and during the next 30 years in most of the Western world (see Figure 7-12). At that point, nuclear energy must incorporate an energy vector that is flexible, transportable, and storable—presumably, hydrogen. Because hydrogen travels well (much like natural gas), the primary energy generators (nuclear plants) can be located far from consumer areas, ending the uneasy cohabitation of today. In addition, they can be extremely large (100 times the size of current plants), making the system again reasonable.

A new continental pipeline network suitable for hydrogen may then be installed during the next Kondratief cycle (1995–2050), instituting the first round of a stable energy infrastructure. Each continent will have a few generation points, presumably located on its shores, that are capable of producing hydrogen in the terawatt range. Like those for the Maglev trains, the signs of such a development should appear in the next 10–20 years.

CONCLUSION

This *tour d'horizon* set out to elucidate problems in the deployment of transportation infrastructures and to identify techniques that might generate consistent descriptions and forecasts. At the level described here, changes generally occur slowly, even when technological progress appears hectic, because social absorption is slow. Thus, choices must be long-sighted and well timed, and this is not easy.

Great breakthroughs are usually controlled by context. Context and its links with innovation can be deepened beyond the cursory analysis presented here, perhaps just through sheer research effort. The most encouraging discovery made in undertaking the analysis was the extreme dynamic stability of the transportation system and subsystems at all hierarchical levels.

REFERENCES

Debecker, A., and T. Modis (Digital Equipment Corp., Geneva, Switzerland). 1986. Determination of the uncertainties in S-curve logistic fits. Paper submitted to the Sixth International Symposium on Forecasting, Paris, June 15–18, 1986.

Doxiadis, C. A., and J. C. Papaioannou. 1974. Ecumenopolis: The Inevitable City of the Future. Athens: Athens Center of Ekistics.

Fisher, J. C., and R. H. Pry. 1970. A Simple Substitution Model of Technological Change. 70-C-215. Schenectady, N.Y.: General Electric Company; see also Technological Forecasting and Social Change 3:75–88, 1971.

Häfele, W., H. Barnet, S. Messner, M. Strubegger, and J. Anderer. 1986. Novel integrated energy systems: The case of zero emissions. In Sustainable Development of the Biosphere, W. C. Clark and R. E. Munn, eds. Cambridge, England: Cambridge University Press.

Haldane, J. B. S. 1924. The mathematical theory of natural and artificial selection. Transactions, Cambridge Philosophical Society 23:19–41.

Kondratief, N. D. 1926. Die langen Wellen der Konjunktur. Archiv für Sozialwissenschaft und Sozialpolitik 56:573–609.

Lotka, A. J. 1956. Elements of Mathematical Biology. New York: Dover.

Marchetti, C., and N. Nakicenovic. 1979. The Dynamics of Energy Systems and the Logistic Substitution Model. RR-79-13. Laxenburg, Austria: International Institute for Applied Systems Analysis.

Marchetti, C. 1983. On a Fifty Years Pulsation in Human Affairs: Analysis of Some Physical Indicators. PP-83-5. Laxenburg, Austria: International Institute for Applied Systems Analysis.

Mensch, G. 1975. Das technologische Patt. Frankfurt, FRG: Umschau Verlag. English translation: Mensch, G. 1979. Stalemate in Technology. Cambridge, Mass.: Ballinger.

Montroll, E. W., and N. S. Goel. 1971. On the Volterra and other nonlinear models of interacting populations. Reviews of Modern Physics 43(2):231.

Nakicenovic, N. 1979. Software Package for the Logistic Substitution Model. RR-79-12. Laxenburg, Austria: International Institute for Applied Systems Analysis.

Nakicenovic, N. 1984. Growth to Limits, Long Waves and the Dynamics of Technology. Ph.D. dissertation. University of Vienna.

Nakicenovic, N. 1987. Transportation and Energy Systems in the US. WP-87-01. Laxenburg, Austria: International Institute for Applied Systems Analysis.

Nukem. 1984. Nukem Market Report on the Nuclear Fuel Cycle. p. 18. NUKEM GesmbH, Hanau, Federal Republic of Germany.

Pearl, R. 1924. Studies in Human Biology. Baltimore, Md.: Williams & Wilkins.

Peschel, M., and W. Mende. 1983. Leben wir in einer Volterra Welt? Berlin: Akademie Verlag.

Verhulst, P. F. 1845. Nouveaux Mémoires de l'Académie Royale des Sciences, des Lettres et des Beaux-Arts de Belgique 18:1–38.

Zahavi, Y. 1981. The UMOT-Urban Interactions. DOT-RSPA-DPB 10/7. Washington,
D.C.: U.S. Department of Transportation.
Zipf, G. K. 1972. Human Behavior and the Principle of Least Effort: An Introduction to
Human Ecology. New York: Hafner. (Facsimile of 1949 edition.)

APPENDIX

The Darwinian behavior of population is described in general in simplified form by the famous Volterra-Lotka equations:

$$\frac{dN_i}{dt} = \alpha_i N_i - \beta \sum_{j=1}^{n} \lambda_{ij} N_i N_j,$$

where N_i is the number of individuals of species i. (The properties of the solutions to these equations have been described by Montroll and Goel, 1971, and in the recent treatise by Peschel and Mende, 1983.) The quantities α, β, and λ are parameters for which a physical interpretation is possible; α_i is the rate of growth of population i in the absence of predation, and λ_i is the cross section of interaction between population i and population j.

Special Cases: The Malthusian Case

A physically intuitive example of this case is a population of bacteria growing in a bottle of broth (Verhulst, 1845). The bacteria act as machinery to transform chemicals present in the broth into bacteria. The rate of this transformation (other things, e.g., temperature, being equal) is proportional to the number of bacteria (the transforming machinery) and the concentration of the transformable chemicals.

All transformable chemicals will ultimately be transformed into bacterial bodies. Thus, to use homogeneous units, one can measure broth chemicals in terms of bacterial bodies. $N(t)$ is therefore the number of bacteria at time t, and $\overline{N}$ is the amount of transformable chemicals at time 0, before multiplication starts. The Verhulst equation can then be written as:

$$\frac{dN}{dt} = aN (\overline{N} - N), \tag{1}$$

whose solution is

$$N(t) = \frac{\overline{N}}{1 + e^{-(at + b)}}, \tag{2}$$

where b is an integration constant, sometimes written as t_0; a is a constant that is independent of the size of the population. Thus, there is no proximity feedback. If we divide both sides of equation 2 by $\overline{N}$, extract the exponential term, and then take the logarithm of both sides, we obtain

$$\log \frac{f}{1 - f} = at + b,$$

where

$$f = \frac{N}{\overline{N}},$$

$\overline{N}$ is often called the niche, and the growth of a population is given as the fraction of the niche it fills. Obviously, this analysis has been done with the assumption there are no competitors. A single species grows to match resources $(\overline{N})$ in a Malthusian fashion.

One-to-One Competition Case

This case was originally treated by Haldane (1924) and reported by Lotka (1956). It deals with the simple case of genetic competition from a mutant; that is, a new variety (1) has a reproductive advantage, k, over the old variety (2). This means that at every generation the ratio of the number of individuals in the two varieties will be changed by $1/(1 - k)$. If n is the number of generations starting from $n = 0$, then

$$\frac{N_1}{N_2} = \frac{R_0}{(1 - k)^n}, \tag{3}$$

where

$$R_0 = \frac{N_1}{N_2}$$

at $t = 0$.

If k is small, as it usually is in biology (typically 10^{-3}), then

$$\frac{N_1}{N_2} = \frac{R_0}{e^{-kn}}. \tag{4}$$

We are now back to equation 2, except for the very favorable fact that we have an initial condition (R_0) instead of a final condition $(\overline{N})$. This means that in relative terms the evolution of the system is not sensitive to the size of the niche, an extremely useful property for forecasting.

Multiple Competition Case

The concept underlying the package developed for multiple competition (Nakicenovic, 1979) is the reduction of multiple competition to a set of double competitions by bunching competitors. The treatment is not general. In fact, oscillatory behavior, a characteristic of the solutions of the Volterra-Lotka equations, does not appear. In the hundreds of actual cases in which this concept was applied, the fits obtained were excellent, and the objects studied did not oscillate.

Derivation of the equation parameters is usually undertaken by least-squares fitting on the Fisher-Pry transform—that is, $\log f/(1-f)$. This may require further investigation, however, because visual fitting by experts results in parameter values that are more efficient for forecasting. An analysis of the effect of noise in the data on calculation of the size of the niche in Malthusian growth has been carried out by Debecker and Modis (1986).

8
Dynamics and Replacement of U.S. Transport Infrastructures

NEBOJSA NAKICENOVIC

This chapter uses several indicative examples to assess the time needed to build new and replace old transport infrastructures and energy transport systems. As the examples will show, both the growth and senescence of transport infrastructures evolve as regular processes, which are describable by S-shaped logistic curves. Not all growth and senescence phenomena can be described by simple logistic functions, however. Sometimes more complex patterns are observed, which are often described by envelopes that can be decomposed into a number of S-shaped growth or senescence phases. Two typical cases are (1) successive growth pulses with intervening saturation and a period of change, and (2) simultaneous substitution of more than two competing technologies. In the first case, successive S-shaped pulses usually represent successive improvements in performance—for example, aircraft speed records in which the first pulse is associated with the old technology, the piston engine, and the second with the new technology, the jet engine. In the second case, simultaneous substitution of competing technologies is usually described by increasing market shares of new technologies and decreasing market shares of old technologies. This chapter will demonstrate that the evolution of transport infrastructure can be described both by the performance or productivity of competing technologies and by their market share (see also chapter 7).

For both of the cases just mentioned, it will be shown that the development of transport networks is subject to regular patterns of change, which can in principle be used for forecasting future trends. Most of the examples are taken from the United States because it is one of the few countries to have well-documented experience of most of the technological changes that have occurred over the last 200 years. Because most of these changes subsequently diffused throughout the world, the examples also indicate the dynamics of these processes elsewhere.

In this chapter, the use of the term *infrastructure* is rather narrow, referring only to transportation and energy grids and networks, and other components of these two systems. These systems are interesting because they have played a crucial role in the economic and technological development process, are very capital intensive, and, in general, have long lifetimes. Analysis of the historical development of these two systems will include a quantitative description of performance improvement, the general evolution of a particular infrastructure, and the replacement of old technologies and infrastructures by new ones in terms of their relative market shares. The term *performance* is used as a multidimensional concept (i.e, as a vector rather than a scalar indicator), and, where appropriate, the size of an infrastructure is measured as a function of time.

The first section of this chapter describes the evolution of transport systems and their related infrastructures. The analysis starts, somewhat unconventionally, with the youngest technologies, aircraft and airways, and ends with the oldest transport networks, canals and waterways. The second section describes the evolution of energy consumption and pipelines as an example of dedicated transport infrastructures. The appendix briefly describes the methods and statistical tests used for this analysis.

TRANSPORTATION

Aircraft

Aircraft are the most successful of today's advanced modes of transportation. Other concepts of rapid transport such as high-speed trains have shown limited success, but they are not used as universally as aircraft. In fact, the rapid expansion of air travel during recent decades has its roots in the developments achieved in aerodynamics and other sciences many decades ago and especially in the engineering achievements made between the two world wars. The DC-3 airliner is often given as the example of the first ''modern'' passenger transport because in many ways its use denotes the beginning of the aircraft age.

The use of aircraft for transportation has increased ever since, and their performance has improved by about two orders of magnitude (about a hundred times). Figure 8-1 shows the increase in air transport worldwide measured in billions of passenger-kilometers per year (pass-km/year). It includes all carrier operations, including those of the planned economies.

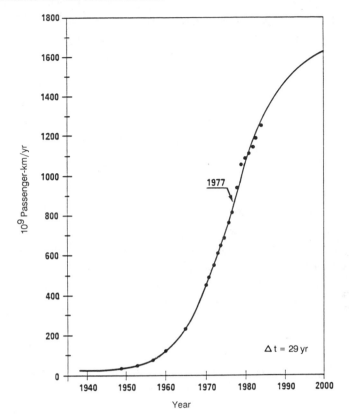

FIGURE 8-1   Air transport worldwide, all operations.

The logistic function has been fitted to the actual data, and it indicates that the inflection point in the growth of air carrier operations occurred about 10 years ago (around 1977). Thus, after a period of rapid exponential growth, less than one doubling is left until the estimated saturation level is achieved after the year 2000. The growth rate has been declining for about 10 years. If the projection here is correct, it will continue to do so until the total volume of all operations levels off after the year 2000 at about a 40 percent higher level than that experienced at present.

Figure 8-2 shows the same data and fitted logistic curve transformed as $x/(\kappa - x)$, where x denotes the actual volume of all operations in a given year (from Figure 8-1, given in millions of passenger-kilometers per hour [pass-km/h]) and κ is the estimated saturation level. The data and the estimated logistic trend line are plotted in Figure 8-2 as fractional

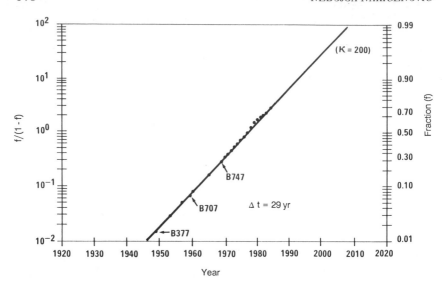

FIGURE 8-2   World air transport, logistic plot.

shares of the saturation level, $f = x/\kappa$, which simplifies the transformation to $f/(1 - f)$. Transformed in this way, the data appear to be on a straight line, which is the estimated logistic function.[1]

Perhaps the most interesting result is that it took about 30 years for world air transport to reach the inflection point (about half of the estimated saturation level)[2] and that within two decades the saturation level will be reached. This raises a crucial question: What will happen after such a saturation? Can we expect another growth pulse, a decline, or the instability of changing periods of growth and decline? Most likely a new period of growth associated with new technologies will follow the projected saturation.

To understand the implications of a possible saturation in world air transport operations and future developments, one must look at the transport system in general, comparing aviation with other modes of transport, and analyze the various components of the air transport system itself. Aircraft, airports, and ground services are the most important components of the air transport infrastructure. The commercial aviation infrastructure differs, however, from the infrastructures of other competing transport systems such as roads or railways in that airports are not continuously connected physically as are pipelines, roads, and railroad stations.

The global fleet of commercial aircraft and how it developed can be described in a number of ways. An obvious descriptor of the fleet is the number of aircraft in operation worldwide. This number increased from about 3,000 in the 1950s to almost 10,000 in the 1980s. During the same time, however, the performance or carrying capacity and speed of aircraft increased by about two orders of magnitude. Thus, the size of the fleet is not the most important descriptor, because much of the traffic is allocated to the most productive aircraft operating among the large hub airports while other aircraft constitute the feeder and distribution system for destinations with a lower traffic volume. The analogy between air transport systems and electrical grids or road systems is very close: large aircraft correspond to high-voltage transmission lines or primary roads.

Figure 8-3 shows the improvement over time of one important performance indicator for commercial passenger aircraft: carrying capacity and speed (often called productivity) measured in passenger-kilometers per hour. Each point on the graph indicates the performance of a given aircraft when used in commercial operations for the first time. For example, the

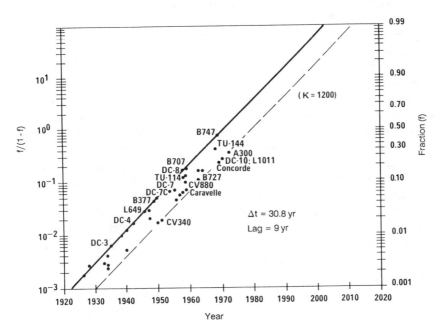

FIGURE 8-3   Passenger aircraft performance. Source of data: Angelucci and Matricardi (1977), Grey (1969).

DC-3 was introduced in 1935 with a performance of about 7,400 pass-km/h (21 passengers at 350 km/h); the B-747 was introduced in 1969 with a performance of about 500,000 pass-km/h (500 passengers at 1,000 km/h). The largest planned B-747s can carry almost 700 passengers. They are therefore about a hundred times as productive as the DC-3 50 years ago.

The upper curve in Figure 8-3 represents a kind of performance feasibility frontier for passenger aircraft because the performance of all other commercial air transports at the time they were introduced was either on or below the curve. Long-range aircraft on the performance feasibility curve were commercially successful; all other planes, whether they were successful or not, are below the curve. Thus, at any given time there appears to be only one appropriate (best) productivity specification for long-range passenger planes. Because the more recent jet transports all fly at about the same speed, the appropriate design for a new long-range transport should allow for a capacity of more than 700 passengers. According to the estimated curve, the asymptotic capacity for the largest aircraft is about 1,200 passengers at subsonic speed (1.2 million pass-km/h or 10 billion pass-km/yr). This implies that the next pulse in aircraft performance, if it occurs, would take place after the saturation phase. It would start at about 1.2 million pass-km/h and grow to much higher levels by at least one if not two orders of magnitude. Thus, after the year 2000, long-range aircraft might be larger and faster. Another interesting feature of Figure 8-3 is that the productivity of all passenger aircraft is confined to a rather narrow band between the performance feasibility curve and a "parallel" logistic curve with a lag of about nine years. This logistic curve represents the growth of world air transport from Figure 8-2.

It took about 30 years for the performance of the most productive aircraft to increase from about 1 percent of the estimated asymptotic performance to about half that performance (for example, the DC-3 represents the 1 percent achievement level and the B-747 roughly the 50 percent mark). In many ways the achievement of the 50 percent level represents a structural change in the development of the entire passenger aircraft industry and airlines. With S-shaped growth (that is, a logistic curve) the growth process is exponential until the inflection point or the 50 percent level is achieved. Thus, at the beginning, the productivity of aircraft is doubled many times within periods of only a few years. Once the inflection point is reached, however, only one doubling is left until the saturation level is reached. In Figure 8-3, for example, this development phase occurred in 1969 with the introduction of the B-747. Because the B-747 can, in principle, be stretched by about a factor of two, it could remain the largest long-range aircraft over the next two decades. Thereafter, a new growth phase with either larger or faster long-range aircraft is conceivable; the more distant future may possibly see both.

Before the inflection point, stretching does not help for more than a few years, given the rather frequent doublings in productivity. Consequently, new solutions are necessary. The necessity for new solutions also means that having a model that performs poorly on the market can be a crucial but nevertheless reversible mistake, provided the manufacturer is able to launch a new, improved performance model after a few years. After the inflection point, however, this strategy is no longer possible because those aircraft that are successful can be stretched to meet market demand through the saturation phase.

Thus, in the late 1960s the introduction of new, long-range aircraft suddenly became riskier because it was no longer possible to launch a new model after a few years. The B-747, for example, had the appropriate productivity, whereas two other competitors, the DC-10 and L-1011, were too small. The introduction of a 700- to 800-passenger aircraft in the near future would be risky because a stretched B-747 can do the same job; the introduction of a smaller long-range aircraft would probably fail because it would fall short of the primary market requirements. The only routes open to smaller, longer range transport such as the MD11 or Airbus 340 are those for which the B-747 is too large.

In the long run, most of the long-range traffic will be between large hubs and will be less in the form of direct traffic between smaller airports. The market niche for long-range aircraft with fewer than 500 passengers will therefore be very limited. A feasible alternative might be to redesign the MD11 and the Airbus 340 as wide-body, shorter range transports suitable for frequent cycles. The design of a cruise supersonic aircraft able to carry 300 to 400 passengers, or a hypersonic transport able to handle 200 to 300 passengers, may therefore be a better strategy for the first years of the next century. To some extent, these principles also explain why the Concorde cannot be a commercial success: with a capacity of 100 passengers, it is 150 passengers short of being a serious competitor for the B-747.

How probable is the development of a large cruise supersonic or hypersonic transport? S-pulses do not occur alone but usually in pairs. Thus, at saturation, structural change will occur, leading to a new growth pulse (probably S-shaped) and in turn to new productivity requirements and therefore to supersonic or hypersonic transport. The alternative is that air transport will saturate permanently over the next few decades, and the wide-bodied families of subsonic transports will actually constitute the

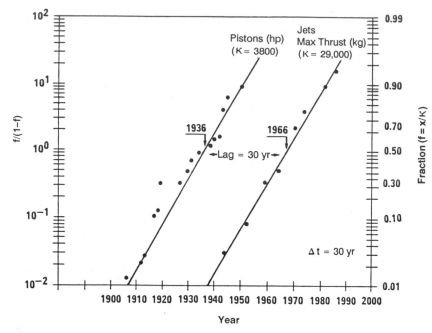

FIGURE 8-4   Performance of aircraft engines. Source of data: Angelucci and Matricardi (1977), Grey (1969).

asymptotic technology achievement. This alternative is unlikely, however, because air transport may become the dominant mode of passenger (long-distance) travel in the next century.

Figure 8-4 shows the improvement in the performance of civil aircraft engines since the beginning of aviation. The first piston engine visible on the plot is the French Antoinette engine, rated at 50 horsepower (hp) in 1906, and the last is the American Wright Turbo Compound, rated at 3,400 hp in 1950. These engines represent an improvement in power of almost two orders of magnitude over 44 years and about 90 percent of the estimated saturation level for piston engines (about 3,800 hp). A parallel development in the maximal thrust of jet engines follows with a lag of about 30 years, starting in 1944 with the German Junkers Juno 004 (rated at 900 kg) and ending with the American Pratt and Whitney JT9D in the early 1980s with 90 percent of the estimated thrust saturation level at about 29,000 kg. Both pulses in the improvement of aircraft engines are characterized by a time constant (Δt) equal to about 30 years. The midpoints (inflection points) of the two pulses, which occurred in 1936 and 1967, respectively, coincided with the introduction of the DC-3 and the B-747. In fact, the Pratt and Whitney Twin Wasp, introduced in 1930, became the power plant for the DC-3. This engine also served as the basis for subsequent and more powerful derivatives such as the Wasp Major introduced in 1945 toward the end of the aircraft piston engine era.

Thus, certain parallels are evident in the dynamics of passenger aircraft development beyond the obvious similarity in the time constant ($\Delta t =$ 30 years). Those engines introduced slightly before the inflection point, such as the Twin Wasp, are "stretched" by doubling the cylinder rows to increase the power. In the Wright Turbo Compound, representing the last refinement in aircraft piston engines, turbocharging was used to derive shaft power. Otherwise, the engine was a direct derivative of the Wright Cyclone series introduced in the early 1930s with Cyclone 9 (which originally powered the DC-2).

The time constant for the development of passenger aircraft is therefore about 30 years. Thirty years after the standard industry design emerged during the 1930s, the B-747, the first wide-body jet to enter service, became one of the most significant improvements in commercial transport, and its productivity represents half of the estimated industry saturation level that may be approached toward the end of this century. Thus, within a period of 60 years the life cycle will be completed: from standardization and subsequent rapid growth characterized by numerous improvements through the inflection point, when the emphasis changes to competition characterized by cost reductions and rationalization. These characteristics of the industry, including steady improvement in performance, are well illustrated by the development of the B-747 family.

The emergence of a new aircraft engine at the beginning of a new phase of growth is very likely toward the end of the century after the projected saturation has been reached. Furthermore, the characteristics of the long-range aircraft in this hypothetical growth pulse are implicit in this analysis. The saturation in the thrust of turbojet and turbofan engines indicates that a new generation of engines will emerge over the next few decades, a generation having much higher thrust ratings and growth potential. The only realistic candidates are the ramjet or scram engines with efficient off-design flight engine characteristics, or perhaps the HOTOL-type air-breathing rocket engines. Thus, a new pulse in the improvements of aircraft engines will most likely be associated with some variant of the variable-cycle air-breathing engine with a high Mach number and perhaps even ballistic flight potential. This trend would single out methane as the fuel of choice between Mach 3.5 and Mach 6, with a small overlap of hydrogen starting at Mach 5. Thus, cryogenic methane-powered cruise supersonic aircraft may become the mode of transport with the highest productivity after the year 2000.

The Automobile

At the beginning of this century, few proponents of the automobile envisaged that its use would spread as rapidly as it did throughout the world. As a commercial and recreational vehicle the motor car offered many advantages over other modes of transportation, especially animal-drawn vehicles. Perhaps the most important advantage was the possibility of increasing the radius of business and leisure transport.

At first the railroads were not challenged by the automobile. Rather, railroads helped the spread of the automobile by offering efficient long-distance transport that combined well with the use of motor vehicles for local urban and rural road transport. Within a few decades, however, the automobile had become an important form of transport for both local and long-distance passenger travel in the United States. Since the 1930s the total mileage traveled by motor vehicles in general has been divided almost equally between rural and urban travel.

The automobile had a relatively late start in the United States in relation to European countries (for example, France, Germany, and the United Kingdom). According to the records, four motor vehicles were in use in the United States in 1894. This was followed, however, with an impressive expansion of the automobile fleet: 16 vehicles in 1896; 90 in 1897; 8,000 in 1900; almost 500,000 10 years later; and more than 1 million after another 2 years. Thus, the United States quickly surpassed the European countries both in production and in the number of vehicles in use.

Figure 8-5 shows the rapid increase in the number of cars used in the United States. The automobile fleet is characterized by two distinct secular trends, with an inflection in the 1930s followed by less rapid growth rates. Because the two secular trends of the curve appear to be roughly linear on the logarithmic scale in Figure 8-5, the automobile fleet evolved through two exponential pulses. Thus, in this example the growth of the automobile fleet did not follow a simple, single S-shaped growth pulse.

The working hypothesis in this case is that the two trends indicate two different phases of the dissemination of motor vehicles in the United States. The first characterizes the substitution of motor vehicles for horse-drawn road vehicles, and the second the actual growth of road transport after animal-drawn vehicles essentially disappeared from American roads (see Nakicenovic, 1986). Only after the completion of this substitution process did the automobile emerge as an important competitor of the railroads for the long-distance movement of people and goods and perhaps as a competitor of urban transportation modes such as the tram, subway, or local train. Thus, the first expansion phase was more rapid because it represents a "market takeover" or expansion in a special niche; the second represents

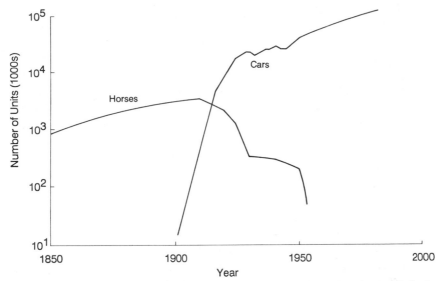

FIGURE 8-5   Number of road horses and mules and automobiles in the United States.

the actual growth of the road vehicle fleets and their associated infra-structures.

The lack of historical records of the exact number of horse-drawn vehicles in the United States soon after the introduction of the automobile in 1895 makes it difficult to describe accurately the assumed substitution of the motor car for the horse during the first, more rapid expansion phase of the motor vehicle fleets. The number of draft animals (road horses and mules) and automobiles given in Figure 8-5 therefore are a rough ap-proximation of this substitution process. Horse and saddle were sometimes used as a ''road vehicle,'' but often more than one horse was used to pull buggies and wagons. City omnibuses used about 15 horses in a single day, and a stagecoach probably used even more because the horses were replaced at each station. Figure 8-5 therefore may exaggerate the number of horse-drawn vehicles if the number of draft animals is used as a proxy for the number of vehicles actually in use. On the other hand, farm work animals are not included in Figure 8-5, although certainly they were also used for transport, especially in rural areas.

Although estimates of nonfarm horses and mules are not very accurate and are unevenly spaced in time, Figure 8-6 indicates that the automobile replaced horse- and mule-drawn road vehicles during a relatively short period and that the substitution process proceeded along a logistic path.[3]

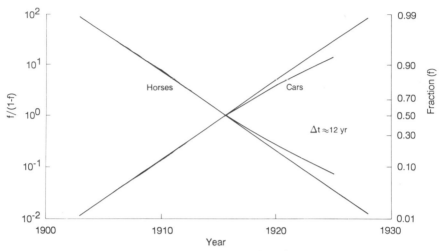

FIGURE 8-6   Substitution of cars for horses, United States.

Motor vehicles achieved a 1 percent share of total road vehicles shortly
after 1900 and a 50 percent share in 1916. A complete takeover occurred
in 1930 when there were 0.3 million road horses and mules and 23 million
cars, an increase from only 2 million cars 10 years earlier. Thus, the
inflection point in the growth of the automobile fleet from Figure 8-5
actually coincides with the end of the replacement of animal-drawn road
vehicles by motor cars and explains the apparent "saturation" in the
growth of motor vehicles observed by many analysts during the late 1920s
and early 1930s. This perceived saturation marks the beginning of a new
phase in the motorization of America, with growth rates comparable to
those of the expansion of horse-drawn vehicles before the automobile age.
Seen from this perspective, the growth in the number of all road vehicles
is a continuous process from 1870 to the present. Figure 8-7 shows the
secular increase of all road vehicles, horse-drawn and motor-powered, as
a logistic growth process with an apparent saturation level of about 350
million vehicles after the year 2030 and a Δt equal to about 100 years.

Because the growth of road transport in general and the substitution of
automobiles for horse-drawn carriages and wagons overlap in time, together they produce two growth trends in the automobile fleet with an
inflection point in the 1930s marking the structural change in the composition of the road vehicle fleets. The growth of all road vehicles results
in one single logistic trend, however. Thus, like aircraft, road vehicles
constitute a kind of distributed infrastructure that expands in time as one
connected system.

Both air and road transport systems require, in fact, elaborate and sophisticated infrastructure. Perhaps the most obvious examples are airports and supporting ground systems for aircraft, and roads and service infrastructures for road vehicles. Airports and railroads were obviously constructed to provide the infrastructure for aircraft and trains, but it is not so clear whether the automobile caused the need for good roads or the construction of good roads caused the development of the automobile industry (this argument was debated in the 1930s; see, for example, Epstein, 1928). Either way, the expansion of road vehicle fleets is paralleled by growth in the mileage of surfaced roads, although the total mileage of all roads increased very slowly from 3.16 million miles (mi) in 1921 to 3.85 million mi in 1981. The total length of all roads, which has remained almost unchanged over the past 60 years, is one of many indicators that do not portray logistic growth trends. It is possible, however, that the mileage of all roads increased during earlier times (during the colonial period, for example) and was saturated 100 years ago or even earlier.

Figure 8-8 shows the total road mileage in the United States and the mileage of urban streets (formerly defined as municipal streets), rural roads, and all urban and rural surfaced roads (bituminous penetration, asphalt, concrete, wood, stone, and other). This figure shows that the growth of surfaced roads paralleled that of all road vehicle fleets while the total mileage of all roads remained almost unchanged. The expansion of surfaced roads preceded the expansion of motor vehicles, however. In

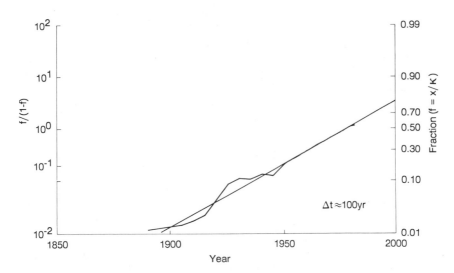

FIGURE 8-7   All road vehicles in use in the United States.

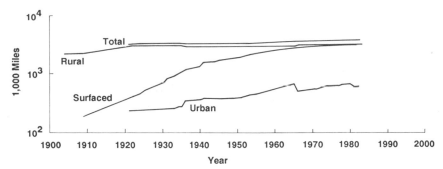

FIGURE 8-8 Mileage of all roads in the United States.

1905, 8 percent of all roads were surfaced, but fewer than 80,000 motor vehicles were in use compared with about 3.3 million road horses and mules (in addition to the 22 million draft animals used for farming). Thus, the early surfaced roads were developed for horses and not automobiles, but motor vehicles quickly expanded into the growing infrastructure.

Figure 8-9 shows the substitution of surfaced roads for unsurfaced roads, a process that lasted about 73 years (Δt). The first rapid-growth phase of motor vehicle fleets occurred therefore while less than half of American roads were suitable for their use. The substitution process shown in Figure 8-9 does not reflect the vigorous road construction effort after the depression years in the United States. Rather, it indicates a lack of such effort during the 1910s and 1920s because the actual expansion of surfaced road mileage was somewhat below the long-term trend during these two decades. A similar underexpansion occurred during the early 1970s, but the deviation from the trend appears to have been compensated for during the last few years. This behavior is reassuring because it confirms the observation that adequate infrastructure is a prerequisite for the expansion of transport systems.

Figure 8-10 shows the increase in surfaced road mileage as a logistic growth process with a saturation level of about 3.5 million mi (almost reached with 3.4 million mi today). This process parallels the substitution process of surfaced roads for unsurfaced roads shown in Figure 8-9. The dashed logistic function represents the growth in the number of all road vehicles from Figure 8-7. Thus, surfaced roads, as an important infrastructure for road transport, appear to be in the saturation phase today; the automobile fleet, on the other hand, is still growing and should reach its saturation phase in about 50 years.

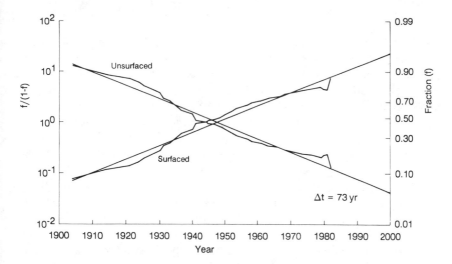

FIGURE 8-9   Substitution of surfaced roads for unsurfaced roads in the United States.

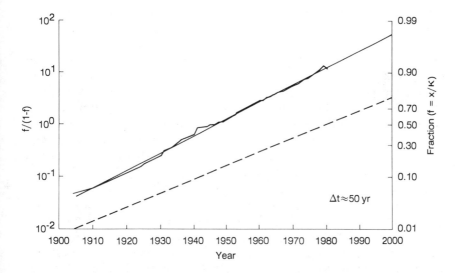

FIGURE 8-10   Mileage of surfaced roads in the United States. The dashed line shows the growth in the number of all road vehicles, from Figure 8-7.

Railroads

Although air transport and the automobile are still expanding modes of passenger travel, railroads are now in the postsaturation development phase, and their position in intercity passenger traffic in the United States is being eroded. A symbol of this decay is the discontinuation of transcontinental railway service in the United States.

The first railroads of significant length were introduced more than 150 years ago; widespread air travel, on the other hand, is only about 50 years old, and the first automobile dates from about 100 years ago. Although railroads were developed largely in Europe, they, like the automobile, had their most dramatic growth in the United States. By 1840, more than 10 years after the first commercial lines went into service, the United States had almost 4,500 km of railroad track compared with Europe's 3,000 km (Taylor, 1962).

The Baltimore and Ohio Railroad, probably the first commercial railroad in the United States, was chartered in 1829; 2 years later, it had 13 mi of track in operation. Many projects soon followed. In 1833 the Charleston and Hamburg Railroad along the Savannah River route, with 126 mi of track, was the longest railroad in the world under single management. By 1835 three Boston railroads were in operation—one to Lowell, one to Worcester, and the third to Providence.

To some extent the early railway lines were feeder lines for canal and waterway transport systems in much the same way that the early commercial motor vehicles were feeders for railways. Tramways (early, dedicated tracks with animal-drawn or steam trains) in the Pennsylvania coalfields augmented canal traffic, and some of the first railroads connecting to the Erie Canal originally served as its branch lines. The early railroads, in fact, were not allowed to compete with the Erie Canal, but they were largely independent transport agents and proved to be sturdy competitors of the older canals. For example, the Boston and Worcester Railway was a competitor of the Blackstone Canal, and when the Providence and Worcester Railroad was completed, it put this canal out of business. The Baltimore and Ohio Railroad took business away from the Chesapeake and Ohio Canal, and the Charleston and Hamburg Railroad was designed to, and did to some extent, divert traffic from the lower Savannah River.

Beginning in the 1830s railroads expanded rapidly in the United States for almost 100 years. Figure 8-11 shows the increase in operated mileage of the first and other main tracks in the United States since 1835.

The mileage increased as a single logistic pulse reaching saturation in 1929 with a Δt equal to 54 years. It declined logistically thereafter with a Δt equal to about 118 years. The actual length of operated main track

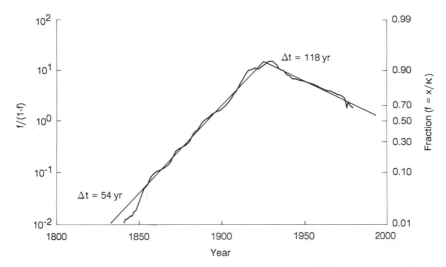

FIGURE 8-11   Growth pulse in main rail track operated in the United States.

infrastructure increased from about 4,500 km (less than 3,000 mi) in 1840 to more than 480,000 km (about 300,000 mi) in 1929—about two orders of magnitude in 90 years. By comparison, the decline was a rather slow process: by the 1980s the length of main track actually in operation had decreased by about one-third to some 320,000 km (about 200,000 mi). Thus, the decline phase (about 50 years up to the present) appears to be slower than the growth phase, probably because older technologies and infrastructures can be put to new uses after they saturate. By doing so, they may avoid complete displacement by new competitors. For example, sailing ships, wood fires, and horseback riding have all become favorite leisure time and sporting activities even though they were replaced by new technologies long ago. In this way, railways may be put to new uses—perhaps for local passenger and tourist traffic similar to ocean cruises—despite their insignificance as a mode of intercity passenger travel. Some canals are already serving such a purpose even though they have not been a profitable means of passenger transportation since the heyday of railroads. Both canals and railroads still offer, however, efficient transportation for low-value goods (per unit weight).

Many technological improvements were introduced in the United States during the first decades of the railroad expansion, including the shift in basic construction materials of rails from wood to larger shares of iron and later steel. Iron rails were a significant improvement because they made the use of heavier locomotives and loads possible, thereby increasing

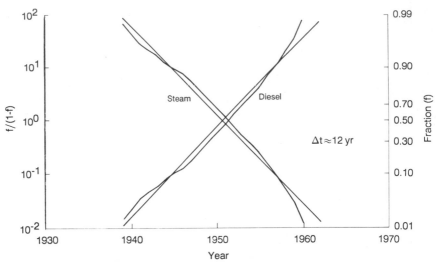

FIGURE 8-12   Substitution of diesel for steam locomotives in the United States.

the efficiency of rail transport. At the same time the energy sources also changed. The draft animals used in the first tramways were replaced by steam locomotives fired by wood, which remained the principal fuel of railroads until about 1870 (Schurr and Netschert, 1960). Wood was then replaced by coal, and later steam locomotives in general were replaced by diesel locomotives. Figure 8-12 shows the substitution of diesel for steam locomotives.

The first diesel locomotive was introduced in 1925 when the total number of locomotives peaked at about 69,000, a few years before the length of main track in operation reached its maximum and started to decline. A few electric locomotives were introduced earlier, but they never gained importance in the United States and remained less than 2 percent of the total locomotive fleet. The replacement of steam by diesel locomotives was a swift process that lasted slightly longer than 20 years (the substitution of automobiles for horses lasted less than 30 years). In 1938 diesel locomotives represented a 1 percent share of all locomotives and by the 1960s more than a 99 percent share. Thus, although the substitution of diesel for steam locomotives was a fast technological change, the continuous increase in performance of the railroad transport system was characterized by longer secular trends.

Since the first generation of designs at the beginning of the last century, the traction of locomotives has increased through improvements in energy conversion and a subsequent increase in horsepower, and through increased weight (possible only because of improvements in tracks and materials). The absolute peak in the total installed horsepower of all locomotives was achieved in 1929 with more than 100 million hp for approximately 60,000 (mostly steam) locomotives. This peak coincided with the maximal length of main tracks also achieved in 1929.

Other indicators of the railroad system in the United States show that the 1920s represented the culmination of railways. For example, the number of passenger train cars in service peaked in 1924 at more than 57,000; the number of freight train cars in service peaked in 1925 at more than 2.4 million. The number of passengers carried (more than 1.2 billion) and passenger-miles (more than 47 billion) also peaked during the same decade (1920). All of these indicators declined subsequently by between 30 and 40 percent of the maximal values reached during the 1920s.

A certain parallel in the development of automobiles and railroads can be detected. In a superficial way, both systems imitated the design of the transport modes they were competing with and eventually replaced. The first motor vehicles were literally horseless carriages; they were almost identical except for the difference in the prime mover. In the same way, early railroad passenger cars were similar to stagecoaches in both design and appearance. Nevertheless, both new transportation technologies represented radical improvements and changes with respect to their predecessors.

More fundamentally, the expansion of main track was only slightly faster than the expansion of surfaced roads in the United States. Both growth processes are characterized by a Δt equal to about 50 years, but the inflection points of the two growth pulses are separated by 56 years— the main tracks reached half the saturation level in 1890 whereas surfaced roads reached that point in 1948. Thus, the growth of these two infrastructures is characterized by a time constant of about 50 years, but the decline of railroad infrastructure appears to have been a much slower process.

Another fundamental similarity in the evolution of the two transportation systems is that while the railroads were saturating, the automobile industry consolidated and introduced important changes that generated subsequent growth. Railways reached their saturation point during the 1920s, the same decade in which the substitution of automobiles for horses was completed. Other fundamental innovations, such as mass production and closed car bodies, were also introduced in the rapidly expanding automotive industry during this period.

It is useful therefore to distinguish two different aspects of the evolution of the two transport infrastructures. Although the growth of main tracks and surfaced roads lasted about 50 years, the technological changes and substitution of new equipment for old equipment is a much faster process of about 10 to 20 years at the level of locomotive or automotive fleets. These processes continue even after the saturation phase is reached, as the substitution of diesel for steam locomotives indicated. Thus, technological changes are important in both growing and declining industries. In growing industries, new technologies are introduced through new additions and replacement, and in the declining industries, new technologies are introduced exclusively through partial replacement of old technologies.

Canals

The similarity in the evolution of rail and road transport systems is perhaps indicative of an invariance in the development pattern of transport systems and their underlying infrastructures. A serious problem arises, however, when comparing these two transportation modes with those that do not depend exclusively on the rigid, man-made links between them. Airways and waterways, for example, rely less on man-made links between nodes because they use the natural environment (air, rivers, and coastal waters). Nevertheless, they require an elaborate infrastructure such as airports, harbors, and canals. Thus, it is difficult to compare the total length of the implicit air and waterway routes and the total length of main railroad tracks or surfaced roads. For both air and waterway routes, however, there are abstract measurements that would, in principle, correspond to the length of the grid: the network of certified route carriers or federal airways in air transport and the total length of continental waterways and canals. Unfortunately, the annual increase in the actual operated mileage length of all air carrier routes and the mileage of used continental waterways and canals is not very accurately documented in historical records. Thus, only sparse accounts and probably inaccurate estimates must be used in this analysis.

The first decades of the nineteenth century in the United States marked the beginning of large roads, canals, tramways, and later railway construction projects. During the so-called turnpike era (1800–1830), several of the roads designed for travel between larger towns or to the West across the mountains were completed. Turnpikes, however, were already being abandoned during the 1820s because of a lack of financial success (Taylor, 1962). During the same period, canal construction was viewed as a more effective means of internal transportation to complement coastal merchant transport while the construction of turnpikes declined. The "canal era" lasted until the railways became the main mode of long-distance transport a few decades later. From this point of view, the 1830s were turbulent years: many turnpikes were abandoned, canal construction was reaching its peak, and some early railway projects were already completed. Thus, since the 1830s at least three different transport modes have to some extent provided complementary services, but they were also competing directly in many market segments. In contrast to turnpikes and railways, canals connected the various natural links of the inland waterway system and did not represent a transport infrastructure in themselves. They can be compared to bridges and tunnels that connect road or rail transport networks. Canals made the inland waterways into an integrated transport system by connecting the lakes in the north with the rivers in the southeast and midwest. The great waterway across the United States never materialized, however.

The first canals were built during the 1780s. When completed in 1793, the Richmond Falls Canal was the first canal to exceed 7 mi in length. From then on the pace of canal construction accelerated: by 1800 the total length of canals exceeded 50 mi, and by 1825 more than 1,000 mi were in operation. Rapid construction continued for another 20 years or so, reaching 3,600 mi in 1850 and leveling off at about 4,000 mi 20 years later. Thereafter the canal business was so seriously eroded by competition from the railroads that many important canals were decommissioned. Subsequently, the length of all canals in use began to decline. In the United States the rise and fall of operated canals paralleled the growth and decline of the main railway tracks but was displaced in time by about 50 years. In both cases the growth in mileage of the operated infrastructure increased rapidly, but after saturation the decline was far less rapid.

Figure 8-13 shows the increase in the length of canals in the United States as a logistic growth pulse with a saturation level of about 4,000 mi after the 1860s. The inflection point, or the maximum rate of growth, was reached in 1832, and the Δt is equal to about 30 years. Thus, canals have a time constant comparable to that of airways but shorter than that of railways and roads. A possible explanation is that both canals and airways represent only one important component of the respective actual transport infrastructure, which for the former includes all waterways in addition to some man-made canals, and for the latter a large infrastructure of supporting systems such as airports and traffic control. On the other hand, railroads and surfaced roads in themselves constitute a large connected infrastructure that is essentially built for a specific purpose. Consequently, it takes longer to construct large infrastructures such as roads and tracks than the selected links (canals or, more abstractly, air corridors) and nodes (airports and harbors) needed to expand a new transport system such as water- or airways into an already available natural environment.

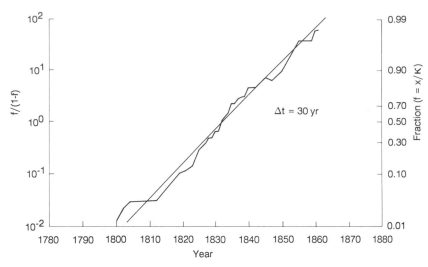

FIGURE 8-13   Length of canals in the United States.

Transport Infrastructure

The difference in the time constants of air and inland water transport systems, on the one hand, and rail and road transport, on the other, indicates that at least at this level of comparison transport systems having more extensive infrastructures may take longer to expand and possibly longer to complete the whole life cycle from growth to saturation and later senescence. To assess whether the time constants are really different, Figure 8-14 shows the substitution of the four transport systems during the last 180 years in the United States in terms of the operated mileage of the competing infrastructures: canals, main railway tracks, surfaced roads, and federal airway route miles. From this perspective the substitution of the four systems over time appears as a regular process.[4]

Several invariant features are inherent to this substitution process. At any given time, at least three important transport infrastructures are competing for shares of the total route length of all transport modes. The longest transport infrastructure is always longer than at least half the total length. Consequently, the second and third longest transport infrastructures are equal to less than half of the total length. This symmetry and the dominating role of the longest infrastructure have been complemented by another regular feature during the last 180 years. The time constant (Δt) increases from less than 50 years for the growth of railway track shares to almost 90 years for surfaced roads and more than 130 years for airway

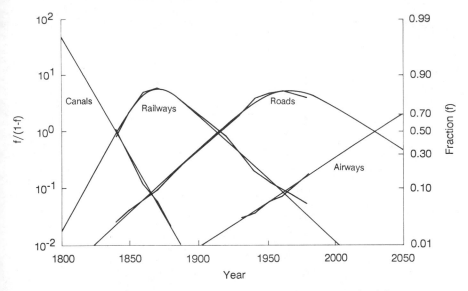

FIGURE 8-14   Substitution of transport infrastructures in the United States.

routes as shares of total length. Thus, the time constant increased by about 40 years for successive infrastructures. The distance between the saturation periods (time of maximal market shares) of railway tracks and surfaced roads is about 100 years.

This result may appear to contradict the earlier observation that the total length of railway tracks and surfaced roads took longer to construct than water and airway routes. In fact, the timetable associated with the substitution dynamics of infrastructure lengths is surprisingly consistent in relation to the duration of growth pulses of the four transport modes during the past 180 years. The apparent inconsistency results from the different ways of measuring the growth rates and life cycles of the respective infrastructures. In the case of market shares the increase in a particular transport infrastructure is analyzed in terms of the length of all networks. Thus, even the rapid growth rate of airway route mileage is translated into a comparatively long time constant because at the same time the total length of all transport networks is also growing rapidly. As a result of these rapid growth rates, the share of surfaced roads has been declining since the 1970s whereas the total length of surfaced roads is still growing toward the saturation level (see Figure 8-10).

Thus, the total length of a transport infrastructure (in this case, canals, railroads, and surfaced roads) can still be growing even decades away from ultimate saturation and final senescence while the shares of its length

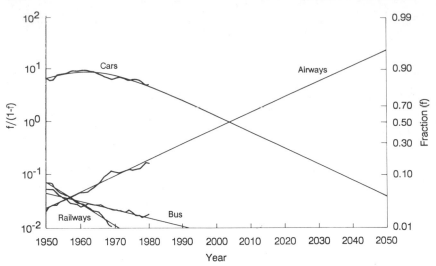

FIGURE 8-15   Intercity passenger traffic substitution in the United States.

in that of all transport infrastructures are declining. The saturation and
decline of market shares therefore precede saturation in absolute growth
in an increasing market, meaning that the eventual saturation of any competing technology can be anticipated in the substitution dynamics in a
growing market.

Although the substitution of younger for older modes of transport is a
regular process when measured in total mileage of the four transport
infrastructures, it is nevertheless only a proxy for the real dynamics of
transportation systems, which should be measured in some common performance unit. Because transport systems provide a whole range of services, such a common descriptor is difficult to define. Two obvious choices
of a common unit are ton- or person-kilometers per year. These units do
not, however, distinguish between freight and passenger transport or between short and long distances. Thus, there is no obvious shortcut, and
it appears necessary to analyze both passenger and freight separately for
both short and long distances (for example, intra- and intercity travel).
Fortunately, the available historical data make it possible to reconstruct
the dynamics of these substitution processes for at least some countries.

For example, Figure 8-15 shows the substitution of different transportation modes in intercity (long-distance) passenger travel in the United
States since 1950. By excluding urban and metropolitan transport (because
explicit statistics are generally lacking), the competition for intercity passenger traffic is reduced to four significant transport modes: railways,
buses, cars, and airways. The shares of each transport mode are calculated

in passenger-miles traveled in a given year. According to this analysis the automobile is still the main choice for most Americans and will remain so into the next century in spite of the market share increases of air travel. The losers are railways and buses. The substitution dynamics indicate that during the next decade the share of airways in intercity travel will increase to almost 40 percent, the share of automobiles will decrease to a little more than 60 percent, and the shares of railways and buses will be virtually eliminated.

Unfortunately, Figure 8-15 does not indicate the full drama of this replacement process because data are not available for the period before 1950. Nevertheless, the substitution process is consistent with the mileage substitution of the respective transportation infrastructures from Figure 8-14. For example, the share of main railway tracks falls to less than 1 percent by the end of the century, and the share of railways in intercity travel phases out even earlier, during the 1970s. During the same decade the shares of both automobiles in intercity travel and surfaced road mileage in total length of the transport infrastructure are saturating. In both cases the shares of airways are increasing and are expected to reach a position of dominance (with control of more than half the "market") during the first decades of the next century. This result suggests that a new growth pulse in commercial aviation may be due in about two decades. Cruise supersonic and possibly air-breathing hypersonic transports might be the only technologies likely to provide the growth potential to be achieved in the next expansion phase of passenger travel.

Obviously, the above description of these complex systems is incomplete. Certainly, there are other illuminating ways of describing the dynamics of these systems. The intriguing aspect of the logistic description of the development of transportation systems is that the systems appear to be interwoven with regular features and a pattern of substitution dynamics over a period of about two centuries. To show that this is not a feature unique to the evolution of transportation systems, the next section of this chapter describes a similar regularity in the evolution of energy systems. Furthermore, future developments in transport infrastructures are related to likely changes in the energy system, especially with respect to energy transport and propulsion for prime movers.

PRIMARY ENERGY

Energy Consumption

At the beginning of the nineteenth century fuelwood, agricultural wastes, and mechanical wind and water power supplied most of the inanimate energy in addition to animal and human muscle power. This poor energy

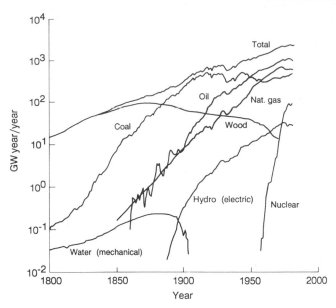

FIGURE 8-16   Primary energy consumption in the United States.

menu (by present standards), however, represented a sophisticated energy system compared to earlier practices. In the nineteenth century a considerable infrastructure of roads (turnpikes) and canals was in place for timber and later coal transport. Mining, manufacture, and irrigation were also usually associated with elaborate systems of dams and waterwheels. Thus, in the early industrial development phase, energy use depended on the transport system, and energy was one of the more important components of goods transported on canals, waterways, turnpikes, and roads.

Fuelwood represented most of the primary energy inputs. Figure 8-16 shows the U.S. annual consumption of fuelwood, fossil energy, mechanical water power, and hydroelectric power since 1800. Data are plotted on a logarithmic scale and show the exponential growth phases in consumption by piecewise linear secular trends.

In the United States, the consumption of fuelwood, once the most important source of energy, has declined since the beginning of the century, although it is still used widely, especially in the developing countries. With the expansion of railroads and the steel industry and the application of steam in general, the use of coal increased exponentially until the 1910s, and it has oscillated ever since. Since their introduction in the 1870s, oil and natural gas have been consumed at even more rapid growth rates. In fact, oil and natural gas curves have the same shape and almost identical

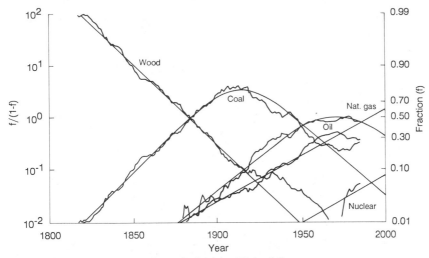

FIGURE 8-17   Primary energy substitution, United States.

growth rates; they are just shifted in time by about 10–15 years. The increased use of oil and natural gas paralleled the growth of the petrochemical and electrical industries and the expanded use of internal combustion and electric prime movers. Because nuclear energy is still in its early phase of development, the steep growth of the last decade may not indicate its future role. Indeed, during the past few years the growth of nuclear energy in the United States and worldwide has declined to more moderate rates.

Energy Substitution

Although for almost two centuries energy consumption did not draw equally from all sources and the use of all energy sources did not increase equally, primary energy consumption (including fuelwood) increased exponentially at an average growth rate of about 3 percent per year. The decline of older energy sources was more than compensated for by the rapid growth of the new sources.

Figure 8-17 shows primary energy substitution in the United States.[5] Mechanical water power (mostly hydro and some windmills) and hydroelectric power are not observable in the figure because of their small contribution to the total energy supply; they barely exceeded the 1 percent level during short periods and were otherwise under that critical level. Thus, before the 1820s fuelwood fulfilled virtually all energy needs in the United States. Coal entered the competition in 1817 at the 1 percent level, and up to the 1880s it was essentially a two-technology market—whatever gains coal made were translated into losses for fuelwood.

Wood remained, nevertheless, an important construction material and source of heat and power well into the last decades of the nineteenth century, enough so that the steam age began in an economy based on wood. The first steamboats and locomotives were fired with wood, which remained the principal fuel used by railroads until about 1870 (Schurr and Netschert, 1960). The iron industry was another large wood consumer. Around 1850 more than half of all the iron produced was still smelted with charcoal. The total amount consumed by manufacturing and transportation was small, however, when compared with the huge quantities used by households. By 1880, the industrial use of wood had declined, so that domestic use accounted for more than 96 percent of the fuelwood consumed (Schurr and Netschert, 1960).

At the same time, coal already supplied almost half of all energy needs, most of it used by emerging industries. In 1880 coal supplied almost 90 percent of the fuel used for smelting iron. The iron was used in turn for construction projects, including larger railroad infrastructures, which by that time used coal as the fuel of choice. Thus, in this respect the end of the last century marks the beginning of industrial development in the United States.

Crude oil and natural gas were first used in the United States at the beginning of the nineteenth century, and both held a 1 percent market share during the 1880s. From then on the use of crude oil expanded, and by 1950 the consumption of crude oil surpassed that of coal. Even as late as the 1920s, however, the consumption of crude oil was not much larger than that of fuelwood. The use of natural gas surpassed the use of coal nine years later. In comparing this period with earlier periods, it is remarkable that the structure of energy consumption changed more during the period of oil dominance than ever before.

The 1950s, when crude oil became the dominant source of energy, represent the beginning of more intense competition among various energy sources, both in the United States and throughout the world. Over the 150-year period (1800–1950), the energy source that dominated the energy supply also contributed more than half of all primary energy consumption; from 1800 to 1880 this source was fuelwood, and from 1880 to 1950, coal. This is similar to the dominance at any given time of one transport infrastructure over all others with more than half of all mileage. This was observed in the substitution of canals, railway tracks, surfaced roads, and airways (see Figure 8-14). During the 1970s crude oil was close to achieving a 50 percent share, but before actually surpassing this mark it began to decline. Thus, during the last three decades, three important sources of energy shared the market without a single source having a pronounced dominance. This is contrary to the pattern observed during earlier periods and the substitution of transport infrastructures.

Figure 8-17 shows that natural gas will dominate the energy picture after the 1980s although crude oil will continue to maintain about a 30 percent market share at the end of the century. The future potential competitors of natural gas, such as nuclear or solar energy, have not yet captured enough market shares to allow definitive estimation of their future penetration rates. The starting point for market penetration of nuclear energy was the 1960s, when nuclear power acquired slightly less than a 1 percent share of primary energy. Allowing for further cancellations of already ordered power plants and the possible decommissioning of those in operation and under construction, nuclear energy could at most double its current market share to about 4 percent by the year 2000. This assumed penetration rate is used for the projection in Figure 8-17, which indicates that more than half of all the primary energy consumed during the first decades of the next century will be natural gas. This result illustrates that not only will the natural gas bubble be absorbed in a few years, but methane technologies will also develop in the future, creating new growth sectors. One of the important sectors for gas in the more distant future may, in fact, be aviation.

This result is unexpected given the numerous energy debates of the last 10–15 years, but it is perhaps reassuring that we may not have to rely on nuclear or alternative energy sources for another 50 years or so after all. The future that emerges would require fewer radical changes, but the challenges of developing new technologies and improving the performance of already employed technologies would remain. Despite the current difficulties in expanding the use of natural gas in a time of worldwide economic slowdown and low crude oil prices, this scenario paints a different picture in the long run. So that readers can better understand how methane might emerge as the dominant energy source of the future, a brief analysis of the evolution of energy transport infrastructures follows.

Crude Oil and Natural Gas Transport

In contrast to crude oil, which is traded globally, and natural gas, which is transported over continental distances, fuelwood was primarily consumed locally, close to the source of timber. Some fuelwood was transported over longer distances, mostly by river flotation, and distributed by waterways or roads. Coal, on the other hand, is a more concentrated form of energy than fuelwood (coal has a higher heat content per unit weight), and coal mines are a more concentrated source than forests. Coal was

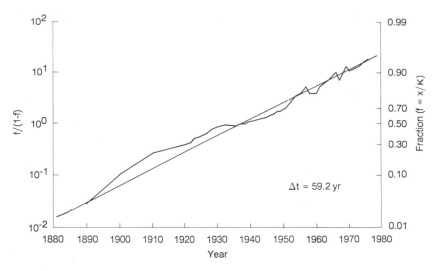

FIGURE 8-18   Pipeline length for crude oil and petroleum products in the United States.

generally transported over longer distances than fuelwood, usually (nationwide) by barges, trains, or "trucks" (horse wagons). In the extreme case modest amounts were transported overseas. Thus, the shift from a wood to a coal economy was accompanied by an expansion of energy transport over longer distances and an increasing number of transport modes. The widespread use of crude oil led to use of yet another transport mode—pipelines. Indeed, pipelines are becoming an important freight transport mode, with market shares in total ton-kilometers per year comparable to those of train and truck transport. They are also comparable to railways in total length of the infrastructure or grid: the 200,000 mi of main railroad track in the United States are slightly shorter than the 230,000 mi of crude oil pipelines. Thus, although the total length of the rail and oil pipeline grids is equivalent, the two infrastructures differ in that since the 1920s the railroad system has been declining while oil pipelines have been expanding. Figure 8-18 shows the rapid increase in pipeline length for crude oil and petroleum products in the United States.

Expansion of the oil pipeline grid parallels the increase in crude oil shares of total primary energy consumption. Oil held a 1 percent share during the 1880s when the rapid increase in oil pipeline mileage began and followed exponential trends until the 1930s (the inflection point occurred in 1937). As if by coincidence, coal, oil's largest competitor, gained a maximal share of primary energy during the same decade. Thus, by

1937 about half of the current length of the oil pipeline network was already in place, and the growth rates declined slowly. During the 1980s the length of the pipeline network should reach the asymptotic level at about the same time that the crude oil shares of total primary energy saturate.

The time constant (Δt) for the expansion of oil pipelines, 59 years, is close to that of the expansion of rail tracks and surfaced roads (about 54 and 59 years, respectively). In the analysis of the expansion of oil pipelines, however, numerical instability was encountered in the values of the estimated parameters with respect to different estimation algorithms used in the analysis. In particular, the result reported in Figure 8-18 is based on an estimated saturation level, κ, of 238,800 mi with a Δt equal to 59.2 years; yet an alternative estimation algorithm (used to test the stability of estimated parameters with respect to changes in the assumptions about the weighing of the observations) gave different estimates—246,500 mi and 78.7 years, respectively. In all other examples the variation in the parameter values was within the estimated uncertainty ranges, as shown in the appendix. Only in the case of oil pipelines was the value for Δt outside this range.

Although crude oil is still the most important energy source, in primary energy consumption it is slowly being replaced by natural gas. In fact, the share of natural gas associated with oil is decreasing in total natural gas production. Thus, greater shares of natural gas transport and end use are based on gas, not oil, technologies (Grübler and Nakicenovic, 1987). This substitution process is also reflected in the increase in natural gas transport and distribution pipelines when compared to the increase in oil pipelines (Figure 8-18).

According to Schurr and Netschert (1960), the earliest recorded commercial use of natural gas in America was in 1821 (coal then supplied just 1 percent of primary energy and fuelwood and draft animals the rest) when it was used as lighting fuel in Fredonia, New York. Natural gas continued to be used sporadically throughout the nineteenth century. The first pipeline was constructed from Murrysville to Pittsburgh, Pennsylvania, in 1883 after the discovery of a large well in 1878.

Despite such pioneering projects by the emerging oil and gas industry, methane was considered a waste product. By 1878 both crude oil and natural gas held more than a 1 percent share of primary energy consumption, but at that time most of the natural gas was consumed in the vicinity of the oil fields.

The natural gas pipeline network began to expand rapidly during the 1890s, or about 20 years after the oil pipelines began to expand. Figure 8-19 shows that this 20-year shift in time persists through most of the

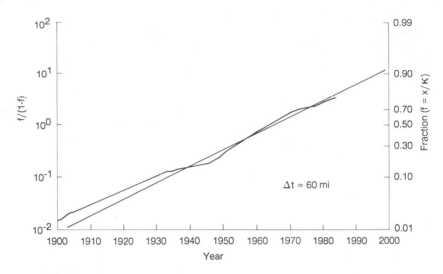

FIGURE 8-19   Natural gas pipeline length in the United States.

growth cycle of the natural gas transport system and distribution infrastructure. The inflection point occurred in 1965, or almost 30 years after
the inflection point in the growth of oil pipelines. Because the time constant
for natural gas pipelines is about 60 years, and therefore longer but still
comparable to that of oil pipelines (59 years), saturation should also occur
more than 20 years later, during the 2020s. Again, this is symmetrical to
the relationship between the growth phases of oil pipelines and oil's penetration of primary energy. The growth pulse started when oil achieved
a 1 percent share of primary energy, inflection occurred when oil became
the second largest energy source (by passing fuelwood), and saturation of
pipeline length was synchronous with the saturation of market shares.
Exactly the same pattern can be observed during the growth pulse of
natural gas pipelines by comparing Figures 8-17 and 8-19. Growth started
toward the end of the last century when natural gas achieved a 1 percent
share of primary energy, the inflection point occurred in 1965 when natural
gas became the second largest energy source (by passing coal), and saturation of both natural gas market shares and length of pipeline should
be achieved during the 2020s.

A large difference between the growth pulses of oil and natural gas
pipelines is the length of the respective transport and distribution networks.
As shown in Figure 8-18 the saturation level for oil pipeline length is
estimated at about 240,000 mi (about the current length of railroad tracks),
while the asymptotic level for the length of natural gas pipelines is esti-

mated at more than 1.3 million mi (more than five times higher). Natural gas is now transported almost exclusively through the pipeline grid. Oil and petroleum products, however, are also shipped by tanker, train, and truck, and for some military uses, even by aircraft. Aside from small quantities of liquefied natural gas and liquid natural gas products, most natural gas reaches the consumer either in a gaseous form or as electricity. The pipeline network for natural gas transport and distribution is therefore much longer than that for crude oil and petroleum products. This, of course, poses the question of whether natural gas will continue to be transported almost exclusively by pipelines in the future, especially if its projected use expands as dramatically as illustrated in Figure 8-17. For liquid natural gas products particularly, it is likely that other transport modes will also be used, conceivably even aircraft. From a technical point of view there are no obstacles to using this transport mode for energy. The question is whether it would be economical and competitive to do so.

This question cannot be resolved here, but in the past, similar solutions were found to meet the ever-increasing need to transport more energy over longer distances. Development of a faster means of transport over larger areas and the use of denser and cleaner energy forms were the technological measures taken then to improve the performance of these systems. One could therefore expect further improvements in the near future, which can be fulfilled by a stronger reliance on natural gas and aircraft until better solutions and completely new systems are devised during the next century. Over the next four to five decades, improved versions of the current energy and transport systems and infrastructures must be relied on because the results of this analysis indicate that the time constants involved in installing new infrastructures are about 50 years.

CONCLUSIONS

The examples analyzed here have shown that the growth and senescence of transport infrastructures can be described as a regular process with logistic secular trends. The time constants (Δt) of these growth processes are clustered around 50 years, with a range of between 30 and 59 years. Considering the poor quality of the historical data on the growth of transport infrastructures, it is remarkable that four network or grid transport systems—railway tracks, surfaced roads, and oil and natural gas pipelines—cluster even more densely between 54 and 59 years. The time constants for canals and performance improvements in aircraft transport are shorter, about 30 years. For canals and railway tracks, senescence lasts much longer than the growth process. The total length of canals, and of railways some 50 years later, declined with a much longer time constant, almost 150 years. Thus, canals are still in use despite a century-long decline.

This perhaps explains the long time constants in the substitution of infrastructures. Although the growth in the length of all network or grid transportation infrastructures was a very fast process—from about 4,000 mi for canals to about 4 million mi for railways, roads, and airways (a growth of three orders of magnitude in about 150 years)—the substitution of transport infrastructures (see Figure 8-14) lasted longer than the actual growth pulses for the four individual infrastructures. The time constant (Δt) of the substitution process increased from 50 years for railway shares to almost 90 years for surfaced roads and more than 130 years for airways, compared with a time constant of 30 years for the growth pulse of canals and about 50 years for railways and roads. These figures illustrate the permanence of infrastructures and their sites. The decline of infrastructure is a slow process. New infrastructures replace the older ones more through rapid growth of the whole transport system than through physical destruction or replacement of older infrastructures.

Despite the remarkable regularity of these growth and substitution processes the variation in the parameter values of different estimation algorithms was outside the uncertainty range for the growth of oil pipelines. Thus, growth processes that follow the simplest possible pattern—a single S-shaped path—can be difficult to measure even when they are almost complete because the saturation levels are a priori unknown and have to be estimated from the data. Technological substitution processes are inherently more complex because market shares of all important (competing) technologies have to be measured. Yet in part because of this higher degree of complexity, they are more stable from the statistical point of view. The most sensitive parameter of the logistic function, the asymptotic saturation level κ, is a priori known in this case. By definition, it can never exceed 100 percent of a given market.

A more consistent analysis of the evolution of transport systems and their infrastructures would require comparison of the performance and services provided by the different modes over long periods. It was not possible, however, to reconstruct such an indicator for the overall transport system. Yet Figure 8-15, which shows intercity passenger travel during the last 37 years, is a good proxy for such a comparison. The substitution of the four major modes of long-distance travel in the United States is a regular process that singles out aircraft as the transport mode with the highest growth potential. The dynamics and general implications of this substitution process are that this result is consistent with the time constants observed for the growth pulses and substitution of the four transport modes—canals, railways, roads, and airways.

The primary energy substitution dynamics (from Figure 8-17) indicate that technological substitution can be characterized by regular time constants, provided the historical data are accurate enough for the analysis. This is possible to some extent for primary energy consumption because different energy sources can be measured in common (physical, energy) units and because their use is relatively well documented. Furthermore, the technological changes in the energy system (i.e., the shift from older to newer energy sources) are also reflected in a parallel evolution of the energy transport infrastructures. For example, both fuelwood and coal were transported largely by canals and railroads in the same way as most other goods. Crude oil and natural gas, however, are transported by dedicated pipeline infrastructures. The evolution of these energy transport infrastructures, then, parallels changes in the energy system, but at the same time their growth patterns are no different from those of other transport infrastructures.

A general conclusion is that technological changes, such as the substitution of road vehicles or locomotives, last a few decades; changes in the transport system and evolution of infrastructures, on the other hand, are longer processes with time constants of between three and seven decades. Thus, the transport infrastructures themselves will not change drastically during the rest of the century, but concurrent technological changes in vehicles, aircraft, and the necessary equipment will improve both the performance and quality of the transport services provided by the current system.

More specifically, road vehicles will remain the dominant form of long-distance transport during the next 20 years, but the importance of airways will increase in time. Both transport and energy systems must, however, meet more stringent economic and environmental requirements over longer distances and in a shorter time. In the United States, these systems appear to be still in the expansion phase as no signs of saturation were detected in the analysis. Rather, it was observed that older, still dominant technologies are slowly being displaced by newer competitors, which in principle offer substantial growth potential.

The next generation of aircraft and natural gas technologies represents evolutionary rather than revolutionary technologies that could meet the more stringent requirements through improvements in current designs and practices over the next two decades. New solutions must be developed during this period for later decades, however. In particular, the performance of transport aircraft is estimated to saturate (in the current growth pulse) at about 1.2 million pass-km/h, which is attainable with current aircraft technology and some improvements. Thereafter, in a new, hypothetical growth pulse, aircraft would have to exceed this level, requiring either large subsonic liners, accommodating perhaps a few thousand passengers, or supersonic cruise or air-breathing hypersonic transport with a more ''modest'' capacity of a few hundred passengers. The first alternative appears unlikely because it would require very powerful turbofan engines, and their rating appears to be saturating along with the aircraft performance (see Figure 8-4). Exceeding the saturation level would also require processing large numbers of passengers at terminals over short intervals, thereby creating new peak load management problems for air controllers, airports, and many service systems. Thus, a new engine (perhaps turbofan/ramjet or ram/scram) could power a supersonic/hypersonic aircraft of the next century with a performance of a few thousand passenger-kilometers per hour. The natural gas economy will provide the necessary liquid methane or other endothermic hydrocarbon fuel, and later cryogenic hydrogen.

APPENDIX

Estimation Methods for the Logistic Growth Function

This analysis of the development of transport infrastructures and systems was based on the hypothesis that technological growth and substitution processes can be described by the logistic function. In the simplest case the logistic growth function describes the technological life cycle from the early development phase through the rapid growth and expansion phase to the eventual saturation phase. Similarly, this function is used in biology to describe growth such as that of organisms and populations in constrained environments.

Here the logistic growth curve is used to analyze the expansion of air travel, aircraft productivity, and the length of surfaced roads, railway tracks, canals, and oil and gas pipelines. This was the simplest case of technology (or infrastructure) growth because in all these examples one single logistic curve described the whole technological life cycle. Unfortunately, although this is the simplest class of examples when compared with the more complex pattern of technological substitution, the statistical problems of estimating the parameters of the logistic function from the empirical data were sometimes substantial, especially in those cases in which the ultimate saturation level has not been reached.

In brief, the problem is to estimate the three parameters of the logistic function

$$x(t) = \frac{\kappa}{1 + \exp(-\alpha t - \beta)} \tag{1}$$

where t is the independent variable usually representing some unit of time, and α, β, and κ are the unknown parameters. Alternatively, the logistic growth curve can be expressed as a linear function of time by moving the (usually) unknown parameter κ to the left side of the equation and taking logarithms of both sides:

$$\ln \frac{x(t)}{\kappa - x(t)} = \alpha t + \beta . \tag{2}$$

This is a convenient form for showing the logistic growth process on semilogarithmic paper because the historical data indicate a linear secular trend (assuming that κ can be estimated from the data or that it is a priori known).

The three parameters are interpreted as follows in terms of the underlying growth process: α denotes the rate of growth; β is the location parameter (it shifts the function in time, but it does not affect the function's shape); and κ is the asymptote that bounds the function and therefore specifies the level at which the growth process saturates (as t tends to infinity, $x(t)$ approaches κ). Thus, all three parameters have clear physical interpretations, although the values of α and β are not necessarily clear intuitively.

The logistic function is a symmetrical S-shaped growth function, with an inflection point, t_0, at which the growth rate reaches a maximum, $\dot{x}(t_0)$ $= -\alpha\kappa/4$. Symmetry implies that the value of the function is half the asymptote at the point of inflection, $x(t_0) = \kappa/2$. Thus, the location parameter of the function can be defined as the point of inflection, $t_0 = -\beta/\alpha$, or, alternatively, as the time when 50 percent of the saturation level κ is reached. The growth rate of the function can be defined alternatively as the length of the time interval needed to grow from 10 to 90 percent of the saturation level κ. The length of this interval is $\Delta t = (\ln 81)/\alpha$. This second set of parameters—κ, Δt, and t_0—also specifies the logistic growth curve (in the same way that κ, α, and β do), but these alternative parameters have, in addition, clear intuitive interpretations.

A nonlinear least-squares regression method was used to estimate the three unknown parameters of the logistic function from the empirical observations. Alternative estimation algorithms were then used to test the sensitivity of the estimated parameter values to different assumptions about the errors and weighing of observations.[6] The estimation methods used in the analysis are reported in Grübler et al. (1987).

The values of the estimated parameters for the logistic growth processes, as well as the correlation coefficient R^2 and uncertainty ranges for the parameters, are given in Table 8-1. Estimation of the uncertainty ranges is based on a Monte Carlo simulation approach by Debecker and Modis (1986) for the three-parameter logistic function. A total of 33,693 different S-curves were generated and subsequently fitted by the logistic function providing values for κ, Δt, and t_0, with known and varying distributions of statistical fluctuations. Debecker and Modis concluded that the value of the estimated asymptote κ is the most sensitive (it varies the most), depending on the amount and accuracy of the data available. Their results indicated that as a rule of thumb the uncertainty of parameter κ will be less than 20 percent within a 95 percent confidence level, provided that at least half of the data are available (at least up to the point of inflection) and that they are at least 10 percent accurate. A more comprehensive treatment of uncertainty ranges and estimation methods is given in Grübler et al. (1987).

In all cases, except Figure 8-18, the values of the estimated parameters were within the specified uncertainty ranges. Even alternative algorithms used to estimate the parameters provided values within the specified ranges.

The Technological Substitution Models and Parameter Estimates

In general, the examples of technological substitution are inherently more complex than the determination of single logistic growth pulses. From a statistical point of view, however, the estimation of substitution processes is much simpler. By setting $\kappa = 1$, a three-parameter logistic function $x(t)$ can be normalized by setting $f(t) = x(t)/\kappa$. For given values of κ, it then reduces to a function with two unknown parameters. In the examples of technological substitution, this known asymptote specifies the size of the "market" in which old technologies are replaced by new ones. In the simplest case, there are only two technologies. The market shares are $f(t)$ for the new technology and $1 - f(t)$ for the old technology (Fisher and Pry, 1971). Thus, only the values of t_0 and Δt must be determined from the observations.

Fisher and Pry used the two-parameter logistic function to describe a large number of technological substitution processes. They assumed that once substitution of the new for the old had progressed as far as a few percent, it would proceed to completion along a logistic substitution curve

$$\ln \frac{f(t)}{1 - f(t)} = \alpha t + \beta \ . \tag{3}$$

Ordinary least squares were used to estimate parameters Δt and t_0 in

TABLE 8-1 Estimates of the Three-Parameter Logistic Function

Figure	Units	κ^a	κ-Range^b	Δt^c	Δt-Range^d	t_0^e	R^{2f}
8-1	10^9 Pass-km/yr	1,747.2	±91.9	30.0	±0.8	1977	0.996
8-2	10^6 Pass-km/h	199.5	±10.5	30.0	±0.8	1977	0.996
8-3	10^3 Pass-km/h	1,224.4	±197.5	30.8	±1.0	1971	0.994
8-4	Pistons (hp)	3,858.4	±137.3	29.7	±0.7	1936	0.977
8-4	Jets (kg)	28,380.0	±910.0	25.6	±0.6	1967	0.968
8-7	10^6 Vehicles	358.8	±76.3	95.5	±3.7	1994	0.997
8-10	10^3 mi	3,485.8	±111.8	58.6	±1.3	1948	0.996
8-11	10^3 mi	319.5	±10.3	54.0	±1.2	1890	0.998
8-11	(Decline)	319.5	(None)	−117.8	±4.8	2001	0.952
8-13	Miles	4,003.9	±128.1	28.9	±0.6	1832	0.991
8-18	10^3 mi	238.8	(None)	59.2	(None)	1937	0.960
8-18	(Alternative)	246.5	±8.5	78.7	±1.8	1937	0.983
8-19	10^3 mi	1,428.8	±56.9	60.2	±1.5	1965	0.993

^{a}Saturation level.
^{b}Range of uncertainty in saturation level.
^{c}Time constant, in years.
^{d}Range of uncertainty in saturation level.
^{e}Date at inflection point.
^{f}Correlation coefficient.

all cases in which one old technology is replaced by a new. Table 8-2 gives the estimated parameter values, the estimation period, and the correlation coefficients for the three examples given in this chapter.

In dealing with more than two competing technologies, a generalized version of the Fisher-Pry model was used because logistic substitution cannot be preserved in all phases of the substitution process. Every given technology undergoes three distinct substitution phases: growth, saturation, and decline. The growth phase is similar to the Fisher-Pry substitution, but it usually ends before complete market takeover is reached. It is followed by the saturation phase, which is not logistic but which encompasses the slowing of growth and the beginning of decline. After the saturation phase of a technology, its market share declines logistically (for example, see the path of railway and road substitution in Figure 8-14 and coal substitution in Figure 8-17).

It is assumed that only one technology saturates the market at any given time, that declining technologies fade away steadily at logistic rates "uninfluenced" by competition from new technologies, and that new technologies enter the market and grow at logistic rates. The current saturating technology is then left with the residual market share and is forced to follow a nonlogistic path that curves from growth to decline and connects its period of logistic growth to its subsequent period of logistic decline. After the current saturating technology has reached a logistic rate of decline, the next oldest technology enters its saturation phase, and the process is repeated until all technologies but the most recent are in decline.

For example, n competing technologies are ordered chronologically according to their appearance in the market, technology 1 being the oldest and technology n the youngest (i.e., $i = 1, 2, \ldots, n$). Thus, all technologies with indices k, where $k < j$, will saturate before the technology with index j, and technologies l, where $l > j$, will saturate after technology j.

The historical time series is denoted by $x(t)$, where the indices $i = 1, 2, \ldots, n$ represent the competing technologies and t the time points (year, month, etc.) of the historical period for which data are available. The fractional market shares of competing technologies, $f_i(t)$, are obtained by normalizing the sum of the absolute shares to one:

$$f_i(t) = \frac{x_i(t)}{\sum_j x_j(t)} . \tag{4}$$

By applying the linear transform of the logistic function to the fractional market shares,

TABLE 8-2 Estimates of the Two-Parameter Logistic Function

Figure	Units	Estimation Period	Δt^a	$t_0{}^b$	R^{2c}
8-6	10^6 Vehicles				
	Horses	1900–1919	−12.3	1916	0.999
	Cars	1900–1919	12.3	1916	0.999
8-9	10^3 Miles				
	Unsurfaced	1904–1982	−72.7	1948	0.967
	Surfaced	1904–1982	72.7	1948	0.967
8-12	10^3 Locomotives				
	Steam	1939–1957	−12.6	1951	0.992
	Diesel	1939–1957	12.6	1951	0.992
8-14	10^3 Miles				
	Canals	1840–1900	−59.9	1841	0.985
	Railways	1840–1860	55.0	1841	0.999
	Roads	1890–1940	86.5	1915	0.996
	Airways	1930–1980	127.5	2030	0.990
8-15	10^9 Pass-km/yr				
	Railways	1950–1980	−47.9	1921	0.982
	Buses	1950–1980	−125.2	1862	0.885
	Cars	(Saturation)			
	Airways	1950–1980	63.3	2004	0.969
8-17	GW-yr/yr^d				
	Wood	1860–1900	−61.9	1883	0.992
	Coal	1830–1895	69.4	1885	0.989
	Oil	1890–1950	70.6	1886	0.960
	Natural Gas	1890–1965	99.0	1985	0.975

[a]Time constant, in years.
[b]Date at inflection point.
[c]Correlation coefficient.
[d]GW = gigawatt.

$$y_i(t) = \ln \left[\frac{f_i(t)}{1 - f_i(t)} \right], \tag{5}$$

a transformed time series with piecewise linear secular trends can be obtained. In fact, only three distinct possibilities exist: a decreasing or an increasing linear trend or a phase of linear increase that is connected by a nonlinear saturation phase to a phase of linear decline. The oldest technology ($i = 1$) always displays a declining linear trend, and the youngest technology ($i = n$) an increasing linear trend (see Figure 8-17). These linear trends can be estimated, including the increasing linear trends of technologies that enter the saturation phase during the historical period.

Ordinary least squares were used to estimate the linear trends for each competing technology. Table 8-2 gave the estimated parameter values for the three multiple substitution processes used here, as well as the estimation period (historical time interval for which the parameters were estimated) and the correlation coefficient. Parameter values were not given for cars in Figure 8-15 because they have been saturating during the entire historical period. Consequently, their substitution path is specified by the model.

Each estimated linear equation with estimated parameters Δt and t_0 can be transported into a logistic function with coefficients α and β:

$$f_i(t) = \frac{1}{1 + \exp(-\alpha_i t - \beta_i)} \tag{6}$$

where $f_i(t)$ is now the estimated fractional market shares of technology i. Because such a logistic function does not capture the saturation phases and represents only growing or declining logistic trends,

$$\sum_{i=1}^{n} f_i(t)$$

may exceed 1 for some value of t, although it must be equal to 1 for all t. Thus, the $n - 1$ estimated logistic equations were left in their original form (6)—that is, as specified by coefficients α_i and β_i—and one of the n equations was defined as a residual

$$f_j(t) = 1 - \sum_{i \neq j} \frac{1}{1 + \exp(-\alpha_i t - \beta_i)}, \tag{7}$$

that is, as the difference between 1 and the sum of the $n - 1$ estimated market shares $f_i(t)$. The latter equation represents the oldest still growing technology, j, such that $\alpha_j \geq 0$ where $\alpha_{j-1} < 0$ and $j > 1$. The selected technology cannot, however, be the oldest technology (i.e., $j \neq 1$), because the oldest technology is replaced by the newer technologies and, consequently, its market shares decline logistically from the start (i.e., $\alpha_1 < 0$).

Thus, initially, there are $n - 1$ technologies denoted by indices $i \neq j$ that follow logistic substitution paths, and one technology, j, that reflects the residual of the market—that is, the complement of the sum of other technologies and 1. Based on the point in time, t_j, at which technology j is defined as a residual, application of the linear transform of the logistic function to the market shares of technology j, defined above, produces a nonlinear function that can be written in the form of equation (5).

This function has a negative curvature. It increases, then passes through a maximum at which technology j has its greatest market penetration, and finally decreases. After the slope becomes negative the curvature diminishes for a time, indicating that $f_j(t)$ is approaching the logistic form. But then, unless technology j is shifted into its period of logistic decline, the curvature will begin to increase as newer technologies acquire larger market shares. Phenomenological evidence from a number of substitutions suggests that the end of the saturation phase should be identified with the point at which the curvature of $y_i(t)$, relative to its slope, reaches its minimum value. This criterion is taken as the final constraint in this generalization of the substitution model, and from it the coefficients for the jth technology in its logistic decline are determined.

Thus, the point in time at which the rate of decrease of $y_j(t)$ approximates a constant is determined. From this point on, the rate of change is set equal to this constant, thereby defining a new logistic function. This point of constant slope is approximated by requiring that the relative change of slope is minimal,

$$\frac{\ddot{y}_j(t)}{\dot{y}_j(t)} = \text{minimum} \tag{8}$$

for $t_j \leq t < t_e$, $\ddot{y}_j(t) < 0$, and $\dot{y}_j(t) < 0$.

If this condition is satisfied (the point in time at which this occurs is $t_{j+1} > t_j$), the new coefficients for technology j can be determined as

$$\alpha_j = \dot{y}_j(t_{j+1}) \tag{9}$$

and

$$\beta_j = y_j(t_{j+1}) - \dot{y}_j(t_{j+1})t_{j+1}. \tag{10}$$

After time point t_j, technology $j + 1$ enters its residual phase. The process is then repeated until either the last technology n enters the saturation phase or the end of the time interval (t_e) is encountered.

These expressions, which have been developed in algorithmic form, determine the temporal relationships between competing technologies.

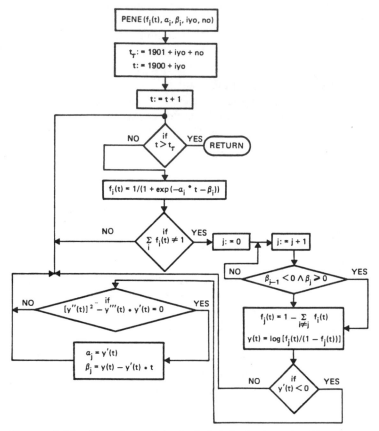

FIGURE 8-20   Flowchart of the logistic substitution algorithm.

Figure 8-20 is a flowchart of the algorithm that describes the logistic substitution process. A more detailed description of this procedure and the software package for the generalized logistic substitution model is given in Nakicenovic (1979, 1984).

NOTES

1. One general finding of a large number of studies is that many growth processes follow characteristic S-shaped curves. A logistic function is one of the most widely applied S-shaped growth curves and is denoted by $x/(\kappa - x) = \exp(\alpha t + \beta)$, where t is the independent variable usually representing some unit of time; α, β, and κ are constants; x is the actual level of growth achieved; and $\kappa - x$ is the amount of growth still to be achieved before the (usually unknown) saturation level κ is reached. Taking logarithms of both sides results in the left-hand side of the equation being expressed as a linear function of time so that the secular trend of a logistic growth process appears as a straight line when plotted in this way. Substituting $f = x/\kappa$ in the equation expresses the growth process in terms of fractional share f of the asymptotic level κ reached—that is, the equation becomes $f/(1 - f) = \exp(\alpha t + \beta)$.

2. This period of elapsed time we call Δt, and we define it as the time elapsed between the achievement of 1 and 50 percent of the saturation level κ (in this example $\Delta t = 30.0$ yr). Given the symmetry of the logistic function the same time is required for the increase from 50 to 99 percent of the saturation level. An alternative definition of Δt is the time elapsed between the achievement of the 10 and 90 percent level. This definition of Δt differs slightly from its first definition, but for all practical applications both definitions can be used interchangeably.

3. A large number of studies have found that the substitution of a new technology for an old one, expressed in fractional terms, follows characteristic S-shaped curves. Fisher and Pry (1971) formulated a simple but powerful model of technological substitution by postulating that the replacement of an old technology by a new one proceeds along the logistic growth curve $f/(1 - f) = \exp(\alpha t + \beta)$ where t is the independent variable usually representing some unit of time, α and β are constants, f is the fractional market share of the new competitor, and $1 - f$ is that of the old one.

4. The fractional shares (f) are not plotted directly but as the linear transformation of the logistic curve—that is, $f/(1 - f)$ (in this more general case, f is the fractional market share taken by a given energy and $(1 - f)$ is the sum of the market shares of all other competing transport infrastructures). This form of presentation reveals the logistic substitution path to be an almost linear secular trend with small annual perturbations. Thus, the presence of some linear trends in Figure 8-14 indicates where the fractional substitution of transport infrastructures follows a logistic curve.

   In dealing with more than two competing technologies, the Fisher-Pry model must be generalized because in such cases logistic substitution cannot be preserved in all phases of the substitution process. Every competitor undergoes three distinct substitution phases: growth, saturation, and decline. This process is illustrated by the substitution path of railway tracks, which curves through a maximum from increasing to declining market shares (see Figure 8-14). In the model of the substitution process, it is assumed that only one competitor is in the saturation phase at any given time, that declining technologies fade away steadily at logistic rates, and that new competitors enter the market and grow at logistic rates. As a result the saturating technology is left with the residual market shares (i.e., the difference between one and the sum of fractional market shares of all other competitors) and is forced to follow a nonlogistic path that joins its period of growth to its subsequent period of decline. After the current saturating competitor has reached a logistic rate of decline, the next oldest competitor enters its saturation phase, and the process is repeated until all but the most recent competitor are in decline. A more comprehensive description of the model and assumptions is given in Nakicenovic (1979).

5. As in Figure 8-14, the fractional shares f are not plotted directly but as the linear transformation of the logistic curve—that is, $f/(1 - f)$ (as the ratio of the market share taken by a given energy source over the sum of the market shares of all other competing energy sources). The form of presentation in Figure 8-17 reveals the logistic substitution path as an almost linear secular trend with small annual perturbations. Thus, the presence of some linear trends in Figure 8-17 indicates where the fractional substitution of energy sources follows a logistic curve.
6. In this particular application the difference was in the assumptions about weighing of the observations in the estimation procedure—for example, whether unit- or data-dependent weights are used.

BIBLIOGRAPHY

Angelucci, E., and P. Matricardi. 1977. Practical Guide to World Airplanes, vols. 1–4. Milan: Mondatori (in Italian).

Debecker, A., and T. Modis (Digital Equipment Corporation, Geneva, Switzerland). 1986. Determination of the uncertainties in S-curve logistic fits. Paper submitted to the Sixth International Symposium on Forecasting, Paris, June 15–18, 1986.

Epstein, R. C. 1928. The Automobile Industry, Its Economic and Commercial Development. Chicago: A. W. Shaw Co.

Fisher, J. C., and R. H. Pry. 1971. A simple substitution model of technological change. Technological Forecasting and Social Change 3:75–88.

Grey, C. G., ed. 1969. Jane's All the World's Aircraft. London: David and Charles Publishers.

Grübler, A., and N. Nakicenovic. 1987. The Dynamic Evolution of Methane Technologies. WP-87-2. Laxenburg, Austria: International Institute for Applied Systems Analysis.

Grübler, A., N. Nakicenovic, and M. Posch. 1987. Algorithms and Software Package for Estimating S-shaped curves. Laxenburg, Austria: International Institute for Applied Systems Analysis.

Marchetti, C. 1979. Energy systems—the broader context. Technological Forecasting and Social Change 14:191–203.

Marchetti, C. 1983. The automobile in a system context, the past 80 years and the next 20 years. Technological Forecasting and Social Change 23:3–23.

Marchetti, C. 1986. Fifty-year pulsation in human affairs, analysis of some physical indicators. Futures (June):376–388.

Marchetti, C., and N. Nakicenovic. 1979. The Dynamics of Energy Systems and the Logistic Substitution Model. RR-79-13. Laxenburg, Austria: International Institute for Applied Systems Analysis.

Martino, J. P. 1983. Technological Forecasting for Decision Making. 2d ed. New York: North-Holland.

Nakicenovic, N. 1979. Software Package for the Logistic Substitution Model. RR-79-12. Laxenburg, Austria: International Institute for Applied Systems Analysis.

Nakicenovic, N. 1984. Growth to Limits, Long Waves and the Dynamics of Technology. Ph.d. dissertation. University of Vienna.

Nakicenovic, N. 1986. The automobile road to technological change, diffusion of the automobile as a process of technological substitution. Technological Forecasting and Social Change 29:309–340.

Reynolds, R., and A. Pierson. 1942. Fuel Wood Used in the United States, 1630–1930. U.S. Department of Agriculture, Forest Service Circular No. 641.

Schumpeter, J. A. 1935. The analysis of economic change. Review of Economic Statistics 7:2–10.

Schurr, S., and B. Netschert. 1960. Energy in the American Economy, 1850–1975: An Economic Study of its History and Prospects. Baltimore, Md.: Johns Hopkins University Press (for Resources for the Future, Inc.).

Taylor, G. R. 1962. The Transportation Revolution, 1815–1860. Vol. 4, The Economic History of the United States. New York: Holt, Rinehart and Winston.

U.S. Department of Energy. 1982. Monthly Energy Review, August 1982. DOE/EIA-0035(82/08). Washington, D.C.: Energy Information Administration.

U.S. Forest Service. 1946. A Reappraisal of the Forest Situation, Potential Requirements for Timber Products in the United States. Forest Service Report No. 2.

9

Air Traffic Congestion: Problems and Prospects

THOMAS CRAIG

Each year, hundreds of millions of passengers are flown all over the United States. They rely on air travel to conduct their businesses and maintain ties with friends and family. Although the airline industry originated more than 50 years ago, it is still a growth industry, with a rate of increase faster than the growth rate of the nation's gross national product (GNP). Moreover, air travel is likely to develop its dominant position because no projected mode of transportation could displace it as the quickest and most efficient way of moving people from city to city. Nor are more exotic forms of communication, such as video conferencing, expected to displace it. By any yardstick, air travel is a success.

Yet this very success has created problems. Because so many people are flying on so many planes, the airports and airways of the United States are no longer adequate to move them smoothly to their preferred destinations.

Airport congestion has many causes—airline marketing policies, airport layout, and noise considerations are examples—but one principal effect: delay. The dollar amount of the cost of annual air travel delay is difficult to state with precision, but it is certainly large (Table 9-1). This cost would be even larger if it were possible to quantify the frustration of millions of travelers who are experiencing more and more delays in an ever more crowded system.

The problems of relieving congestion in the air and in airports do not have simple solutions. The authority and responsibility for tackling them clearly lie with the Federal Aviation Administration (FAA). But the au-

TABLE 9-1   Estimated Annual Cost of Air Traffic Delay, 1984

Cost of Delays	Amount
Aircraft	
Average delay per operation (minutes)	6.8
Air carrier operations (thousands)	10,839.5
Total delay (thousands of hours)	1,228.5
Average cost of delay per hour	1,647.0
Total cost of delay to aircraft (millions of dollars)	2,023.0
Passengers	
Passenger hours lost (millions)	117.9
Value of passenger time lost (dollars per hour)	22.3
Total cost of delay to passengers (millions of dollars)	2,629.3
Total cost of delay (passengers plus aircraft) (millions of dollars)	4,652.3

SOURCE: Transportation Systems Center. Airport Capacity Enhancement Plan. 1986. Cambridge, Mass.

thority for relieving congestion on the ground is divided among many entities and is thus a controversial and highly politicized issue. Consequently, constructing new airports and improving old ones are slow, painful processes. Under the circumstances, there is little hope that many, if any, new airports will be built in the United States during the rest of this century.

Although its authority is clear, the FAA still faces a difficult task in tackling the problems of delay due to congestion in the air because solutions require federal funding and the cooperation and agreement of various parties. Congress, faced with extremely high deficits, is slow to provide adequate funding to upgrade the air traffic control (ATC) system. Moreover, most of the proposed solutions are technical, and controversy and delay surround the implementation of each new proposed piece of advanced technology. In many cases the parties involved cannot concur because they genuinely disagree on the technical merits of alternative systems. Improvements are also delayed because the various factions involved take divergent stances on the merits of the National Airspace Plan, which is the overall FAA blueprint for reaching multibillion-dollar partial solutions to the congestion problem. Although the FAA is the sole designated authority for operating and improving the federal airways system, it is still subject to the wishes of Congress and the public as expressed in federal legislation. The FAA administers the law; it does not create it.

CAUSES OF AIRPORT CONGESTION

Airline marketing policies, which are driven by passengers' preference for prime-time flying, contribute significantly to the problem of air travel

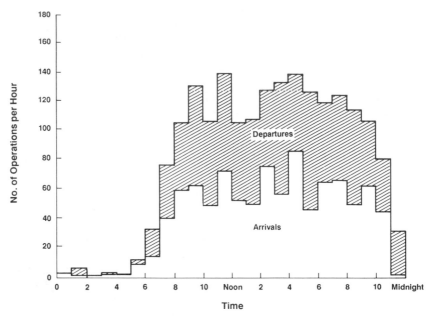

FIGURE 9-1   Scheduled operations at Atlanta's Hartsfield International Airport.

demand exceeding supply. As a result the number of planes scheduled to arrive and depart almost simultaneously at an airport can overwhelm the system (Figure 9-1 and Table 9-2). For example, as shown in Table 9-2, 41 aircraft operations are scheduled for the first 10 minutes of the hour at Atlanta's Hartsfield Airport; unscheduled flights raise the number even higher. Such situations can generate backups and cause delays that last throughout the day. A New York area airport official, in summing up the problem of schedule bunching, stated, ''When there are delays, they (the airlines) say, 'Others will blink first.' Well, nobody is going to blink.''

Aircraft weight classes and differences in speeds contribute to congestion because these variations affect air traffic control processing. Within the terminal area, radar separation that must be maintained between planes is established at 3 nautical miles (NM). Arriving aircraft that are following a heavy jet, however, must be separated by 4, 5, or 6 NM, depending on the weight class of the subsequent flights. All departing planes following the heavy jet are under the same constraints. Consequently, as the number of heavy jet operations increases, an airport's actual arrival and departure capacity can be significantly reduced, thus increasing congestion and delay (Figure 9-2). Because of these variations in terminal area and approach speeds, controllers must ensure that initial spacings exceed the required

TABLE 9-2 Atlanta-Hartsfield Scheduled Traffic for 1 Hour in November 1985[a]

Time	Arrivals	Departures	Cumulative	Time	Arrivals	Departures	Cumulative
11:00	8	4	12	11:30	3		70
11:01			12	11:31	1		71
11:02	1		13	11:32	3		74
11:03	1		14	11:33			74
11:04	1	2	17	11:34	3		77
11:05	2	7	26	11:35	8		85
11:06		1	27	11:36	2		87
11:07		2	29	11:37	3		90
11:08	1	2	32	11:38			90
11:09	2	1	35	11:39	1		91
11:10	3	3	41	11:40	7		98
11:11		1	42	11:41			98
11:12	3	1	46	11:42			98
11:13			46	11:43			98
11:14		2	48	11:44			98
11:15		2	50	11:45			98
11:16			50	11:46			98
11:17			50	11:47	1	5	104
11:18		1	51	11:48		2	106
11:19	1	1	53	11:49		2	108
11:20		3	56	11:50		7	115
11:21	2		58	11:51		2	117
11:22	1		59	11:52		1	118
11:23	1		60	11:53		1	119
11:24	2		62	11:54		1	120
11:25	1		63	11:55		4	124
11:26	1		64	11:56			124
11:27			64	11:57		2	126
11:28	1		65	11:58		2	128
11:29	2		67	11:59		1	129

[a]Add 6.5 percent for typical nonscheduled traffic.

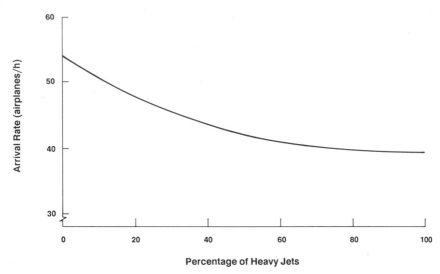

FIGURE 9-2   Influence of heavy jets on arrival throughput. The figure assumes the airplane mix is composed of large and heavy jets.

distance when a slower aircraft is leading so that the distance between the planes is not less than the allowed minimum when the leading aircraft crosses the landing threshold. The resulting spacings can double the target minimum separation as aircraft are vectored to the final approach course at various distances on the landing runway. When the trailing aircraft is slower, separation increases at the threshold to more than the minimum and throughput is lost. The same is true when planes with different climb speeds depart consecutively.

One obvious way of reducing congestion lies in increasing the size of airplanes so that more passengers travel on each flight. This strategem can succeed, provided allowance is made for the increased wake vortex separation required when the maximum gross weight of the airplane exceeds 300,000 pounds (see Figure 9-3).

The layout of an airport can also affect congestion, either positively or negatively. Runway spacings, the point of intersection of the runways, the location and turnoff angle of exits, and runway length are all relevant factors when considering an airport's capacity. Figures 9-4 and 9-5 show typical diversity in airport configurations. The air traffic control procedures developed for the variety of airport configurations must include safety margins that can limit operations when necessary, particularly in the case of bad weather. Such safety margins are required because pilots and controllers still rely in part on their ability to see approaching traffic. Thus, for example, at Chicago's O'Hare Airport and at Dallas-Ft. Worth, triple arrival streams to a set of parallel runways and one intersecting runway are used only in daylight with a ceiling of at least 1,000 feet (ft) and 3 miles' visibility—and, in Chicago, when runways are dry.

Several procedures tailored to runway spacings have been developed for use in any weather conditions at busy airports. Such procedures include parallel approaches to runways separated by at least 2,500 ft, using reduced spacings (2 NM) between arrivals on the adjacent instrument landing system (ILS) localizer courses; and simultaneous ILS approaches to parallel runways separated by at least 4,300 ft.

At Newark International Airport, tests are being conducted to reduce the in-trial spacing between successive arrivals to that required to accommodate minimum runway occupancy time (ROT). The tests are based on the concept that when the average ROT is 50 seconds (s) or less, a separation of 2.5 NM is adequate unless wake turbulence rules apply. The

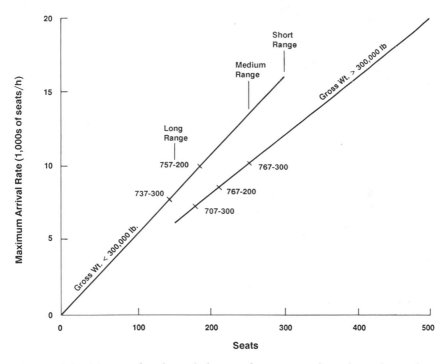

FIGURE 9-3 Impact of wake turbulence rules on seat throughput. Increasing airplane size to increase seat throughput can produce a reduction in throughput if airplane gross weight exceeds 300,000 pounds.

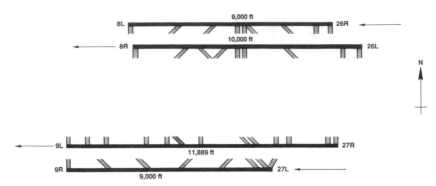

FIGURE 9-4   Runway operation patterns at Atlanta's Hartsfield International Airport. West flow operated 60 percent of the time; reverse or east flow operated 40 percent of the time.

procedure cannot be used at all airports, however, because the 50-s average is not attainable at some locations.

Airport capacity can also be affected by congestion on the ground. The O'Hare Airport runways and air traffic control system currently can process more traffic per hour than the gates will accommodate. Many ground delays are caused by this situation.

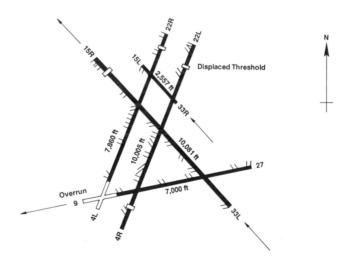

FIGURE 9-5   Runway operation patterns at Boston's Logan International Airport: four configurations with the west flow configuration operated 42 percent of the time.

TABLE 9-3   U.S. Air Traffic Forecasts

| Year Beginning | Traffic Volume (billions of RPM[a]) | | | | Size of U.S. Jet Fleet (number of units) | |
| | Boeing | | FAA | | | |
	Domestic	Int'l.	Domestic	Int'l.	Boeing	FAA
1986	293	77	279	68	3,248	3,031
1990	351	88	341	82	3,446	3,412
1997	480	119	479	119	3,821	3,976

[a]RPM = revenue passenger miles.

Environmental concerns and local noise abatement rules influence the capacity of many, if not all, major airports. If noise problems limit the airport to a single initial departure track when actually multiple runways are available, the airport's departure capacity can be reduced by two-thirds or more. Arrival track location requirements can also limit capacity. The Charlotte-Douglas Airport offers a classic example of this situation: only one of the three runways may be used during church hours, and only two may be used during the school year.

Some airports experience particularly serious congestion or delay when weather conditions do not permit visual approaches. Denver, San Francisco, St. Louis, and Minneapolis all fall into this category. Arrival capacity can be reduced by 50 percent or more when visual separation procedures cannot be used.*

PROSPECTS FOR IMPROVEMENT

FAA forecasts offer no prospect of relief from airport congestion and delay, at least as far as scheduled air carrier operations are concerned. Tables 9-3 through 9-6 show both FAA and Boeing projections for certain classes of commercial air traffic. Table 9-3 shows, for instance, that both the FAA and Boeing forecast continued growth in the volume of air traffic and modest increases in the size of the U.S. jet fleet. Both sets of projections convey the same message: air taxi/commuter operations are making, and will continue to make, heavy demands on airport and airway facilities without moving a commensurate share of the traffic.

Defining this situation is not meant as an indictment of the air taxi/commuter airlines. They are, in fact, doing precisely what the architects

*The author is indebted to Boeing Air Traffic Control Systems Analysis for this discussion of conditions contributing to airport congestion.

TABLE 9-4 Boeing and FAA Projections of Commercial Air Carrier Operations Including Air Taxi/Commuter Operations (in millions of tower operations)

Year	Air Carrier Operations		Air Taxi/Commuter Operations	
	Boeing	FAA	Boeing[a]	FAA
1986	11.8	11.9	—	7.3
1990	13.1	13.4	—	8.7
1997	14.2	15.2	—	11.2

[a]Boeing has no forecast of air taxi/commuter operations.

of deregulation envisioned—providing service to smaller communities that want the speed and convenience of air travel. Nevertheless, the impact on major facilities is unacceptable. The system cannot afford to have 42 percent of commercial air carrier movements account for less than 8 percent of the passenger enplanements.*

One proposed way of easing the growing congestion at major hubs is to bypass, or overfly, these cities. Unfortunately, most air travelers in the United States either come from a large hub or want to get to one. In fact, about 92 percent of all passengers begin and end their journeys at a large hub, regardless of the route flown in between. This limits the amount of relief that might be achieved by overflying.

In short, airport congestion will continue to be a major air travel problem throughout this century. Solutions require cooperation among the many interests involved, each of whom approaches the problem from a slightly different point of view. The FAA must be involved, along with the local airport authority; the community; special interest groups that represent environmental concerns, the airlines, and the airframe and engine manufacturers; Congress; the financial community, which must float bonds; and finally, the passenger, who pays the penalty for delay in lost time and frazzled nerves. The chances of an agreement among these various entities on a set of actions designed to relieve airport congestion seem remote.

The FAA now has in place a plan to meet its responsibilities for relieving airside congestion. First released in December 1981 the plan includes four main air traffic control programs. The cornerstone of the plan is a new

---

*Each time a passenger actually boards an airplane is a passenger enplanement. For example, one person traveling from Carmel, California, to Buffalo, New York, would represent four enplanements if routed over San Francisco, Chicago, and New York City on four different carriers.

TABLE 9-5   Projected Commuter Air Traffic in Relation to Total
Passenger Enplanements (in millions)

Year	Scheduled Passenger Enplanements		
	Total	Commuter	Percentage
1986	413.1	25.9	6.3
1990	500.3	35.0	7.0
1997	693.1	54.5	7.9

SOURCE: Federal Aviation Administration. February 1986. FAA Aviation Forecasts,
Fiscal Years 1986–1997. Washington, D.C.: U.S. Department of Transportation.

state-of-the-art computer system, which provides the increased capacity
needed to handle growth in traffic. The new system will also integrate
and automate control services both in the terminal and en route. The first
installation was completed in Seattle in late 1986; the system is expected
to go on-line in June 1988. Initially, the computers will use the existing
air traffic control computer program. All computers are expected to be in
operation 6 months after delivery.

An advanced automation system is the second component of the plan.
The advanced system uses minicomputers to improve controllers' productivity through modernized software and controller hardware. Third,
the voice-switching and control system will automatically switch any in-
trafacility voice communication between controller positions. Fourth, the
consolidation of 200 terminals and en route radar facilities into 23 area
control facilities will bring significant savings in manpower and costs.
When the fully modernized system is in place by the late 1990s, it will
be able to handle 25 percent more operations than was possible in 1980,
with a controller work force of fewer than 10,000.

The plan to modernize the nation's air traffic control system is now
being put into operation, but budgetary problems are jeopardizing its timely
completion. Congress must reauthorize the funding for the plan each year.

TABLE 9-6   Projected Commuter Operations as a Share of Total Air
Carrier Operations (in millions of tower operations)

Year	Air Carrier	Total (including commuters)	Commuter Share (percentage)
1986	11.9	19.2	38.0
1990	13.4	22.1	39.4
1997	15.2	26.4	42.4

SOURCE: Federal Aviation Administration. February 1986. FAA Aviation Forecasts,
Fiscal Years 1986–1997. Washington, D.C.: U.S. Department of Transportation.

Some parts of the plan are already 1 to 2 years behind schedule. The delay is due to a combination of factors: an $80-million shortfall in FAA operating funds, the pressures of the Gramm-Rudman-Hollings Act, the failure to use the aviation trust fund surplus, and congressional mandates that govern criteria for awarding contracts.

Reducing congestion is further complicated by the FAA's mandate to keep the airways safe. One way to ensure safety is to control the flow of traffic. One metering system for this purpose is already in place. But as air carriers plan to offer more flights to meet increased consumer demand, it seems safe to predict that air travelers will still be plagued by delays in the years ahead.

Air travel has helped to create modern cities. In urban areas, however, the quality of life is an important concern to most of its inhabitants, and there is no doubt that wasted time and inefficient transportation systems are negative elements of city life. For air carriers and government agencies charged with managing the air transport system, the need is growing to compromise and so break the logjam of delays. It would be an ironic twist if air travel played a major role in the cities' failure to provide a high-quality way of life. The survival of the cities depends on transportation systems that can also grow and survive without paying the penalty of delay and inefficiency.

10
Combining Communications and Computing: Telematics Infrastructures

DEAN GILLETTE

Today's combinations of computers and telecommunication devices to form new infrastructures are as important to national economies in the twentieth century as the combination of steam engines and carts to form railroads in the nineteenth. The new infrastructures support the development of businesses and industries of the "information society"—businesses and industries that provide jobs for over half of the U.S. work force.[1] Of all the names suggested for the new combination the most commonly used is *telematics*. It is the anglicized version of *télématique*, a word coined by Nora and Minc (1980) in their book *L'Informatisation de la Société*.[2]

Telematics today is directly used in almost every sector of our socioeconomic structure. For example, many people find automatic teller machines convenient for personal financial transactions. A *Wall Street Journal* reporter types a story into a word processor in New York, and the paper is printed and published in Chicago, San Francisco, and Miami the same day as in New York. Automobile manufacturers tailor production schedules to fill dealers' orders for cars with specific arrangements of features. And the federal government relies on telematics for functions ranging from agency management to command and control of national defense systems, which themselves contain integrated communication and computer infrastructures.

The technical and economic feasibility of such a range of telematics uses was achieved well over a decade ago. Newspapers and magazines, as well as learned journals, constantly describe new applications of telematics and growth in the variety and sophistication of old applications.

233

Much can be done with existing telematics components by imaginative applications and by building new infrastructures based on them. Even more will be possible as improvements are made in critical areas. One such area is the cost of high-speed data communication; another is the flexibility and cost of terminals. Fortunately, there is vigorous research and development in the underlying technologies, including solid-state electronics, and advances in the field should lead to decreased costs and other improvements. A third area of concern is the lack of uniform standards for the interconnection of facilities and protocols for interaction between computers of different manufacture. Progress is being made in achieving these goals also, both domestically and internationally.

The evolution and application of telematics, however, have also exacerbated certain existing social problems and introduced new ones. Theft by telecommunication is now possible, and new threats to privacy have appeared. New dichotomies between rich and poor are growing domestically and internationally. Private managers and governmental bodies face new challenges in acquiring the benefits of telematics while mitigating its harms.

This chapter reports on the nature and status of telematics infrastructures and on opportunities for improvements. It also touches briefly on prospects for future telematics systems and a few of the social issues such systems raise.

COMPONENTS OF A TELEMATICS INFRASTRUCTURE

Computer functions have been used in communications since about 1900, first with the introduction of the dial-controlled switch to make automatic telephone connections and, more obviously, since the 1950s when computers were attached to the telephone network to measure usage and computer charges. (The switching and billing computers, however, are internal to the network and are not accessible to the telephone user after a connection is made.) Communication lines carry information among processing, storage, control, input, and output functions in a computer. Indeed, transmission speed and data transmission capacity are critical, sometimes limiting, factors in designing advanced computer systems.

The interaction of computing and communications in telematics differs from the use of computers in communications. In telematics, at least one terminal on a communications connection is a computer, and information is sent over the communications network in machine-sensible form, normally in formats and at speeds completely incomprehensible to humans.

Each telematics system has both physical and logical parts. The physical parts are the data transmission channels, the associated data switching systems, and the computers at terminals or nodes in the network. The logical parts are the standards and protocols for interconnecting and using the physical parts. In applications in which data processing is distributed, as with automatic teller machines in banking, the organization of this distribution is an aspect of the logical part. Except for such distributions, the computers that are part of a telematics infrastructure can operate equally well standing alone and not attached to data transmission facilities. To adapt the computers to telematics applications, two types of changes are needed: the computer must be physically adapted to treat the transmission facilities as devices for input and output, and the software must be prepared to permit interaction with the data network, terminals, and other computers on the network. Thus, from the vast infrastructure of computing, we may take as unique components of telematics the logic of standards and protocols and the plan for geographical distribution of processing, both of which are to be represented in software. The applications programs of computing are not a part of the telematics infrastructure, but the infrastructure helps make their results widely available.

Data Transmission Facilities

The first electrical telecommunication system transmitted a digital signal—the Morse code of telegraphy. Today, although some communication facilities are limited to telegraph data transmission rates—fire alarm and traffic light control networks, for example—the vast bulk of communication channels are designed to transmit voice signals. Because it is readily available and can be adapted to carry data signals, the technology for telephony is the foundation of the data transmission facilities in telematics.

A component of a telematics infrastructure could be a voice-grade channel in the telephone network. A pair of wires, a "loop," connecting a home or office to a local switching system network could be such a component. The channel could be a connection through the public switched telephone network or a private, dedicated voice channel in the network of facilities that make up the communications infrastructure.

Almost any voice channel in the telephone network can transmit data at 1,200 bits per second (b/s), and 1,200-b/s modems cost less than $200. Although some pairs must be adapted, most wire pairs and all voice channels in carrier systems can carry data at a rate of 9.6 kilobits per second (kb/s). High-speed modems cost about $5,000.

In addition to voice channels, the telecommunications infrastructure contains a hierarchy of facilities that transmit digital signals at various rates. At the bottom, or zero level, of the hierarchy, we find devices that encode a continuously varying voice signal into a 64-kb/s digital signal. At the first level of the hierarchy, 24 of these signals are "time division

TABLE 10-1   The U.S. Digital
Transmission Hierarchy

Level	Data Rate (Mb/s)	Equivalent Telephone Channels
0	0.064	1
T1	1.5	24
T1A	3.1	48
T2	6.3	96
T3	44.7	672
T4	274.2	4,032

multiplexed'' into a single 1.5-megabit per second (Mb/s) stream.[3] Forty-eight 64-kb/s signals are combined at level 1A. Table 10-1 shows the hierarchy of digital signal transmission in the United States.

To begin to appreciate the potential of these existing facilities, note that the text of this chapter (about 5,000 words) could be transmitted in 0.1 s at the T1 level, and the text of all the chapters in this volume could be transmitted in 1 s at the T2 level.

The signal transmitted over any transmission medium may be at any one of several of these levels. A pair of wires with regenerative repeaters spaced at 1-mile (mi) intervals can carry a T1, T1A, or T2 level signal. A coaxial cable or microwave radio relay system, either terrestrial or satellite borne, can carry a T4 level signal. An optical fiber system can carry at least two T4 level signals, and its capacity is increasing as research and development continue.

Any digital channel in the telephone hierarchy can carry any data signal compatible with the maximum bit rate in that channel. Thus, instead of using a 64-kb/s data channel for a single voice signal, we might use it for six 9.6-kb/s data channels multiplexed in a digital logic of choice. A level 3 channel could either carry 672 voice channels or a properly encoded entertainment-grade television signal. Because the assignment of the meaning of the bits in any channel is arbitrary, these transparent channels of the communications infrastructure can be the components of a telematics infrastructure—provided a protocol to define the meaning of a stream of bits has been established.

Data Switching Facilities

The function of switching is to choose the path a message will take while traversing a communications network. The message coming into a switching system must in some way contain, or be accompanied by, an instruction to the switching system regarding the outgoing channel—a 10-digit telephone number, for example. Each switching system contains an internal connection network that establishes a path between an incoming and an outgoing transmission channel, and it contains a control function that responds to instructions to establish that path and order the connection network to do so.

Over the years, three technologies have been developed and used in switching: electromechanical, electronic, and digital systems.[4] Because almost all new transmission systems are digital, the choice of digital switches is economical in telephone systems and is natural in telematics.

Telephone network switching systems connect one voice channel to another to establish a unique circuit between the calling and the called parties. At present, 5 s or more are needed to set up a cross-country connection through local and toll switches by circuit switching. But in 5 s, 50 pages of single-spaced text could be sent on a 1.5-Mb/s data link; thus, for some applications, the time involved in circuit switching is just too long.

An alternative is to structure the network to operate like the postal service—that is, to send the address of the receiver together with the message and have them forwarded together from switching center to switching center. In such a store-and-forward system, the entire message is passed from one node and stored at the next before transmission to the subsequent node. Alternatively, a long message may be divided into "packets" of specified length—say, 1,000 bytes—each numbered and transmitted with the address of the recipient. In one protocol the packets are reassembled into the original message on reception. In another the first packet establishes a "virtual" circuit through the network for successive packets to follow.

In addition to its speed advantage, packet switching is far superior to circuit switching for transmitting messages to multiple receivers; with a change of address at the head end of the packet, messages can be sent simultaneously to many locations.

Terminals

Terminals on a telematics network are referred to as "smart" or "dumb," depending on whether they have internal data processing capabilities; a microcomputer thus is a smart terminal, and a teletypewriter is dumb. Smart or dumb, the terminals must either generate a data signal in a format acceptable for transmission or connect to an interface unit that converts formats.

Beyond the physical interconnection level, however, are the logical levels vital to computing. Two computers may have different codes for letters, different methods of structuring stored information and messages, different access procedures, and, generally, different protocols. Unless the whole telematics infrastructure is built to a single set of standards and protocols, an interface message processor (IMP) may be needed between a terminal and the network.

Aggressive development of personal computers (PCs) in the last few years has made the notion of a dumb terminal almost obsolete. PCs with startlingly great capabilities are now advertised for a few hundred dollars—prices lower than those of dumb terminals only a few years ago. Because software for logical interaction over a telematics network can now be lodged in a relatively inexpensive smart terminal, the need for IMPs should decline.

Distributed Processing

The first digital computers sat in solemn majesty in air-conditioned space, and users, like acolytes, traveled to them. Comparisons with ancient oracles were obvious. With the advent of telematics, not only could users communicate instead of traveling, but computers could be joined for work in concert on a common problem. The hierarchy of computers that support a large bank's statewide distribution of automatic teller machines is an example of such distributed processing.

The concept of geographical distribution is powerful, but exploitation of the idea to its fullest extent is difficult. One thorny problem, for example, is that of storing widely needed data. Should storage be in one place with relatively expensive communications to each computer, or should each computer store part of the data and use communications for limited access and updating? If the latter method is used, what is the logic of distribution and the plan for changes?

Parallel processing, a common term in contemporary computer design, refers more directly to the use of multiple processing units *within* a computer than to the use of distributed processing. Development of strategies and programming tools for efficient parallel processing is a formidable task expected to lead to new levels of processing speed. Such a task is distinct, however, from the effort that arranges the geographical distribution of processing that characterizes telematics.

Standards and Protocols

Interconnection standards are necessary in any physical system: rail separation in railroads, voltage level and frequency precision in power distribution, maximum pressure and pipe thread shape in water systems, frequencies of the tones in push-button telephone systems, number of lines in a television picture, and on and on.

Circuit-switched telephone networks need another layer of standards to define the process by which a connection is requested and completed. After a voice channel connection is made, however, a voice circuit is free of protocols except for limitations on bandwidth. Any language can be used, speech can be fast or slow, and two people can even talk simultaneously, if incomprehensibly.

In data communication, switched or not, additional layers of standards are needed for compatibility. Such standards cover data rates, the representation of letters and numbers, the structure in a block of bits, and the length of a packet. All such questions must be answered unambiguously before a digitally encoded message can be transmitted. In telematics, yet another level of standards is needed to achieve software compatibility among computers and between computers and terminals that may have access to several different kinds of computers.

Some aspects of standards and protocols are susceptible to analysis: choice of analog-to-digital encoding for reproducibility, for instance. Other choices, such as block length in packet switching, are more arbitrary.

If one company manufactures all the parts of a system or can completely specify a portion for an outside manufacturer, standards may be set by that company, and any arbitrary choices will be determined by fiat. Three examples are AT&T's standards for its nationwide telephone-to-telephone public switched network before the Federal Communications Commission (FCC) permitted customer-owned terminals and competitive long-distance service; IBM's System Network Architecture (SNA) for extensive telematics systems; and Xerox's Ethernet standard for local area networks. Occasionally, a private standard becomes a de facto industrywide standard, either because the initiating entity dominates the industry, as AT&T did for its telephone network plan, or because it is more convenient to adopt an existing standard than to develop a new one, as some other suppliers found in the case of Xerox's Ethernet.

When a system is not the sole responsibility of a single supplier, a forum for agreement among the many suppliers must be established. In the United States, standards may be set by professional societies (for example, the Institute of Electrical and Electronics Engineers [IEEE]) industry associations (for example, the Electronic Industry Association), government agencies, or independent groups. The American National Standards Institute (ANSI) has established rules for the structure of standards groups and the processes by which they develop and publish standards.

The International Telecommunications Union (ITU), originally established as the International Telegraph Union and now headquartered in Geneva as part of the United Nations, has been the forum for setting transborder standards for nearly 120 years. "Recommendations" for data communications are made by the Consulting Committee for International Telephone and Telegraph (CCITT). The CCITT "X.25" recommended protocol for packet switching, for example, is now almost universally used.

The International Standards Organization, which is also based in Geneva, provides another forum. Its recently published open systems interconnection (OSI) reference model for computer-to-computer communications quickly became the foundation of telematics protocols. The OSI model is an architecture that distinguishes seven layers of standards and protocols so that the task of setting standards is less likely to drift into irrelevancies. The lowest three levels are primarily concerned with data communications, and the upper three with the software issues unique to telematics. The intermediate fourth level involves data processing that helps control communications.[5]

ARRANGEMENT OF TELEMATICS SYSTEMS

Topologies and Data Flows

Data transmission channels have directionality. For example, a 1.5-Mb/s digital channel carried on a pair of wires with repeaters spaced at 1-mi intervals transmits data in only one direction; for two-way communication a second pair of wires is needed.

A one-way data channel is referred to as "simplex." A two-way channel is "full duplex," whether it uses a single medium, as in telephony, or a coordinated pair of media, such as the two simplex channels in a 1.5-Mb/s digital trunk. "Half duplex" uses a single medium alternately for transmission and reception, as in "press-to-talk" citizens' band radio communications.

The basic topologies of telematics systems are the star, bus, tree, ring, and compound arrangements shown in Figure 10-1. In the star network, all terminals, indicated by T's in boxes, are connected to a central point, and the connections must be duplex. In the bus topology, all terminals are connected to a single medium, which must be duplex; the ring is like the bus except that it uses simplex transmission. A tree might be used for one-way distribution from a single node, as in cable television; a return channel requires duplex transmission. In the star, bus, tree, and ring topologies, only one path exists from one terminal to another. In the

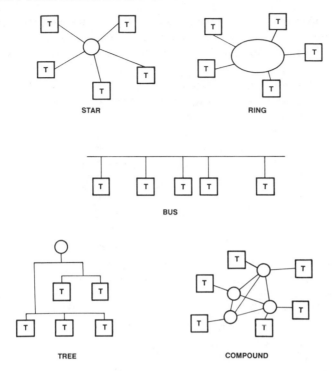

FIGURE 10-1   Local area network topologies.

compound topology, any of several paths can exist from one terminal to another, and alternate routing is possible to avoid an overload or a damaged facility. Either simplex or full duplex channels are used.

In the star and compound topologies, switching functions at the nodes control traffic flow. They use either circuit or packet switches, but they assign channels and times of transmission uniquely according to internal protocols and the addresses presented. The compound arrangement is characteristic of the public switched telephone network, which uses full channels, and nationwide packet-switched networks, which use simplex channels. The star is characteristic of a switching office serving local telephones or a telematics system in which point-of-sale terminals are polled in turn to ask if they have a transaction to carry out.

In the bus and ring topologies, the control of data flow is distributed. Each terminal may be assigned a unique time slot or frequency for transmission, and each "listens" to all slots and frequencies for messages addressed to it. These protocols are referred to, respectively, as time division multiple access (TDMA) and frequency division multiplexing

(FDM). An alternative is to provide a single channel accessible by all terminals and establish a protocol to avoid simultaneous transmission. One such protocol is token passing, in which transmission is permitted only by the terminal that has the token or password. If that terminal has no message to transmit, or after it transmits a specified block length of data, it passes the token to the next terminal in line. Another popular protocol is carrier sense multiple access with collision detection (CSMA/CD), under which all terminals listen for a signal generated by the channel when a message is being transmitted. If a terminal has a message to send and the carrier signal is absent, it transmits. If two terminals transmit simultaneously, each can detect the other's signal and that a collision has occurred. In that event, both terminals stop transmitting, wait a randomly determined period of time, then transmit again if the channel is clear.

Networks

Local area networks (LANs) are, as the name implies, data networks that serve a small area, such as a university campus or an industrial park. A star topology entered through telephone lines in a local private branch exchange may be used if data rates are low and the efficiency of packet switching is not needed. More frequently, LANs use a bus or ring topology with high-speed channels in coaxial cable or optical fibers. One example is Ethernet, which sends data at 10 Mb/s on a coaxial cable in a bus configuration and uses the CSMA/CD protocol.

Nationwide networks provide communications among LANs and among widely dispersed individual users and computers. Some nationwide networks are private, such as those in military applications, and are built to a single set of protocols. Other networks are public and must accommodate users with a variety of equipment and connecting LANs with a variety of protocols. Interface message processors may be needed to connect terminals to the network, and "gateways" may be needed to connect one network to another. Both are responsible for format and protocol conversion.

One example of a nationwide, indeed worldwide, network is BITNET, which was started in 1981 by Yale University and the City University of New York with support from IBM Corporation. It operates at 9.6 kb/s and is a store-and-forward message network. Other public networks are the Advanced Research Projects Agency Network (ARPANET) and GTE Corporation's TELENET.[6]

SOCIAL ISSUES

The development and application of the computer has been accompanied by social concerns about invasions of privacy, job displacement, the dichotomy between information-rich and information-poor populations in the United States, and a new form of Third World economic lag. The introduction of telematics has not only exacerbated these problems but has brought new ones, the most prominent of which are remote computer intrusion and a slowdown in the innovation process.

Computer Intrusion

Tapping a telephone line to listen to people talking has been a federal offense for years, and in the fall of 1986 it became a federal offense to tap a data stream. Although there are state laws, as in California, that prohibit the unauthorized use of a computer, there are also federal sanctions for an electronic intruder in, for example, Arizona who readjusts financial accounts in a California bank. Computer intrusion for the discovery of personal facts (invasion of privacy), for financial gain (theft), or merely for the "pleasure" of prying or to prove that entrance is possible ("hacking") has become prevalent enough to be a plot theme in popular movies. Fortunately, owners of data bases have become aware of their vulnerability if telephone line access is possible and are developing security measures. The ultimate security, of course, is to use closely guarded, private, dedicated communication channels or not to use telematics at all but to return to the central, noncommunicating computer, exchanging efficiency for security.

The Innovation Process

Before the advent of telematics the markets of the computer and telecommunications industries did not overlap. AT&T was barred from any business except communications by the 1956 consent decree that concluded the federal antitrust suit begun in 1949 against the company. Computer companies, on the other hand, were busy enough exploiting a rapidly advancing data processing technology. As telematics emerged as the successor to stand-alone computing, however, the distinction between communications and computing began to blur.

As this convergence of technologies was occurring, the nation's regulatory bodies were becoming disenchanted with regulation itself and were seeking ways to introduce competition as a preferred mechanism to protect consumers. One consequent action was to force AT&T to divest itself of its local telephone operations in return for relief from the provisions of the 1956 decree.[7] The expected result was "fairer" competition in intercity telecommunications and increased competition in computing.

With the removal of AT&T as the proprietor of the bulk of the national telecommunications network, two changes in the evolution of telematics have occurred: AT&T can no longer set de facto protocols and standards for the nation, and the regulatory pressure to keep depreciation rates low has evaporated. The result of the first change is that revision of standards and protocols will be slowed by the need to have competitors agree, although, as discussed earlier in this chapter, there are already forums for such deliberations.

The possibility of more rapid depreciation may be more subtle. When AT&T had its monopoly under regulation, it designed, built, and installed equipment for long lifetimes and low maintenance costs. Two hours of downtime in 40 years was an objective in the development of switching systems. Annual operating expenses were low, consonant with a regulatory desire, but the introduction of new services was also slow. With regulatory restraint gone, less will be spent on long-lived equipment, and new services will be introduced more rapidly. Shorter lifetimes, however, are equivalent to more frequent repairs. Together with the elimination of the Bell System as the end-to-end service supplier, these factors have made it more important for telematics users to develop the competence to select communication options from the variety available in the market. The management task is not new; it is similar to that needed in selecting vehicles for car pools and computers for corporate support.

PROSPECTS FOR THE FUTURE

Components

Solid-state electronics technology is fundamental to all physical aspects of telematics, including computers, switching systems, and transmission systems. The current vigorous and fruitful research and development in this area indicate that there will be at least another decade of improvements to capability and reductions in cost.[8]

Transmission systems of greater capacity and lower cost will continue to be developed as the costs of integrated circuits decrease and manufacturing experience is gained, particularly in optical fibers. There will probably be a pause in additions to the armada of U.S. communications satellites as the space shuttle program is restructured and as new unmanned launch vehicles are developed, but the deployment of optical fiber systems should bridge most gaps in the interim.[9]

As digital switches replace space division switches in the telephone network, the time needed to carry out circuit switching will decrease. Further improvement will occur as central control of interoffice switching (CCIS) is extended. CCIS is a scheme in which the addresses, or numbers, of the calling and called parties are sent to a central computer connected by data links to all switches in a network. The computer finds a route for the desired connection and orders all the necessary switches to close simultaneously. Connection times can be in tens of milliseconds.

Both switching systems and computers will benefit from improvements in integrated circuits. Although development of even faster and more capacious computers will increase the demand for improved data communication networks and more sophisticated gateways and IMPs, the technologies seem to be available to meet that demand.

Thus, substantive progress is evident in most technologies fundamental to advances in the physical aspects of telematics. Yet improvement in terminal apparatus that is now expensive or cumbersome still awaits new discoveries or technical approaches. True end-to-end electronic mail will not become a reality until a combined typewriter and hard-copy printer is available for under $100, and video display units will continue to occupy a substantial portion of a desk until a flat screen display as flexible and inexpensive as a cathode ray tube is created.

The current diversity of protocols and standards causes difficulties and extra expense in arranging telematics systems. Exploitation of the seven-level OSI protocol structure should help avoid incompatibilities. Some of this is already happening. Digital Equipment Corporation, for example, intends to modify its DECnet protocols to conform to OSI, and both the Boeing Company and General Motors Corporation have adopted OSI for their private networks.

Facilities Arrangements

Cost reductions in transmission may come more swiftly to some users through the rearrangement of existing facilities than through the development of new ones. For example, buying and installing a ground station for transmitting and receiving satellite communications to serve an office complex may be less expensive than leasing the equivalent capacity from telephone companies. This method is justifiably called the bypass method. Its use is a political issue because regulators are concerned that the loss of the profits from overpriced business telecommunication services will force local telephone companies to raise the price of residential services to compensate for losses due to underpricing in that market. Regulators have taken little corrective action, however, and businesses are increasing their use of bypass facilities for many long-distance communication services, including telematics.

U.S. regulators have limited the options of some telematics system designers—for example, through FCC decisions that prohibit AT&T from making any protocol conversions and from using some level 4 protocols in structuring networks for the services it offers others. In principle, however, another entity could provide the IMPs and gateways and then lease digital circuits from AT&T to provide a complete service after negotiating with AT&T for interconnection protocols. AT&T, of course, is trying to convince the FCC that the restrictions should be removed.

Social Issues

The social issues accompanying the introduction of telematics are being addressed by appropriate legislative, institutional, and business groups. Opportunities for damage by computer intrusion should decrease as new laws are passed and as data base managers introduce access controls and tighten security. The market issues are more difficult to assess, however, because the telematics industry structure was so altered by the breakup of AT&T. We will never know how rapidly innovation would have occurred in the old framework and can only hope that delays in the revision of standards will be outpaced by advances in technical developments. Perhaps, too, the improvements in reliability that are accompanying the newest in technology will help keep service levels up as we enter an era of deliberate obsolescence in telematics equipment.

Continuing Evolution

The agent for continued evolution of telematics infrastructures is technology, particularly solid-state electronics and software. Strong research programs in both areas can be found in private industry as well as in universities. The federal government both supports research and encourages private industry to create new services. And private industry is eager to accept the opportunity to capitalize on a growing need. Nor is the United States alone in providing new telematics services: foreign entities either provide or support the development of telematics systems. Nippon Telephone and Telegraph's CS-1 and CS-2 communication satellites respectively provide transparent communication and teleservices using the OSI protocol structure. The European Research Community, the United Kingdom, Ireland, Australia, and Canada are also continuing aggressive development of telematics systems.

Moreover, in cooperation with the CCITT, various nations are developing plans for an integrated services digital network (ISDN) that eventually will provide voice, data, and image transmission services over a single network incorporating both packet and circuit switching with CCIS control. The deployment of a 64-kb/s voice and data transmission capability is expected in the United States in the late 1980s. Overall, it appears that telematics infrastructures can serve today's needs well; it also appears that foundations to meet our future needs are in hand or are being developed.

NOTES

1. Two analyses that both established the 50 percent figure but were carried out in entirely separate ways are in Porat (1976) and Abler (1977). In the decade since this work, U.S. information industries have continued to grow while jobs in manufacturing and agriculture have declined; thus, the former has become even more critical to the U.S. economy.
2. This reference is a report to the president of France on the importance of telematics to the French economy. The translation (Nora and Minc, 1980) includes a foreword by Daniel Bell.
3. Multiplexing is a technique for reducing the cost of transmission by using a single medium to communicate several messages simultaneously. In frequency division multiplexing (FDM), each message is impressed on a different carrier frequency at the transmitter and separated at the receiver by a tuner that responds only to that frequency. One application is found in contemporary cable television systems, which use FDM to carry scores of TV programs to a residential channel selector.

    FDM is the oldest of the multiplexing methods. In fact, Alexander Graham Bell tried to send several telegraph signals over a single pair of wires by having each turn a unique frequency on or off to send the elements of a message. His experimental apparatus for such a "harmonic telegraph" was actually the one that carried the famous first telephone message. His knowledge of the science of speech led him to understand the significance of the result, even though he was working on another problem.

    If each of several messages is encoded as a string of ones and zeros, as in a data signal, time division multiplexing (TDM) can be used. With TDM a single high-speed transmission medium carries sections of each of several lower speed channels alternately in time. A T1 channel, for example, carries 8 bits from channel 1, then 8 bits from channel 2, and so on for 24 channels; the T1 channel then starts again with the next 8 bits from channel 1. As the natural complement of digital transmission, TDM has become the dominant technique in new communications systems.
4. The earliest of the switching technologies were electromechanical systems, which used relays for both the control function and the network connection function. Although data signals at a few hundred bits per second will pass easily through a relay connection network, the logic in relay control systems is simple and inflexible and not adaptable to the more exotic demands of some data communications. Electronic switching was introduced in the early 1960s when relays were used for connections, but the control function was a special-purpose, stored-program computer that could accommodate complex logic and software changes. Both electromechanical and electronic switches are referred to as space division switches because the input and output channels for both

consist of discrete wire pairs with which the switches make physical, electrically continuous connections. Either switch makes connections in tenths of a second.

In the mid-1970s, digital switches were introduced. The control function in such switches is, again, a computer controlled by a stored program, but connections are made in a totally different fashion. Input and output channels are time slots in a time division carrier system. Connections are established by assigning the block of bits in a time slot in an incoming digital channel to a specified time slot in an outgoing digital channel, perhaps after a delay of a few hundred microseconds. The process is referred to as time slot interchange or time division switching and is the obvious complement to time division multiplexing or transmission. New connections can be established in milliseconds.

If incoming signals are on loops or analog carrier systems, they are converted to a digital format before presentation to the digital switch. If outgoing trunks are analog, a digital-to-analog converter is introduced between the switch and the trunk. Such conversion may seem cumbersome, but the complement must be accomplished if the incoming and outgoing signals to a space division switch are in a digital format.

5. Voelcker (1986) gives an excellent description of the OSI seven-level structure.
6. The periodical *IEEE Communications* is a good source of information on data networks. A new IEEE publication, *Network,* which first appeared in January 1987, is an excellent source for the newest in data communications.
7. Shooshan (1984) provides excellent essays on the economic, policy, and regulatory issues leading to divestiture by individuals responsible for many of the decisions.
8. Several relevant technological projections are given by Mayo (1985).
9. The potential for reduction in transmission cost is thoughtfully described by Lucky (1985).

REFERENCES

Abler, R. 1977. The telephone and the evolution of the American metropolitan system. P.1 in The Social Impact of the Telephone, I. De S. Pool, ed. Cambridge, Mass.: MIT Press.

Lucky, R. W. 1985. Telecommunications research and development: A look at the next twenty years. Paper presented at the Fifth Convocation of Engineering Academies, London, June 10–15, 1985. Also in The Bridge 15(3):2–6.

Mayo, J. S. 1985. The evolution of information technologies. Pp. 7–33 in Information Technologies and Social Transformation, B. R. Guile, ed. Washington, D.C.: National Academy Press.

Nora, S., and A. Minc. 1980. The Computerization of Society: A Report to the President of France. Cambridge, Mass.: MIT Press.

Porat, M. U. 1976. The Information Economy. Palo Alto, Calif.: Stanford University; and Washington, D.C.: U.S. Government Printing Office.

Shooshan, H. M. III. 1984. Disconnecting Bell—The Impact of the AT&T Divestiture. New York: Pergamon Press.

Voelcker, J. 1986. Helping computers communicate. IEEE Spectrum 23(3):61–70.

11

Reflections on the
Telecommunications Infrastructure

HARVEY BROOKS

This chapter raises a set of issues critical to the telecommunications infrastructure by exploring three basic questions: (1) What are the implications of the shift in the United States from a planned telecommunications infrastructure to one driven by market forces and largely dominated by a few large users with highly sophisticated requirements (Borrus et al., 1984)? (2) How will the growth of telecommunications and the redistribution of "information power" within organizations and among different groups in the population affect human settlements and organizations (Downs, 1985)? and (3) How can we best describe and project the evolution of the telecommunications infrastructure (Borrus, 1986; Borrus et al., 1985)?

THE MARKET SHIFT

Probably the most important environmental factor determining the future evolution of communications infrastructure in the United States is the shift from a regulated monopoly to market-driven competition (Borrus et al., 1984). Whereas the pace and direction of technological innovation were once determined mainly by systems engineering and the goal of expanding channel capacity and decreasing unit costs per bit, they are now driven by the needs and requirements of a few of the largest telecommunications users. The emphasis in the field is shifting from the transmission and switching infrastructure to the increased sophistication of equipment and "value added" on the user's premises (see chapter 10). The new environment has been described in striking terms by Mayo (1985, p. 23):

249

For decades electronic technologies have been pulled into the marketplace as fast as humanly possible. Today's technology, however, is so rich that it can do more things than society might find useful. Increasingly, marketing resources are required to sort out innovations, to contain the scope of development, and to focus investment on the applications that will win in the marketplace. . . . Such a give-and-take relationship between markets and technologists has long operated in low-technology fields such as soaps and toothpaste. Today, there is a similar, rapidly evolving relationship in fields of the highest technology, especially in computers, software, and telecommunications.

The question that cannot yet be answered is whether this new, market-driven system will automatically ensure optimization of the infrastructure from a societal standpoint. For example, will the system continue to meet the needs of smaller users, local communities, and the public sector, especially the public sector below the federal and international level? How will this new system affect the original ideal of a universal, affordable service?

In a way the Bell System represented an ideal case of the success of a planned economy encapsulated within the free enterprise system. It was much more successful than any true planned economy, perhaps in part because it continually defended itself with free enterprise rhetoric. It was a case in which systems engineering of the whole subeconomy of tele-communications worked well. It produced a single product—telephone service without terminal frills—that was an ideal target for a planned economy.* This ideal was predicated on the assumption that there were what economists would call large positive externalities associated with the maximum dispersal of customer connections that could not be fully captured in the competitive price chargeable to the individual customer. This positive externality justified some kind of collective subsidy that actually took the form of a cross-subsidy from high-density traffic to low-density traffic, and from sophisticated high value-added services to minimal basic services. As long as the requirements of large users could essentially be met by simply increasing the number of plain old telephones within the organization, the old system was in a position to satisfy all users with the same basic technology; all the sophistication was built into the public network. But as it became technically possible to provide more and more sophisticated services on the user's premises (value added) outside the public network, the needs of different kinds of users became more and more differentiated, and pressures for a different system of

---

*For an illuminating exposition of the philosophy and achievements of the "old" Bell system, see Bode (1971).

managing the supply of new technology became irresistible (Oettinger, 1984, 1985).

The justification for the old telephone system was technical integration—that is, the maintenance of the technical integrity of the system as new technology and new user services were incorporated into it. The question has become whether this technical integrity can be maintained in the face of much greater diversity in sources of technology and in user requirements. How can the benefits of technical integration, standards, quality control, and compatibility of different vintages of very long lived and long-depreciation-life equipment be preserved in the new system while realizing the advantages of more experimentation and competition? How can present and potential users be more integrally involved in the planning of new telecommunications systems? Because the service provided by the old system was a basic standard commodity that the network could be optimized to produce at minimum cost, customers were little affected by the technical design of the network except through the cost and reliability of the service they received. The only problem of the network was the actual production of the service; it did not have to be tailored to the specific needs of a variety of customers.

A closely related question is the extent to which the new deregulated system will be degraded by the phenomenon of "cream skimming" as high-volume services in dense information corridors are tailored to the needs of large, sophisticated users and the cross-subsidization of services used sparsely by large numbers of people is rigorously eliminated because such services are relatively unprofitable. Will the trickle-down effect of new technology developed for, and delivered to, the most sophisticated and performance-oriented users automatically serve the needs of large numbers of small users? Will a higher rate of innovation in a market-driven system offset the decreased attention to users with less market power? What objective function is in effect maximized by the new market-driven system (i.e., what parameters of the communications system will it tend to optimize), and how will its configuration and performance differ from that of the old regulated system?

EFFECTS ON HUMAN SETTLEMENTS AND ORGANIZATIONS

Will information power become more concentrated and less accessible to all, or will the abundance of information resources and channel capacity lead to greater equality of access to the power conferred by the control of information? Generally speaking, the various visions put forward in Japan of a future information society anticipate equalization of information power both regionally and among different groups of the population. Such visions picture the information society as a force for democratization and participation (National Institute for Research Advancement, 1985). In the West the view tends to be more in the direction of information power giving an advantage to large organizations and to a few urban communications and transportation hubs with world-scale access. Most advocates of the Third World see information technology, and particularly telecommunications, as widening the gap between the industrialized countries and the Third World in such a way that the industrialized countries will greatly increase their power to dictate to the Third World and arrange the world economy to their own advantage. Others foresee this effect not only between the First and the Third Worlds but also between regions and cities within the industrial countries. Which view is likely to be more correct? To what extent is there a choice, and how can that choice be influenced (United Nations Centre for Science and Technology for Development, 1986; Society for International Development, 1985)?

What will be the effect of modern telecommunications on the future configuration of a city? Will it make possible more dispersion to the suburbs and even to the countryside, or is face-to-face contact still sufficiently important that its advantages will not soon be replaced by sophisticated telecommunications? What is the prospect for the diffusion of person-to-person video communications? What external factors are likely to influence that prospect? Why did the Picturephone prove to be a technical success and a market failure (Bode, 1971)?

What will be the influence of telecommunications on the comparative advantage among different kinds of urban centers? Will telecommunications, possibly in combination with air transport, reinforce the hierarchy among urban centers ranging from world-scale economic and communications nerve centers to local niche cities, or will the abundance of information channels make possible many more centers with approximately equal connectedness to the world economy? The Japanese have attempted some answers to these questions: they see the new information society as decreasing the relative importance of such centers as Tokyo and Osaka, pointing to the characteristics of communications technologies that tend to make the cost of communication almost independent of distance (National Institute for Research Advancement, 1985).*

In fact, Japan has systematically linked its plans for regional devel-

---

*One source of information in this area is the proceedings of the International Symposium on the Impact of New Communication Technologies on Local Government (1984) held at the U.S. Department of State, Washington, D.C., from December 3–5, 1984. See also Urban Innovation Abroad (1985). The symposium addressed different approaches taken in Japan, the Federal Republic of Germany, and the United States.

opment to telecommunications technology, actually building experimental cities (that were going to be built anyway) incorporating all the latest telecommunications technologies in such a way that their usefulness can be tested. An example is Minato Mirai 21, a new city for 190,000 residents near Yokohama. According to the summary of the 1984 International Symposium on the Impact of New Communication Technologies on Local Government, the new city "will be a resort showplace and will feature wide-band communications systems, videotext, and interactive systems." This development is all part of the Japanese ambition to become a model "information society" in the next century (Urban Innovation Abroad, 1985). The tone is optimistic, and the thrust is toward integrated experiments to test advanced concepts in operation in new cities.*

By contrast, the study of a series of small-scale demonstration projects in the Federal Republic of Germany places greater emphasis on their economic, political, and social effects than on their technological effects. The approach being developed by the Bundespost seems to be one of caution and indeed technological pessimism, although, as reported in *Urban Innovation Abroad* (1985), "local governments in Germany are actively pushing their federal and state level counterparts for more active experimentation and deployment of telecom technologies," seeing "the technologies as helping to create a more democratic society where citizens have access to information from a variety of sources." Thus, there is a second thrust in the German approach emphasizing local influence in shaping the future of telecommunications technology in that country.

The dominant feature of the U.S. approach is diversity and heterogeneity under the guiding influence of the market. The *Urban Innovation Abroad* summary of the international symposium stated:

As a result of their experiences to date with telecommunications, the U.S. participants talked less about grand schemes for how the technologies would change their organizations and communities, and instead focused on the need to develop a set of skills for planning, managing, and evaluating their use of telecommunications in each of the three local government roles—consumer, broker, and sustainer of local democracy.

An avoidance of the "big picture" seems to pervade the U.S. approach. The U.S. group, mainly represented by local officials, described telecommunications as

---

*See National Institute for Research Advancement (1985), pp. 93–99, for a discussion of such concepts as Teleutopia, teleports, and the relation of telecommunications to regional development and regional disparities in access to information.

a complex web involving technology they knew little about, private sector vendors who have done little to earn the trust of public officials, an intergovernmental system that is oriented to deregulation despite the expressed concern of local officials, intraorganizational concerns over how telecommunications will affect jobs and responsibilities, and a citizenry that, for the most part, seems only to want basic transmissions and diverse entertainment services at low cost. (Urban Innovation Abroad, 1985, pp. 4–5)

What can be said about the effect of information technologies on the nature and structure of organizations? Will the ease with which the center of an organization can monitor and control its far-flung activities tend to reinforce bureaucratic, hierarchical structures with a high degree of functional specialization? Or will it lead to the creation of horizontal, and relatively flat, networklike organizations with quasi-autonomous nodes capable of coordinating their activities horizontally through instant access to a common data base and to each other, either directly or by updating their input to the common data base? In other words, will information technology increase the capacity of a few big brains to control the activities of more and more people, or will it increase the capacity of many "little brains" to concert and coordinate their activities in a way that is equivalent to, but much more effective than, one big brain that cannot keep everything at the forefront of attention continuously, no matter how sophisticated the information terminal (Brooks and Schneider, 1985)?

Different countries have different attitudes toward this problem. The Japanese characteristically take an optimistic view and have adopted an aggressive attitude toward the creation of planned sophisticated networks in the expectation that they will lead to democratization of access to information services and a reduction in social differences arising from such differential access (National Institute for Research Advancement, 1985).

Will modern information- and communications-intensive manufacturing and office technologies make possible dispersed, flexible specialization of the kind envisioned by Piore and Sabel in *The Second Industrial Divide* (1984)? Flexible specialization in their view means that modern computerized manufacturing systems can be profitable with much shorter production runs and can produce a larger variety of products with the same capital equipment, thus making it possible to respond much more rapidly and economically to changes in customer requirements and in the demand mix for products. Flexible manufacturing has in fact advanced much further in the manufacture of electronic, telecommunications, and computer equipment than it has in metalworking industries (Borrus et al., 1984). Furthermore, flexible manufacturing, combined with telecommunications, makes possible a much higher degree of decentralization and smaller plants than in the past. If so, how will this affect the division of labor between the industrialized and the developing worlds? Will the trend toward smaller economic units promote the decentralization of labor-intensive components of an integrated production process to areas where the cost of labor is low, or will the trend toward just-in-time inventory management and the closer integration of design, production, and marketing tend to drive companies to repatriate economic activities that had previously been dispersed to take advantage of low labor costs (United Nations Centre for Science and Technology for Development, 1986; Society for International Development, 1985)? As the fractional labor content of both goods and service production becomes so small that labor costs are no longer a major consideration in relation to inventory costs and the use of capital, will the attraction of cheap labor disappear?

MEANINGFUL MEASUREMENT AND PROJECTION

What are the most meaningful measures of the volume of telecommunications services when the service increasingly consists of value added by terminal equipment on the customer's premises rather than the flow of bits between customers? Is it possible to analyze the future volume of information services in a way that parallels Marchetti's (see chapter 7) and Nakicenovic's (see chapter 8) analyses of the level of activity of various transportation modes? In telecommunications, is it possible to project a saturation such as Marchetti and Nakicenovic have projected for air transport at about twice the present annual passenger-kilometer volume? Can we foresee developments in telecommunications technology analogous to the Mach 8 aircraft in air transport that could generate a new pulse of exponential telecommunications growth? Would a breakthrough in software production—a change from the labor-intensive art that it is today to a mass-producible technology—be a possible source for such a pulse? What new functions for information technology could such a breakthrough make possible?

Within the telecommunications system, to what extent is there regular substitution of one mode for another? Historical experience may suggest that substitution is less likely than some kind of ecological symbiosis among old and new systems. It is unlikely, then, to be a question of wires, cables, and so forth being superseded by satellites or of satellites being superseded by optical fibers. The question is how these technologies will fit together in an optimal system. What are the factors that govern this optimization, and how can government-mandated rate structures influence the future mix among different communications modes?

CONCLUSION

The telecommunications infrastructure presents a different problem from that of the rest of the infrastructure picture discussed in this book. A theme in current debates is the decay of infrastructures and the general lack of investment in and adoption of technological innovations that could increase their productivity. This theme is by and large not valid for the communications infrastructure. Here, investment appears to be adequate to the major needs, technological innovation is proceeding at a breathtaking pace, and new technologies are adopted rapidly. Indeed, the problem is that the life cycle of telecommunications technologies is shortening, and the proliferation of new technical opportunities is outpacing the ability of society to choose among them and to plan a coherent structure. The main problem for the United States is whether the new reliance on the market to determine the direction of innovation and infrastructure investment in telecommunications will serve the public interest more effectively than the old system of regulated monopoly, systems engineering, and technical integration. That question may apply particularly to the "public goods" aspect of the telecommunications infrastructure. It is too early to tell how the new national experiment in telecommunications will come out.

REFERENCES

Bode, H. W. 1971. Synergy: Technical Integration and Technological Innovation in the Bell System. Murray Hill, N.J.: Bell Laboratories.

Borrus, M. 1986. Japanese telecommunications: reforms and trade implications. California Management Review 28(3):43–61.

Borrus, M., F. Bar, and I. Warde (with J. Millstein and P. Cogee). 1984. The Impacts of Divestiture and Deregulation: Infrastructural Changes, Manufacturing Transition, and Competition in the U.S. Telecommunications Industries. Berkeley Roundtable on the International Economy project for the U.S. Congress Office of Technology Assessment. Berkeley: University of California Press.

Borrus, M., F. Bar, P. Cogez, A. B. Thoresen, I. Warde, and A. Yoshikawa. 1985. Telecommunications Development in Comparative Perspective: The New Telecommunications in Europe, Japan, and the U.S. Berkeley Roundtable on the International Economy. Berkeley: University of California Press.

Brooks, H., and L. Schneider (with K. Oshima). 1985. Potential impact of new manufacturing technology on employment and work in industrial and developing countries. Harvard University, Cambridge, Mass. Mimeograph.

Downs, A. 1985. Living with advanced telecommunications. Society 23(3):26–34.

International Symposium on the Impact of New Communication Technologies on Local Government. 1984. Papers. Washington, D.C.

Mayo, J. S. 1985. The evolution of information technologies. Pp. 7–33 in Information Technologies and Social Transformation, B. R. Guile, ed. Washington, D.C.: National Academy Press.

National Institute for Research Advancement. 1985. Comprehensive Study of Microelectronics 1985. Tokyo: NIRA.

Oettinger, A. G. 1984. The information evolution: Building blocks and bursting bundles. May draft. Program on Information Resources Policy, Harvard University, Cambridge, Mass.

Oettinger, A. G. 1985. The abundant and versatile digital way. June draft. Program on Information Resources Policy, Harvard University, Cambridge, Mass.

Piore, M. J., and C. F. Sabel. 1984. The Second Industrial Divide: Possibilities for Prosperity. New York: Basic Books.

Society for International Development. 1985. Informatics: Is there a choice? Development 1.

United Nations Centre for Science and Technology for Development. 1986. New Information Technologies and Development. Advanced Technology Alert System Bulletin 3(June).

Urban Innovation Abroad. 1985. Impacts of new telecommunications technologies on local governments in Europe, Japan and the U.S. explored in international symposium. Urban Innovation Abroad (April):4–5.

12

Water Supply and Distribution: The Next 50 Years

ROYCE HANSON

Taken as a whole, the United States has plenty of water, now and for the future. The problem is, of course, that no one lives in the United States as a whole: we live in specific communities, and not all communities have, or will have, enough water.

If the world would just stand still, most places could get by with the water now available or with the water that is in the process of being made available through a combination of conservation measures and improved management of available resources. Although some distribution and treatment facilities should be improved or replaced, state and local governments can probably finance the solution of more than 90 percent of the problem themselves (Congressional Budget Office, 1983).

The world will not stand still, however, and population migration continues to areas that must import water. Other problems also exist. Excessive "mining" of water from some aquifers threatens both municipalities and agriculture. Coastal communities are experiencing salt intrusions into groundwater where withdrawals have exceeded the rate of recharge or where rapid development has lowered water tables. In older cities the deterioration of distribution systems due to age, poor initial construction, and inadequate maintenance causes enormous amounts of water to be wasted and results in the need for repair and replacement of facilities.

For two generations, federal water programs in the arid states have provided water to communities at prices lower than the cost of producing it. We are now scraping the bottom of this federal pork barrel. In regions that have depended on interbasin transfers, there may be enough water to meet current demands, but there is not enough water to meet projected growth based on current rates of consumption and reuse.

An additional constraint on supply arises from growing environmental sensitivity. The protection of minimum levels of streamflow, concern for the quality of the drinking water supply, and increasing conflicts between the need to protect water supplies and dispose of toxic and hazardous materials add to the costs and complexity of maintaining adequate supplies of water for urban and rural settlements.

Almost all of these problems can be solved through the usual incremental policy process. Most of the solutions are not costly, especially if we consider management alternatives to the historic pattern of building to meet, or even feed, demand. Household water use, for example, could be reduced by as much as 10 percent by requiring the installation of water-saving devices, some of them as inexpensive as putting bricks in flush tanks. The revision of plumbing codes to require conservation devices in new construction could cut water use in these buildings by about one-third, according to studies by the U.S. Environmental Protection Agency (1981). There are numerous other methods in addition; for instance, Tucson, Arizona, has been able to reduce per capita water use by 24 percent through public education in the use of water-saving devices and by price increases (Postel, 1984).

Recycling water used for agriculture and industry is also highly cost-effective. Through recycling, other countries such as Sweden and Israel have achieved reductions in industrial demand of from 50 to 70 percent (Postel, 1984). Using figures on water use and potential reuse and recycling for U.S. industries produced by the Departments of Commerce and the Interior, Postel (1985) estimates that it would be possible for water withdrawals for manufacturing in the year 2000 to be 45 percent lower than they were in 1979.

Other water supply and distribution problems may also be well within our capacity to solve. Estimates of the "need" for replacement and repair of existing public water systems and for the development of new systems based on traditional water demand studies are often overblown. Replacement costs based on the age of facilities are highly untrustworthy, in part because the age of a water main has little correlation with its failures (O'Day and Neumann, 1984). Moreover, a number of solutions to many of the problems of water mains are more cost-effective than replacement. For instance, it may be possible to "loop" parts of the system, producing the capacity for backup service to an area affected by a break. This procedure allows the replacement of the failed section of line without interrupting service and also avoids the greater cost of replacing large sections of line that may be good for many years. In addition, the adoption of effective management and maintenance programs can extend the life of the existing facilities and reduce the cost of new or replacement construction.

If the American water problem were simply defined as the urgent need to improve management and maintenance and to finance development of the marginal amount of new sources and distribution systems required to maintain adequate supplies for agricultural, industrial, and municipal users, it would not be a matter of serious national concern. In this context, the water problem is a minor aspect of the little debate going on in the country over what to do about our infrastructure.

But the U.S. water problem is not that simple. Two long-term trends cause us to redefine it: (1) the impact of the "greenhouse effect" on geographic regions and the urban system, and (2) the continuing pollution of groundwater and surface water. In light of these trends, water becomes an organizing issue on which hinges a great strategic debate about the future settlement patterns of the country. Both require near-term choices with long-term consequences, and the choices made affect more than water. They involve all other infrastructure, and they require the rethinking of some of our most settled institutional arrangements.

THE IMPACT OF CLIMATE CHANGE ON WATER SYSTEMS

There is now widespread agreement among scientists that in the next 50 years the average temperature of the earth could increase by 2° C or more (Ciborowski, 1985a; National Research Council, 1983). This increase will be the consequence of the accumulation of heat-trapping gases, principally carbon dioxide, in the atmosphere. The rapid expansion of fossil fuel use and the depletion of forests are major causes of the buildup of these gases, which produces the greenhouse effect. As warming occurs, the melting of polar ice and thermal expansion of ocean water should produce a rise in sea level. The highly uncertain estimates of this rise, a phenomenon that would profoundly affect infrastructure worldwide, range between approximately 20 centimeters (cm) and 200 cm by the year 2100.

Globally, a warmer climate will bring about an intensification of the hydrologic cycle. Evaporation will be more rapid, and in some areas streamflows and soil moisture will be reduced. Extreme drought could be more common. In areas where the climate is drying, water tables will fall while the demand for irrigation may increase. It will become necessary to irrigate areas that do not need irrigation today. In some areas, of course, rainfall and streamflows will increase. When that occurs, rising water tables and broader floodplains will produce a different set of infrastructure problems.

TABLE 12-1   Comparison of Water Requirements and Supplies[a]

Water Region	Present Climate—Ratio of Requirement to Supply	Warmer, Drier Climate	
		Percentage Change in Supply	Ratio of Requirement to Supply
Missouri	0.43	−63.9	1.18
Arkansas/White/Red	0.18	−53.8	0.39
Texas Gulf	0.35	−49.8	0.70
Rio Grande	0.91	−75.7	3.72
Upper Colorado	0.99	−39.6	1.65
Lower Colorado	1.19	−56.5	2.68
California	0.41	−43.9	0.74
For seven regions together	0.43	−53.0	0.90

[a]Assumes a 2° C increase in temperature and a 10 percent reduction in precipitation.

SOURCE: Revelle and Waggoner (1983), p. 423.

Municipalities that currently have adequate supplies may find that they are facing both periodic and chronic shortages in the future. Reduced streamflows will affect both the quantity and the quality of water. Cities such as Washington, D.C., which draw most of their water from flowing rivers, will be especially hard hit. Those with storage reservoirs will find that faster evaporation and slower refilling after drawdowns will change their planning and management practices. Coastal cities that have been drawing water from the ground faster than it can be recharged will face increased threats from seawater intrusion.

Table 12-1 shows one estimate of the effect of a drier climate on a number of river basins in the United States. In the example, if Western rivers experienced a flow reduction of as much as 40 to 70 percent, the supply in a number of basins consequently would be insufficient for agricultural and municipal needs. This situation could also be expected to produce political pressure for transfers of water from basins with surpluses. Alternatively, agricultural cultivation dependent on irrigation would have to be restricted to zones in which water was available. Urban development would also have to be limited to areas in which local surface water and groundwater supplies were adequate. If the transfer option were chosen, the cost would be substantial. Estimates for the Missouri basin alone, for the period from 2000 to 2025, range from $1.6 billion to $2.8 billion a year. Costs at this level could lead to the advancement of saltwater conversion technologies, particularly for urban use.

In some regions, changes in the water supplied by the atmosphere may be accompanied by irreversible reductions in water that can be "mined" from underground.

With the depletion of the Ogallala aquifer under the High Plains of the Midwest likely by 2030, a major agricultural region of the country will face a severe change in its water supply. The nearest available sources are the Great Lakes. This raises questions of cost and interregional conflict within the United States, and would also involve negotiation of an international water budget with Canada.

POLLUTION AND SUPPLY

The contamination of water supplies has been and still is one of the most serious environmental problems in this country. Since the enactment of the Federal Water Pollution Control Act in 1972 (Public Law 92–500; 33 U.S.C. 1251 et seq.), limited progress has been made in improving the quality of some surface waters. Yet the net condition of the nation's surface waters has not improved or worsened much since the early 1970s (Conservation Foundation, 1984). The quality of U.S. groundwater, on the other hand, appears to be deteriorating. The Office of Technology Assessment estimated in 1983 that 29 percent of the groundwater drinking supplies of 954 cities with more than 10,000 people were contaminated (Office of Technology Assessment, 1983).

Little is known about groundwater movement and the intrusion of pollutants into groundwater. Land disposal of wastes was long regarded as safe, but the discovery of contaminants in groundwater many years after disposal sites had been closed and the appearance of toxic materials in groundwater located far from suspect disposal sites have raised new issues about the steps that should be taken to protect groundwater.

A major source of concern is the increased use of nondegradable toxic and radioactive materials, which is generating a disposal problem of enormous magnitude. Federal legislation has addressed the control of toxic substances and their applications in agriculture and industry, the disposal of hazardous wastes, the siting of disposal sites for nuclear waste, and the cleanup of hazardous waste sites. Many states have enacted supplementary legislation. Yet there is still great concern about the contaminants already in the hydrologic system from old disposal sites that remain undiscovered or have not yet been cleaned up, from years of application of herbicides and pesticides to agricultural and urban lands, and from the dumping of such materials into sanitary and storm sewers.

Thus far, toxic materials are the most dramatic source of contamination, but they are by no means the most frequent (Pye et al., 1983). Saltwater contamination has also become a serious problem, whether it is caused by pumping out fresh water faster than it can be recharged, by the use of chemicals to de-ice roads, or by the percolation of irrigation water into the ground, carrying dissolved salts. Other contaminants include bacterial and viral materials from septic tanks, feedlots, or improper sewage disposal and nitrates from fertilizers and sewage.

The consensus is that groundwater pollution is getting worse in spite of considerable efforts to address the problem (Conservation Foundation, 1984). The implications for the nation's water infrastructure are that such pollution endangers some existing supplies or restricts the rate at which they can be used, or both. In addition, to the extent that groundwater pollution is not arrested, it limits the use of groundwater as a future supply for many cities. Even if further contamination can be halted and the effects of previous pollution reversed, the process will be costly. In developing new sources of water, special care will have to be given to ensuring its safety.

As we learn more about various contaminants and their health effects, it may be necessary to retrofit many of the nation's older water systems with technologies that cleanse the water of these substances. We can probably look forward to more stringent standards for drinking water, increased monitoring and regulation by federal and state governments, and the development of new technologies designed to protect drinking water quality (Senate Committee on Environment and Public Works, 1984). Here again, it may be desirable to advance the development of cost-effective seawater conversion technologies and apply them to other contaminated supplies.

CLIMATE CHANGE, GROUNDWATER POLLUTION, AND WATER POLICY

Climate change and pollution are related phenomena because changes in climate may make some water supplies more vulnerable to pollution or to higher concentrations of contaminants. Although these factors frame the nature of the water problem for the nation, they do not suggest their own solutions. What is known is that it is extraordinarily difficult to reverse the effects of actions (i.e., pollution) that have already taken place, as demonstrated by the difficulty of implementing the superfund law.

It is easier to ameliorate or reverse pollution from some sources than from others. Because pollution is a widely acknowledged problem, there is a good chance that policy changes can be made now to retard future contamination. It will be much harder to muster the resolve—a course of action that must be taken soon—to adopt policies that can have a material effect on the rate of climate change. Such policies would involve substantial reductions in fossil fuel consumption by the economically advanced nations (Ciborowski, 1985b), a course of action that would be resisted. One of the causes of such resistance is that most of the world has a heavy investment in fossil fuel as a source of energy. Climatic change occurs too slowly to generate politically salient support for policies designed to prevent or materially retard the change. In addition, effective change would require concerted international action. Lacking a compelling "silent spring" rationale for anticipatory action, policymakers are more likely to consign themselves to reacting to shortages after they have occurred and to an inertial system of accommodation to the new conditions as they develop.

In fact, this passive/reactive scenario best describes current policy. Worldwide, forests are being depleted, and fossil energy use is still growing. With the recent reductions in oil prices, the consumption of fossil fuels may actually accelerate in the short run. No attempts are being made to guide settlement patterns in the United States to slow the long-term growth of regions most prone to water shortages. On the contrary: such areas are among the fastest growing parts of the country. Contributing to the process, water supply policy continues to be driven by the utility concept—the duty to provide water to meet the demand for it. Cities appear to be adjusting to the depletion of their existing water supplies less by adopting conservation measures than by promoting the development of new sources of supply.

We can expect continuing migrations to regions that will be vulnerable to water shortages as climate changes occur, particularly in the southwestern and mountain states and some of the coastal states of the Southeast and New England. The water infrastructure for many of these areas is relatively new, and much of it is currently operating below its ultimate capacity. Thus, it is unlikely that water infrastructure constraints will limit settlement in the next decade. In addition, although no new federal water infrastructure projects have been added to the federal budget in many years, several major projects still to be completed are designed to provide additional water to arid municipalities and agricultural areas during the next 25 years.

Nevertheless, if this business-as-usual scenario should unfold, the areas now experiencing the greatest rates of growth will have severe water crises on their hands soon after the turn of the century. Then the major policy issue will be whether to try to keep urban populations and economic activities in place by building interbasin water transfer systems far greater than anything now in use, to develop (and probably subsidize) technologies such as desalinization, or to let the ravages of "nature" depopulate these areas and redirect industry and agriculture to the areas with enough water to sustain them. In the latter case a more modest increment of infrastructure for urban and agricultural water distribution might suffice. One approach would be to let the ''market'' decide: if people living in arid regions want to stay there, they must pay the full cost of water transfers or the full cost of advanced technologies for purification and recycling of polluted water.

In this light, water infrastructure policy for the next 25 to 50 years is likely to focus on four major issues:

1. repair, replacement, and rehabilitation of systems serving older cities;
2. conservation of existing supplies;
3. interbasin transfers of water to meet municipal, agricultural, and industrial demands; and
4. restructuring of the water market and redesigning of the institutions that allocate water to regions and to users.

THE IMPROVEMENT OF EXISTING SYSTEMS

Whatever the long-term aspect of the water problem, there is little doubt that much of the existing plant has been allowed to deteriorate. From dams and aqueducts to mains and laterals, much of the public water system built during the last 100 years needs repair. Some of it should be replaced.

Age alone is not the culprit, however. Invisible until it breaks, the water distribution system in many cities is the victim of systematic neglect in operations and maintenance management. This suggests that a purely capital-intensive response is unnecessary and insufficient. It is unnecessary because many of the problems can be overcome by improved management. Such management may take the form of improved identification and monitoring of conditions for which replacement is necessary and of cases in which improved maintenance, repair, or other measures are more appropriate and cost-effective. A purely capital-intensive response is insufficient because, unless changes occur in the management of water systems, a new injection of capital is unlikely to have a lasting effect.

Management changes need to encompass more than improvement of the maintenance programs of water agencies and companies. Such changes must go to the heart of the system of pricing water and controlling quality and performance throughout the system. In many if not most cities, the price consumers pay for water is less than the water costs, particularly if capital depreciation, preventive maintenance, and upgrading to meet evolving water quality standards are included. This situation may be changing, however; in a few instances, such as the rehabilitation of the Baltimore water system, bond buyers are beginning to require cities to covenant to maintain a price structure that is adequate to finance the upkeep of the system (Humphrey, 1983).

The price of water has a demonstrable effect on the conservation of supplies. Cities that have imposed price structures that reward conservation and punish waste and peripheral uses have experienced substantial drops in the per capita rate of consumption, forestalling the need to expand supply sources.

Most cities base charges to both new and old customers on the average price per gallon of all water delivered in the system. This means that old customers usually subsidize new customers and that incremental additions to the size of the system cost the new consumer little more than connecting to the existing system, assuming it has the necessary service capacity. Charging the marginal cost for new water services would, alone, probably not have much effect on urban development patterns. If charging the marginal cost for water services were combined with the use of marginal cost pricing for all new infrastructure, however, such a policy could be expected, at a minimum, to substantially reduce the level of public subsidies now provided to private development and to redirect some of the development pressure from raw land to areas with underused facilities, thus increasing capital productivity.

Improved management and planning techniques can appreciably reduce estimates of the need for repairs or replacements based on such rules of thumb as age of facilities or projections of demand. Frequent inspection and computerized monitoring of water mains can locate leaks, which falsely magnify demand. Simply by developing policies for water rationing during emergencies, Washington, D.C., metropolitan area water planners were able to reduce the cost of emergency water supply facilities by two-thirds. Further savings in projected costs were achieved by intergovernmental agreements to interconnect independently operated systems to provide improved distribution of water during periods of spot shortages for particular suppliers.

The repair, replacement, and revitalization of urban water systems should not be presumed to be principally a capital problem, even though it may be possible to document a substantial number of physical defects and deficiencies. Rather, the physical requirements should be seen as part of the overall capital management system of a city. Noncapital approaches should be favored where possible. When a capital improvement is required to solve a problem, it should be shown to be cost-effective and the responsible authority should demonstrate its fiscal and managerial capacity to maintain and manage the facility once it has been improved. From an investment point of view, federal and state governments, as well as the raters and buyers of municipal and state bonds, would be making more secure decisions if they were to insist that continuous, effective management be an integral part of any capital improvement package. Institutional reform is, at this point, probably more important than money to the quality of infrastructure (Peterson, 1984).

CONSERVATION

Conservation should be one of the highest priorities of any comprehensive management program, whether at the city, regional, or national level. In the urban context, conservation measures not only save and stretch existing supplies but may actually enhance them. A particular pricing policy can induce users to conserve by increasing unit costs as consumption increases. For such a pricing policy to be effective, however, service must be metered; thus, a conservation tool produces a management benefit for the system by helping it keep track of users and uses.

Development regulations that protect floodplains and aquifers and require the retention of storm water can assist in recharging aquifers and in improving streamflow and water quality (Urban Land, 1983). In addition, plumbing codes can require the use of equipment that cuts consumption without decreasing the quality of service. Some cities have also established "water budgets"; under this plan, major water users must stay within a fixed usage budget or pay high surcharges. These measures encourage industrial recycling of water and force irrigators to pay more attention to the weather and soil conditions instead of following a fixed schedule of water releases (Wrenn, 1983).

At the regional level, agricultural irrigation offers enormous potential for conservation. As long as water for agricultural use is priced at only 19 percent of the cost of producing it, however, inefficient use is almost guaranteed. New investment in more efficient irrigation technologies will be required for the full potential of conservation measures in this area to be realized.

A number of the new irrigation techniques have proved to be quite cost-effective. The surge technique, introduced in Texas, is a good example of these technologies. Surging involves the use of valves that release water at specific intervals; in field tests, it reduced water and energy consumption by 10 to 40 percent. Another new technique, which applies water close to the crop through drop tubes rather than spraying from a center pivot, could pay for itself in 5 to 7 years merely through the savings it provides in water and energy. Upgrading all the center pivots in the high plains to this new system could save more than 2 billion cubic meters of water a year in withdrawals from the Ogallala aquifer (Postel, 1985). As long as water is priced below its value, however, it is unlikely that farmers will make the capital investments required to irrigate using one of these new techniques (Caswell and Zilberman, 1985).

Greater conservation of agricultural water would make it possible to use the saved supply for urban areas. The Metropolitan Water District, which serves most of southern California's urban areas, has been negotiating with agricultural users for rights to water that is now wasted. There is enough such water to meet the projected needs of the district for many years, even at current rates of use, and the district sees this water as a means of avoiding further ill-fated interbasin transfer schemes. Arizona, in looking at projections of its water needs and expected supplies, is encouraging the conversion of agricultural lands to urban and industrial uses as a means of conserving water and ensuring the availability of supplies for its cities. (One of the major trade-offs to be considered in planning for future water needs is whether to retire large areas of irrigated land from agricultural use to allow for urbanization of the region.)

Changing methods of irrigation and farming and changing crops are the likely results of a passive/reactive approach to climate change, regardless of the short-term conservation measures that may be employed. These measures would, however, have a useful conservation effect if introduced earlier rather than later. Switching from corn to sorghum as a feed grain in the high plains, for example, would reduce water demand by about one-fifth, with little loss in the nutritional value of the crop as a feedstock. In the high plains, there is increasing interest in more dryland farming, and with farm prices temporarily low, some marginal lands are being retired from active cultivation.

Sharp increases in the price of irrigation water and changes in agricultural practices are necessary in certain areas of the country. Without such changes, both agriculture and the cities will face shortages far sooner than necessary. With the changes, more may be wrung out of existing regional sources than is now possible.

INTERBASIN TRANSFER

The interbasin transfer of water is a technological answer to the problem of not having enough water where the people are. Historically, interbasin transfer has provided a workable solution for many cities. The Colorado River, for example, provides water to southern California and to Denver. New York City draws much of its water from the Delaware River basin. Oklahoma City transports water from southeastern Oklahoma. Interbasin aqueducts are an engineer's or bond attorney's dream. In recent years, however, these large-scale public works projects have run into difficulty, both for political and environmental reasons.

Politically, such projects are classic cases of turf protection. Those who have the water are reluctant to part with it because water increasingly has come to symbolize a capacity for growth. Consequently, within states, citizen opposition has resulted in the disapproval of transfers. The Oklahoma Water Resources Board recently denied the application of Tulsa to extract up to one-seventh of the water in Tenkiller Ferry Reservoir in eastern Oklahoma (Shelley and Wijeyawickrema, 1984). In 1982 voters in northern California successfully petitioned for a referendum and defeated the construction of the peripheral canal, which would have transported water from the Sacramento River to southern California. Recent murmuring about the transportation of water from the Great Lakes to other parts of the United States has produced snarls from the governors of the Great Lakes states and the premiers of the adjacent Canadian provinces. Those who have water now seem to have begun to understand the basic creed of the have-nots: "(1) get it first; (2) get someone else to pay; and (3) if you have to pay, shift as much of the burden as possible away from water users" (Miller and Underwood, 1983, p. 638).

Since the adoption of the National Environmental Policy Act (NEPA) and its many state "little NEPAs," large-scale transfer projects have come under sharp attack for their environmental impacts. Impoundments in particular have been the subjects of protracted administrative hearings and litigation brought by environmental groups concerned with the protection of free-flowing rivers, natural scenery, and wildlife. In many respects the environmental challenges to water projects have brought a new national force to a negotiating table that historically had been dominated by those locally benefiting and the federal and state water management agencies.

Environmental concerns have grown particularly acute in interbasin transfer controversies. The government of Canada, for example, took strong exception to a feature of the Garrison diversion project in North Dakota, which would have transferred water from the Missouri River basin into the Red River watershed. Manitoba and Canada were concerned that this would affect water quality in the Red River basin. Canadian opposition, combined with that of American environmentalists, resulted in a considerable scaling down of the Garrison project.

For the immediate future, turf and environmental politics will almost certainly limit sharply the number and size of public interbasin transfers approved by state and federal water management authorities. Small-scale transfers are likely to continue, however. In fact, the private market for interstate water will probably grow, with prospective users purchasing water from those who have rights to its use.

Several states have enacted legislation aimed at preventing the transfer of water out of the state. Yet such laws have serious constitutional defects because the U.S. Supreme Court has held that water is an article of commerce and as such may be sold and transported across state lines (*Sporhase* v. *Nebraska ex rel. Douglas*, 458 U.S. 941 [1982]). States may regulate commerce in water to the extent that their regulations do not conflict with federal laws or unduly interfere with, burden, or affect interstate commerce. What this means precisely is anybody's guess. Clearly, it does not mean that states may establish priorities that conflict with federal priorities for the use of water (*Arizona* v. *California*, 373 U.S. 546 [1963]).

States may control water in federal reservoirs to the extent that their control is not inconsistent with specific congressional directives (*California* v. *U.S.*, 426 U.S. 645 [1978]; *Consolo* v. *Federal Maritime Commission*, 383 U.S. 607 [1966]). Thus, a state as the owner of part of the water behind a federal impoundment might sell it for use in another state or region, as long as the sale did not interfere with a larger federal purpose such as maintaining water levels sufficient for navigation or supply to irrigators. South Dakota recently tried to sell some of its water in the Oahe reservoir to a private company for use in a pipeline that would convey coal slurry from Wyoming to Arkansas. Downstream states successfully opposed the sale on the navigation issue. Based on this case, it would appear that a state might be unable to prevent a similar transfer among private parties unless it could demonstrate that there was a compelling state interest in preventing the sale. Conceivably, a state could prevent transfers when their cumulative impact on the state's own water needs reached a critical point (*Kleppe* v. *Sierra Club*, 427 U.S. 390 [1976]).

RESTRUCTURING MARKETS AND REDESIGNING INSTITUTIONS

The next generation of infrastructure managers will have to reinvent the system of markets and public institutions that provide and produce public water. Neither appears capable of working as they will have to work in a time of physical scarcity and fiscal constraint.

Water systems function in a managed market that is created by public policy and heavily influenced by it. Public agencies produce water directly or license private companies to produce it for municipal use. State law establishes the rights and priorities of users of natural and man-made bodies of water. Prices are set by the operating agencies or approved by regulatory agencies. From the consumer's viewpoint, there generally is only one supplier of municipal water, whether it is the government itself or a regulated private utility. At a given location there is no competition for either service or price.

Historically, this government-created market has been more interested in equity than in efficiency. There has been a strong consensus behind water policy that all kinds of users should have as much water as they want, wherever they want it, and that it is government's job to make this happen. At the local level, water is perceived as an unlimited birthright (Ingram and McCain, 1977).

Until recently, there has been little concern with efficiency, either in the allocation of water to different users or in the consumption of water by classes of users. On the contrary, there has been an effort to increase water use by pricing it below cost. To the extent that low-cost water has been an intentional subsidy for urban and agricultural development for much of the country, it is a subsidy that has worked. There is considerable doubt, however, that the subsidy has produced a net benefit, especially in urban development. It is probable that the facilitation of urban growth in arid zones of the southwestern and mountain states has occurred at the expense of other urban areas.

The areas and groups that have benefited from cheap water now have a considerable stake in their water "rights." In fact, as water becomes scarcer, the value of their equity interest increases. Thus, the equity issue takes on its second meaning. Depriving people of this interest, which they attained in good faith and in reliance on public policy at the time, raises questions of legal and political fairness. Nevertheless, there is an obvious need to improve the efficiency of the water system as an increasing number of people will be willing to pay far more than the current prices for water and as the rest of the country realizes the magnitude of the subsidy it has provided.

There is a third dimension to the equity and efficiency issues. Some water supplies, such as major aquifers, are not renewable, at least not on a politically realistic time scale. Their pollution or depletion leaves the next generation without that source of water and imposes the need to pay premium prices to obtain water elsewhere. Although some water policy analysts favor the replacement of the existing managed market with a free market, such an approach does not deal well with the intergenerational equity issues.

This third dimension suggests that a major task for water policy is to restructure the water market in ways that make use of free market principles to increase efficiency in the system but that stop short of promoting or allowing the unrestricted consumption of reserves needed for the future. As noted above, this restructuring should have the result of inducing higher levels of conservation and improving allocations among users. To the extent that it induces conservation, it partially addresses the issue of intergenerational equity. The nature of the system, however, tends to obviate competitive pricing and service. "Market" mechanisms tend to be limited to cost-based pricing and bidding by prospective users.

Market approaches therefore will have to be complemented by a revision of the regulatory regimes that govern the water market. In some cases, for example, reallocations by regulation may be required to prevent waste. Both the regulation and taxation of excess use or pollution may prove to be more effective means of promoting the kind of development that protects supplies and the quality of groundwater reserves. Where subsidies are continued, they will have to be more narrowly aimed than they are at present and also better justified, from both an economic and an environmental perspective.

A major factor in restructuring the market for water will be the size and character of the federal role. A sharp reduction in the level of federal participation (traditionally, 70 percent of the costs of projects) will mean that states and localities will pay more. This change in itself should encourage the elimination of all but the most efficient projects (Congressional Budget Office, 1983). Combined with rate reform, conservation measures such as taxes on waste, and marginal pricing for service to new development, a reduced federal role should reduce effective demand for water and thereby materially affect estimates of need.

Law also plays a major role in the market for water and governs other behavior in water policy. It is important institutionally in its effect on the politics and economics of water supply and in its determination of the "rules of the game" for extending water service to new development.

Eastern and western states are governed by different doctrines of water law: eastern states follow the riparian doctrine, and western states apply the doctrine of prior appropriation. A few states use parts of each system.

Under the riparian system, a landowner adjacent to a body of water is entitled to "reasonable use" of the water as long as the rights to use of the water by downstream users is not unduly impaired. Under the prior-appropriation doctrine, the first person to make "beneficial" use of the water is entitled to continued diversion and use of that much of the water. That person's right has priority over the rights of all users who come later. Neither doctrine is well suited as a legal basis for the allocation of a scarce resource. Indeed, a few states have begun to recognize that the legal regimes under which they operate impair the rational management of water as a public resource.

Both doctrines give certain users vested property rights in the water, and these rights may be condemned and purchased under the power of eminent domain for a public purpose or benefit. They may also be regulated, but any such regulation must meet tests of reasonableness. Unreasonable regulations will be voided by the courts, and there is doctrine, but no actual cases, suggesting that if a regulation "goes too far" in depriving owners of the economic use of their property rights, the regulation will be considered to be a taking, and compensation must be paid (*Pennsylvania Coal* v. *Mahon*, 260 U.S. 393 [1922]; *Penn Central* v. *City of New York*, 438 U.S. 104 [1978]). Whether or how these same doctrines apply to groundwater is uncertain.

Some western states have recognized that the long-range implications of the prior-appropriation doctrine for management of their water resources could be devastating. For example, they could be faced with the need to compensate owners of water rights for water needed by the public even though the owners had never used the water and had no present plans to use it. In 1973 Montana enacted a law that allows government agencies to acquire prospective water rights. Thus, a river such as the Yellowstone, from which relatively little capacity has been appropriated by prior users, can be protected for future public needs. In 1980 Arizona enacted the Groundwater Management Act, which requires users of groundwater to accept conservation measures and taxes to achieve, by 2025, safe yields, in which withdrawals will not exceed the rate of recharge. New development can be approved only if it shows proof of an assured water supply. After 2006 the state is authorized to purchase agricultural land and retire it from that use if conservation measures alone appear to be inadequate.

These states are nibbling at the edge of a powerful legal doctrine that is as old as the Roman empire but that has not yet been broadly applied to water law, especially for groundwater. The doctrine of public trust asserts that the government holds certain rights in trust for the public and has the authority to exercise continuous supervision to protect the people's common heritage. The doctrine has been invoked to protect shorelines and wetlands and to allow states to reclaim rights that had been previously granted to private interests for the use of marine lands. In 1983 the California Supreme Court invoked public trust doctrine to declare that the state could reconsider and revise the "rights" of the Los Angeles Department of Water and Power to divert water from the Mono Lake basin (*National Audubon Society* v. *Superior Court of Alpine County*, 33 Cal. 3d 419; 658 P2d 709 [1983]). The court held that no one could claim a vested right to divert waters once it becomes clear that the diversion harms interests protected by the public trust. Thus, the state is not confined to stand by its past decisions if they look incorrect in the light of current knowledge (658 P2d at 712).

Given the magnitude and complexity of the problems the nation will face in the next 50 years concerning the adequacy of water supplies, their allocation to uses, and their geographic distribution, it is already past time to rethink the foundations of water law in the United States. Public trust doctrine may be a useful place to start in reconciling eastern and western law and in rationalizing the basis for both the market and public decisions that will have to be made (Casey, 1984; Dunning, 1983; Huffman, 1983).

In addition, it will be necessary to decipher just what it means for water to be an article of commerce, subject to regulation both by Congress and, to some extent, by the states. Ultimately, federal legislation will probably be necessary to establish the limits of interbasin and interstate transfers. Public trust doctrine may provide useful tools in dealing with issues such as intergenerational equity and the limits of state regulation of privately held water rights.

Both the federal government and the states need to redesign the decision-making processes used at federal and regional levels for setting and carrying out water supply and distribution policies. Coordinated planning for the development, conservation, and use of water supplies will be needed at the national level as it becomes clear that climate changes and pollution threaten to change the value of water and place some parts of the country in serious economic jeopardy. It will also be necessary to think seriously about how planning for this basic resource and for the infrastructure necessary to use it efficiently and equitably relates to the development of a system of cities in the United States that will advance our capacity to compete with the rest of the world in an information-based economy (Hanson, 1983).

Coordinated policy planning does not necessarily imply that the result will be a nationally managed water market. Even a decision to encourage a free market in water will take concerted action to free such a market from the institutional barriers that current law and bureaucracies have erected. The eventual solution is likely to be a mixture of market management, and much of the management is likely to be decentralized to the states and regional agencies.

It is important, however, to take a hard look at the existing morass of treaties, compacts, and agencies governing water decisions at various levels of the federal system. All the flows of some rivers have already been allocated to uses that do not fit current, let alone future, realities (U.S. General Accounting Office, 1979). Agencies that deal with water quality are often separate from those that deal with water supplies. It is not essential that they be consolidated; it is critical that they participate in the decisions that determine the future of the supply system.

Changing the rules of the game for water politics would be helpful, however difficult it might be. At the national level, Congress concerns itself with specific water projects while the President tries to develop a national water policy. The system is a classic case of distributional politics in which the decisions benefit a small segment of the population but do not visibly harm the rest, who nevertheless end up paying for them (Lord, 1980). The process needs to be changed so that the distribution of costs and benefits and the questions about how these decisions will affect settlement patterns and economic activities can be better understood. Yet in some respects, initiating such a change would generate more rather than less conflict. This assumption suggests that the modest steps taken in setting up the Water Resources Council, which has been abolished by the Reagan administration, should be retraced, but this time the council should be given more clout in the development of a national water policy. It is also important that the Congress consider and act on a unified national water policy rather than on individual projects. If Congress can be persuaded of the need for a comprehensive policy to deal with the impending changes in climate and world economies, such a deliberative process may actually be possible.

At the state and regional levels, similar action would be desirable. Informal and quasi-governmental organizations on a regional scale already have some potential for developing into more than marching and chowder societies dedicated to the protection of their own turf. One promising model is the International Coalition for Land and Water Stewardship in the Red River Valley. This grass-roots association of citizens and governments in Minnesota, North Dakota, and Manitoba was organized in response to local frustration from trying to get the public agencies to coordinate their efforts in flood control, irrigation, and water supply. The coalition is organized according to watershed and aims to build a consensus in the region for a comprehensive conservation and use program. Currently, it is funded by donations from members and foundations.

Watershed and basinwide organizations can deal adequately with issues that are internal to their regions. There will be a need, however, for ways to mediate and determine interbasin disputes and arrangements. One of the central issues of national and interregional policy by the turn of the century will be the extent to which large-scale transfer projects should be provided. If these decisions are not made by that time, aqueducts cannot be in place by 2025 when significant effects of climate change could begin to be felt. By that time, decisions made for transfers of water will be too late to sustain urban settlements that have already occurred, and the nation might face the need to depopulate certain large cities.

CONCLUSION

What oil has been to the twentieth century, water may be to the twenty-first century. Its inefficient use, maldistribution, and absolute scarcity will be a basis for political conflict in the United States and possibly for military conflict in other parts of the world. The presence of an adequate supply will be the sine qua non of urban development and a healthy agricultural economy. Its presence will give some regions of the country comparative advantages they do not currently realize.

Water infrastructure for the twenty-first century will still require dams and treatment facilities and pipes. But more than at any time in national history, it will also require the development of new institutions of markets, law, and governance.

REFERENCES

Casey, E. S. 1984. Water law—Public trust doctrine. Natural Resources Journal 24(3): 809–825.

Caswell, M., and D. Zilberman. 1985. The choice of irrigation technologies in California. American Journal of Agricultural Economics 67(2):224.

Ciborowski, P. 1985a. The greenhouse problem: Physical dimensions and consideration of risks. Paper prepared for the World Resources Institute, Washington, D.C.

Ciborowski, P. 1985b. Societal response to a greenhouse warming. Paper presented at the University of Washington Quaternary Research Center Seminar, April 30, 1985.

Congressional Budget Office. 1983. Public Works Infrastructure: Policy Considerations for the 1980s. Washington, D.C.: U.S. Government Printing Office.

Conservation Foundation. 1984. America's Water: Current Trends and Emerging Issues. Washington, D.C.: The Conservation Foundation.

Dunning, H. C. 1983. A new front in the water wars: Introducing the public trust doctrine. California Journal (May).

Hanson, R. 1983. Rethinking Urban Policy: Urban Development in an Advanced Economy. Washington, D.C.: National Academy Press.

Humphrey, N. 1983. Strategies for Financing Maintenance. Report No. 2 for the Urban Infrastructure Network. Washington, D.C.: The Urban Institute.

Huffman, J. 1983. Instream water use: Public and private alternatives. In Water Rights: Scarce Resource Allocation, Bureaucracy and the Environment, T. Anderson, ed. Cambridge, Mass.: Ballinger Publishing Company.

Ingram, H., and J. R. McCain. 1977. Federal water resources management; The administrative setting. Public Administration Review 37(5): 448–455.

Lord, W. B. 1980. Water resources planning: Conflict management. Water Spectrum 12(Summer):3.

Miller, J. R., and D. A. Underwood. 1983. Distributional issues in western municipal and industrial water supply. Water Resources Bulletin 18(August):4.

National Research Council. 1983. Changing Climate: Report of the Carbon Dioxide Assessment Committee. Washington, D.C.: National Academy Press.

O'Day, D. K., and L. A. Neumann. 1983. Assessing infrastructure needs: The state of the art. Pp. 67–109 in Perspectives on Urban Infrastructure, R. Hanson, ed. Washington, D.C.: National Academy Press.

Office of Technology Assessment. 1983. Technologies and Management Strategies for Hazardous Waste Control. Washington, D.C.: Office of Technology Assessment.

Peterson, G. E. 1984. Financing the nation's infrastructure requirements. Pp.110–142 in Perspectives on Urban Infrastructure, R. Hanson, ed. Washington, D.C.: National Academy Press.

Postel, S. 1984. Water: Rethinking management in an age of scarcity. Worldwatch Paper 62. Washington, D.C.: Worldwatch Institute.

Postel, S. 1985. Conserving water: The untapped alternative. Worldwatch Paper 67. Washington, D.C.: Worldwatch Institute.

Pye, V. I., R. Patrick, and J. Quarles. 1983. Groundwater Contamination in the United States. Philadelphia: University of Pennsylvania Press.

Revelle, R. R., and P. E. Waggoner. 1983. Effects of a carbon dioxide-induced climatic change on water supplies in the western United States. Pp. 419–432 in Changing Climate: Report of the Carbon Dioxide Assessment Committee. Washington, D.C.: National Academy Press.

Senate Committee on Environment and Public Works. 1984. Safe Drinking Water Act Amendments of 1984. Hearings before the Subcommittee on Toxic Substances and Environmental Oversights on S. 2469. Washington, D.C.: U.S. Government Printing Office.

Shelley, F. M., and C. Wijeyawickrema. 1984. Local opposition to the transfer of water supplies: An Oklahoma case. Water Resources Bulletin 20(October):5.

Urban Land. 1983. Stormwater retention protects water supply. July.

U.S. Environmental Protection Agency, Office of Water Program Operations. 1981. Flow Reduction: Methods, Analysis, Procedures, Examples. Washington, D.C.: U.S. EPA.

U.S. General Accounting Office. 1979. Water Supply in Urban Areas: Problems in Meeting Future Demand. Washington, D.C.: U.S. General Accounting Office.

Wrenn, D. M. 1983. Water availability: A factor of cost. Urban Land (July).

13

The Urban Wastewater Infrastructure

BERNARD B. BERGER

The urban wastewater treatment infrastructure is by tradition, preference, and engineering necessity either underground or so remotely located as to be out of sight. Still, system shortcomings or malfunctions are in time inevitably impressed on system users—and almost always in disagreeable ways. It would be tempting in this overview of system evolution to set aside for the moment the problems of today, to take a bold leap into the future and describe where we should like to be and therefore expect to be 50 years from now. Unfortunately, the problems of today cannot be ignored or solved simply by fiat; their solution will shape the wastewater infrastructure of the future.

The function of the wastewater infrastructure is of course to protect public health and decency by carrying wastewaters away from those who generated them, to dispose of such wastewaters in ways that will not harm aquatic ecosystems or wildlife, and to present no significant hazard or displeasure to humans. The wastewater treatment infrastructure is not intended, and should not be depended on, to produce an effluent clean enough to keep a pristine receiving stream unchanged in purity and of drinking water quality. The main defense of the quality of drinking water is the drinking water treatment plant, not the wastewater treatment infrastructure. The systems are of course sequentially related, and sometimes they are combined. Separate infrastructures are traditional, however, and this arrangement, which has worked satisfactorily for years, is reflected in our political and professional institutions.

The main physical components of the urban wastewater infrastructure are the collection system, the treatment plant, and the water body that receives the plant effluent. The tasks these components present to the ''keepers'' of the infrastructure go beyond improvements in technology, multiple and difficult as they are. The responsibilities of water pollution control authorities include developing more effective and reliable planning techniques for projecting system growth and modification, resolving current uncertainties in setting water quality standards for water bodies receiving wastewater discharges, solving the troublesome problem of treating wastewaters of industries using the public sewerage system, coming to grips effectively with the problems of combined sewer overflows and nonpoint runoff, finding acceptable ways for permanent disposal of sludge, and establishing an adequate and equitable funding base for operating, maintaining, and upgrading the wastewater disposal system. To place these tasks in perspective, the following sections of this chapter will describe the evolution and outstanding problems of the system's major components.

THE COLLECTION SYSTEM

The existing sewerage systems of most large municipalities, particularly the older cities of the eastern United States, are patchworks of pipes and conduits of various ages and sizes. Some were installed to convey both household sewage and industrial wastewaters, some serve only to collect and carry away storm-water runoff, and some are designed to transport both wastewater and runoff. The applicable terms are sanitary sewer, storm sewer, and combined sewer, respectively. Chronologically, the sequence of development and use should be storm sewer, combined sewer, and sanitary sewer. Until about the 1830s, with only rare exceptions, collection systems, many just open ditches, were designed for the sole purpose of carrying off storm-water runoff. Household wastes were to be placed for final disposal in privy vaults or cesspools, many of which served multiple families. Deposition of household wastes in storm drains was banned by law to prevent creating noisome conditions and public nuisance.

This policy, which presumably reflected the best professional judgment of the late eighteenth and early nineteenth centuries, proved disastrous in a short time. This was evident in the filthiness of the city environment of the day, as suggested by Hogarth's well-known drawings and as attested to by writers of the period. A particularly vivid picture of an early morning in Edinburgh in Queen Anne's time is painted by G. M. Trevelyan in *English Social History*:

Far overhead the windows opened, five, six, or ten storeys in the air, and the close stools of Edinburgh discharged the collected filth of the last twenty-four hours into the street. It was good manners for those above to cry 'Gardy-loo!'

(Gardez l'eau) before throwing. The returning roysterer cried back 'Haud yer han,' and ran with humped shoulders, lucky if his vast and expensive full-bottomed wig was not put out of action by a cataract of filth. The ordure thus sent down lay in the broad High Street and in the deep, well-like closes and wynds around it making the night air horrible, until early in the morning it was perfunctorily cleared away by the City Guard. Only on a Sabbath morn it might not be touched, but lay there all day long, filling Scotland's capital with the savour of a mistaken piety. (1942, pp. 437–438)

The Combined Sewer

The discovery in 1849 of the role of the backyard cesspool in spreading cholera through a contaminated drinking water system, a landmark in protecting the public health, led to a reversal in wastewater policy and practice. Soon thereafter, household wastewaters had to be discharged into the nearest storm drain to be conveyed away from human habitation as quickly as possible. Thus, the storm drain became the combined sewer. From a cost–benefit point of view, the use of a combined sewer rather than separate sewers seemed to be obviously advantageous, and it soon became standard practice in the cities of Europe and the United States. The sizing of combined sewers was based on accepted assumptions about the extent of area to be served, population density, per capita wastewater contributions, wastewater discharges from commercial and industrial establishments, rainfall intensity and duration, and physical characteristics of the ground surface.

The combined sewer, which was so logical a development a century and a half ago, has in the past 25 years presented a major problem. This conclusion is based on the fact that it is simply not feasible from an engineering or economic point of view to provide sufficient capacity in such sewers to transport all of the runoff resulting from a heavy storm. Even moderate storms may produce flows far in excess of the combined sewer's carrying capacity, which is usually limited to about three times the average daily dry-weather flow. Overflow or relief devices are therefore provided in the combined sewer to prevent the backup of sewage into basements at times of sewer surcharge. The overflows are discharged without treatment into nearby watercourses.

Given the apparent logic of the planning assumptions, design engineers of the early city systems believed that the life and utility of the combined sewer would be affected only by deterioration of materials, which could readily be repaired. Unfortunately, in many cities the planning assumptions proved to have their own life expectancies, and over time they failed to hold up. The populations connected to the sewer increased, as did the per capita sewage contribution. In many cities the area served by main sewers grew far beyond what was expected and designed for as a result of community growth, intensive land development, and annexations. Overflows that initially occurred rarely and lasted for only brief periods increased in frequency and duration. Many examples of stream pollution by overflow from combined sewers may be cited; a well-documented case is the shoreline and coastal waters of Boston Harbor, into which more than 100 overflows discharge. Long an insignificant source of water pollution, sewer overflows have now become one of our most important and intractable pollution problems, one that will continue to trouble us as far ahead as we can see. Unless this shortcoming of our municipal wastewater infrastructure is corrected, the benefits we expect to result from capital investment in wastewater treatment plants will not be fully realized. Even if treatment plant effluents were given the quality of distilled water, the receiving water bodies would still be polluted at times by the discharges from combined sewer overflows.

It may appear surprising that water pollution control agencies have been so slow to recognize the problem. In retrospect it seems so clear: populations, per capita water use, and contributory areas were all increasing, but the combined sewers remained the same in size and carrying capacity. It would seem, again in retrospect, that anyone with common sense should have seen the problem developing. Many environmental engineers did, of course, and where conditions approached the unendurable, sewer improvement programs were undertaken despite their high cost and the extreme disruption they produced. What appears to be a failure in problem perception is more likely the result of the priority given to construction of treatment plants and to preoccupation with this latter task.

Engineers believed at first that the solution to the problem of overflow from combined sewers would be found in a sewer separation program: The existing combined sewer would receive wastewater from only households and commercial and industrial establishments for conveyance to the treatment plants; the storm sewer would collect runoff for discharge to the nearest watercourse. The idea of separate systems was a sound one, but the enormous cost of such a program, apart from the disruption associated with it, was a major deterrent to aggressive planning. Whatever support remained for sewer separation, except in special cases, weakened further with findings that street wash (runoff) could be highly pollutional: the first flush from the storm sewer could be stronger than raw sewage, and the pollutional character could persist throughout the discharge.

Some engineers suggested that the problem could be controlled by constructing storage tanks at each overflow. The tanks would permit the return of overflow to the sewer when dry-weather flow resumed. Alternatively, the tank contents could be chlorinated and discharged to the watercourse. This approach was generally rejected except in special situations because of the difficulties and costs of land acquisition at overflow locations, problems in controlling settleable solids, and the enormous cost of operating and maintaining storage chambers, pumping equipment, and chlorinators at what might well be a hundred or more locations in the city.

A unique solution to the combined sewer overflow and storm runoff is seen in Chicago's Tunnel and Reservoir Plan (TARP), which was proposed initially in 1962 (Dalton and Rimkus, 1985). Here, 131 miles (mi) of tunnel (47 mi completed by the end of 1985) 9 to 33 feet (ft) in diameter and 150 to 350 ft below street level will intercept all excess sewage and runoff for conveyance to underground reservoirs sized to contain the largest rainfall in Chicago's history. When dry weather returns, the diluted sewage will be pumped back and treated before discharge into the canal system. A plan similar to Chicago's multibillion-dollar project was proposed in 1963 for the city of Boston but was never accepted (Horsefield, 1968).

Urban Hygiene

The Chicago plan, heroic in concept and size, would probably be applicable at only a few locations. More generally, a solution for the problem of overflow from combined sewers must entail either capture and management of the overflow or separation of sewers. The difficulties that occur with the latter have already been described. Still, urban storm-water collection systems are used extensively, and therefore ways of minimizing the pollutional impact of such discharges must be considered. The obvious solution is to keep our urban land surfaces, paved and unpaved, as clean as possible. This means more than frequent street cleanings; it signifies the recognition of a new and heightened perception of urban cleanliness or urban hygiene, which should include special collection and disposal of potentially hazardous chemicals used in the home, cleanup of unmapped and perhaps forgotten dumps and sites once used for disposal of concentrated industrial liquid wastes, and rigorous control of animal wastes. More fundamentally, it means the initiation of an education program in which urban hygiene is equated with personal hygiene. Although one cannot expect that the pollutional character of urban nonpoint runoff could be reduced to zero or even near zero, an effective urban hygiene program may provide a basis for rendering such pollution innocuous.

Land Use Management

The ultimate utility of a deep tunnel and reservoir plan or any other plan will of course depend on the long-term accuracy of the assumptions used in the planning process. To minimize the chances of recurrence of the existing overflow problem, a prudent policy for protecting the sewerage system is required. At the least, such a policy should include adequate control of land use and development and careful assessment of programs of regionalization and land annexations for which sewerage service rights may be granted.

The converse of the issue of granting sewerage service rights is that, although the wastewater infrastructure is an important determinant of the distribution of population and allied service industry, it is by no means exclusive. Population and industry move to outlying or extraurban areas as a result of many forces, including improved and expanded systems of public and private transportation and new housing developments, which offer attractive opportunities and facilities for education, recreation, and employment. The predicted widespread introduction of household telematic systems may, by weakening the need for central work sites, result in further redistribution of population to outlying areas. The sewerage system, which represents a very substantial public investment, is of course fixed in place. A policy or urban development strategy that results in redistribution of population and industry could reduce the use of portions of the existing sewerage system and the revenue derived from it. This reduction in turn could adversely affect system operation and maintenance. The strategy of urban land use planning should be to foresee such consequences and, to the degree possible, try to preserve the values inherent in the existing infrastructure.

Although the focus here is on the collection of urban wastewaters, the impact of nonurban, nonpoint sources of pollution, such as from rural and agricultural lands, cannot be ignored. Such sources, particularly the runoff from agricultural land, may place a heavy burden on the receiving water body and at times reduce markedly the benefits of urban wastewater management. The significance of agricultural land runoff is evident: such runoff contains high concentrations of oxygen-demanding substances, suspended solids, bacteria, pesticides, and nutrient chemicals. The remedy lies in use of agricultural practices and land management techniques designed to minimize and control the storm runoff. Unfortunately, concern over this problem occupies a low position in the current hierarchy of agricultural priorities. In the long term, this need will have to be addressed.

WASTEWATER TREATMENT AND THE RECEIVING WATER BODY

The wastewater treatment plant and the receiving body of water are linked components of the municipal wastewater system. In principle, the nature and design of the treatment processes depend directly on the water quality standards set for the water body. In practice, the mandatory requirement for universal secondary treatment—that is, treatment that provides separation of settleable and floatable solids and stabilization by microbial communities of oxygen-demanding substances—usually suffices. This treatment amounts to an acceleration of the processes of self-purification occurring naturally in the stream.

Biological Wastewater Treatment

Universal compliance by municipalities with the requirement for secondary (i.e., biological) wastewater treatment meeting conventional performance criteria would remove a major pollutional burden from the nation's waters. The U.S. Environmental Protection Agency (EPA) reports, however, that although industry (i.e., those businesses that are not served by public sewers) is doing an acceptable job in cleaning up its discharges, municipalities are lagging. In fact, EPA reports that about 30 percent of publicly owned wastewater treatment plants fail to meet the effluent criteria. Several reasons for such dereliction have been cited, but the reason most frequently noted is an insufficient number of adequately trained plant operators.

This condition stems in the main from the nature of the federal program of grants to municipalities for the construction of wastewater treatment plants. Provision for such an incentive was contained in the original 1948 enactment of the Federal Water Pollution Control Act, but the Federal Water Pollution Control Grant Program was not adequately funded until passage of the 1966 amendments. The size of these federal grants was increased in subsequent legislation and in 1972 amounted to 75 percent of a plant's contruction cost. Many states supplemented the federal grant with a 15 percent state grant. The combined grant covered construction only, however; it did not extend to plant operation and maintenance. Given the conservative inclination of consulting engineers in the wastewater field and their understandable concern with reputation and with liability, few viewed with enthusiasm EPA's efforts to move them toward seeking innovative, alternative methods of wastewater treatment. The conventional processes were generally installed. These processes require trained technicians for plant operation and maintenance because of the nature of the mechanical and electrical equipment being used and the need for routine sensitive microbiological and chemical testing for process control. Too often, municipalities consider the costs of such requirements excessive. The result is a low-quality effluent, a degraded water body, and a capital investment that has been improperly employed.

What is needed here and can be provided by imposing adequate sewer service charges is a sufficient and assured funding base for operation and maintenance as well as for additions and replacements to physical plants. What is now general policy for many public water supply systems should be adopted by the wastewater agencies. Many communities have already adopted a service charge policy; whether the charge is adequate depends on the availability and adoption of a rigorous method of auditing system management.

Federal funds amounting to nearly $50 billion have been granted to municipalities since 1972 for the construction of wastewater treatment plants. Still, the job is far from completed. EPA has estimated that another $39 billion will be needed by the year 2000 for plant construction (Journal of the Water Pollution Control Federation, 1985). Congress did not intend that the federal construction grant program be permanent; the 1972 legislation specified its termination in 1982. It is no great surprise, however, that this did not occur because the pressure by states and municipalities to continue the program was too great. Funds are now appropriated year to year, and many observers believe the program will be terminated in the near future. This in fact seems to be the current will of Congress. The 1987 Clean Water Act amendment, which Congress passed over the President's veto, authorizes a fiscal year 1987 expenditure of $1.2 billion for direct construction grants to municipalities but calls for an end to this program by 1990.

Physical and Chemical Methods of Wastewater Treatment

Until about 1960 the bulk of research and development on wastewater treatment was directed toward improving biological treatment processes. In that year the U.S. Public Health Service, which was then the agency responsible for conducting the federal water pollution control program, undertook an examination of a broad span of physical and chemical principles that seemed to offer promise in solids separation. A review (Koenig, 1983) of such processes, excluding those already widely used in wastewater treatment, includes the following:

Centrifugation	Adsorption
Magnetism	Electrokinetics
Surface tension	Electrophoresis
Foam fractionation	Electro-osmosis
Froth flotation	Electrodialysis
Solvent extraction	Freezing
Stripping	Hydration
Distillation	Microfiltration and
Osmosis	ultrafiltration
Chemical oxidation	Ion exchange
	Reverse osmosis

Thus, we have experienced a dual trend in research and development, encompassing on one hand a most efficient employment of the processes occurring in nature and on the other the application of an advanced and presumably more costly technology. This duality, however, should not be viewed as necessarily reflecting competition. The fact is that advanced techniques for separating solids are commonly considered processes that supplement rather than replace secondary treatment, enabling the effluent to meet rigorous standards of water quality.

Concern with wastewater treatment is worldwide; yet the industrialized countries exhibit few major differences in approach to the technology of wastewater treatment. Goals may vary, and those of the United States are among the most stringent, but the basic methods for meeting these goals are similar.

Therefore, we can foresee that the wastewater treatment infrastructure for urban areas will continue to consist of primary and secondary treatment, modified as experience justifies, in addition to tertiary treatment as required to meet water quality standards for the receiving water body. Decisions on the design and operation of such systems, including selection and use of major system components, will continue to be based on what has become the customary analysis of life-cycle costs within a context of restricted system funding.

The shortcomings in our existing wastewater treatment infrastructure therefore are not the result of an absence of effective technology for pollutant separation or destruction; a broad range of candidate solids-separation processes is available. We can if necessary treat sewage to a degree that meets the most stringent requirement of drinking water. The health effects and public acceptability of such direct reuse as well as the costs of treatment are now being studied by the city of Denver. In that project the biologically treated sewage effluent is being further treated by a complex train of processes for microbial destruction and for separation of solids (Lauer, 1985). The goals are to lower process costs, improve plant operation and maintenance, and develop acceptable ways of disposing of sludge. There are additional and equally difficult challenges: the establishment of reasonable water quality standards and the control of wastewater discharges from industry into the public sewerage system.

Water Quality Standards

The Federal Water Pollution Control Act Amendments of 1972 (33 U.S.C. §1251 et seq.) define pollution as "the man-made or man-induced alteration of the chemical, physical, biological, and radiological integrity of the water''; they also set a national goal of "elimination of discharges of pollution into navigable waters." Accomplishing this feat will require at least that we know what pollutants reach the sewerage system and what concentrations of such substances may be tolerated with repeated exposure by humans, aquatic life, and wildlife. We have made, and continue to make, substantial advances in techniques for detecting, identifying, and measuring synthetic organic compounds in extremely low concentrations. As we do so, however, we complicate the problems of assessing risks and determining maximum tolerable concentrations, which are the basis of water quality standards. We make the task even more complex by misrepresenting the real world in which exposures rarely involve single compounds in pure solution but instead entail multiple compounds in mixture.

Numerous workers have emphasized the uncertainties associated with extrapolating the results of animal tests, the paucity of useful epidemiologic knowledge because of the rarity of illness caused by organic compounds of industrial origin in water solution, and the weakness of assumptions of toxicity based solely on chemical structure. For any given pollutant (or mixture of pollutants) the questions remain: How does the level of risk in a given water sample vary with concentration and exposure time? What risk may be tolerated by humans? How is such knowledge to be translated into water quality standards and limits on treatment plant effluent? Such knowledge is essential to municipal acceptance and control of industrial wastewater discharges and to the design and management of the wastewater treatment plant.

William D. Ruckelshaus, former EPA administrator, has commented on this issue:

"Risk assessment" is the device that government agencies such as EPA have adopted to deal with this quandary. It is the attempt to quantify the degree of hazard that might result from human activities—for example, the risks to human health and the environment from industrial chemicals. Essentially, it is a kind of pretense; to avoid the paralysis of protective action that would result from waiting for "definitive" data, we assume that we have greater knowledge than scientists actually possess and make decisions based on those assumptions. . . .

Despite this uneasiness, there appears to be no substitute for risk assessment, in that some sort of risk finding is what tells us that there is any basis for regulatory action in the first place. The alternative to not performing risk assessment is to adopt a policy of either reducing all *potentially* toxic emissions to the greatest degree technology allows . . . or banning all substances for which there is any evidence of harmful effect, a policy that no technological society could long survive. Beyond that, risk assessment is an irreplaceable tool for setting priorities among the tens of thousands of substances that could be subjects of control actions—substances that vary enormously in their apparent potential for causing disease. In my view, therefore, we must use and improve risk assessment with full recognition of its current shortcomings. (1985, pp. 26 and 27)

In his examination of this issue, Alvin M. Weinberg (1985) emphasizes the practical impossibility of developing clear-cut methods for predicting the health consequences of chemical pollutants present in trace concentrations. He suggests several ways to provide some assurance of safety despite the uncertainty: by "technological fix," that is, by the inherent character of the design, and by application of the principle of de minimis (Weinberg, 1985). The first method presumably would require specific pollutant sensors in the plant effluent that could feed data back to process controls. The second would be applicable to situations in which there is natural exposure to chemicals of concern and in which man-induced exposure is low by comparison. The technological fix presents a challenging assignment to research workers. The de minimis approach presumably could be used only in cases in which the natural background exists; given the synthetic nature of most pollutants of industrial origin, few opportunities would be likely.

In an earlier day the procedure was simpler, and uncertainties were few and seldom troublesome. Some of our older coworkers will undoubtedly remember the time when "dilution is the solution to pollution" was accepted as doctrine. At that time, one proceeded confidently on the basis that 2.5–4 ft^3/second of streamflow could assimilate safely and without nuisance the raw sewage produced by a population of 1,000 people. This primitive procedure was set aside in 1925 with the development of the Streeter-Phelps dissolved oxygen level. This equation, refined and elaborated, is still used when dissolved oxygen is a critical water quality criterion. Such occasions are less frequent now that all municipal wastewater treatment plants (except for a few waivers for coastal cities) must provide secondary treatment of wastewater. The stream's capacity to assimilate dissolved oxygen-demanding substances is, for all practical purposes, not now available to wastewater dischargers.

Pretreatment of Industrial Wastewaters

The occurrence of significant concentrations of heavy metals and non-biodegradable, possibly toxic, organic substances in wastewaters reaching the treatment plant presents problems few biological treatment plants are designed to handle. Unless such potentially harmful substances are separated and removed in the sludge, whose utility and value are reduced thereby, they appear in the plant effluent and in the receiving water body. Most of these pollutants are discharged into the sewer by industrial plants despite the requirements of the Federal Water Pollution Control Act that such dischargers pretreat their wastewaters. This program has generally proved difficult and ineffective. Although control of such pollution is absolutely essential to the success of the national program for water pollution control, pollution from these sources continues to be a burden to treatment plants and a potential hazard in water bodies.

Perhaps it is unrealistic to expect small industrial plants connected to the urban sewer to provide effective control of their wastewaters as required by the Federal Water Pollution Control Act. Such control would include familiar and difficult tasks, including defining the character of the wastewaters, treating these wastewaters sufficiently and reliably, and monitoring dependably the treated effluent before discharging it into the public sewer. Few industrial plants have had to cope with such responsibilities, and few have the experience, staff, and laboratory resources required for this task. It is hardly surprising therefore that compliance by the industry with pretreatment requirements has been poor, despite the availability of private consulting firms to provide the services desired.

A bold remedy might be considered: the initiation of a municipal industrial wastewater acceptance program through which the municipality would assume responsibility for industrial wastewater characterization, treatment, and monitoring. This responsibility should not be solely the municipality's, however; industrial plant management must have the opportunity for adopting in-plant controls that could reduce the pollutional load. The cost of the municipal program must of course be borne by the industry served.

The concept of the acceptance plan is not new. Two decades ago the state of Maryland instituted a program providing state acceptance of municipal and industrial wastewater discharges (Butrico and Coulter, 1972). Even now, many cities provide services approaching those that would be covered by the municipal industrial wastewater acceptance plan.

Sludge Management

Disposal of sludge satisfactorily and permanently remains a persistent and often frustrating challenge. The use of sludge as fertilizer, an accepted practice in an earlier day, is commonly in disfavor today because of fear that it may contain toxic substances. Sludge can be disposed of in a number of ways: It can be discharged into coastal waters (usually with gross consequences as in Boston); it may be placed in landfills as a component of the municipality's solid wastes; or it may be incinerated, in which case resulting air pollution must be controlled. With few exceptions, current modes of sludge disposal by large cities are temporary, expensive, and productive of complaint and stress. The development of innovative methods for permanent and acceptable sludge disposal for medium-sized and large cities remains a high-priority need in the wastewater infrastructure of tomorrow.

COMPREHENSIVE PLANNING

The importance of planning in the nationwide program of water pollution control was recognized in the initial federal legislation, which stated the "Surgeon General (of the U.S. Public Health Service) shall . . . prepare or adopt comprehensive programs for eliminating or reducing the pollution of interstate waters and the tributaries thereof, and improving the sanitary condition of surface and underground waters" (U.S. Congress, 1948). In the main, the federal government's procedure was to help the states develop or update their river basin plans and to work for national uniformity in setting water quality standards and treatment plant performance criteria. This initial approach contributed to an acceptance of the concept of uniformity and to the process of cooperation among the states. In other respects the federal program of comprehensive planning proved to be of only limited value. The plans that evolved could not accommodate unforeseen growth and shifts in population or the relocation of industrial plants. The program did not foresee the federally imposed universal requirement for biological treatment of wastewater from municipalities or for "best-available" treatment for industries. It gave little thought to pollution from combined sewer overflows and to nonpoint sources of pollution.

In the eyes of many experienced wastewater engineers, an important shortcoming of the program was its primary emphasis on a basinwide approach and its failure to focus adequately on the need to clean up the largest wastewater discharges, namely, those from the cities located at the mouths of interstate river systems. Ironically, cleanup of these latter discharges would have little effect on the pollution in the river system itself.

The far-reaching 1972 amendments to the National Water Pollution Control Act shifted the planning focus to those areas where industrial and urban wastewater problems were highly complex and difficult—that is, to the large urban areas. The areawide planning programs, the so-called Section 208 programs, were instituted throughout the nation; through them, planners tried to come to grips with problems of regionalization as reflected in the integration of planning by central cities, satellite communities, and industries, and they searched for ways to control the nonpoint sources of pollution. These programs were generally conducted by regional planning agencies that were strongly imbued with the ideal of environmental quality restoration and preservation. The programs aspired to the development of coherent plans for integrating regional point and nonpoint wastewater collection, treatment, and disposal systems and for realizing effective programs of urban hygiene. These goals could seldom be reached, however, because the impediments were too great. Solutions to existing problems remained elusive. And institutional barriers could not be effectively removed: agencies responsible for design, construction, and operation of wastewater collection and treatment systems differed in training, experience, and outlook from those engaged in Section 208 planning. Even so, in many areas these programs gave impetus to comprehensive wastewater management planning; unfortunately, with the termination of these programs, such positive improvements seemed to weaken.

CONCLUSION

This chapter focuses on physical structures, policies, and practices that represent weaknesses in many urban wastewater management systems. Wastewater discharges that are still poorly controlled include overflows from combined sewers, storm-water runoff, and contributions from other nonpoint sources. To these must be added, in many areas, treatment plant effluents, which too often fail to meet minimum performance conditions and moreover may contain toxic substances that conventional treatment processes are not intended to remove. The sources of pollution and the problems they present may be readily visualized; their solutions, although apparent in many cases, are often difficult to achieve.

Chicago's Tunnel and Reservoir Plan, although enormously costly, may be a prototypical solution for large urban areas that experience frequent and protracted overflows from combined sewers and excessive pollution from storm runoff. Other remedial measures can also be described, but at this time they do not justify a high level of enthusiasm.

The task of setting maximum allowable concentrations of toxic substances by balancing the costs and benefits of reducing or eliminating them, if in fact such balance is sought, will continue to challenge us as long as basic essential information is lacking. In the absence of reasonable and protective maximum allowable concentrations, questions about equity, as in requirements imposed on industrial waste dischargers, will persist, as will questions about the adequacy of the wastewater management program.

Four additional aspects of the urban wastewater management infrastructure require improvement: (1) pretreating industrial wastewater discharges, (2) upgrading the operation and maintenance of treatment plants,

(3) strengthening metropolitan areawide systems of wastewater management, and (4) disposing of sludge. The fourth problem is ubiquitous, persistent, and, in view of the large quantities produced, almost always an awkward, temporary, and costly operation.

The efficiency of urban wastewater infrastructures depends on our ability to solve the problems of system structure, standard setting, funding, management, and planning. The utility of long-range planning is of course influenced by the extent to which we can rely on predictions of population and industrial growth and shifts, and on management of service area extensions and annexation. This statement propounds nothing new, but it is worth repeating because the urban system is not static and the urban picture changes from generation to generation. Population grows, moves into and out of, and shifts within the area. New industries move in, often at the periphery of urban areas, and many exert an unanticipated demand for sewerage service. Isolated communities in the metropolitan area expand or fuse their wastewater treatment systems and in the process create needs for regional systems.

Regulations on water uses and standards are not necessarily fixed in perpetuity and may be altered to reflect new knowledge and reasonable compromises with regard to equity, resource use, and protection of environmental quality. Still, change is slow and, to a degree, manageable; plans can be modified in timely, realistic ways. There are few major surprises, and those there are usually arise from a failure to perceive what is there to be perceived. Adherence to a soundly conceived and frequently updated plan would ensure the usefulness of the wastewater infrastructure for the indefinite future.

REFERENCES

Butrico, F. A., and J. B. Coulter. 1972. Statewide management—what does the future hold? Journal of the Sanitary Engineering Division, Proceedings of the American Society of Civil Engineers. 98(February):247–256.

Dalton, F. E., and R. R. Rimkus. 1985. The Chicago area's Tunnel and Reservoir Plan. Journal of the Water Pollution Control Federation 57(December):1114–1121.

Horsefield, D. R. 1968. Deep Tunnel Plan for the Boston area. Journal of the Boston Society of Civil Engineers (October):231–251.

Journal of the Water Pollution Control Federation. 1985. 1984 needs survey—U.S. Environmental Protection Agency. The Journal 57(May):355.

Koenig, L. 1983. Fundamental considerations in the removal of organic substances from water—a general overview. Pp. 1–25 in Removal of Organic Substances in Water and Wastewater, B. B. Berger, ed. EPA-600/8–83–011. Washington, D.C.: U.S. Environmental Protection Agency.

Lauer, W. C. 1985. The current status of Denver's potable water reuse project. Journal of the American Waterworks Association 77(July):52–59.

Ruckelshaus, W. D. 1985. Risk, science, and democracy. Issues in Science and Technology 2 (Spring):19–38.

Trevelyan, G. M. 1942. English Social History. New York: David McKoy Co., Inc.

U.S. Congress. 1948. Federal Water Pollution Control Act. Section 3, Comprehensive Program for Water Pollution Control. P.L. 80–845.

Weinberg, A. M. 1985. Science and its limits: The regulator's dilemma. Issues in Science and Technology 2(Fall):59–72. (Also pp. 9–23 in Hazards: Technology and Fairness. Washington, D.C.: National Academy Press, 1986.)

14
New Construction Technologies for Rebuilding the Nation's Infrastructure

C. WILLIAM IBBS AND DIEGO ECHEVERRY

The tools and services of the American construction industry are essential to the rebuilding and maintaining of this country's infrastructure. Construction engineers focus on the basic building blocks common to many structures: building components, materials, foundations, and the other elements that are combined to create bridges, hospitals, roads, and other infrastructure facilities.

In recent years, construction engineering has made substantial technological progress. This progress extends across various subfields of the industry: materials science, materials testing, new construction technologies, robotics, and the application of computers to infrastructure construction and management.

This chapter presents examples of technological progress in these subfields and in the construction industry in general. The examples reflect both the kind of innovative work being carried out and its level of sophistication. It should be noted that some of the important innovations in the industry are managerial rather than technological. Contractual risk sharing, labor productivity improvement programs, and project financing schemes fall into this category. This discussion, however, will be limited to the "hard" side of construction engineering and management technology.

THE CURRENT PROBLEM

Current concerns about the nation's infrastructure arise from two factors. First, modern life as we know it could not continue without it. Second, there is a growing body of literature that suggests much of the infrastructure in the United States is in a critical stage of decay.

Anecdotal and statistical evidence substantiates this claim of decay. Overall, the U.S. Federal Highway Administration estimates that 28 percent of the nation's 270,000 bridges are in need of repair or replacement (Constructor, 1986). The Commonwealth of Pennsylvania alone has more than 53,800 highway bridges in use. More than 44 percent of them are 40 years old or more (26 percent are at least 50 years old, and 5 percent are at least 80 years old) (Hoffman, 1986). Older does not necessarily mean worse, but the passage of time has brought problems for many of these bridges. Some 9,400 have been judged structurally deficient or functionally obsolete because of inadequate lane widths, unsafe curve radii, and similar flaws. In Pennsylvania alone the cost of upgrading the bridges to a "desirable status" is projected at $5.7 billion.

Sewers, another critical part of the infrastructure, also need overhauling. For example, roughly three-fourths of Boston's sewers were built in the nineteenth century. The system has decayed to the point where some 15 percent of its flow is lost to leaks. New York City water and sewer lines, which may have had design lives of 75 to 100 years, are replaced long after. City engineers there have called for the replacement of 30 percent of all water mains (2,200 miles) within the next 10 years, with costs estimated at $2.45 billion (O'Day and Neumann, 1984).

Choate and Walter (1983), whose book *America in Ruins* sparked much of the revived interest in public works facilities, estimate that combined government spending from all levels will have to reach $3 trillion in the next decade to maintain the present level of service. A partial list of the most expensive infrastructural items and the estimated cost of their refurbishing includes:

- highways and bridges outside urban areas, $1 trillion;
- city streets, $600 billion;
- municipal water systems, $125 billion;
- water pollution controls, $100 billion;
- ports and inland waterways, $40 billion; and
- prisons and jails, $15 billion.

The total amount needed for public works facilities represents an amount roughly equal to planned national defense outlays over the next 10 years. We are committing only about one-third of this needed sum today.

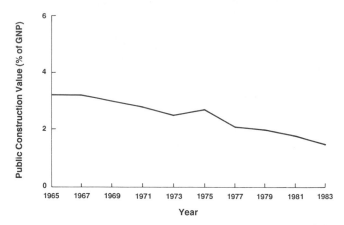

FIGURE 14-1   Recent governmental expenditures on the physical infrastructure as a percentage of the gross national product. Source of data: Construction Review, Washington, D.C.: U.S. Department of Commerce.

Several factors help to explain this situation. One is the decreasing percentage of public funds spent on government construction (U.S. Bureau of the Census, 1970, 1975, 1986). In less than 20 years, these expenditures have dropped by almost half (see Figure 14-1).

Industry inflation compounds this decline in expenditures. As shown in Figure 14-2, annual price increases in the construction industry have ranged up to 20 percent above general economic inflation (U.S. Bureau

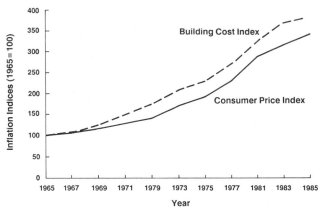

FIGURE 14-2   Inflation in the American construction industry. Source of data: Construction Review, Washington, D.C.: U.S. Department of Commerce.

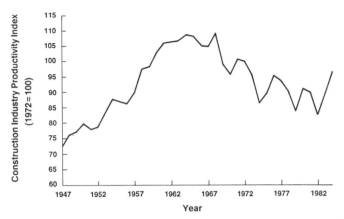

FIGURE 14-3   U.S. construction industry productivity over time. Source of data: Construction Review, Washington, D.C.: U.S. Department of Commerce.

of the Census, 1970, 1975, 1986). Thus, governments are not only spending proportionately fewer dollars today, but, taking inflation into account, they are getting less value for their money than they did 20 years ago.

Moreover, construction productivity, here interpreted as the value or output generated per unit of input, has been uneven over the past three decades by virtually any measure. For example, the composite labor and capital productivity index has been highly erratic and, recently, about 10 percent below the peak years of 1961–1969 (Figures 14-3 and 14-4; Cremeans, 1981). Construction productivity is also low in relation to other components of the national economy (Table 14-1; American Productivity Center, 1984).*

Multiple factors explain this decline in productivity: regulations; changing work force demographics; extremely large and complex projects, such as nuclear power plants, that some construction managers were unprepared to handle; and the economic boom of the 1960s all figure into it. Managerial complacency coupled with labor militancy may also have been a factor. Regardless of the reasons, the results of the decline have been traumatic and far-reaching. Easiest to understand, perhaps, has been the pronounced shift to more prefabrication and modularization. It is not uncommon, for example, for an entire sewage treatment facility to be assembled offsite and then shipped to its final destination in one piece.

Another outgrowth of the cost–productivity trap has been the astonish-

*For a discussion of issues related to construction productivity and for other sources of information in this area, see National Research Council (1986).

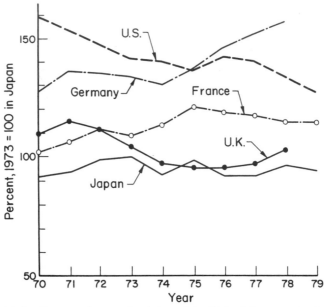

FIGURE 14-4   Construction productivity of the United States and other selected nations over time. Reprinted with permission from Civil Engineering.

TABLE 1   Average Annual Rates of Change (percentage) in Productivity of Labor[a] and Capital,[b] Selected Sectors, 1948–1983

Sector	1948–1983	
	Labor	Capital
Business economy	2.3	0.1
Goods-producing industries	2.9	0.2
Service-producing industries	1.8	0.2
Construction	0.4	−2.3

[a]Labor productivity = output per hour.
[b]Capital productivity = output per unit of capital.

SOURCE: American Productivity Center (1984).

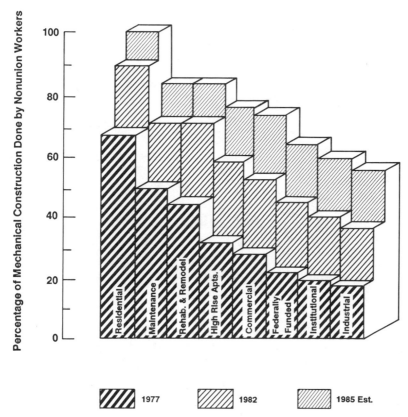

FIGURE 14-5 Growth of nonunion construction in the U.S. mechanical trades over time. Reprinted with permission from Civil Engineering.

ing growth of the open-shop labor movement. Relaxed work rules and lower wage rates and fringe benefits have cost construction trade unions significant amounts of market share. Figure 14-5 shows the experiences of the mechanical trades, as one example. In total, some 70 percent of U.S. construction today is "merit shop" labor, open without prejudice to union and nonunion workers. Ten years ago, that figure was less than 30 percent.

A third major change in the American construction industry recently has been the explosive growth in foreign competition. At one time, American builders regularly captured all domestic work and a principal share of the large international projects. Today, as shown in Figure 14-6, that role is being threatened by a number of other nations, depending on the

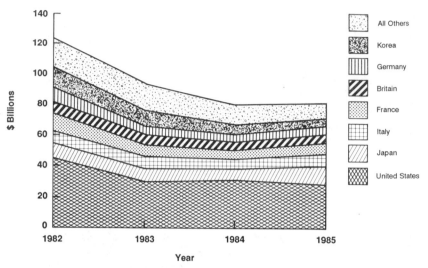

FIGURE 14-6   International construction market shares of various nations. Source of data: Various issues of Engineering News-Record from 1982 to 1985.

market (Pinyan, 1986a). Perhaps even more tellingly, foreign contractors and designers are increasing their stake in this country, which is, for example, the fourth largest foreign market for British contractors. The vast majority of the Japanese automobile plants being built here are designed and constructed by Japanese firms. And Swedish and German firms have acquired equity shares in several large American construction firms. Figure 14-7 captures the spirit of this pronounced change (Pinyan, 1986b). In summary, the American construction industry has experienced a severe interruption in economic and technological progress. Yet there are signs that it is reviving. The following sections describe some of the technologies that are making construction more efficient and cost-effective.

NEW MATERIALS TECHNOLOGY

Over the past several decades, rapid technological change has occurred in various subfields of materials science. Although less visible than the computer technology revolution, these innovations nevertheless have been as pronounced and lasting. Today, the construction industry routinely uses steels twice as strong as those of 15 years ago and concrete mixes three times the standard of 3,000 pounds per square inch (psi) of two decades ago. Other important advances have taken place in corrosive, extreme temperature, and other hostile environment applications. The next section describes several clear cases in which new materials technology has had a positive impact on infrastructure performance and cost-effectiveness.

Research in concrete technology has yielded numerous innovations that have been successfully applied in the field. One is the development of superplasticizers, which, when added to concrete, cause dispersion of the cement particles of a concrete brine. This lessens the amount of water required to mix the concrete, and as a result, the hardened concrete is much less porous and consequently much stronger. Superplasticizers have made possible the appearance of commercial brines of 15,000 psi (100 megapascals [MPa]); in laboratory conditions, strengths of more than 20,000 psi (140 MPa) have been obtained (Mindess and Young, 1981). These high strengths permit much more cost-effective designs for concrete structures, at an additional cost of 5–10 percent.

The inclusion of metallic or polymer fibers in concrete to enhance tensile strength and toughness is another important technological development. Applications have ranged from using fibers as overlays in pavements, to the solid construction of blast-resistant structures (Mindess and Young, 1981). Many other recent developments in concrete technology can lower

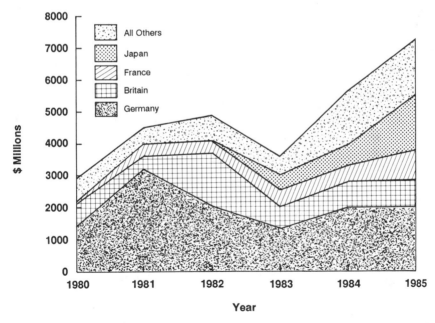

FIGURE 14-7 Foreign contractor shares of the U.S. market over time. Source of data: Various issues of Engineering News-Record from 1981 to 1986.

costs and heighten the effectiveness of infrastructure facilities. (Polymer-impregnated concrete and the use of cement-replacing admixtures and accelerants are two examples.)

One of the most interesting and simplest recent material technology innovations has been the concept of roller-compacted concrete (RCC). This material is a combination of portland cement and selected on-site clays and silts mixed together to form a low-strength composite.

The most noteworthy application of RCC has been at Willow Creek Dam in Oregon, a facility designed and owned by the U.S. Army Corps of Engineers. The success of this project can be measured in several ways, all of which are related to the new material. The construction time was 1 year (a rockfill dam would have required 3 years); it cost about $10 million less than the second cheapest method explored; and the cost of concrete per cubic yard was one-third the cost of traditional concrete. These results were obtained by combining novel ideas with known techniques. Figure 14-8 shows the construction methods used in putting this innovative material in place.

RCC has two important advantages over traditional concrete: (1) lower cement content and (2) reduced handling and placing costs. When fresh, RCC resembles a silty gravel and thus can be spread and compacted with earthmoving equipment. The labor costs associated with this procedure are much lower than those typical of labor-intensive systems of handling and placing concrete.

The successful implementation of these innovative ideas is due in part to good management practice. Work on the Willow Creek Dam had to start in the early spring; all of the RCC had to be in place by late fall. The initial program planned 122 days for placing the concrete, and it was actually performed in 124 days. In spite of the new techniques used and the crews' inexperience with this type of project, the work was finished on schedule and with a relatively low cost overrun of 12 percent (Schrader, 1982; Civil Engineering, 1985).

The practical benefits of better materials are also visible in the technology of metals, particularly corrosion protection. Metals, especially steel, are present in reinforced concrete structures, underground pipelines, bridges, storage tanks, and many other structures. New corrosion-resistant alloys, as well as enhanced corrosion protection methods, should significantly reduce maintenance and repair costs of these facilities.

NEW MONITORING AND SENSING TECHNOLOGIES

As in other fields, computerization and miniaturization have profoundly affected monitoring and construction equipment. Improvements have been

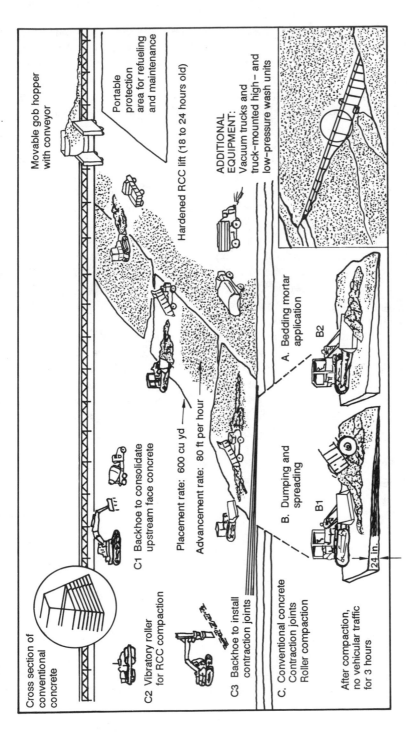

Movable gob hopper
with conveyor

Portable
protection
area for refueling
and maintenance

Hardened RCC lift (18 to 24 hours old)

ADDITIONAL
EQUIPMENT:
Vacuum trucks and
truck–mounted high– and
low–pressure wash units

C1 Backhoe to consolidate
upstream face concrete

Placement rate: 600 cu yd

Advancement rate: 80 ft per hour

A. Bedding mortar
application

B2

B. Dumping and
spreading

B1

Cross section of
conventional
concrete

C2 Vibratory roller
for RCC compaction

C3 Backhoe to install
contraction joints

C. Conventional concrete
Contraction joints
Roller compaction

After compaction,
no vehicular traffic
for 3 hours

24 in.

FIGURE 14-8 Schematic representation of the roller-compacted concrete (RCC) construction process. Reprinted with permission from Civil Engineering.

made in earthmoving operations, for example, by adapting sensors to bulldozers and scrapers to improve placement tolerances and operators' fields of vision. Electronics systems now conduct actual real-time, non-destructive testing by acoustical and x-ray diffraction means. And longer wearing, more heat-resistant brake pads have permitted the development of haul trucks with a capacity of 150 tons, something unimaginable only a few years ago.

Computerized monitoring is improving safety and efficiency during and after construction. For example, Florida's Sunshine Skyway Bridge is now being replaced with one of the longest cable-stayed bridges in the world, with a main span of 1,200 feet (ft). Embedded within the concrete segments of the bridge deck and bridge piers are strain meters and temperature sensors. With the assistance of a microcomputer-based system, these instruments monitor various deflections and deformations of the structure during and after construction. The Florida Department of Transportation can thus assess the structural condition of the bridge and accurately record its performance over its service life (DiVietro, 1986). A similar computerized monitoring of a nuclear containment structure is described by Pinjarkar (1982).

Energy-efficient, safer, better organized buildings are operated with computers and control systems that monitor and adjust temperature, the degree of illumination of public areas, ventilation, and other variables. The tools to automate water and wastewater systems are also available today in a technology that consists of automated control devices linked through microwaves with a computerized control device (Bishop and Schuck, 1986).

NONDESTRUCTIVE TESTING

Nondestructive testing techniques promote increased confidence in the quality of built components. At the same time, they reduce the cost of inspection and testing. Most of these techniques are used on concrete structures and pavements, although some are also applied to underground pipelines.

One important class of devices used for nondestructive testing employs different types of electromagnetic or ultrasonic waves. One such technique is the ultrasonic pulse velocity method for measuring the strength of concrete. Others are the radar and x-ray devices that locate and identify reinforcing bars inside a concrete element. Employing a similar principle, ground-penetrating radar is used to locate underground objects. In some areas, optical devices are moved to inaccessible places for the visual inspection of facilities. (For example, television cameras are used to evaluate the internal condition of sewer systems.)

Another type of device applies a known force at the surface of the material with a special hammer and measures the resulting deformation to infer the strength of hardened concrete. A variety of devices, all based on this approach, are used to determine the properties of pavement.

NEW CONSTRUCTION METHODS

Improved construction methods are having important effects on the initial costs of facilities, the speed of their completion, and the quality of service provided to users. An important area of potential savings in time and money is the construction, repair, and reconstruction of pavement. The savings are proportional to the size of the existing investment and the volume of annual spending in this area—an estimated $10 billion (Forsyth, 1985). A number of new methods are currently being used. For instance, the development of filter fabrics for pavement drainage and different types of synthetic fabrics for crack control have helped to reduce costs and extend the useful life of many pavements. New or improved equipment that produces higher quality pavement at lower costs includes electronically controlled slipform pavers and new pavement breakers (Ray, 1986). Pavement recycling technology is another recent innovation for cutting reconstruction costs. This method uses the old pavement as a raw material for new pavement. At the same time, pavement maintenance costs may be reduced by the construction of so-called zero-maintenance pavements. In combination with subgrade and enhanced drainage, pavements can provide virtually maintenance-free service for their first 20 years (Saxena, 1982).

Bridge construction and repair are also top candidates for improvements and savings through innovative construction techniques. The repair of the Zilwaukee Bridge, currently in progress in Michigan, clearly demonstrates the kind of savings that are possible. During its initial construction in 1982, this bridge suffered huge displacements in essential parts of its structure, largely because of foundation shifts. In the past the only recourse would have been to demolish and rebuild the bridge. Instead, using new construction techniques, the engineers repaired the affected pier and columns and saved some 6,000 tons of high-strength concrete. During the repair work the ground that supported the damaged pier was frozen to increase soil resistance while construction crews built additional support. Hydraulic rams were used to restore the columns to a vertical position (Arnold, 1986).

New techniques for tunneling and pipeline construction are also promising to improve the infrastructure. One example is the successful use of hydraulic jacks to force hollow concrete units into the ground. This method minimizes the disturbance of surface activities and is economically competitive with open-cut construction (Phillips, 1984). Successful preliminary experiences have also been reported using robotics for tunnel construction; robots can carry out faster and more precise tunneling (Shimomura and Sonoda, 1984).

CONSTRUCTION ROBOTICS

Indeed, the promise of construction robotics is becoming a reality as advances in machine vision, mobility, and navigability lead to prototypes. Developers must proceed carefully, however, because construction robots are much more complex instruments than factory robots. A construction robot moves to a work task; a factory robot is stationary, and the work moves to accommodate the assembler. Moreover, construction robots face a range of loads, changing terrains and dynamic environs, and a highly variable weather environment.

Nevertheless, robotics research has been spurred by the promise of better quality control, productivity, health and safety, and cost-effectiveness. Today, modest research programs in construction robotics are in place at Carnegie Mellon University, the University of Illinois, M.I.T., and other institutions. The recent application of construction robotics includes the tethered robot that assisted in the cleanup of the damaged Three-Mile Island reactor. REX, a robot designed at Carnegie Mellon University, has proved useful for excavation near leaking gas utility lines.

Most of the pioneering research and development in construction robotics is taking place in Japan. The Japanese have tested a variety of applications, including prototypes for exterior building wall tile inspection, concrete floor slab placement and finishing, three-dimensional structural steel erection, and abrasive water jetting for tunneling.

The most advanced Japanese robotic experiment involves a fireproofing system (Yoshida et al., 1984). The SSR-2 robot used in the system consists of four key components: a base, vertical and horizontal arms, and a wrist (see Figure 14-9). This manipulator has six degrees of freedom and is driven by a playback-control system consisting of light friction-type cylinders; a potentiometer at the end of the arm senses the position of the arm relative to the steelwork to be fireproofed. Both the SSR-2 and its predecessor, the SSR-1, must be "trained," in the sense of being led through the first of many similar passes. A small 16-bit computer control and power system is tethered to the mobile unit. The dimensions of the

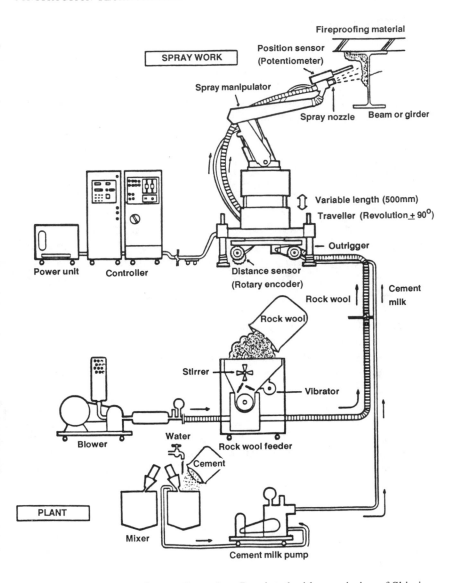

Fireproofing material

SPRAY WORK

Position sensor
(Potentiometer)

Spray manipulator

Spray nozzle   Beam or girder

Variable length (500mm)

Traveller (Revolution ± 90°)

Outrigger

Power unit   Controller

Distance sensor
(Rotary encoder)

Rock wool   Cement
milk

Rock wool

Stirrer

Vibrator

Blower

Water   Rock wool feeder

Cement

PLANT

Mixer

Cement milk pump

FIGURE 14-9   Japanese fireproofing robot. Reprinted with permission of Skimizu
Construction Co., Tokyo.

unit are approximately 2 meters (m) by 3 m with a vertical reach of 3 m. The unit weighs about 800 kilograms.

The true test of the viability of this robotic sprayer is whether it costs less than conventional methods. Only limited full-scale testing has been completed thus far. But in one experiment involving a 20-story office building, 100 units of various sizes and lengths were coated by the machine and an equal number by human crews. The robot took a total of 62 hours (h) to set up, transport, spray, and finish; the human team took 112 h. Moreover, the quality of the final product was substantially better when the fireproofing was placed mechanically.

Today, robotic and other intelligent machines are finding new applications at a steady pace. A part of this application pattern can be ascribed to the considerable research and development investment that has already been made; part is also attributable to the slowdown in worldwide construction activity. Nevertheless, it is predictable that robotic construction will soon have a place alongside more traditional building activity.

NEW MANAGEMENT TECHNOLOGIES

Another set of technological innovations is developing in the field of construction management control. Traditionally, management information systems have been good vehicles for reporting *data* but have been deficient in reporting *information* and providing control.

Several new approaches, however, may replace the old systems. Two advances involve sophisticated applications of mathematical simulation. The first advance grew out of work by Paulson at Stanford University. It is the actual modeling and "what if" analysis of construction field operations—that is, the flows and balances of equipment, labor, and material on large projects. An interactive, graphical tool, Paulson's INSIGHT system is becoming more accepted and valued (Ibbs, 1985). The second, a simulation model, AROUSAL, deals with the project management aspects of construction (Ibbs, 1985). AROUSAL is the brainchild of Landsley at the University of Reading (U.K.). It models such decisions as personnel staff assignments, hiring, and skill training. Several firms in the United Kingdom and the United States are using this system.

The greatest advances in management control technology promise to be in another computer-aided construction field: the relatively new science of artificial intelligence. Knowledge-based expert systems (KBES) in particular are being seized on by researchers and practitioners alike almost as panaceas. Today, KBESs exist for project risk assessment, evaluation of a contractor's safety program, and project goal setting.

One specific application of KBES technology that attempts to solve a long-standing problem is being carried out at the University of Illinois. Ever since builders and managers began to represent project flows mathematically, they have faced problems analyzing construction schedules for adequacy and completeness. Project owners need summary schedules to forecast completion, phased occupancy dates, and cash flow requirements and to prepare and defend against contractor claims for extra costs. CONSAES, a construction schedule analysis expert system under development at the University of Illinois and the University of California, Berkeley, is a serious attempt to provide the U.S. Army Corps of Engineers with such a management tool. The system checks schedules initially and during the project and updates them in terms of cost, time, and constraints inherent in the logic of construction tasks. For example, the cost module analyzes cost-weighted schedule activities to ensure that unreasonable "front-end loading" is not present.

CONSAES is now being tested at a number of Corps locations worldwide. Continual updates are being made, and a study is in progress to assess the payoff of the investment. The consensus is that this tool and its underlying technology are so valuable to construction management that many other applications will soon be tested.

DATA BASES FOR MANAGEMENT

Data bases, automated data-collection devices, and their linkage and support systems are also contributing to better management in ways that help keep construction and repairs to a minimum. If a computerized inventory of infrastructure facilities contains information on operating characteristics, maintenance and repair needs, and other data, it can provide excellent assistance when budgeting and setting priorities for resource allocation. The same inventory can be used to support a computerized system for scheduling maintenance and repair activities. In several jurisdictions, data bases are already being used for these purposes.

The state of Washington has been a pioneer in computerizing the inventory of infrastructure facilities. In 1978 Bellevue, a suburb of Seattle, developed a fully operational data base of its water supply system. By 1984, an automated mapping system was installed and running, designed to manage information on the lot sizes and topography of Bellevue. Today, several other data bases, such as those for building permits and the associated property improvement activity, are being developed or are in use. At the same time, the city is developing software to integrate all the data bases to facilitate data sharing among systems. A maintenance operations and management system is also being designed to improve the efficiency of the maintenance departments. This effort has already resulted in better planning and management of the infrastructure of Bellevue (Godfrey, 1985).

In another example, the Pennsylvania Department of Transportation set up a bridge management system in 1986 to manage data from more than 50,000 bridges larger than 8 ft. The system is designed to keep updated records of the facilities, recommend bridge maintenance and repairs, and estimate costs. Although not especially sophisticated, this system will put bridge maintenance and repair on a more rational basis and should make it easier to set priorities and plan budgets (Hoffman, 1986).

In summary, new materials and innovative technologies will play significant roles in our attempts to rebuild and maintain the nation's infrastructure. Today, these technologies are being used to create maintenance-free pavements and metal bridges more resistant to corrosion. At the same time, construction technologies are making it possible to build elements of the infrastructure more efficiently, safely, and cost-effectively. Technology is also improving management through such tools as computerized project planning systems and data base management methods.

In all of these areas, the technology is still developing and will continue to develop. Meanwhile, solutions to the immense problems posed by our deteriorated national infrastructure will demand every new technology that construction researchers can devise and that practitioners can implement.

ACKNOWLEDGMENT

This material was based on work supported by the National Science Foundation under grant no. MSM-84-51561, Presidential Young Investigator's Award. Any opinions, findings, conclusions, or recommendations expressed are those of the author and do not necessarily reflect the views of the sponsors.

REFERENCES

American Productivity Center. 1984. Productivity and the U.S. Economy. Houston, Tex.: American Productivity Center.

Arnold, C. J. 1986. Salvaging the Zilwaukee. Civil Engineering 56(4):46–49.

Bishop, D. F., and W. Schuck. 1986. Water and wastewater: Time to automate? Civil Engineering 56(1):46–48.

Choate, P., and S. Walter. 1983. America in Ruins: The Decaying Infrastructure, M. Barker, ed. Washington, D.C.: Council of State Planning Agencies.

Civil Engineering. 1985. Dam pioneers concrete variant. (July):42–45.

Constructor. 1986. Washington, D.C.: Associated General Contractors of America. November.

Cremeans, J. E. 1981. Productivity in the construction industry. Construction Review 27 (May-June):4–60

DiVietro, P. 1986. Monitoring a bridge's pulse. Civil Engineering 56(3):54–55.

Forsyth, R. A. 1985. Recent developments, future needs and opportunities in pavement technology and management. P. 39 in Proceedings of the Conference on Infrastructure for Urban Growth. New York: American Society of Civil Engineers.

Godfrey, K. A., Jr. 1985. Data base in your city's future. Civil Engineering 55(10): 66–69.

Hoffman, G. L. 1986. Bridge management: Computer aided priorities. Civil Engineering (May):62–64.

Ibbs, C. W. 1985. Proceedings of a Workshop for the Development of New Research Directions in Computerized Applications to Construction Engineering and Management Studies. Construction Research Series Technical Report No. 19. University of Illinois.

Mindess, S., and J. F. Young. 1981. Concrete. Englewood Cliffs, N.J.: Prentice-Hall.

National Research Council. 1986. Construction Productivity: Proposed Actions by the Federal Government to Promote Increased Efficiency in Construction. Washington, D.C.: National Academy Press.

O'Day, K., and L. A. Neumann. 1984. Assessing infrastructure needs: The state of the art. Pp. 67–109 in Perspectives on Urban Infrastructure, R. Hanson, ed. Washington, D.C.: National Academy Press.

Phillips, S. H. E. 1984. Tunnel and bridge construction with minimum disturbance to overhead service. Pp. 172–183 in Proceedings of the Conference on Rebuilding America: Infrastructure Rehabilitation. New York: Metropolitan Association of Urban Designers and Environmental Planners.

Pinjarkar, S. G. 1982. Data acquisition and process control. Journal of the Technical Councils of ASCE 108(May):89–95.

Pinyan, C. T. 1986a. Foreign contracts inch upward. Engineering News-Record 217(3): 38–42.

Pinyan, C. T. 1986b. Foreign contracts inch upward. Engineering News-Record 217(22): 12–13.

Ray, G. K. 1986. Progress in paving equipment and construction methods. Concrete Construction 31(5):439–445.

Saxena, S. K. 1982. New structural systems for zero-maintenance pavements. Transportation Engineering Journal 108(TE2):169–182.

Schrader, E. K. 1982. The first concrete gravity dam designed and built for roller compacted construction methods. ACI Concrete International (October):169–182.

Shimomura, Y., and T. Sonoda. 1984. Tunneling by robots—Shield driving automatic control system. Proceedings of the Workshop on Robotics in Construction. Carnegie Mellon University.

U.S. Bureau of the Census. 1970, 1975, and 1986. Statistical Abstract of the United States. Washington, D.C.: U.S. Department of Commerce.

Yoshida, T., T. Veno, M. Nonaka, and S. Yamazaki. 1984. Development of spray robot for fireproof cover work. Proceedings of the Conference on Robotics in Construction. Carnegie Mellon University.

15
Longevity of Infrastructure

GREGG MARLAND AND ALVIN M. WEINBERG

The infrastructure of our society is largely determined by the set of capital-intensive and generally long-lived structures and devices that allow us to get what we want, get rid of what we do not want, communicate with each other, and hold the fabric of society together. This set includes the structures and devices that mediate the production and flow of the primary elements of the economy (energy, food, water, waste, materials, and finished goods) and those primarily involved in socialization (education, religion, communication, corrections, and governance). Focusing on the structures and devices of the first type, we are concerned with power plants, transmission facilities, dams, roads, bridges, and the major civil engineering works of man.

Our interest here is with the longevity of these structures—their mortality. Infrastructure is capital intensive; yet items of infrastructure may last much longer than the time required to pay for them. If these structures approach immortality, then they exist as part of the inheritance of each generation, and each generation needs only to maintain its inheritance and to add infrastructure capital as the systems grow. If, on the other hand, the major capital items of infrastructure are relatively short lived, then each generation has both a greater obligation to supply its own infrastructure capital and a greater opportunity to affect the character of its own infrastructure.

This chapter poses three ostensibly similar questions about the longevity of infrastructure: How long does it last? How long could it last? How long should it last? These questions are in fact distinctly different and are by nature historical, technical, and ethical, respectively.

THE IMMORTALITY OF INFRASTRUCTURE

These questions all raise an initial question about when and why structures are judged to be no longer serviceable. Why are structures replaced, and what determines their lifetime? The following considerations are limiting:

- Devices wear out.
- Operation and maintenance become too expensive—often because parts become difficult to replace or because operations are too labor intensive and labor costs escalate.
- Competing systems and technologies become available and are cheaper, less polluting, more attractive aesthetically, or of a scale (usually larger) better suited to achieving the system's purpose.

The following section presents a brief, anecdotal view of the history and longevity of several types of structures (power plants, dams, bridges, and roads) and then returns to ruminate over the last two questions: How long could they last, and how long should they last?

Electric Power Plants

Analysis of the longevity of energy-producing devices raises a moral issue: what responsibility do those who build polluting and possibly dangerous electric power plants owe to future generations? It could be argued that, insofar as these devices are inexpensive to operate, the generation that paid for their construction was compensating later generations for any such burden with the gift of relatively cheap electricity—provided the later generation does not have to rebuild the power-producing devices.

In an article in *Energy Policy*, this argument was presented, based on an analysis of the costs and longevity of systems for producing inexhaustible power from dams, fission and fusion reactors, and solar devices. The burden of the argument was as follows:

If plants last very much longer than their design life, and if their maintenance costs do not grow excessively, then the product of such plants will eventually become remarkably cheap. If the plants produce electricity from one of the inexhaustibles—solar, fission breeders, or fusion—then the cost of electricity can be expected to become very low, perhaps around 1¢/kWh. . . .

Ordinary economics discounts the future at a rate that reflects our uncertainty

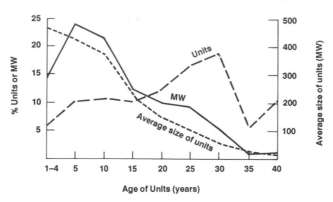

FIGURE 15-1   Age of the total U.S. thermal electricity generating capacity (coal, oil, gas, nuclear). SOURCE: Electrical World (1985). Reprinted with permission.

about the future, as well as the realities of today's money markets. Should we discover that these gadgets last "forever," economic doctrine would still forbid our investing in them rather than in more immediate gadgets whose lifetime, and pay-off, is much shorter. Large "immortal" energy systems might acquire much the same status as roads and bridges—part of society's infrastructure, for which society is prepared to pay more than strict economic accounting would dictate. Thus a political decision, one dictated by the broad concern for the future, may be the only way to switch to the low cost "immortal" energy system. (Weinberg, 1985, pp. 58–59)

Electricity from long-lived plants will be cheap only if fuel costs in these plants are low. This is the case for solar-based devices—solar cells, dams, wind turbines—for which the primary energy, sunlight, is "free." To a lesser extent this is true also for nuclear energy sources—fusion and breeder reactors—for which the fuel cycle costs are expected to be low and practically independent of the supply of uranium. Even nonbreeder reactors have fuel cycle costs that are below the fuel cost of fossil plants. The actual lifetime of these low-fuel-cost devices can hardly be based on experience since nuclear reactors, fusion reactors, and solar plants are either nonexistent or have yet to reach the scheduled end of their lives. The oldest large power-producing reactors, located at Calder Hall in the United Kingdom, are still in operation. Although these graphite reactors are 30 years old, their operating licenses recently have been renewed.

Figure 15-1 and Table 15-1 summarize the age distribution of large electrical generating plants in the United States. As of 1982 about 73 percent of all electrical capacity was in plants that were less than 20 years old; only 9 percent was in plants more than 30 years old. Some 24 percent

TABLE 15-1   Age Distribution of U.S. Electric Power Generation Capacity, 1982

Age	Nameplate Capacity in Megawatts		Percentage of Thermal	Hydro	Percentage of Hydro
	Total Capacity[a]	Thermal			
9 years of less	266,503 (42)[b]	241,855 (38)	44	13,988 (2)	22
10–19 years	193,555 (31)	175,545 (28)	32	14,729 (2)	23
20–29 years	113,103 (18)	94,385 (15)	17	18,346 (3)	28
30 or more years	56,603 (9)	38,775 (6)	7	17,705 (3)	27
Totals	629,764 (100)	550,560 (87)	100	64,768 (10)	100

[a]Pumped storage is included in the total but is not included in either the thermal or hydro columns.
[b]Figures in parentheses are percentages.

SOURCE: Hudson (1983).

of this older capacity was hydroelectric, whereas only 10 percent of the total capacity (and even less of the total generated energy) was hydroelectric.

Modern electrical generating plants have usually been designed to last 30 to 40 years. This lifetime was determined not so much because the power plant wore out after that time as because the efficiency of newer power plants exceeded the efficiency of the older ones. The newer plants therefore used less fossil fuel per kilowatt-hour (kWh) and thus were cheaper to operate than the older plants.

Two developments have changed our outlook on how long a power plant should be able to operate. First, fuel cost in a nuclear power plant is less important than in a fossil fuel plant; improvements in efficiency are therefore less telling in the nuclear case than in the fossil case, especially if the improved efficiency requires higher capital cost. Second, the thermodynamic efficiencies of fossil power plants have tended to plateau at about 35 percent; reaching higher levels places heavy demands on the materials of construction. Thus, the original incentive to retire an old fossil plant—lower thermodynamic efficiency than its newer replacement—is no longer compelling.

The electric utility industry and its suppliers have devoted much attention recently to the extension of the life of existing power plants, both fossil and nuclear. In a full-page advertisement in the February 5, 1986, *Wall Street Journal* entitled "Life Begins at 30," the General Electric Company announced a new service dedicated to the renovation of old power plants. The economics appear to favor renovation over new construction by a wide margin. General Electric claims that to renovate a fossil plant costs an average of only $250/kW; on the other hand, to construct a new plant might cost almost 10 times as much. Our impression is that few completely new full-scale power plants will be built in the United States during the next 20 years or so. Instead, old fossil and nuclear plants will be renovated, thus avoiding the building of many megawatts of new central station capacity.

A related issue is the siting of new fossil or nuclear power plants. In the United States there are now more than 50 nuclear power plant sites and more than 400 fossil plant sites with capacities of 400 megawatts (MW) or more. Given the difficulty of finding new sites that are acceptable to the public, we would expect these sites, if not the devices and structures on them, to be used for a very long time. This is particularly true of the nuclear sites; yet because it is doubtful that any new nuclear plants will be built during the next 20 years, the issue may not be put to a test before the turn of the century. The geography of our electricity producing system has largely been set by the location of the existing sites.

Burwell and Lane (1980) pointed out that the existing nuclear sites, on which are located plants capable of producing about 110 gigawatts (GW) of nuclear power, could eventually accommodate at least 340 GW of nuclear capacity. Such multiple-reactor sites are the rule outside the United States. Thus, France's 66 reactors occupy 21 sites, or about 3 reactors per site, whereas in the United States, 129 operating and planned reactors will occupy 76 sites, or 1.7 reactors per site. Although the evidence is less clear for fossil power plants, it seems likely that new, large fossil power generators will be added to existing sites rather than being built on new sites.

Dams

The longevity of dams has been highly variable. Many dams have lived long, useful lives, but other dams have led quite short lives and suffered dramatic terminations. Many dams have experienced drastic repairs, rebuildings, and replacements. By and large, however, dam building has progressed tremendously, and major advances have often been triggered by major failures. Changes in size and structure of dams reflect improvements in theory, materials, construction methods and equipment, and computational capability. It is striking that dams have also seen dramatic changes in function. The earliest dams were built for irrigation; dam building for water supply, flood control, transportation, and water power followed in sequence. By the 1890s the generation of electricity had begun to attain worldwide importance, and dams were used to produce hydro-electric power. Today's multipurpose dams also include soil conservation and recreation among their purposes.

Although the oldest known earth dam was built nearly 5,000 years ago, real understanding of earth dam theory was not complete until around 1940 (Smith, 1972). Before about 1870, dam building was largely an empirical process, and the failures were numerous.

The useful life of a dam varies widely. The Teton Dam in Idaho was a 91-meter (m)-high modern structure completed in 1975. It failed during the initial filling. By contrast, two irrigation dams built in the second and third centuries A.D. at Mérida in western Spain are still in service (Smith, 1972). Both dams at Mérida are nearly 20 m high and have had a series of repairs over the centuries. The 2-kilometer (km)-long dam of the Lake of Homs, Syria, was built by the Romans about 284 A.D. and kept in use nearly 1,700 years. A bigger dam was built on top of it in 1934. Of eight dams built to supply water to Constantinople around the sixth century A.D., four are still in operation. Norman Smith observed in his book, *A History of Dams*, "While there is nothing to suggest that any of them survived in the original form, there is no doubt that some of the ancient dams still standing on the Kur (Persia) are Archaemenian in origin'' (Smith, 1972, p. 56), and they date to the fifth and sixth centuries B.C. Kebar Dam (Persia) was built by the Mongols around 1300 and is still intact at 26 m height despite being badly silted. Tenth-century Moslem dams still meet irrigation needs around Valencia, Spain. The Alicante Dam on Rio Monegre in Spain was completed in 1594 and, at 41 m, stood as the world's tallest dam for almost 300 years.

These dams highlight the trial-and-error successes; a rational approach to dam building did not appear until the middle of the nineteenth century. Along with the successes were many failures, the consequences of which have increased with the size of the dams. The first serious dam disaster of modern times was in 1802 when the Puentes Dam in Spain failed and cost 608 lives. A new structure was erected at the same site.

Among the oldest dams still in use in the United States is the 4.5-m Espada Dam built on the San Antonio River in the mid-eighteenth century. During this same era, many small dams served and were eliminated, either purposely or through neglect. The Jones Falls Dam in New York was the highest (19 m) in North America when completed in 1832, and it remains in sound condition today (Smith, 1972).

Many early dams established sites that were either rebuilt or enlarged but that remained as dam sites. The Ponte Alto Dam in Italy was 4.9 m high when first completed in 1613. With periodic heightening, it had reached 37.8 m by 1883 when another dam was built a short distance downstream to support the lowest 25.3 m of the upstream dam. A dam at Whinhill in England was completed in 1746, failed in 1815, was rebuilt in 1821, and failed again in 1835. Rebuilt a second time, it is still functioning.

''The first half of the nineteenth century was essentially a period when dams were built in markedly increased numbers but with little improvement in design and still no proper understanding of their structural behavior'' (Smith, 1972, p. 191). The first seriously designed dam was the Furens Dam, completed in 1866, at Saint-Étienne, France.

At about this same time, two major dam failures focused attention on dam design, theory, and engineering. The 35.7-m-tall Habra Dam in Algeria was completed in 1870 but failed completely in 1881 when water rose 4 m above the intended maximum; in 1895 the 14-year-old, 15-m-high Bouzey Dam in France failed with a loss of 150 lives. The failure of what were thought to have been rationally designed dams led ultimately to a significantly improved understanding of dam principles.

The first all-concrete dam, the 52-m San Mateo Dam near San Francisco, was completed in 1889. With improvements in the design and construction of dams, the 1920s were the last decade with an appreciable number of dam failures. By the 1930s, major modern dams were being built, but improvements in all aspects have continued to the present. For example, rock mechanics is an area of recent advances in knowledge. Improvements in engineering have brought significant increases in efficiency and reliability in existing hydroelectric plants.

There have been two major U.S. dam failures in the last 20 years. In addition to the 1975 Teton Dam failure, the Walter Bouldin Dam in Alabama experienced a 90-m-wide breach in 1975 (the 50-m-high earthfill dam had been completed in 1957). Although the failure caused no loss of life, there was extensive flooding, and the 225-MW powerhouse was destroyed. The dam was reconstructed.

Major modern dams can have extensive service periods, although they require much more maintenance than did the simpler structures of previous centuries. The Hoover Dam and the Bonneville Dam celebrated their fiftieth anniversaries in 1986 and 1987, respectively. The Grand Coulee Dam remains the marvel it was when completed in 1942. A current list of U.S. electrical generating plants contains at least six small dams that were first put into service before the turn of the century.

One consequence of the increasing number of dams is the exhaustion of the best sites. Improved understanding of basic principles now permits the construction of safe dams in less attractive sites. An interesting question is whether and how major dams or dam sites might be abandoned. History offers many examples of dams rebuilt on a given site and a few examples of sites abandoned after failures. With larger dams and more intensive land use, the abandonment of good sites seems more unlikely. Smith (1972) describes several specific instances in which dams that were inadequate by current standards were essentially replaced by being drowned by new impoundments built downstream from the existing structures.

A Tennessee Valley Authority (TVA) dam, the Great Falls Dam on Caney Fork River in Tennessee, was recently considered for retirement. This is a 28-m dam with a 31,860-kW generating capacity and an 8.5-km^2 reservoir with 193 km of shoreline. The primary use of the reservoir is for recreation. The dam was completed in 1916, received major modifications in 1925, and was acquired by TVA in 1939. A 1983 TVA evaluation noted four significant deficiencies: dam instability, insufficient spillway capacity, leakage (which totals as much as 5.5-m^3/second under and around the dam); and deterioration and inadequacy of the power generation facilities. The TVA evaluation said in part, "based on current design criteria, the dam is not safe against overturning or sliding" (TVA, Hydropower Planning Section, 1983, p. 12). Dam removal was rejected as an option because of silt release and public disapproval (especially reservoir property owners) and because the dam area was considered a prime hydroelectric site. Another possibility that was considered (and rejected) was to run the dam to failure because the risks associated with failure were judged to be small.

A major dam that *was* abandoned by TVA was at Hales Bar on the main stream of the Tennessee River. The Hales Bar Dam, which was begun in 1905, completed in 1913, and acquired by TVA in 1939, had an extremely poor foundation. Serious leakage was first noted 11 days after the last concrete was poured, and efforts to control the leakage continued until the decision was made to abandon the dam 50 years later. The dam was abandoned by constructing another major dam (Nickajack) 10.3 km downstream, which brought the reservoir to the initial pool level, and then dismantling the top of the older structure to avoid a hazard to navigation (TVA, Division of Water Control Planning, 1963; TVA, Office of Engineering, 1963).

Siltation, another major reason dams lose their usefulness, has brought TVA to abandon powerhouses and sell dams to communities for nominal fees. A case in point was the Davy Crockett Dam in Tennessee: the dam, which was 90 percent silted up, was converted into a wildlife refuge. Lake Meade, Arizona, is estimated to have lost 3 percent of its storage capacity in 14 years and Lake Mangla in northeastern Pakistan more than 11 percent in 20 years as a result of siltation (Smith, 1972). Although such problems as siltation may shorten the useful life of a dam, TVA engineers seem to believe that at modern dams, such as Norris on the Clinch River in Tennessee, the concrete will last forever.

Bridges

How long does a bridge last? There seems to be no consensus on the answer to this question. George Latimer, mayor of St. Paul, Minnesota, is reported to have said in August 1984, "Just two weeks ago our 95-year-old historic link across the Mississippi River, the High Bridge, was prematurely closed because it had rusted beyond safety standards" (National Research Council, 1985, p. 27). Henry J. Hopkins, in his book *A Span of Bridges*, writes, "It is rare for any metal bridge in western civilization to last more than 150 years" (1970, p. 175), and "by modern standards anyone who built a bridge that lasted 100 years would be judged a complete master" (p. 19). Yet noting that a few Roman arch bridges are still functioning, Hopkins observes, "The magnitude of the Roman achievement can only be assessed by bearing in mind that, statistically speaking, it is virtually impossible for a bridge to last 2,000 years'' (p. 20). And J. W. Gregory agreed: "The survival of any Roman bridge is very improbable, as a modern masonry bridge, unless carefully maintained, is estimated to last for only 70–100 years'' (Gregory, 1931, p. 71).

At the same time, many bridges have had lifetimes measured in days, and some have even failed to survive the removal of the construction supports. The useful lives of bridges have been ended by flood, fire, wind, rust, rot, foundation scour, war, collision, weathering, inadequacies of width or carrying capacity, and changing concepts of aesthetics. Long-lasting bridges are those that have had good form, materials, construction, abutments, and maintenance—and no military damage. Throughout history, sociopolitical factors have militated against the preservation of bridges, one important reason being that efficient maintenance requires a stable central authority.

The earliest specimen of a Roman arch still intact in Rome is over a drain in front of the temple of Saturn, built between the sixth and fourth centuries B.C. Other Roman bridges are more than 2,000 years old. The Ponte d'Augusto at Narni, north of Rome, was built around 220 B.C. It had four arches, one with a span of 32.3 m, and stood 33.5 m high and 8.2 m wide. Its gradual disintegration was initiated by war damage, but one arch still survives.

In other places an important site has been occupied by a succession of bridges. The first record of a bridge at the site of the London Bridge was in 963, and it referred to a timber bridge. The bridge was reconstructed at least twice before a stone bridge was begun in 1176.

As in other civil engineering works, bridge building has progressed through a sequence of building materials and construction methods with a large empirical foundation and gradually emerging science. "In the construction of early bridges, principles of scientific design were unknown. A bridge was built and if it failed the next one was built of heavier material'' (Christensen, 1973, p. 113). The eighteenth-century civil engineer Jean Perronet, a pioneer of modern bridge building, employed good science to build many French bridges and during the 1700s mastered the masonry bridge. His Pont de la Concorde was completed in 1791 and still serves Paris.

The stone arch has been the world's main bridge type for 2,000 years, and many early nineteenth-century stone arches remain in use in the United States. Materials and methods have limited bridge dimensions; early arch bridges had semicircular arches and hence relatively short spans. By the nineteenth century, spans reached nearly 50 m. The largest stone arch in existence today is the Ponte Adolphe in Luxemburg, which was completed in 1903 with a span of 85.3 m. In 1758 the longest bridge span was a 120-m timber truss at Schaffhausen, Switzerland.

In the United States, covered bridges were designed to protect the bridge deck and structure, particularly joints, from weathering. The life expectancy of early covered bridges was much enhanced by the development of paints and other preservatives. The longest timber bridge remaining in this country is a 140-m-long covered bridge built in 1866 on the border between Vermont and New Hampshire.

As technological development continued in the United States, however, timber and stone gave way to metal and other materials. The nation's first cast-iron bridge was completed in 1836 in Brownsville, Pennsylvania; the first large bridge built of structural steel was the Eads Bridge in St. Louis, completed in 1874 with three 150-m arches. Concrete was first used in a U.S. bridge in 1871; in 1889 the first U.S. reinforced concrete bridge was built in Golden Gate Park, California, ushering in what the U.S. Department of Transportation (DOT) has called the "great bridge era" in the United States. This period between 1900 and World War II saw rapid growth in the number and size of bridges and in related technical knowledge, of which the most important was the development of reinforced concrete (DOT, Federal Highway Administration, 1977). The first use of prestressed concrete in a U.S. bridge, the next major technical step forward, was in Philadelphia in 1951.

Advances in design capability made it possible to improve the serviceability of bridges. Thus, by 1870 engineers were able to do stress and moment analyses for structural design. Today, the advent of computers has made possible even more refined analyses of more complex structures in less time.

Our inheritance of older bridges in the United States includes many that continue to perform in exemplary fashion and many that continue to perform in spite of what we now consider to be inadequacies of one sort or another. The Federal Aid Highway Act of 1970 included a bridge replacement program. Seven years later, the U.S. Department of Transportation reported that, although many of the most deficient had been replaced, "There are thousands of bridges on the Federal-Aid system that are posted as having limited capacity of carrying truck traffic" (DOT, Federal Highway Administration, 1977, p. 442). "Today, the city of Chicago owns, operates, and maintains more movable bridges than any other public agency in the world. Many of those existing structures are more than a half-century old, yet they continue to serve the purpose for which they were built. . . . That they can be taken for granted testifies to the excellence of the original design and to the never-ending inspection, maintenance, and repair program'' (Christensen, 1973, p. 113).

Roads

Roads and trails on earth date to man's basic need to seek food and water. Long-distance routes were the result of the irregular distribution of important materials, such as flint, amber, tin, and silk. The most precisely determined of the prehistoric long-distance roads were those across west central Europe (for the trade in amber) dating back to 2000 B.C. Some ancient "ridgeways" in England, however, seem to have been in use for 6,000 years. The credit for building the first "made" road is generally given to the Romans, but well-made roads were built long before this time. There were probably stone roads in 3000 B.C. for hauling blocks for the Great Pyramid of Cheops (Gregory, 1931); and the Carthaginians are said to have made a system of stone-paved roads in the fifth century B.C., although no remains have been found.

The Roman Empire prepared an entire continental system of well-built roads for administrative purposes; indeed, as Gregory (1931, p. 62) said, "roads made the Roman Empire possible." The *Itinerary of Antoine*, published during the reign of Diocletian, consists of a list of 372 roads totaling 85,237 km in length. Some Roman roads in England still have paving in place, especially where they have been buried by soil or new roadways.

Once routes are established, they tend to be preserved, although the utility of the road itself depends heavily on its maintenance. After the Roman army withdrew from England, maintenance was not continued, bridges collapsed, and roads were lost to use. Similarly, Gregory observed in 1931 that the imperial roads in many parts of China had fallen into decay through lack of repair. He noted, "It is said that in China a road is good for seven years and then bad for 4,000" (Gregory, 1931, p. 107). Throughout history, good road maintenance has generally been the product of stable central and local authority. An early formal recognition of this truth came in 1555, when the English Parliament passed the first statute to put road maintenance under the control of elected authorities.

The permanence of travel routes is nowhere more apparent than in the United States where the history of roads is relatively short. In the United States, we can document relatively easily the passage of a route from Indian trail to pioneer road to country road to modern highway. "In a host of instances our highways and roads follow for many miles the general line of the routes of the buffalo and Indian on high ground" (Gregory, 1931, p. 11). Although new demands and vehicles, new materials, and new construction and maintenance methods have continually forced changes on our roads, routes and rights-of-way have often been maintained.

We notice repeatedly this continuity of basic major routes in spite of changing demands and minor route changes. The coastal highway, now U.S. Route 1, was substantially in place south to Charleston, South Carolina, by the time of the War of 1812. As reported by the U.S. Department of Transportation in 1977,

There were over 2,350,000 miles of rural roads and city streets at the time of the advent of the automobile. . . . [W]hat we have been doing for 73 years is highway improvement planning. . . . Most of the mileage added has been in the expanding suburban areas. . . . Most of the planning has been directed toward upgrading the early roads on or close to their original locations. Notable exceptions are seen in the Interstate System . . . and in . . . Alaska. (p. 264)

As vehicles have evolved, becoming faster and heavier, roads have become obsolete because of inadequate alignment, grade, width, and sight distance. Many roadways have been upgraded and many relocated with the old roadway relinquished to local authorities. Narrow bridges and bridges with low load capacities, sharp curves, and unbanked turns have gradually been eliminated. Much new right-of-way has been required to straighten and widen roads. Insufficient capacity and the choking traffic of strip development have been other causes of obsolescence for long-distance routes. After a trend toward widening existing roads in the United States has come the development of special, high-capacity roads. In fact, the evolution of the nation's roads reflects their changing role in human affairs in addition to the changing technology of roads, road building, and road use. That role has been shaped by numerous influences including the development of bicycles and cars, concerns about mud and dust, conflicts between urban and rural interests, changing perspectives about who should pay for and maintain roads, safety considerations, the availability of improved building materials, and the evolution of quantitative engineering principles. Perhaps the most recent factors to play a major role in the evolution of roads have been the social, economic, and environmental aspects of the highway system.

Chicago, like most cities, has struggled with the quality and capacity of its roads. The city was platted in 1830 with roads 66 feet wide, but this size has proved inadequate in many instances and there has been considerable restructuring. A citywide plan was developed in 1907 by Daniel Burnham, many parts of which were gradually implemented over the subsequent half century. When Michigan Avenue was widened between 1914 and 1929, 8,700 property settlements were required, although many who received damages were surprised to find themselves rewarded in addition with increased property values. The "backbone of Chicago," the Eisenhower Expressway, was envisioned by Burnham but not completed until 1956. Other events also mandated change in the city's streets; for example, the adoption of a sewage system plan in 1855 required raising the grade of many streets to provide the correct slope for the sewer system. Yet the continuity of routes in the face of changing styles, times, and needs, is exemplified by the Dan Ryan Expressway:

The Vincennes Trace, carved out by the wheels of the early settlers' wagons, connected the pioneer village of Chicago with Vincennes, Indiana. The "trace" followed earlier trails formed by moccasined feet of Indians. The $300 million Dan Ryan Expressway, opened to traffic in 1962, retraced this ancient thoroughfare with multiple lanes of reinforced concrete. (Christensen, 1973, p. 158)

Drawings from Robert Phillips in 1737 (Figure 15-2) show that the durability of road surfaces 250 years ago was not qualitatively different from that of modern roads. Gregory gives some hint of the life expectancy of road surfaces in 1931: waterbound macadam, 3 years; tar macadam, 9 years; asphalt macadam, 12 years.

A 1949 national survey of the U.S. interstate system found that the average age of road surfacing was 12 years and that 13 percent of roads in the system were more than 20 years old and "nearing the end of their useful lives" (DOT, Federal Highway Administration, 1977, p. 165). Griffin (1986, p. 52) writes that U.S. "interstates are designed to last 20 years before major repairs are necessary, but many do not." The quality of the road surface is rated "good" in only 57 percent of the interstate highway system; almost 10 percent is rated "poor." This is because of failure of the initial estimates to anticipate traffic volume, especially of heavy trucks. The damage from heavy traffic volume can be seen in New York City, which patched half a million potholes in 1985 (Bedard, 1986).

HOW LONG COULD ELEMENTS OF INFRASTRUCTURE LAST?

The foregoing examples show that the lifetimes of power plants, dams, roads, and bridges are distributed over a wide range. The Grand Teton Dam failed immediately when the reservoir was filled; the Alicante Dam remains serviceable after nearly 400 years. The Tacoma Narrows Bridge failed after 4 months; the Brooklyn Bridge still stands after 100 years.

In many instances a power plant or a bridge is taken out of service not because it no longer can perform its original function but because a competing device can perform the same function less expensively or because the original function is no longer very useful—for example, the bridge is too narrow for the increased traffic it must now carry. In the following paragraphs, however, the focus is on the narrower issue of physical obsolescence or failure: Can we identify in the design and construction of

PLATE XIV.

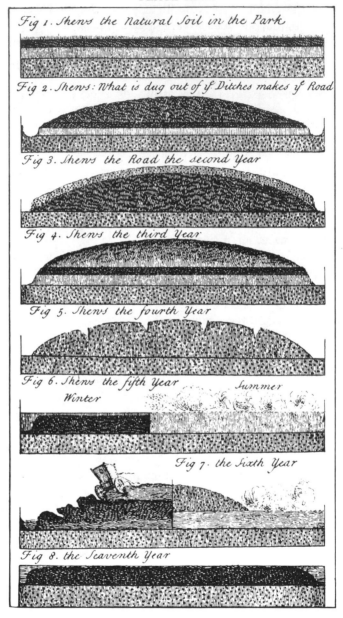

FIGURE 15-2   The road's progress as predicted by Robert Phillips to the Royal
Society, 1737. SOURCE: Gregory (1931).

TABLE 2   Failure Frequency of Dams

Years of Building	Percentage of Dams Failing Within 20 Years of Construction
1850–1899	4.0
1900–1909	3.5
1910–1919	2.5
1920–1929	2.0
1930–1957	0.5

SOURCE: Germond (1977).

these structures trends that portend longer life for the coming generation of basic structures than for the previous generations?

The answer is almost surely yes. A single instance of a Newcomen steam engine lasting for almost 150 years proves the existence theorem: Devices of this class can in principle last a long time. Research ought to reveal why they last a long time, and therefore research should lead to devices that are longer lived.

For centuries, both dams and bridges were designed empirically. As designers learned the principles of mechanics and of the strength of materials, the building of bridges and dams gradually became more scientific and catastrophic failures became less frequent (Table 15-2). This trend toward fewer catastrophic failures can be expected to continue as technological innovation continues, bringing improved materials, better monitoring of the status of these devices, and improved design for the easy replacement of deteriorated components.

Three examples illustrate these points. First, the steel used in the pressure vessels of older light-water reactors is sometimes sensitive to radiation embrittlement. The elimination of copper impurities in these steels is expected to increase their resistance to embrittlement. Second, the new St. Petersburg–Ft. Myers suspension bridge will be monitored extensively for stress and temperature by a system of sensors, all feeding information into a central computer. Such elaborate monitoring ought to give early warning and therefore help forestall incipient failures. Third, early pressurized water reactors in nuclear plants were designed under the assumption that the steam generators would last as long as the plant. This has not been the case, and in addition, defective steam generators in these plants are awkward and expensive to replace. Reactor designers now realize that steam generators can be expected to fail and design them to be replaceable.

In some sense, the longevity of these devices reflects the prejudices and traditions of their designers. Cathedrals in the Middle Ages were expected to be eternal. Because of this tradition, great care and expense went into their construction: many such cathedrals are now 500 or more years old, although most have been rebuilt and require extensive maintenance.

By contrast, roads in the United States have usually been perceived as having a short lifetime; in general, they have been built to last 20 years, whereas the autobahns in Germany are still serviceable 50 years after Hitler began their construction as military arteries. Of course, Hitler perceived his Third Reich as lasting 1,000 years. Albert Speer in his memoirs writes that in anticipation of such "immortality," he experimented with various concretes to determine their resistance to the elements.

Power plants traditionally have been expected to last 25 to 30 years, largely because history has shown them to become noncompetitive by then, and their design was geared to this perception. Today that perception has changed, in part because the plants have reached a thermodynamic ceiling. As a result, some Russian reactors now are reported to be designed for 70-year lifetimes.

The issue in some sense is always one of economics: the projected lifetime of a device can generally be lengthened if enough money is put into its construction. But if the perception of obsolescence is strong, then the amount that is worth spending in the first place is limited. A power plant, for example, must pay for itself over its lifetime. As that lifetime decreases, the amount we can afford to pay at the outset is lessened, and such penury by and large reduces the lifetime of the plant.

One would expect that research and development in materials, monitoring, and design ought to lead to devices that deteriorate slowly without requiring unreasonable additional capital investment. Indeed, R&D aimed at lengthening the life of infrastructure could be an important step toward improving our country's vital systems.

HOW LONG SHOULD INFRASTRUCTURE LAST?

As long as an element of infrastructure fulfills its function satisfactorily, economic forces will encourage its survival rather than its replacement. Once the structure or device has been amortized, it becomes a "free" good bequeathed by a prior generation to its successors. At that time the capital carrying cost of the old device falls to zero. Unless the maintenance and operating costs of the old device become so high that they exceed the combined fixed and operating cost of its replacement, it is less expensive to keep the old system than to replace it.

Obviously, devices designed to be "immortal" are more expensive than throwaway devices. How much more expense is warranted to make a device immortal can hardly be estimated in general. It can only be hoped that the cost of immortalization will continue to fall as our technology improves.

A powerful argument against immortalizing infrastructures lies in our uncertainty about the future. Despite our most confident predictions we can never know how much a city will grow in the next 50 years. Thus, a magnificent bridge, built for immortality in 1880, may prove inadequate 100 years later, not because the bridge has deteriorated but because it has become a bottleneck to growing traffic.

Arguments such as this underlie the recent trend toward smaller units in power plants. Because growth in a plant's electric load is so hard to predict (and the predictions of the 1970s have almost without exception been far too high), many utilities have responded by forswearing large (1,000 MW), long-lived power plants for much smaller (~200 MW) plants. This stratagem sacrifices economy of scale to gain the reduced risk of guessing wrong on load growth. By choosing smaller plants, the utility maintains a flexibility it forgoes when it builds mammoth facilities that may require more than 10 years to build.

Is there any evidence for what is perceived to be a growing reluctance to build new infrastructure in very large units and instead to emphasize smaller, decentralized elements, simply because the smaller elements allow greater flexibility? We can only see such a trend clearly in the case of power plants. On the other hand, we cannot ignore the many trends in our social ethos that glorify decentralization and the idea that "small is beautiful." Should these trends continue to acquire political status, we might expect future infrastructure to be built on a smaller scale, to be more flexible, and possibly less longed lived. The connection between immortality and size is not clear. Many utilities install relatively small gas turbines that tend to have intrinsically short lifetimes. And in a rough way (approximate surface-to-volume ratio), a large bridge might be expected to last longer than a small one. We cannot claim, however, to understand the relation between longevity and capacity.

Nevertheless, there are powerful incentives to continue along the traditional line of large, centralized, long-lived infrastructure. Many elements of infrastructure, especially power plants, emit pollutants. The treatment of pollutants is cheaper on a large scale than on a small one. Economics thus would favor the centralization of systems that deal with pollutants, including waste disposal facilities.

A second incentive toward centralization of facilities is to be found in the current reluctance to accept any device that the public finds environmentally threatening, whether it is a dam, power plant, transmission line, or waste disposal facility. The situation is perhaps most clear-cut for power plants; no one wants a new power plant in their "back yard." This suggests that new power plants, if they are to be built at all, are likely to be built on existing sites. Thus, even if the power-producing devices themselves are mortal, the sites are probably immortal. What is true of power plants is probably true of transmission lines and waste disposal facilities: their sites, once chosen, are likely to remain in operation long after the original devices have crumbled and decayed.

It may be that the siting of new infrastructure, insofar as it requires new sites, will prove to be the most serious impediment to the renewal of our vital systems. Certainly the electric power industry's experience in the siting of transmission lines and of coal- and nuclear-fired generating plants gives us little assurance that the creation of future infrastructure will be easy and without political ferment. Perhaps this characteristic, more than any other, will argue for maintaining the existing infrastructure, or at least the existing sites, rather than arousing the passions of those who would be inconvenienced by, or who might even believe themselves to be susceptible to harm as a result of, new infrastructure.

GENERAL OBSERVATIONS

The challenge in the field of infrastructure is one of anticipation and optimization. If today a bridge is judged to be inadequate for whatever reason, this does not necessarily demean its functioning to date, nor does it justify construction of a bridge whose capacity will not be required until 50 years hence. On the other hand, if it appears that a bridge at this location will be a permanent part of our infrastructure, can we design it so that its physical structure and life expectancy are optimized for an evolving role, perhaps for incremental changes or periodic replacement?

A further part of the challenge is that as items of infrastructure increase in size and complexity, the consequences of failure or misjudgment become greater. It is this sort of recognition that has led to the construction of electric power grids in such a way that service can be maintained despite the failure of part of the system and to highway repaving methods that permit one lane to remain open to traffic while the adjacent lane is resurfaced.

But how much flexibility is it possible to incorporate into our infrastructure? It has been pointed out that one of the dangers of long-term climate change (for example, as a consequence of increasing concentrations of atmospheric carbon dioxide) is that our infrastructure "grows up" dependent on the current physical environment.

Hazardous waste presents a particular challenge. We are caught between our immediate, pressing need to do something with waste and the possibility that in the future we will discover better ways for dealing with it. Certainly, for nuclear waste, it is necessary to design a system that has virtual immortality. As was pointed out for all the systems discussed in this chapter, designing for immortality implies both a well-engineered structure and a stable central authority to care for it. It is this kind of concern that has led one of us to contemplate something approaching a religious order that would harbor the long-term commitment to stewardship of waste sites. We can assert that one of the real problems in dealing with hazardous waste now is that we have done so poorly in the past, both in original engineering and in stewardship.

CONCLUSIONS

From this brief review of several elements of physical infrastructure, one is left with the impression that some elements last much longer than their expected design life whereas others do not. The energy-generating system, although it is aging, seems likely, by and large, to last longer than was expected. On the other hand, there is little evidence that roads, even modern ones, will last much longer than their design lifetimes— that is, unless they undergo costly repairs. Modern dams and bridges probably will last considerably longer, on average, than their design lives.

What does seem clear is that even if the elements of infrastructure are themselves not "immortal," the sites that they now occupy probably are. This trend has been accentuated in recent years as popular opposition to new large and intrusive structures and processes has grown. This trend further suggests that the geographic backbone of our society is probably well established and is unlikely to change.

REFERENCES

Bedard, R. 1986. Car and Driver, August 1986, p. 56.

Burwell, C. C., and J. A. Lane. 1980. Nuclear Site Planning to 2025. ORAU/IEA-80-5(M). Oak Ridge, Tenn.: Oak Ridge Associated Universities, Institute for Energy Analysis. May.

Christensen, D., ed. 1973. Chicago: A History. Department of Public Works, City of Chicago. Chicago: Rand McNally and Co.

Electrical World. 1985. How old are U.S. utility powerplants? (June):103.

Germond, J. P. 1977. Insuring dam risks. Water Power & Dam Construction. (June):36.

Gregory, J. W. 1931. The Story of the Road. London: Alexander Maclehose Co.

Griffin, L. 1986. The state of the interstates. Car and Driver, August 1986, p. 52.

Hopkins, H. J. 1970. A Span of Bridges: An Illustrated History. New York: Praeger Publishers.

Hudson, C.R. 1983. Age and Capacity Profile of Electric Generation Plants in the United States. ORNL/TM-8510. Oak Ridge, Tenn.: Oak Ridge National Laboratory.

National Research Council. 1985. Technological Alternatives for Urban Infrastructure.

Building Research Board, J. P. Eberhard and A. B. Bernstein, eds. Washington, D.C.: National Research Council.

Smith, N. 1972. A History of Dams. Secaucus, N.J.: The Citadel Press.

Tennessee Valley Authority, Division of Water Control Planning. 1963. The Nickajack Project. TVA Report 44-100. Norris, Tenn.

Tennessee Valley Authority, Hydropower Planning Section. 1983. Project Rehabilitation Feasibility Report, Great Falls Project. TVA Report WR28-1-13-101. Norris, Tenn.

Tennessee Valley Authority, Office of Engineering. 1963. The Hales Bar Problem—A Summary Report. TVA Report 44-4. Norris, Tenn.

U.S. Department of Transportation, Federal Highway Administration. 1977. America's Highways 1776–1976: A History of the Federal-Aid Program. Washington, D.C.: U.S. Government Printing Office.

Weinberg, A. M. 1985. "Immortal" energy systems and intergenerational justice. Energy Policy 13(1):51–59.

Contributors

JOHN S. ADAMS is professor of geography, planning, and public affairs at the University of Minnesota. From 1975 to 1976 he was Fulbright Professor at the Interdisciplinary Institute for Spatial Organization at the Economic University in Vienna, Austria. He has taught at Pennsylvania State University and the University of Washington and has consulted and lectured at many campuses throughout the United States, Canada, Europe, and Japan. He has authored, coauthored, and edited articles, books, and reports on the American city, regional economic development and planning in the United States, and intraurban migration in American cities. Dr. Adams received his B.A. degree in economics from the College of St. Thomas and his M.A. degree in economics and statistics, and the Ph.D. degree in economic geography from the University of Minnesota.

SIAMAK A. ARDEKANI is assistant professor of civil engineering at the Virginia Polytechnic Institute and State University. His current research is in transportation management issues in the aftermath of major urban disasters such as earthquakes and floods. He has coauthored numerous journal articles on urban traffic management and operation. He is associate editor of the *Transportation Science Journal* and a member of the American Society of Civil Engineers, the Operations Research Society of America, the Institute of Transportation Engineers, and the Transportation Research Board, where he serves as a member on the Committee on Traffic Flow Theory and Characteristics. He received his Ph.D. degree in civil engineering from the University of Texas at Austin.

W. BRIAN ARTHUR is Morrison Professor of Population Studies and Economics at the Food Research Institute, Stanford University. From 1977 to 1982 he was with the methodology group at the International Institute for Applied Systems Analysis in Laxenburg, Austria. His current research, for which he received a 1987–1988 Guggenheim Fellowship, is on the implications of increasing returns and nonconvexities for economic theory and demography. He has worked on a variety of subjects including probability theory, the economics of technology, industry location theory, optimization theory, mathematical demography, and the economics of intergenerational transfers. Dr. Arthur holds a Ph.D. degree in operations research from the University of California, Berkeley.

JESSE H. AUSUBEL is director of the Program Office of the National Academy of Engineering. Mr. Ausubel became a resident fellow of the National Academy of Sciences in science and public policy in 1977. He then served for 2½ years as a research scholar in the resources and environment area at the International Institute for Applied Systems Analysis, near Vienna, Austria. From 1981 to 1983 he served as a National Research Council staff officer principally responsible for studies of the greenhouse effect. Mr. Ausubel's interests generally revolve around long-term interactions of technology and environment.

MARTIN BECKMANN is professor of economics at Brown University and professor of applied mathematics at the Technical University of Munich, Federal Republic of Germany. He has taught at the University of Chicago, Yale University, the University of Heidelberg, and the University of Bonn. He is author or coauthor of 11 books and 200 articles on economic theory and operations research. His research interests are in the economics of location and transportation and in the theory of organizations. He has received honorary doctorates from the universities of Umea (Sweden), Karlsruhe, and Hamburg.

BERNARD B. BERGER, professor emeritus of civil engineering, was director of the Water Resources Research Center and professor of civil engineering at the University of Massachusetts from 1966 to 1978. From 1941 to 1966 Dr. Berger served in the Commissioned Corps of the U.S. Public Health Service. In 1954 he was named chief of water supply and pollution control research at the Robert A. Taft Sanitary Engineering Center and in 1963 became assistant chief for research in the Division of Water Supply and Pollution Control. In 1965 he was appointed deputy chief of the Office of Resource Development. During 1968–1969, he worked as a water resources specialist in the Office of Science and Technology of the Executive Office of the President and served as chairman on the Federal

Committee on Water Resources Research. Dr. Berger has been consultant to several foreign governments on river sampling and water planning and has served as chairman and U.S. representative on related bilateral and international conferences and committees. Dr. Berger received an honorary doctorate of science from the University of Massachusetts in 1979. He is a member of the National Academy of Engineering.

HARVEY BROOKS is Benjamin Peirce Professor of Technology and Public Policy, Emeritus, and Gordon McKay Professor of Applied Physics, Harvard University. He came to Harvard from General Electric in 1950 as professor of applied physics. He became dean of engineering and applied physics in 1957 and served in that capacity until 1975, when he was appointed professor of technology and public policy and transferred most of his teaching and research to the Kennedy School of Government, where he heads the Science, Technology, and Public Policy Program. Dr. Brooks has served in many government and quasi-government advisory positions, including those with the President's Science Advisory Committee, the National Science Board, and various project advisory committees to the Office of Technology Assessment. Dr. Brooks is a member of the National Academy of Engineering, the National Academy of Sciences, and the Institute of Medicine.

THOMAS R. CRAIG is director of market research at the Boeing Commercial Airplane Company, where he is responsible for economic, air passenger, air cargo, and product forecasting. Mr. Craig joined Boeing in 1958 and has served as sales and marketing research analyst, manager of air freight market research, member of the corporate planning staff, and manager of passenger traffic forecasting before being named to his present position. From 1948 to 1958, Mr. Craig served in the U.S. Foreign Service as a consular officer in Hamburg, Federal Republic of Germany, and Prague, Czechoslovakia. Mr. Craig holds a B.S. degree in economics from Rutgers University.

EDGAR DONA received his M.S. degree in transportation at Virginia Polytechnic Institute and State University. He was an International Road Federation Fellow and is now practicing civil engineering in the Philippines.

DIEGO ECHEVERRY is a doctoral candidate at the University of Illinois and the University of California.

DEAN GILLETTE is Henry R. Luce Professor of Information Technology and Society at Harvey Mudd and Claremont McKenna colleges. From 1953 to 1984, Dr. Gillette was a member of the technical staff at Bell

Telephone Laboratories and served as director of military systems analysis, executive director of transmission systems engineering, and executive director of corporate studies. He is the author of numerous publications on telematics and telecommunications. Dr. Gillette has served on committees and advisory boards of the Office of Technology Assessment and the Institute of Electrical and Electronic Engineers, among other organizations, for international communications and telecommunication policy research. Dr. Gillette received his B.S. degree in chemistry from the Oregon State University, and his M.A. and Ph.D. degrees in mathematics from the University of California, Berkeley.

SHEKHAR GOVIND is a research engineer assistant at the University of Texas at Austin, where he earned an M.S. degree in civil engineering in 1984, majoring in structures. His work toward a Ph.D. degree in transportation in 1988 was related to pavement fatigue damage due to applied stress.

ROYCE HANSON, professor of public affairs and planning, joined the Hubert H. Humphrey Institute of Public Affairs, University of Minnesota, as associate dean in 1983 after a career spanning academia, politics, research administration, and public service. In the late 1960s, he was president of the Washington Center for Metropolitan Studies, an interuniversity urban research institute. During the 1970s, he served as chairman of the Montgomery County Planning Board of the Maryland National Capital Park and Planning Commission. In 1981 Dr. Hanson served as study director on the National Research Council Committee on National Urban Policy. He is the author or editor of numerous publications on urban development and policy. Dr. Hanson received his A.B. degree in economics from Central State University in Edmond, Oklahoma, and M.A. and Ph.D. degrees in government and public administration and a law degree from the American University.

ROBERT HERMAN is L.P. Gilvin Centennial Professor, Emeritus, in civil engineering and sometime professor of physics at the University of Texas at Austin. Before assuming his present position in 1979, Dr. Herman was with the General Motors Research Laboratories and headed the Department of Theoretical Physics from 1959 to 1972 and the Traffic Science Department from 1972 to 1979. Dr. Herman's research has covered a wide range of both theoretical and experimental investigations, including molecular and solid-state physics, high-energy electron scattering, astrophysics and cosmology, as well as operations research, especially vehicular traffic science and transportation. With Ralph Alpher in 1948, Dr. Herman made the first theoretical prediction that the universe should now be filled with a cosmic microwave background radiation, which is key evidence for the validity of the Big Bang model of the origin of the universe. Dr. Herman is a member of the National Academy of Engineering. He received his B.S. degree in physics at City College, New York, and his master's and Ph.D. degrees in physics from Princeton University.

PAUL M. HOHENBERG is professor of economics at Rensselaer Polytechnic Institute. Dr. Hohenberg has taught economics and economic history at Stanford, Cornell, and Concordia universities. He is the coauthor of *The Making of Urban Europe* with Lynn Hollen Lees and coeditor of the *Journal of Economic History*. Dr. Hohenberg received a bachelor's degree in chemical engineering from Cornell University, an M.A. degree in economics from the Fletcher School, Tufts University, and a Ph.D. degree in economics from the Massachusetts Institute of Technology.

C. WILLIAM IBBS is associate professor of civil engineering in the construction engineering and management program at the University of California, Berkeley. Dr. Ibbs moved to California from the University of Illinois, Urbana, in 1987. Before assuming his academic positions, Dr. Ibbs acquired substantial industrial experience in the private sector. This has allowed him to develop an extensive research program, for which he received the Presidential Young Investigator's Award in the Building System and Construction Engineering program of the National Science Foundation in 1985. Dr. Ibbs earned his B.S. and M.S. degrees in civil engineering at the Carnegie Mellon University and received his Ph.D. degree in civil engineering from Berkeley.

LYNN HOLLEN LEES is professor of history at the University of Pennsylvania, where she has taught since 1974. Dr. Lees has been a visiting fellow at the Joint Center for Urban Studies of Harvard University, the Massachusetts Institute of Technology, the Shelby Cullom Davis Center of Princeton University, and at the University of Leicester in England. She has written numerous publications on topics in European economic and social history, including *The Making of Urban Europe* (Harvard University Press, 1985), which she coauthored with Paul M. Hohenberg. Dr. Lees has served on the executive boards of the Council for European Studies and the Social Science History Association and has been a consultant for the National Endowment for the Humanities and the Social Science Research Council. Dr. Lees received her B.A. degree from Swarthmore College and her Ph.D. degree from Harvard University.

CESARE MARCHETTI is a research scholar at the International Institute for Applied Systems Analysis (IIASA) in Laxenburg, Austria. Dr. Marchetti came to IIASA from the European Community Research Center, where he had been head of the Division for Development of Materials and Technologies from 1959 to 1973. Dr. Marchetti's fields of interest extend from energy systems, technology of heavy water separation, and applied surface physics to the history of technology and general systems theory. Dr. Marchetti received his education in physics at the University of Pisa, Italy. In 1977 he received an honorary degree in science from the Technical University of Strathclyde, Glasgow, Scotland, for his work in systems analysis.

GREGG MARLAND is a staff scientist in the Environmental Sciences Division at Oak Ridge National Laboratory. From 1975 to mid-1987, he was at the Institute for Energy Analysis at Oak Ridge Associated Universities and before that he was assistant professor of geology at Indiana State University. He is the author or coauthor of many scientific papers on energy systems, energy resources, and the environmental impacts of energy systems, in particular the CO_2-greenhouse issue. Dr. Marland holds a B.S. degree from the Virginia Polytechnic Institute and State University and a Ph.D. degree in geology from the University of Minnesota.

NEBOJSA NAKICENOVIC is a research scholar at the International Institute for Applied Systems Analysis in Laxenburg, Austria. He was formerly with the Nuclear Research Center, Karlsruhe, the Federal Republic of Germany, where he worked in the field of nuclear materials accountability. His broader research interests are in econometrics, game theory, global modeling, technological and social change, and information and data processing. His extensive study of economic and technological changes during the past three centuries evolved as his doctoral dissertation *Growth to Limits*. Dr. Nakicenovic received his M.A. degree in economics from Princeton University and his doctoral degree from the University of Vienna, Austria.

ALVIN M. WEINBERG is a distinguished fellow of the Institute for Energy Analysis, Oak Ridge Associated Universities, Oak Ridge, Tennessee. Dr. Weinberg was director of the Oak Ridge National Laboratory from 1955 to 1973; director of the Office of Energy Research and Development, Federal Energy Office, in 1974; and director of the Institute for Energy Analysis from 1975 to 1985. He has made numerous contributions to the design, development, and safety of nuclear reactors and the formulation of science policy. Dr. Weinberg is a member of the National Academy of Engineering and the National Academy of Sciences.

Index

X